EYE OF WITNESS

EYE OF WITNESS

A JEROME ROTHENBERG READER

Edited with commentaries by

Heriberto Yépez and Jerome Rothenberg

Black Widow Press
2013

Poems from *Poems From the Game of Silence*, *Poland/1931*, *New Selected Poems*, *That Dada Strain*, *Vienna Blood*, *Khurbn & Other Poems*, *The Lorca Variations*, *A Paradise of Poets*, *Seedings & Other Poems*, and *A Book of Witness* used courtesy of New Directions Publishing Corporation. BWP thanks New Directions Press and Declan Spring for their help with this book.

In addition poems and other works were drawn from books originally published by the following presses: City Lights Books, 1959; Hawk's Well Press, 1960; Trobar Books, 1962; El Corno Emplumado, Mexico, 1966; Fulcrum Press, London, 1967; Black Sparrow Press, 1968; Something Else Press, 1966, 1968; Circle Books, London, 1968; Unicorn Press, Santa Barbara, 1969; Tree Books, 1971; Tetrad Press / Spot Press, London, 1972, 1982; Perishable Press, 1973, 1975; Singing Bone Press, 1975; Membrane Press, 1976, 1995; University of California Press, 1985, 1995; Pennywhistle Press, 1989; Zasterle Press, Spain, 1989; Sun & Moon Press / Green Integer, 1994, 1989, 2001; Farrar Straus & Giroux, 1992; Meow Press, 1998; Granary Books, 2001, 2005; Exact Change, 2002, 2004; te/let books, 2003; Chax Press, 2004; Kadle Books, Spain, 2004; Wesleyan University Press, 2004; Ahadada Books, 2006; Veer Books, London, 2007; University of Alabama Press, 2008; Marrick Press, 2009; Black Widow Press, 2010; Junction Press, 2011. Grateful acknowledgement to all concerned.

Black Widow Press is an imprint of Commonwealth Books, Inc., Boston, MA. Distributed to the trade by NBN (National Book Network) throughout North America, Canada, and the U.K. All Black Widow Press books are printed on acid-free paper, and glued into bindings. Black Widow Press and its logo are registered trademarks of Commonwealth Books, Inc.

Joseph S. Phillips and Susan J. Wood, Ph.D., Publishers
www.blackwidowpress.com

Cover art: *Asmodea*, 1821–1823, by Francisco Goya, Museo del Prado, Madrid
Cover design: Kerrie Kemperman
Book production: Kerrie Kemperman

ISBN-13: 978-0-9837079-9-8

Printed in the United States

10 9 8 7 6 5 4 3 2 1

TABLE OF CONTENTS

GALLERY ONE: PROLEGOMENA TO A POETICS

A BOOK OF OTHERINGS

POETICS & POLEMICS 1: TOWARD AN ETHNOPOETICS

GALLERY TWO: THE WORLD TURNED UPSIDE DOWN

A BOOK OF EXTENSIONS

POETICS & POLEMICS 2: EYE OF WITNESS

GALLERY THREE: A CRUEL NIRVANA

POETICS & POLEMICS 3: TOWARD AN OMNIPOETICS

NEW POEMS: DIVAGATIONS & AUTOVARIATIONS

INTRODUCTION

A Re-Vision of Jerome Rothenberg's Poetry and Poetics

Jerome Rothenberg's poetic work began in the late fifties. It was after his stay in Europe that his writing took the form of what would become a lifelong program. His first published book, *New Young German Poets* (1959), already showed his characteristic interest in translation, poetics, avant-garde writing, and their relation to the human condition as a deeper presence *restructuring the poem.* Although his work can be associated with that of his early group—David Antin and Armand Schwerner, among others—Rothenberg's work is unique. He shares techniques, contexts and a literary/cultural field with others, but his ends are sui generis.

In this first period of his work, Rothenberg saw image and emotion (however suspect) as primordial dynamic—and daimonic—forces giving life to the poem and as powers capable of introducing and re-producing a non-visible dimension. The interaction of this visionary aspect of his poetry and his commitment to experimental writing, which came from his international outlook and from aspects of the North-American avant-garde, is the force that gives shape to his poetry as a whole.

Rothenberg's poetics of vision follows the Romantic tradition. Blake was a strong influence from the start. But if we want to understand the newness of Rothenberg's position we need to take into account that—in contrast with many other American poets of the post-war period—he developed his literary work in wide-ranging communication with other traditions. He took Charles Olson's interests in ancient cultures in a new direction and energetically researched and translated from other languages and texts. Rothenberg was one of the first innovative North-American poets to develop in the context of a contemporary multi-national poetry community across the Americas and Europe. He is both American at core and as post-American as possible in practice.

Rothenberg was not the only one interested in Lorca or Neruda, for example, or in early avant-garde and post-war European poetics—though this spectrum was not at all typical in the U.S.—but his approach was very different from previous ones. Where Olson, say, was only interested in ancient Mayas, just one decade later Rothenberg, like Paul Blackburn and Margaret Randall among others, entered into an active relationship with a number of contemporary Latin American writers. And most importantly he decided to construct his own work strongly bolstered by a growing network of transnational contacts. This participation was not simply a matter of a pioneering effort to reach out and establish bridges between writers from different national literatures and languages but was also an element that triggered and permanently altered his literary practice.

This international context may well be one of the factors involved in the somewhat marginal position he was given in the "New American Poetry" that was then emerging. Rothenberg was not just one more important "American" poet appearing to readers in the sixties. He was a pioneer Pan-American writer, with a profile different then from those of the Beats and other counterpoetics movements and still separate today from those of the mainstream poetry and post-language-poetry scenes.

But again, this emergent global aspect did not appear by itself but in tandem with Rothenberg's belief—explicit at the beginning of his career and implicit later in an almost semi-secretive way— in an underground reality for which poetry is a door or window. And this is where his "deep image" poetics takes on full meaning, as is best seen in the small but very significant collection of poetics, translations and collaborations in his *Poems from the Floating World* (1959–1963), both a mini-magazine and a cross-cultural anthology, that was, in Foucault's term, a heterotopia.

Although it may not be obvious, Rothenberg's first poetry collection *White Sun Black Sun* (1960) was born out of this same interaction between an older visionary paradigm and a new post-Western and radically innovative approach to writing. *White Sun Black Sun*'s title, for me at least, reflects the encounter of Western ("white") critical poetics and other cultures and dimensions ("black"). This combination of a powerful and conscious technical interest and an underworld vision quest, results in a verbal structure increasingly ruled by parataxis, collage, disjunction, assemblage, juxtaposition, enantiodromia, but also an enterprise based on egalitarianism, collective creation, and an ongoing search for new centers.

With the expansion of the experimental, international and historical aspects of his poetics, some of the early Romantic elements lost their centrality. Emotion gave way to a full exchange between vision and experiment, in which the logic of entangled sightings (entries into the other world through poetic percepts) and "deep image" as such disappeared from Rothenberg's main vocabulary, making his poetics go from a search for a mystic source out-of-and-into darkness to a decentered poem and (perhaps more importantly) a decentered subject. Rothenberg suppressed his original visionary "I" only to engage in a range of experiments with multiple "I's" and eyes.

One can see the gradual change from a Romantic American Deep Image to a post-Romantic plural vision in the transition from *Between 1960–1963* to *The Gorky Poems* (an edition which by the way involved binational and bilingual work). Although Rothenberg himself seemed to have completely abandoned "deep image" and even came to see his work there in a self-critical way, there is certainly a continuity between the understanding of this earlier period and the new period in the making.

A new dimension in Rothenberg's work began in the second half of the sixties. The key concept now was *ethnopoetics*—a continuation, among other things, of Olson's travels into Mexico, of Pound's explorations in global collage, of his own readings of anthropological sources, and with that too he brought a logical conclusion to the project of European avantgardists like Tristan Tzara (and the European avant-garde in general), to bring to light a heterogeneous range of poetries from other geographies and with an opening as well to other, often occluded levels of consciousness. In Rothenberg's case, there was also a systematic impulse to build a new image of poetry worldwide and to subvert Western poetic understandings using materials from other strains and cultures.

One can easily bypass the heart of Rothenberg's poetics—especially once ethnopoetics appears and attracts attention—not only because Rothenberg does not openly insist on the metaphysical nature of his poetics (he is in fact skeptical about it) but also because so much contemporary experimentalism (at least in its post-sixties phase) has a strong connection to positivistic, postmodernist and anti-metaphysical tendencies (from analytical philosophy to deconstruction), according to which language is a cultural surface or network, with a consequent lack of any real sense of depth. As time passed, Rothenberg's work came to be understood in the context, for example, of Language Poetry, most of whose poets (but not all) define their poetics in opposition to any metaphysical or religious claims. But Rothenberg's poetics does contain metaphysical premises: ethnopoetics is not only a poetics of multiculturalism and a post-colonial mapping but also a search for a primal poetics, an investigation into the relation of the non-conscious mind and its cultural forms of expression.

Rothenberg has been very careful in establishing parallelisms between shamanism and contemporary poetry and art. He doesn't want to draw premature conclusions, but putting the relation of *shaman* and *poet* into discussion was a frontal part of his ethnopoetics project—though he later preferred the trickster figure as a closer model for comparison, probably because of the more ambivalent and absurdist nature of the trickster's cultural function. His assemblage *Technicians of the Sacred* (1968) opened our historical consciousness to the range of poetries across the globe and shattered for some of us the basic Eurocentric beliefs that still dominate the literary domain, "a concerted assault," as Charles Bernstein described it, "on the primacy of Western high culture and an active attempt to find in other, nonwestern/nonoriental cultures, what seemed missing from our own." And yet it was at the same time a more than 500-page-long manifesto on the skills and epistemic possibilities of ritual/performance and of oral and visual image-making, wherever found.

His famous appropriation of Eliade's phrase "technicians of the sacred" takes on a new meaning when viewed in the light of Rothenberg's Janusian writing. As another example of Rothenberg's contradictory pairings, "technicians" here means experimentalists concerned with cultural invention and transmission, while "sacred" refers to whatever may be taken as the hidden domain. Technicians of the sacred then means experimentalists of the invisible. But the "total translation" that Rothenberg's poetry frequently asks for also instructs us not to subordinate either of the elements of the implied dichotomy, not to kill the paradox. Technicians of the sacred, *experimentalists of the invisible*, are those agents occupied with renovating *form* and at the same time investigating the *bottomless*. (Please note that this is the same conceptual and secret play of opposites active in other key Rothenberg titles, like his 1960–1970 anthology *Poems for the Game of Silence*, where "game" refers to the reordering of the poem's formal-cultural aspects while "silence" may refer to a kind of crypto-mysticism.)

Ethnopoetics thus seen is at least triadic: experimentalist in literature, multicultural in politics and esoteric in religion. To read his poetry fully, we need to understand that the changes his work has gone through do not follow a linear order in which prior discoveries or principles get pushed aside for newer ones. Rothenberg's work is braid-like.

*

Poland/1931 (published in 1974, but in preparation since the late sixties) is an experiment in an altered ethnopoetics, a turn from the early primitive, archaic and indigenous explorations (first in *Technicians* and then in *Shaking the Pumpkin*) to a playful investigation of his own immigrant and Jewish imaginaries. At this point in his work, Rothenberg is using different voices to recall fragmentary memories that re/dis/cover image and sound legacies coming from disparate (and desperate) archival and phantasmagoric sources.

His ethnopoetic assemblage projects continued in the seventies with magazines like *Alcheringa* and *New Wilderness Letter* and the anthologies *America A Prophecy* and *A Big Jewish Book*. At this point in his career, Rothenberg was centrally linked with "ethnopoetics" though I think few thoroughly understood that ethnopoetics as a form of poesis is a collage including cryptohistory—a call for the simultaneous renewal of cultural forms and a reconfiguration of consciousness, a matter of making new cultural and spiritual constellations available.

And it is at this level that *ethno*poetics—as the creative research on how culture produces poiesis—involves an *etho*poetics—how poiesis in turn produces communities and subjectivities *(ethos)*. Each of Rothenberg's successive books of poetry can then be read as an increment in voices and memories, a present that never stops uncovering new pasts. From *A Seneca Journal* (1978) to *That Dada Strain* (1983), Rothenberg saw a new transition coming (and again marked it with a retrospective gathering of his work, *New Selected Poems* [1986]). It is at this *etho*poetic level, that Rothenberg's can be read not as a project mainly occupied with exterior entities—other traditions, composition techniques, etcetera—but as that of a poet undergoing a process of metamorphosis through different phases. The movement from Deep Image to Ethnopoetics was part of an *ethopoetic* desire to construct a post-Romantic—but still visionary—poetry.

During the ethnopoetic stage, Rothenberg made adjustments—which again let us see more clearly the *etho*poetical aspect of his becoming—going from an ethnopoetics centered on the other(s) to an ethnopoetics centered in his own Jewish-Western imaginary. Accordingly the new 1985 edition of *Technicians of the Sacred* included European materials, and in the nineties Rothenberg's translation work would concentrate on avant-garde figures like Lorca, Schwitters, Nezval, and Picasso, and his new big project in the 1990s would be a global reordering of modern and post-modern poetries in the first two volumes of *Poems for the Millennium* (with Pierre Joris).

But none of this can be fully understood only at the level of books and texts. Performance is a crucial part of Rothenberg's poiesis. As in other cultural contexts, in his work as a poet the strengthening of performance can be seen as a sign of the birth of new forms. Performance is not "form"—a closed or at least recognizable form—but an unsettled form-process, a form-in-becoming or even a form-that-will-not-accomplish-itself—a kind of ephemeral or liminal transition between one form and another in which culture goes through a crisis to transform and make sense and non-sense during the struggle, an interplay of resistance and emergence.

This is why performance is so important in Rothenberg's poetry, and one can see that many of his transformational peaks are located precisely around those series of poems that most clearly involve performance: the Navajo and Seneca "total translations" (chants), for example, and the poems dedicated to the older Dada poets. These high performance works from the 1970s and 1980s announce a change in Rothenberg's poetic subjects and his (conscious and unconscious) writing methodologies. If performance is how we go from one form to another, without the need or help of rational means—and with body as a catalyst—it is not the individual poet who performs but who himself becomes the subject of performance.

Performance occurs when the body enters into a strong field of non-standard language. The eye of performance is the eye of the hurricane: the central ego disappears and is replaced by the void produced by the intense movements of energetic language around it. Performance is also used by Rothenberg to make texts come into living material conditions—a fulfillment of the verbi-voco-visual soma. With Rothenberg, performance gives full life to poems through the revival of voices coming, he seems to tell us, from the elsewhere—as the performer's body and identity are altered by the very action of performance.

In a related sense Rothenberg's use of the word "Pre-Face" is yet another turn of phrase that signals *etho*poetical transformations. The word itself became idiosyncratic in Rothenberg's work starting with the now classic pre-face to *Technicians of the Sacred* (which also included a post-face). Pre-Face here implies a change of identity, and it is no accident that Rothenberg's prose frequently takes the form of prefaces or postfaces. His poetry collections use them further as a kind of explanation or commentary on the circumstances, procedures, intentions and ideas behind the writing. The presence of these pre/post-faces is an unequivocal key to understanding the whole of Rothenberg's work, poems and poetics alike, as a series of experiments in trans-forming the poetic subject and per-forming the language inside of which the poet becomes an-other.

Through these pre-faces—as in his other essays and even in his *commentaries*—Rothenberg became one of the most persistent practitioners of "poetics" as a literary, even a poetic genre of its own. Probably no other

North-American post-war poetic movement—with the clear exception of various feminist tendencies—had the potential to become a field of study in its own right as did ethnopoetics. Ethnopoetics as a proto-social-science opened a hybrid discourse that freely merged poetry and anthropology, and in a more subterranean way implied something like a psychohistory, that is, a discourse on the manifestation of forms and contents belonging to the dead in the embodied consciousness of the living individual, a pairing that was best captured in the poems and title of *Poland/1931*—where "Poland" can be read as a sign of the past, of the dead and others, and "1931" (Rothenberg's birth year) as a sign of the personal: a collaboration between a ghostly otherness and a private body by means of an unconventional language that blends the communication between the two sides of the equation. Vision and perception mediated by a gatekeeper who refuses to simply translate.

The dead are the portal into our own identities, the undercurrent of memory, of the past flashing into our current imagination, self, and senses. We lack the proper skills to understand the activity, "the presence of the dead," as Rothenberg once put it, in our daily lives. The individual is not a single entity, but an indivisible congeries of others. In the search to better understand this, some form of art and poetry may serve us as a kind of speculative speech, a playful and uncanny set of representations on the impossibility of a language exclusively created by a single entity. Rothenberg's persona (that is, the mask through which all speech emerges) grew in voices, sources, archives, traditions, techniques, forms, audiences, both on the page and in performance. Then, after *That Dada Strain*, his poetry took yet another turn.

*

Rothenberg's first poetry period had occupied itself with the descent into darkness, a vision that he kept exploring: the abyss, wilderness, hells, flower-worlds, paradises, mystical dimensions, and all sorts of underworld characters and scenes, using a complex collection of avant-garde and post-romantic methodologies to call them out. His journeys into new regions have continued from the eighties into the present century through his masterful explorations of new times and places: from the death camps of *Khurbn* (1989) to the openings and furtive glimpses of *Gematria Complete* (2009); from his scattered poems derived from travels into old geographies and cultures to the surge of fresh translations in *A Paradise of Poets* (1999) and the darkened worlds and rooms embedded in *Concealments and Caprichos* (2010). These multiple landscapes are "cruel nirvanas," imaginal space-times of suffering.

As such they call us to become many, an other or a series of others, of voices coming from all roles, levels and directions.

If after Deep Image came Ethnopoetics—with the former not so much going away as merging in the helix of his total project—after this Deep Ethnopoetics came a poetics of witness. Where "testimony" as an act of witness was present almost from the beginning, the figure of the witness as such has only slowly emerged as a new conceptual center in Rothenberg's work: a plural-I that describes the world at the same time that it intervenes in it. The witness here is as much an ethnographer and historian as a survivor and magician; he still belongs to the oneiric dreamworld but is plagued by the human capacity for cruelty. The witness wants to portray the world in words that include the activity of the occult and occulted in the "real" world. He uses the "barbaric" precisely to write "poetry after Auschwitz." He does not peacefully contemplate the world or merely name it—the many voices that the witness includes are often mean, obscure, cruel. Witness is wizard and warrior, executioner and victim, trickster and tyrant. And is always paying the price of pain. He is from elsewhere but belongs to this world. He participates in History. He is Many. He likes to incorporate the mouths, the voices and the words of others (not only in his poems but also in the form of otherings, variations, transcreations and appropriations, even of words from his own poetic past). And he is almost always speaking "on borrowed time."

Poet-as-witness is post-shamanic. It is no accident that this figure-function gains importance after *That Dada Strain*, whose last poem (in the book of that title) is dedicated to the rise and fall of María Sabina, the Mazatec shamaness, a kind of rite of passage to separate from the shamanic dream she symbolized. Rothenberg knows that late poets cannot be shamans. (There's no visible tribe, pure Myth does not exist in a world after Hollywood, nor can the shaman holistically heal because he or she is historically wounded.) But Rothenberg refuses to accept that a poet is just a plain writer and that language is merely cultural. The I and spirit that a certain post-modernism dismissed reappears in the mud. Psyche is undeniable. Language is vertiginous. Poetry is soul-re-making—if only by chance.

Poet-as-witness is still in the making, and it may well be Rothenberg's main contribution to poetics, though a more subtle one than ethnopoetics as an open field and Deep Ethnopoetics as a project still to be understood in its complete scope. Probably we will have to become "post-post-modern" (G. Oppen) to understand the importance of Rothenberg's version of the "witness", a mode in which poetry is neither neo-shamanism nor pure artifice, neither Romantic nor Post-Romantic. The witness, besides, throws light on the previous stages of Rothenberg's poetic past, showing the nature of his own experiments with North-American experimentalism, an experimentalism in which discontinuity is not just an aesthetic technique but also a way to call up the presence of death, and parataxis a way to aesthetically render the superimposition of this and the other world.

Rothenberg's witness is the marker of a new kind of poet—its pre-face—in which two apparently opposite drives coexist: an acknowledgement of poetry as a perpetual and radical change of form—and thus the willingness to not retain any-thing—and a desire to construct a total poetics, or—to use a recent word of Rothenberg's—an *omnipoetics*: to say in every form possible what cannot possibly be said.

HERIBERTO YÉPEZ
Tijuana/Berkeley
2013

PRE-FACE

The opening to poetry came to me before the poems and writings covered in this book. The last world war had been over for several years, but the memory of war and its attendant holocausts was strong and stayed so: a sense of violence and cruelty, the dark side of what makes us human, more powerful in its way than the hope the war's ending had also engendered. That much is retrospective, of course, as are by now the years and decades that followed, that opened up new wars and wounds, and made still greater the need for a new language, a new way to speak and see the world—"against the fascination which forms of expression exert on us," as Wittgenstein put it for philosophy. For me it was poetry that played that central role, spread, I would like to believe, across the full span of my work and life.

The opportunity of a Reader like this, then, is the opportunity to assert a wholeness in the work, in the way at least that I've long imagined it for myself. In that sense it takes a step beyond a selection of poems, although the poems of course are at the heart of the work—as always. For many of us the life of poetry is a many-sided endeavor, *a grand collage* in which the poems as such interact with our attempts to create & to explore a new poetics, a new idea of poetry, & has more often than not been fought out through polemics & manifestos, both individual & collective. The way from poems through poetics brings with it a range of other writings & doings: performance pieces, plays & soundplays; translations & variations drawing from the works of others; large assemblages alongside simpler books of poems. The totality of the work, now covering a lifetime, is for me as for others more than a single gathering can hold, for which what follows is a summary or mapping, an attempt to show the range of works & treat them as a whole: an anthology of my own works on the model of my other anthologies, the mix of poems and gatherings that came before.

It is late in the game now, but the perspective that that gives me is in some sense worth the wait. The work-and-life, as Heriberto Yépez and I present it here, traces on its poetics side a line from *deep image* to *ethnopoetics* to a *poetry of witness* (as I still struggle to define it), and to the idea of an *omnipoetics* that hopes to bring it all together. In that progression, it seems to me, changes happen and contradictions abound, but nothing is ever wholly lost, while each individual element can both be read for itself and in relation to the other elements that come before and after. For me this is more than a matter of theory, more like a single large assemblage from what has been my life—a history as well of loves & friendships embedded largely in the poetry itself.

The structure of the book is meant to keep the mix alive. The elements at our disposal are those I've spoken of already, and the intention, as Yépez and I decided from the start, was to keep the boundaries between them as porous as possible. We began therefore with the construction of three "galleries," following, with a minimum of editing or revising, a loose chronology of early, middle and later works respectively, in which poems as such predominate, interlaced with short essays and manifestos and with excerpts from letters and related documents. For the bulk of the poetics in the book, however, we set up three independent sections of "poetics and polemics" and we also created two sections more specifically focused on aspects of my writings to which I wanted to call special attention and that could best be seen, we thought, by juxtaposing works across the decades.

In the first of these two sections, "A Book of Otherings," we extend the practice of translation to include a range of works in which the voices and words of others enter or direct the process of individual composition: appropriation, collage, "total translation," and beyond all these a sense of poetry as a collaborative or collective enterprise, the product of a language we all share, even while we bend it to our special needs and singularities. I have written elsewhere about collaboration, not as something that diminishes us but rather as a necessity of our lives as social beings, and a number of my bigger works have been the result of such collaborations, as have translation projects which allowed me to work through languages outside of my own range as a writer and reader.

In another section of this book, "A Book of Extensions," other collaborations come into play, along with singular works that explore the boundaries and limitations of our acts as poets—visual and performance works foremost. The question of absolute originality is beside the point here, and part of my own predilection in fact is to be as conscious as I can be of the sources and origins of our most experimental works, part of a searching of the past as another route into the future. Performance, both musical and theatrical, is an inherently ancient and collaborative work, which has allowed me, beyond my solo efforts as a reader/performer, to work with a number of musicians and with ensembles like The Living Theater on an exploration of what our poetry could be—what we could make it be—as an art of sound and gesture. In a number of visual works as well I have proceeded on my own grounds but still more interestingly, I think, with others, to open anew—or with renewed emphasis—to the force of writing and the visual word and to the intersection in a single space of word and image.

If all of this was set in motion in the last century, a final section of "new poems" allows me to bring the work up to the almost present with selections from two series of poems, "Divagations" and "The Jigoku Zoshi Hells: A Book of Autovariations," along with a complete new work, "A Poem of Miracles," written in preparation for my eightieth birthday. With the autovariations in particular I come into a revisioning or othering of one of my own earlier works, *The Seven Hells of the Jigoku Zoshi*, some poems from which appear elsewhere in these pages. In that sense I turn the tables on myself or follow the directives I quote from Matisse, *that one should be able to rework an old work at least once ... [to] change course, search for something new.* At this point in my life I feel this both as a closing of the circle and as a signal for the new century now in progress and for the new/old work to come.

Two final points then in summation: first, my pursuit of a kind of transcultural or global poetics: a poetry rooted in its place but capable of crossing borders and languages to become a virtual *omnipoetics.* And secondly that that move in its later stages explores a multivocal poetry of witness—the ubiquity of an I-as-speaking-subject that we all share—personal and transpersonal at once. From there, while incorporating my own expanded books, the anthologies that have themselves incorporated so much of what I've come to know, I find myself on the verge of what Robert Duncan, speaking for himself, once called "a grand collage." If my own version of that is differently constructed from his and others', that's only to be expected. And while I could say more about both of these points—and will or have done so elsewhere—suffice it for now that a book like this gives me a final retrospective view, which, if there were time enough and space to show it, would lead to that greater vast anthology-of-everything toward which our lives and thoughts have long been moving.

Thanks & Acknowledgements

The question has come up of collaboration, and with it an idea of poetry, for all its idiosyncrasies, as a collective work. That makes it a riposte in a sense to the various anxieties of influence propounded by Harold Bloom and others that tend to override and conceal the creative pleasures of the work, present and past, that we make in common. In the course of my workings over the years, and surely for much of it covered in these pages, there are many who have been close to me, some of them as coworkers and all of them as friends. Of those whose work coincides with mine in some of these pages or with whom I've collaborated on works and projects here and elsewhere, Pierre Joris has long been a principal figure, and others with whom I've joined forces on anthologies and magazines include David Antin, Steven Clay, Harris Lenowitz, George Quasha, Diane Rothenberg, and Dennis Tedlock. Beyond these there are a number of others, from arts outside of poetry, who appear in these pages and whose presence has brought my own work into new arenas—Eleanor Antin, Arman, Susan Bee, Larry Fink, Arie Galles, Tom Phillips, and Ian Tyson among the artists, and Charlie Morrow and Bertram Turetzky among the musicians and performers. And those with whom I've worked in the making of translations include Richard Johnny John, Harris Lenowitz, David McAllester, Milos Sovak, and Yasuhiro Yotsumoto.

That this book is itself a collaborative effort and a work across boundaries and borders with Heriberto Yépez is another point worth noting. It is with him in fact that the idea arose to assemble the older works into a new collage of our joint devising. In the process of our work together, he stands with Mayra Luna and Diane Rothenberg as my true companions in this venture. If I could offer a dedication to a work co-authored as this one is between us, it would be to him and them.

JEROME ROTHENBERG
Encinitas, California
2013

GALLERY ONE

PROLEGOMENA TO A POETICS

By degrees we beheld the infinite Abyss, fiery as the smoke of a burning city. Beneath us, at an immense distance, was the sun, black but shining. Round it were fiery tracks, on which revolved vast spiders crawling after their prey, which flew or rather swam in the infinite deep, in the most terrific shapes of animals sprung from corruption; and the air was full of them, and seemed composed of them. These are Devils, and are called Powers of the Air. I now asked my companion which was my eternal lot? he said, "Between the black and the white spiders."

—William Blake, from *The Marriage of Heaven & Hell*

"A LITTLE BOY LOST"

They took me from the white sun and they
left me in the black sun, left
me to sleep among long rows of overcoats:
I was a city boy lost in the country, a
wound in my hand was all I knew about willows
Can you understand, do you hear the wide
sound of the wind against the cow's
side, and the crickets that run down my
sleeve, crickets full of the night, with
bodies like little black suns? try as I will
there is only this cry in my heart, this cry:
They took me from the white sun, and they
left me in the black sun, and I
have no way of turning now, no door

THE NIGHT THE MOON WAS A SPIDER

The night the moon was a spider
we ran.
The sky grew as black as your eyes.
It was starting to rain.

Sails in the air
broke loose.
Red sails.
You laughed.
The moon was a spider.
A ribbon of blood reached down
from the sky
to the roof of our house.
Red and black.
We were trying to sing.
It was cold.
In the net of the sky
where the bones were hanging
I saw what
I thought was your face.
The scraping
of wheels over rock
in the dark of the moon.
Begin:
The night the soldiers drove by
I rose from our bed,
my hands bound behind me,
and looked.
You were trying to dream.
An icicle broke from the sky
and entered my heart.
The moon was a spider.

WHY DEEP IMAGE?

When we speak about "deep image," we renew a demand that poets get at the reality of things by turning inward: that the process of self-perception be united as far as possible with our means for perceiving the world around us. This sort of concern leads naturally to a reconsideration of whether a "poem" is something other than the structure of its words, even while being integrally connected to that structure, which gives it a shape and name.

The question which presented itself at the start, before image in any sense had clearly entered the picture, was where the poem took root (what its source was)—or, as it later developed, whether certain elements in what, by the cut of the lines, we distinguished as a "poem," were "poetic" in their very nature: in short, if there existed a special kind of poetic activity. I was by then convinced that there was a long-standing confusion between the structure of words we call a poem and the event-of-a-poem's-happening: all the more elusive because structure and event could coincide in the same space—and probably should, as likely in the nature of things. But I did feel too that not all events that occur in a poem—and certainly not in most poems written today—are in this sense the happening-of-a-poem.

The event that seemed to me most clearly central to the happening-of-a-poem was what we came to call "deep image." The word *deep* wasn't intended to convey a sense of profundity, pseudo or otherwise, but to show that the direction of seeing in this kind of image is into a man rather than outside him: not a habit of the eye so much as a penetration of the self to refocus on the world through the eyes-of-feeling. This means that we have to try to see the world in all its natural and contemporary detail as if no differences existed between the seer and the things he sees. To see in this way—through the self (emotively)—results in certain necessary changes on the material emerging in the poem:

> a heightened sense of the emotional contours of objects (their dark qualities, or shadows);
>
> their free re-association in a manner that would be impossible to descriptive or logical thought, but is here almost unavoidable;
>
> the sense of these objects (and the poem itself) being informed with a heightened relevance, a quickened sense of life;
>
> the recognition of the poem as a natural structure arising at once from the act of emotive vision.

The power of the deep image is its ability to convey a sense of two-worlds-in-one—directly—with no concept to come between the inner experience and its meaning. With this comes a new attack on the mystery of the real, in which all our habitual perceptions are continually being put into question. The poet discovers the unknown by creating it from the vast resources of his inner life, the savings of an experienced world still rich in meaning: he delivers, as deep image, the life-giving vision that he could in no other way explain.

In spite of this essential directness of communication, the recasting of the world in the self's image will seem to some a distortion of whatever world they habitually take for "the real one." Some such discomfort has accompanied the introduction of deep image by other modern poets. But any disruption of a bad habit should be welcome. The deep image brings with it a demand for new visions of the world, new creations into thought: in short for poetry in its creative aspect, in which, as Baudelaire first had it, the poem "will contain, at one and the same time, the object and the subject, the external world and the artist himself."

INVINCIBLE FLOWERS

The flowers here are so sad, I could cry.
Not one of them acts like a flower, or carries itself like a flower.
Not one grows red overnight in the sudden anguish of spring.
They lie in wax wrappers and fidget.
Or sometimes, a head peers over a vase, half alive:
they've surrendered.

Colors die out as innocence fades in the eye of the florist.
Adjusting his watch he strides past the roses.
Shouting orders at something—the evening perhaps—he will smother
the lilies.
Only the ferns will survive his cigars (and then for how long?)
Tulips, asters, begonias, etc. are squeezed in a single dark box full of
wadding,
sent out every day to hospitals, weddings and graves.
Eternal observers, these silent, terrible flowers.

No! Give me plastic flowers, flowers in granite and ice,
proud flowers cut into monuments, honoring God, the flowers of
poverty,

flowers formed by the hands of young girls in lofts in the Bronx,
cut out of papers in Tokyo, hidden in shells,
flowers pasted on walls in great bunches, painted on bottles, on stones,
enticing "real bees" to my table.

But sometimes, not meaning to, I find that I forget.
I find that I remember things that are better left forgotten.
Perhaps when it rains in my room,
and the window is open, the sheets are thrown like sand on the floor,
and my hand like a falcon is diving on quarries of paper,
I hear (at first in the distance) the sound of a great Flower
crying out loud in the sun.
And the thought of something I would not betray grows wild in my
heart.
The light is enclosed on each side by the darkness of flowers.

A POEM FOR THE PRESIDENT

In the subways of water
the president
talks with his mice:
the trains are covered
with nets,
the mice never speak.
And deep under Brooklyn
children with faces of zinc
are praising the president,
mirrors tied to the rails
deliver
the pledge of allegiance:

silently
silently
night has crept from her garden:
with breasts the color of kettles
she faces the sun,
and the president
breaks through the ground

in a smock,
nearing the place where she sits
in the second darkness of Brooklyn:

death in the tenements
covers a mirror:
the president waves:
the children
are praising the mice:

the mice never speak.

A SMALL POEM

Something, an iron door
closing, small
fingers touching
a stalk, has frightened
me: walking the lake
at dusk there was ice
and some crows: dark
travelers, nothing
to fear but
myself.

THE STATIONMASTER'S LAMENT

I have buried her under a stone
The eagles fly past our house with umbrellas
The grey forms rise in the grass
I have buried her solemnly
Speaking the words that she knew:
And the chairs have stood by my side
The trains have been constant in death

The trains have been constant
The conductors who watered our plants have dropped by:
Nodding their pale Busterkeaton-like heads

The brakemen have played farewells on their cellos
Have rendered their final farewells
And the chairs have stood by my side

The chairs have been constant
The chairs with their arms full of wires were dearer to me than my
friends
I will never forget them
They and the eagles both loved us (as only our plants had before)
They came when I called them
They wept dark tears made of burlap
And stood by my side

I have buried her under a forest
The conductors who walked with her coffin were there
The benches were there with white thermoses turning her sheets
With burning black eyes the telegraph keys called the wind
Now they sleep at her feet
And the brakemen play their farewells

We have paid our farewells with her plants
Where the grey forms were rising commuters climb ramps through the
night
They throw in their fistfulls of earth and bad dreams
They run to the edge of the night where no one will follow
Past lakes of blue darkness where furnaces holler like bulls
And I sit with the three-hundred chairs of my dreams
They have stood by my side
I will never forget them

And the trains have been constant in death

THE REAL REVOLUTION IS TRAGIC

The face of America buried under
a stone, and the rain that falls through my needle
silently enters this room in the night.
Ships cry: the passengers
race through a forest of wheels:

and I and my love and America
battle the streets with mirrors and chalk,
and the night with dark kisses.

Over a town that runs inward
I bend and pick from the floor
an egg full of hours (voice
of the graveyard pressing my skull,
this graveyard of voices):
                                        oh listen,
we're dying again in
America, dying
the deaths of our highways and houses,
and love's the gaud least attained.

Tonight the face of my secret America
will float on the water, the banners
of hair take root like red trees,
spreading fire over these cities.
Why are the eyes of it burning,
meeting my gaze with percussions and glass?

Ah,
      this sunrise is old, with its puddles of death
and its motors: the rain of wet dollars
pours through my shirt in
the night, in the days without hope,
in the years that are falling.

A CONCILIATION

Ce sont des villes!—Rimbaud

The cities hold dark rain,
and we will die.

The cities hold plaster,
and faces scribbled by children,
and hair: we

will pass through the long rooms
again, and come to a sudden
cold place where the river ceases,

remembering. What?
To have been with you,
breath against breath,
some hot summer.

What cities!

IMAGE & MODE:
A LETTER, 1960, TO ROBERT CREELEY

New York
November 28, 1960

Dear Bob,
I hesitated for some time before sending off the last letter, wondering if, without addressing myself to the question of the poem as an aural entity, etc., the rest would not still seem vague and generalized. Finally decided to let it go and continue with this.

To begin with, I pretty much agree that in some sense "speaking, or writing, itself becomes a 'percept' and in this guise a deep influence on the 'thing said.'" I'd only want to qualify it by speaking of two kinds of percept: a) what you call "mode," etc. which is, to my mind, *percept internal to the poem*, and b) the *referential percepts* (image etc.) which at least seem to have external counterparts, i.e. can be taken in that sense as direct analogues to meaning, reality, etc. (The latter might also include the sense of an actual dialogue in time—percept internal to the speaker—that's so strong in your own work; or should that be considered as different again? Well…) It seems to me that such distinctions, which I feel necessary for clarity, could again make one infer that image is prior to line or rhythm (or vice versa), yet this is deceptive—from the first opening into the poem, the referential elements are themselves sounds or patterns of sound and pulse, etc., so that it's still possible to think of the emergence of the whole poem (sound and "content") as a concurrent unity. Something like this, anyway, is how I'd want to consider "form" in the poem: as a progression and patterning of all the elements of language and vision integral to the poem's organic movement.

Well, to get to the problem of "craft" from another direction—Duncan in a letter somewhere—to Kelly or me, I forget which—asked how we'd distinguish the poem from any other visions? I think we would, of course, almost too simply, "because the poem is the vision of a poet," i.e. by here reintroducing the concept of the Makar.[1] But if poems are to be the visions of Makaris, they must be of Makaris who see. In other words, I don't think we should be trapped into a hasty equation of poetry and verse-making, and that's what I see as the danger where structure and/or measure are treated as isolated factors, i.e. abstractly. (Or if you're going to make this your focus, reducing the poem to sound and/or manner, shouldn't you take it as far as Stein did? The referential area of a poem, when present but neglected, has a way of turning back on the poet, betraying him into an apparent triviality.)

So, my concern so far is whether the internal percepts, when separated from vision (particularly where referential elements persist) can really lead to a poetry in depth. For myself, I feel image (free referential percept) central in this sense, as focus, if only that I still believe this, from moment to moment can take the naïve world on faith, to move from there. (And if I lost the referential percept also, would turn perhaps to something almost music, dropping the content altogether.) But to take form as center (in a poem that retains referential elements) seems to me almost necessarily to act toward a distortion or weakening of vision: since vision (to invert and paraphrase Zukofsky) often involves the assertion of form thru something like privation of it, or by its consideration as inseparable from the referential percepts which it voices. But maybe it's all a question of what one stresses to begin with.

It's come to me here, having taken it this far along the first two lines mentioned, that it's really the 3rd thing—sense of a dialogue in time—that most strongly concerns you. Somehow, probably because of the emphasis Duncan put on it in earlier letters, I'd read your speaking-and-writing-as-itself-percept in terms of so-called Melos, which I suppose is implied there but not really key. Do I read you right to say you conceive of "mode" as the reality of the poem at a given point in time: the structure, perhaps, of its emergence into speech? If so, would the poem's tension be seen resulting from the almost physical effort to voice it, to make it actual? Hence

[1] Scots word for the poet (plural: Makaris), as it turns up in William Dunbar's "Lament for the Makers," etc.

organic to the conceptual impulse, etc.? This, anyway, is something I can confirm from my own experience of it, though I don't believe that there's no other way in, or that the movement toward image isn't derived from the same source. What confuses me is the apparent equation of this with craft; at least I find it possible to consider craft in various ways, depending on the poem: the poem's being fashioned to do what it's about, which may be other than the presentation of a thinking-out-loud. I mean, I can't deny the validity of poems that are largely a kind of thinking-out-loud (and most good poems are that somewhere in their history), but feel this again as too narrow a center, leading to "dry manner" or substanceless psychological oozings, the sense of a great strain directed toward the statement of nothing. (And in your own work, I find this often averted precisely as the content emerges, moving toward an intense fullness: and in THE DOOR, etc. being transformed into a total poetry, which I would praise sans slightest hesitation.)

You raise a question about translation, its supposed dangers, etc., which I take it is with reference to use of it in *The Fifties*, *Floating World*, elsewhere. I obviously can't go along with you here, since I wouldn't ever have given that much time to translation as simply "informational." I think we can agree about key areas of the poem not really being "translatable" (the logopeia, the thinking-out-loud element, etc.) if you're speaking of giving equivalents in any way exact. But precisely this is what makes it ever really worth bothering: an area left open in which (sometimes) a new poem can be written. This involves some sense of re-creation: sympathetic submergence into the generalized circumstances of the original, etc. But aside from this I think there's an area of poem that's much more nearly (tho not completely) translatable, of image, etc.: so I'd be disagreeing with the old Frost chestnut of poetry being what's lost in translation, or only that. Anyway, I feel it's for us to cut across boundaries where we can: I'm too much out of it ever to be a nationalist, even in poetry, and while I draw a lot from where I stand (especially the structure of language, as order of the speech I know), believe we have to learn to talk also across the level of "deep image" and vision: and where the practice of it's grown rusty in present surroundings, will look to see it done wherever it's open to me and then—transforming as far as I can the part that would be lost—to hear it back in my own voice, etc.

I've been warned too, but would strongly disagree, that certain of these elements are so locked in, say, the Spanish tradition and "climate" as to be unusable by poets here. Yet Neruda's Chile isn't Lorca's Spain, more I gather like Norway in terrain and with mixtures of Basques, Indians, Celts, etc.; so too for Celan's Germany and/or Rumania, Breton's Paris, Lawrence's England, the America that's given us the sometimes emergence of this in Whitman (out of the fuzzier depths of Emerson), Stevens ("hunting tigers in red weather"), even Pound ("Thou art a beaten dog beneath the hail, A swollen magpie in a fitful sun / Half black half white"): most of our good poets somewhere in their work, yourself included. So it's these elements that move across languages, in contrast to those that inhere, that we must also keep ourselves open to see. Our tradition even now is great enough to hold whatever new approaches we bring to it, if only we fit them in with passion, etc. In the next *Floating World*, too, I've tried to include a few "ancient" texts translated into the native idiom but with the image kept strong or even re-enforced: all of this with the feeling that there's other ways into the poem than what we've so far gotten from Pound and Williams: other ways too of music and craft: and ultimately that each of us must come to his own "truth," etc. from whatever direction: the unique coherence and rightness of each poem.

In terms of the above differences suggested and your readings, say, of poems in *White Sun*, I think part of the difficulty too may be in my normal use there of a cumulative rather than a sharply hesitant line, the latter more heavily associated with the effect of thinking-out-loud (at least in the "Black Mountain" development, etc.): uninterrupted rather than interrupted movement. If that's the trouble—for the ear at least—could you perhaps re-read some of the poems in terms of it, if not to dig at least to see that it's not done without some care. (Also you might re-read "Taste of Joy" and "Conciliation," images aside, for the interrupted movement that's in fact there: something first learned from you, Denise, others, and of more importance as I've gone on.) But to prove you wrong where you think I falter, there's no other way in the end than thru image, and to see that is perhaps more a question of satori than reasoned discussion. Or sleight-of-hand, if I turn out simply wrong.

As ever,
Jerry

THE LIGHT BULB & THE COCKEYED QUEEN OF POLAND

There is something
following you…

But when I looked
behind me
the two women pointed—
at what?

The sun in the bowl
isn't cautious.
Why should she wonder?

No dignity in that.
My shoes?

A turn of the lock
equaled death.
The two women pointed.

There is something
following you…

The sun in the bowl
isn't cautious.

But when I looked
behind me—
a turn of the lock
equaled death.

No dignity in that.

The two women pointed—
at what?

There is something
following you…

My shoes?

A turn of the lock
equaled death.
Why should she wonder?

The two women pointed—
at what?

The lightbulb
& the cockeyed queen of Poland.

No dignity in that.

HOW TRAGIC IT IS TO BE A KING & LIVE IN A PALACE & NEVER HAVE TIME TO BE GAY

Something about it was sad.
You could tell it was sad.
Either the King or the Queen
or Myself was mad,
but something was sad.
It was terribly sad.
It was wrong.
You could tell it was wrong:
the king had been ailing for days
so loud and so long
that his ermine robe couldn't take any more
and blew out its spots.
Oh yes it was sad.
It was ridiculous too, but first it was sad
and second it was wrong
and third it was cold.
It was terribly cold.
It was coldest under the throne.
It was everything under the throne.
I think said the Queen it is mice.

I think it is rain said the King.
I think it is night.
It is oddly and strangely like night.
The hand of the moon
the hand on my shoulder is white.
It is terribly white.
It is wrong.
The Queen ran into my bed.
The chamberlain stood by the door.
The King tripped over the floor:
he fell down and landed head last
on my canopy.
I think said the Queen it's the King.
I think it's the spring said the King.
I think it's the wind.
It sounds like the wind.
It is oddly and strangely the wind.
It is oddly and strangely like night.
Or the rain.
Or the wind.
I'm sure said the King it's the wind.
I'm sure said the Queen it's the King.
After she said it
they carried him out.
After she said it again
they brought him back in.
He was too thin to laugh so we cried.
He was too fat to fart so he died.
And we buried him under a royal bed
of the Queen's own favorite royal begonias,
except for his head
sticking out of the ground
like a flower.
And then we wept.
Christ how we wept.
Buckets we wept.
It's sad said the Queen.

And it was.

A FIRST MANIFESTO 1960

The poem is the record of a movement from perception to vision.

Poetic form is the pattern of that movement through space & time.

The deep image is the content of vision emerging in the poem.

The vehicle of movement is imagination.

The condition of movement is freedom.

A DEATH FUGUE *after Paul Celan*

Black milk of morning we drink you at dusktime
we drink you at noontime and dawntime we drink you at night
we drink and drink
There's a man in this house who cultivates snakes and who writes
who writes when it's nightfall *nach Deutschland* your golden hair
Margareta
he writes it and walks from the house and the stars all start flashing he
whistles his dogs to draw near
whistles his Jews to appear starts us scooping a grave out of sand
he commands us play up for the dance

Black milk of morning we drink you at night
we drink you at dawntime and noontime we drink you at dusktime
we drink and drink
There's a man in this house who cultivates snakes and who writes
who writes when it's nightfall *nach Deutschland* your golden hair
Margareta
your ashen hair Shulamite we scoop out a grave in the sky where it's
roomy to lie
He calls jab it deep in the soil you men you other men sing and play
he tugs at the sword in his belt he swings it his eyes are blue
jab your spades deeper you men you other men play up again for the
dance

Black milk of morning we drink you at night
we drink you at noontime and dawntime we drink you at dusktime
we drink and drink
there's a man in this house your golden hair Margareta
your ashen hair Shulamite he cultivates snakes

He calls play that death thing more sweetly Death is a straw boss *aus Deutschland*
he calls scrape that fiddle more darkly then hover like smoke in the air
then scoop out a grave in the clouds where it's roomy to lie

Black milk of morning we drink you at night
we drink you at noontime Death is a straw boss *aus Deutschland*
we drink you at dusktime and dawntime we drink and drink
Death is a straw boss *aus Deutschland* his eye is blue
he hits you with leaden bullets his aim is true
there's a man in this house your golden hair Margareta
he sets his dogs on our trail he gives us a grave in the sky
he cultivates snakes and he dreams Death is a straw boss *aus Deutschland*

your golden hair Margareta
your ashen hair Shulamite

Translation from German

WALKIN' AROUND *after Pablo Neruda*

It just so happens that I'm tired of being a man.
It just so happens that I walk into tailor shops and movies,
withered, impenetrable, a flannel swan
that steers across a sea of origins and ashes.

The odors from a barber shop can start me bawling.
I only want a little rest from stones and wool.
I only want to see my last of institutes and gardens,
of merchandise, of eye glasses, of elevators.

It just so happens that I'm tired of my feet and my nails
and my hair and my shadow.
It just so happens that I'm tired of being a man.

And yet how delightful it would be
to threaten some accountant with the head of a lily
or murder a nun with a blow on the ear.
How beautiful
to go through streets with a green knife
and holler out loud till I die of frostbite.

I don't want to keep on being a root in the darkness,
irresolute, pulled from all sides, till a dream leaves me shaking,
dragged down through the seeping bowels of the earth,
absorbing and thinking, stuffed with food every day.

I don't want all that grief on my shoulders.
I don't want to keep on as a root and a tomb,
alone underground, a wine cellar stocked with the dead,
frozen stiff, half gone with the pain.

So the day called Monday starts burning like oil
when it sees me pull in with my face of a jailhouse,
and it howls on its way like a wounded wheel,
and leaves tracks of hot blood in the direction of night.

And it shoves me into certain dark corners, into certain moist houses,
into hospitals where the bones sail through the windows,
into certain shoemakers' shops with their odors of vinegar,
into streets full of terrible holes.

There are birds the color of sulfur and horrible guts
that swing from the doors of houses that I hate,
there are false teeth forgotten in a coffee pot,
there are mirrors
that ought to be crying from shame and terror,
there are umbrellas wherever I look, and poisons, and belly buttons.

I walk around with my calm, with my eyes, with my shoes,
with my anger, with my memory failing,
I move on, I wander through offices and orthopedic shops,
and courtyards where clothes are hung from a wire:
underdrawers, towels and nightgowns that cry
slow tears full of dirt.

Translation from Spanish

A SIDE OF BEEF

1
The meat hooks are black, covered
with flies licking
the blood, these black meat hooks

In the air a late fly
hovers: it will find a window
& rest there

& I will find no one:
no one will find us
come closer! sit with me here

The windows are burning

2
The meat hooks are black
with white flies
They are licking them, ah
the black meat hooks

Ah the black meat hooks
the presence of death
in a room where a meat hook
swings from the ceiling

The meat hooks are black
with black flies
They are watching over them, ah
the black meat hooks

3
But listen, won't you?
listen to the blade
as it swings
& the meat hooks

& the black meat hooks
where the sunlight
falls from the ceiling

where the fire burns
how many animals
come to eat from your hand?

A face cut in two:
in the blood that covers each eye
a black meat hook

4
They come toward where I am
but we are further away
still further
every time they reach us

we are further away
for being here, for watching
the black meat hooks

It is not light enough
to see you, when I look around
your shadow burns

your shadow turns from me,
the meat hook swings around
a further corner

THE COUNTER-DANCES OF DARKNESS

THE TEXT

All life is oriented to the light from which life comes. The bees in their dances are oriented to the sun and, if it is dark, will dance in relation to a candle flame.

Robert Duncan, *The Day Book*

THE COMMENTARY

1
But that the bee could be seeking death, oblivion, was also clear & would, in some sense, make that dance more fierce—more precious too? We noticed other movements as well, movements away from light, of the animals who burrowed in our hill, the night creatures stiffened by beams from my flashlight, the roots of all things curving back into earth's belly, the penis into the womb of the woman. Could light teach us the whole dance without the counter-dance of darkness?

2
There is no light or darkness that, in itself, can orient us to where we become, but only a constant shift of planes between the two—light & darkness, life & death, speech & silence, sight & blindness. "The dark," wrote Lorca, "wants to become light," but the Gabon pygmies told us, "The light becomes darkness / the night & again the night / the day with hunger tomorrow."

3
Both sides are made real—one not subordinated to the other, but as functions of a total movement born from, productive of, each other. That the child is born is no truer than that the man dies; & sometimes the distance between birth & death is no more than a moment, part of an hour at best. Yet the narrow dimensions of that child's life is no stranger than that our whole universe, whose limits move away from us at speeds approximating

to the speed of light, will return someday to the undifferentiated mass of its first beginning, to a heavy & dark brilliance the size of Mars's orbit. Had Lawrence visioned this when he wrote: EVERYTHING IS MEANT TO DISAPPEAR. EVERY CURVE PLUNGES INTO THE VORTEX AND IS LOST, RE-EMERGES WITH A CERTAIN RELIEF AND TAKES TO THE OPEN, AND THERE IS LOST AGAIN. Between light & darkness we wait, we dance, like the Evening Star he sang of, BETWEEN THE SUN AND THE MOON, AND SWAYED BY NEITHER OF THEM... THE EVENING STAR THAT IS SEEN AT THE DIVIDING OF THE DAY AND NIGHT, BUT THEN IS MORE WONDERFUL THAN EITHER.

4

We are not only the victims of the forces that will destroy us, we are their children. And it is given us, at times of passionate concentration, to celebrate the movements of our being-in-the-world. The light will kill the bee & the darkness guard the root, & it will finally not matter. But the celebration matters NOW—whether darkness is my source, or light my goal, or both—whether I walk between the darknesses & dream of light, or blinded by that light, seek darkness. We are all in movement.

THE DANCES

The penis, this other miracle, enters the dark, the body enters the dark & will soon be wed to the darkness—
which of these will keep sight of the heavens, will seek light as its first, its only source?
& the root that presses deep in the earth—what does it seek?

The myriad roots that turn from the light—into earth, the darkness
how does the loss of the heavens sit with them? or their place in the total design?

. . . .

1

The dancers move forward—I am last in the circle, changing
my body, pretending to be with those who had died in the fire
my love a deceit, starting from the lowest level of what I would soon become—
fire, fire, the smoke asleep in their golden veins, as with fire & blood.

2
Someone to speak to me, someone to answer me where I stand—
your light is a mystery over these hills, twining me, whispering through
   me,
the first rain over my hands as it hurries to touch me—in that light
your shadow had yet to appear, it was a conciliation, but clearer than that,
   a beginning.

3
There is a movement in its rooms no longer—
a locket that was shaken by the wind
& a dead body that rests with the other dead bodies—
evening, my shadow touched by the headlights from a passing truck
while across the road other shadows cover other dead bodies—
I had forgotten where it began,
I can only remember the ache in your fingers
so cold, so in need of my breath to wake them.

4
As I dreamed my stature (mad dream!) as in the pasture at night
among the freaks, the many-headed cattle, loiterers—
that I could match their size—that bewildering bruteness,
could be set apart where I walked to be mocked—
this monster, this debaser, broken & degenerate & eternally damned &
   alone—
only not to be whole—a part of that order, the goad for its senseless
   stars—
not to give life & watch it taken back again—
what wars in a single lifetime! what slow deaths worse than all wars!
what bliss as the body dissolves, turns sour, returns to its pitiless earth!
does a flower offend you?
does the sun make you cringe that opens every inch of you with careless
   fingers
for this I had made myself monstrous!
how many others must die to force one moment of doubt to your throat?

5
The silence will open—as a hand will open against your hand
though its fingers will not open—or will open only to my breath that
   moves them

or as the wind moves the curtains to show a field, the corner of this sky
the corner of your eye that sleeps inside me—
in the shadow of the eaves the trigger spoke, uncoiled the spring broke
  loose,
clouds big with thunder, golden shapes of birds leaped skyward
fell & crushed themselves against my hands—
still others will crush themselves against my hands
& when the dead return, there will be other ways of telling time
& many strange words then—
& there will be a language also—of our own.

6

The existence of the horrible in every particle of air—
among its roots, submerged in droplets—vision!
You were not immune to it—neither at evening with the rain still in your
  hair
nor in the garden at noon—not the first to be spared, to raise a cry
against its stars—what imbecile regrets for all your nights of silence!
No one had dreamed your pain then—how it would draw the fingers
  back
would drive its roots inside you—muscle & joint, the knot, the hard en-
  closure—death?
Around you the air was suddenly alive—
whole cities full of the "luckless dead"—pavilions—marchers
but your heart couldn't contain it—like the universe it shrank, became
  your fist
abandoned in the rain, the odor clings to it—
& there are places in the dark where no light enters,
where a hand moves slowly through the silence, on the wall
a pressure that was like the earth, took color from it—
your shadow in my blood—for we were someone's dream of vengeance.

7

Not in a meadow—the dead who are dead & the dead who will be dead
& the bull driven to a slope below the house, a dark, terrible shadow
& your darker shadow, the moon—
for this we delayed, for the night, just started, to end
for time to lose all dimension—only the kiss at your throat, the warm
  touch of you

curve of my blood through yours—but the dead were with us from the
start
it was a circle, a habit of repetition,
first sensed in the breaking of bread, the heifer's dance into life
the mother cow swollen her bag hanging down to the earth
also a root through the earth—all swollen, all broken
you woke to it under the moon, but in darkness—
in darkness it had begun—in darkness, in darkness it will be ended.

IMAGE & MELOS: A LETTER, 1960, TO ROBERT DUNCAN

September 27, 1960

...following with great interest your interchange with Kelly. On the basis of your first letter to reach here (only one I've seen, other 2 being described) *I feel no real disagreement as to melos, etc., being other vehicles for manifestation of "floating world"* (source) within the poem, tho if you define yourself as a poet of "word-magic" primarily, my own direction in these last years has probably been toward "image-magic"—yet it doesn't seem to me that any of the "powers" are totally to be denied, nor can they where the poem is allowed to happen. Certainly I find image occurring at many points in your work, & can only hope for myself that sound & music do not automatically leave where image enters. In the act of uncovering the poem, in fact, my personal experience has been that the other elements we are said to be slighting are especially insistent; where they don't assert themselves (emerging concurrently) the image feels unreal and slack—a lightweight, lifeless counterfeit.

But image still appears to me as the thing sought once I am into the poem. Or more precisely the under-world of hidden painful (joyful) forms. As in the Thomas gospel:

When you see your likeness, etc.

Here I have to enter without any of the old certainties: to go out and search for that world, never knowing for sure if what I find is real or dross, except in so far as *I can accept the data emerging from the poems—mine and others.* In this way the poem creates the reality that then exists for us: a unique (one hopes) and certain thing, that can yet be shared. It is, I think, because of the initial disbelief / skepticism (perhaps despair) that prompts the surrender to the under-world (to find & create forms & images therefrom) that I cannot—as you can, perhaps—really utilize other data—allusory, historical, etc.—in the composition of the poem; & in the presence of other poems I can surrender only where the impact of the search & the resultant world it has created overwhelms me with its presence. So for a while much of your writing in the [Opening of the] Field, etc., was closed to me, largely for the "intrusion" of the tradition you prize so highly—and I too, once I understood the way to the source, to the reality of the poems. But, for myself, as a way of making the poem, I must still come on the source directly, as a head-on confrontation; in other words, I can't build it up yet through intermediaries, but have to create it new in order to accept it. For this reason, I think, the image becomes for me the *prima materia.* If I were fixed enough in a tradition (able to write from it, not just in its light) so I might build with blocks of data largely—as I find you doing—then melos, logos, etc. might come first to hand—the image-symbols being there to start with. (This happens in translation.) But it has not yet become, for me, a question of *arrangement* (I don't use the word disparagingly) but *discovery at every point I meet the poem.* Now, where this is really the case (& I find it historically in the poetry of the "deep image," whether among 20th Century disbelievers or earlier figures—isolated mystics, etc., figures cut off from the mainstream of dogma), I feel a new power released, nameless for now, a result of that "self-abandonment to that which is not known". So that I don't take the "rootlessness" you've spoken of in earlier letters as a liability—I don't assume you mean lack of precedents, history being full of the uprooted—rather it seems to me, once met in its own terms, like the dark voyage Melville described in the great *Lee Shore* chapter of *Moby Dick*:

> But as in landlessness alone resides highest truth, etc.

For, then, this seems to be the great adventure of spirit in our time, & (why not) particularly the burden of the American poet, where the destruction of the old certainties has gone further & strange cultures oppress consciousness with their conflicting demands. In your work I see this answered, partly, by a re-arrangement of older elements—probably not far distant from the new-creations of the deep image poets. In this way I find it stronger and fuller than the early poems of Creeley (before the Door, etc.) where melos, etc., seemed to me to be pursued in isolation from any real sense of deep image, *almost* as a decoration of the trivial.

(Stein seems to me the better example of how far the under-world can be explored without utilization of deep image, & I'm glad for that reason that you mention her.)

THE JOURNEY BETWEEN SUMMERS

To Robert Kelly & Octavio Paz

Dissolution of your names,
two cities

hidden in her lips, a
frightened dust

& the portion of my eye
that still sees

watches morning, this
green light

across the bed.
The mountain leaves us.

Shivers. I
think of
Paris, white
water

& black trees. I
hold her close.

We sleep: the
movement

between poems
is half my life,

the other half
your voices.

A thought. A nerve
detached from sleep,
forcing a passage,
rains

against the further door.
We force it.

Strangers we stand
unknowing

in a stranger's house.
Somos

desconocidos, strangers
to your love.

Yet the same grass holds us,
where you slept we

also sleep, the grass
is warm with your shapes.

With strangers. My body
covers hers. The grass

swarms with old alphabets.
A god once walked here,

bent to your voices.
And when it's dark

on the porch of some
old farmhouse,

because the sky
is that much darker

or hearing the voices
from below the earth

of animals, I form
the letters of your names

in light. Or draw them
from her lips.

It is that still.
Death awaits us

in what's nearest.
Only a voice.

It is enough. It
is enough.

It doesn't last. We
leave this mountain

too. It is enough.
I wait here

& the old woman,
nearly dead across the way

screams. Another name.
I have no voice

to say it. It is
enough, no name to give it

but death, this
radiance

across the room
we move to

as I cup her face,
my hands

reach up to it
& fold

as you would say,
in sleep.

THE DEEP IMAGE IS THE THREATENED IMAGE

And he said to me 'He is lost who takes a boat & takes no risk.'

And he told me that part of a man's salvation is imperiling himself.

And the waves came, lifting what was beneath, & cast it on the shore.

*And he told me that the surface of the sea is unattainable light, & its bottom unfathomed darkness, & between are the perilous whales.**

By an arrogant act of creation, the poet defies death & the nightmare-void : he tries to be a god & fails. But his failure has taken him into new country, where the struggle continues. A strange terrain too, but only for the self-deluded. Here he can touch reality, feel its dark outline beneath his hands, its breath against him. His center has become the world's. The rhythm of the struggle is the rhythm of creation. Defiance is a palpable surrender.

Courage & skill : without them, nothing. Without them, dizziness & loss. Extinction. The darkness rises up to drown him. A word more or less, a wrong step, & the mind is plunged into chaos, the chaos of the un-created, shapeless, empty. The poem's meaning is the only meaning possible at a given moment in the struggle.

U n a t t a i n a b l e l i g h t . . . u n f a t h o m e d d a r k n e s s . . . & b e t w e e n a r e t h e p e r i l o u s w h a l e s . There is no hope of victory, for death outlasts him. He can only move & shape. Poetry becomes a passage & an act of desperation. The poet writing to survive, rejoicing in each new survival, with something like the hunter's joy. The last free man, fighting the darkness on his own terrain & in his own terms. The terms—his weapons, his means—must be his own. Those who refuse to turn back, who cannot turn back, have been the real poets, the heroes of the word.

The "deep image" is the poetic image struggling with the darkness. The image rescued from the lie of the unthreatened. Not as a literary prescription, for writing better poems or nurturing the language, but from an impasse in the soul, in which the protective "reality" & false emblems of the inherited past have drawn a blank. Not as a neurotic outcry either, from the weakness of a self-pity, but in the wholeness & fitness of the poet's vision.

The world as it existed for the first man still exists. It taunts us & breaks into our dreams. The poet dares to face it without hope & to create from pure desire, from pure love. The world as it existed before man. The primal world, not yet hardened into the mold of law, but a new law to be imposed on it in the daily encounter. A return to the beginning. A struggle to shape the world through the power of the creative moment, the flash of light that overthrows the darkness & is itself a greater darkness. Creation struggling with death: the final death of man which may itself come as a blinding flash of light. Poetry as a total & desperate act. This is where the real song begins.

October 1961

*Then everything came to me with a sword in its hand. When he said "Escape" I asked "Where?" And he said "Fall in the darkness." And I fell in the darkness & saw myself. And he said "Never see any man but yourself & never come out of the darkness until I take you out : & if I take you out I will show you myself, & you will see me: & if you see me you will be the furthermost of the furthest."**

---

*an-Niffari, 10th Century Arab writer

A CANTICLE FOR SUICIDES

I'm sick of it!
Right up to here I'm sick of it!
I'm sick of the life-song
I'm sick of the windows that don't let the air in
And the windows that don't keep it out!
I'm sick of it
I'm sick of the dead who isn't dead anymore?
I'm sick of the hammers that tear open the earth that dirty the streets
with the smell of water
I'm sick of the smell of water
I'm sick of the faces that scream with boredom in the sexual night
I'm sick of my own face staring back at me from a mirror

Who isn't dead anymore?
The water cries from my lungs
The black water rises inside me and hurts me with its far smell
But I go on living
I go on breathing the air and living in the shadows
You live beside me in the shadows
And every night the water gets deeper every night the houses vanish in
the small rain
Who isn't dead anymore who hasn't fallen who isn't falling from the
lonely roofs

from the nights of desire and the tight hands that stretch toward us
from the small rain the rain of the last day, the judgment

I'm sick of it!
Right up to here I'm sick of it!
I'm sick of the faces and the hands I'm sick of the bodies that can't hold
in their own smell
I'm sick of the smell and the dark sexual water
I'm sick of the stone under the water the stone in my chest in my lungs
I'm sick of you
I'm sick of myself
I'm sick of the corridors and mirrors I'm sick of the way I look at myself
in the night
Because it's always myself that I end up facing
It's always myself that I can't see
Myself in the mirror in the sink myself staring back from the water

This is the water of self
This is the stone under the water, the death's head
This is the worm under the stone tear it out of your sight
This is the mirror under the stone tear it out of your sight
This is the silence under the stone tear it out of your sight
Tear it out of your sight!
This is the house spun by worms who isn't dead anymore?
This is the sound of tears in the shadows
This is a house in the shadows
This is a house with all the world's shadows in its corners
With all the world's waters beating at its doors
This is the water of self tear it out of your sight

FOUND POEMS FROM "THE EMERGENCE NOTEBOOKS"

1

A season in the mind
of hell, the furthest
opening, a passage
starting from the eye

then journeys
downward, further down
it meets itself
the meeting
is another start,
the passage out
returning

2

:
in mud, the silt
from Euphrates' banks
he saw

THE CREATION

This was the silence of the beginning
& spoke

TIAMAT
APSU (abyss)

A woman without hands
with pierced sex crying

Who dreamed it: was it death
or hunger then: in whose mind
was the water born, whose image?

CHAOS
was its name

& there were colors in it, lines
in all directions, such fine animals
of every kind & faces without end

: chaos with colors with bright eyes

*

& ATUM grew restless
too but found no woman

bathed in NUN he felt
his member swell, its lips
would open toward him
then he took it in his hand

3
(These were the notes, the words written in the first phase. I read them over until they blurred, until they were words no longer but music, until the music was music no longer but light, until the light split into small suns & moons & spun around me. What did I see? What could I report to the others? So deeply imbedded as no longer to be a part of me. Light we cannot hold, but goes from us

4
& filled it with shapes
                    bending around the curve
                    a star breaks
                    two stars
a yellow tree grows toward the opposite light
as song

foliage of morning, water
                    & your body that fills
                    the empty light no longer
                    your body in the morning air
                          forgive me
                    your body in its latitudes
                          forgive   forgive me
as the yellow tree was music
grew   that I will know you
                    only for a day
forgive me

5
where does it start in us?
                    each time I draw breath
                    the pain

feels even deeper,
signals a loss
that leads beyond my escape to it
the face
detestable face
smiling at me over the black lamp
breaks the spell, hope
dies again
always the procession
of the eternal marchers
begins
but
"willing to stake your life & risk madness"
(writes Snyder)
how far already
when even the poem
is more than I wanted

6

A KEY. TO SPEAK THESE WORDS IS TO BE DELIVERED: AVOID TERROR AT ALL COSTS, OR ELSE KNOW DREAD AS ITSELF A KIND OF JOY: IT IS NO LONGER THE EYE THAT SEES, BUT SIGHT EXTENDS FROM THE OPEN POINT TO WHERE MOTION IS FIVE-DIRECTIONAL AND ETERNAL: FROM HEREON THERE IS NOTHING THE MIND KNOWS THAT IS NOT REAL

7

for Robert Kelly

Strange
that it takes so long to die

: my father's words
stay with me   are heard
as impulse   as the image
say, or pivot
lingers (Duncan tells us)
in the *melos*
all the rest is
senseless

although we sing it
(as the garden spinning
turns
to join her body)

& in perfect health begin,
hoping to cease not till death

From THE SEVEN HELLS OF THE JIGOKU ZOSHI

The First Hell: *of measures, where swindlers measure fire in iron boxes*

How can any of you know
what it feels like
to count coins in Hell

You have the rest of it to keep you busy
Your eyes are troubled enough

But down here
the nights are longer
& the days are senseless
Down here
the rain falls
upside-down
from iron boxes

The smoke inside the narrow room
pulls back
It winds around the bedposts
like a colored cloth
around a leg that's bleeding

Violet & green
with pain

What should we say to our fingers?
Should we remind them

of the cool silk yards
they handled behind counters

The healing lotions
rolled between the palms

Should we tell them that the earth
crawling with black grief
at least was wet

1
2

Blue coins of disaster
are ringing in the night
The distant call of metal birds
is like the rhyming
in bad poems
before your birth

You would not know me now

The fire at my ribs
has emptied me of flesh & words
I stand here with the others
counting

letting the numbers fill my head
An outlaw

1
2
3
4
5

I want to turn aside
but Hell won't let me
Hell is the outraged customer

who slams the cashbox
against my hands

A candle drips
along the sidewalk
Wax covers the windows of a small store
& blurs the sun

A darkness full of crates
through which I walk
thinking of other hells than this

The skin cries under the brand
of intellect
Deceit of numbers
raising questions in the mind
that's helpless
The fevered brow

Smash it to hell
You have a right to it

1
2
3
4
5

The white eye watches
through the window
Where we live is where
we always lived
The sea of death

THE SECOND HELL: *of thieves, where thieves are ground in mortars*

The thieves the thieves the lovely thieves are no more
The shore is washed by the sea
The sea is combed by the wind

The wind sleeps all day in the chimney
It moves through the house in the evening
It wakes us, it opens a door for the sea
It walks where the thieves walked
It leads us into a night without windows
Comfort me stay with me light of my eyes
The lovely thieves are no more

The thieves are crying
Their voices are crying from Hell
Their tears fill the snow with lost coins
Their tears burn my fingers
My fingers that move through your hair
How gentle your voice is
Respond to them Answer them
Think of the pain they bear in their skin
The thread that runs from their skin to your voice
From your voice to the wind
Respond to them Answer them

The thieves the thieves the lovely thieves are no more
The shadows are silent
The silence has entered your voice
Your voice is asleep in the shadows
Wake again in the night wake again full of fear
Wake to the shadow of death at your window
The ladders that hung from the sky are falling
The thieves are falling their blood is filling the earth
The earth that awaits you
The earth that destroys you
The earth that has stolen your voice

The earth's voice is crying with hunger
A single grave waits for us all
A single stone grinds us to water
The water flows to the sea
The sea is asleep in your voice
Your voice that could flood Hell with tears
That could ease the pain of the dying

But only the thieves cry tonight
They cry where no one can hear them
Their voices cry from the stone
Their voices cry where we sleep without dreams
The thieves the thieves the lovely thieves are no more

The Fifth Hell: *of unclean food, for those who served unclean food to others*

        The fattened sky
resting at the door of this
        white butchershop
carries the old wounds:
The poor meat stands without skin & streams blood,
it covers flowers & roots in the window
flows in slow rivers under the paws of a cat
The butcher sees me & smiles
        the red steam coating his apron
The breasts of the housewives are heavy with salt

Our looks across from a distance:
        I feel the grass part
in his smile, the soft paws brushing the earth
Why should this butcher concern me?
Why should I want to run or cry out?
        to rise like a river of teeth?
Why should I look so long at those rows of sweet flesh,
the flanks black with flies, the white tiles?

His breath is stirring the hair of these women,
like dry smoke it moves down the aisle
        past the register
        comes to rest on the scales
Salt & fire, dismemberment, blood, old commitments
marigolds stuffed into jars in the sun
the flesh caving in, the warm center
        Now they come in small groups
to watch the skulls behind glass

the gouged eyes, the hills of flayed bones
the blue despair of the sinews
the soft hairy flesh

The butcher prods the young leaves:
          Someday
when the dawn has grown old
we will face each other across the wet roofs
(like the priests of Xipe watching the Spaniards draw in)
And the bones will tell us that life eats life & grows fat
          that we claw at each other
(Have I said enough now? Are you sick enough of this meat?)

          Sitting at tables
stuffing our skulls with the tag-ends of life
we will go on as before
          forgetting
changing flesh into words, words into paper
lying in wait for each other
eating ourselves on this miserable earth
          And if sometimes
we should pass a window
          strewn with flowers & flesh
& the old memory of the old wounds should begin
& the sweet smell stick to our throats:
We will know again
          that image of a dark bull
bathed in its entrails
          a shroud of wild heavy flowers
that draws us to worship in silence
the sorrow of all this poor meat

The Seventh Hell: *of smoke, where fire-raisers try in vain to escape from a shower of hot sand falling from a cloud*

The houses of men are on fire
          Pity the dead in their graves
          & the homes of the living

Pity the roofbeams whose waters burn till they're ash
Pity the old clouds devoured by the clouds of hot sand
& the sweat that's drawn out of metals pity that too
Pity the teeth robbed of gold
The bones when their skin falls away
Pity man's cry when the sun is born in his cities
& the thunder breaks down his door
& pity the rain
For the rain falls on the deserts of man & is lost

If the mind is a house that has fallen
Where will the eye find rest
The images rise from the marrow & cry in the blood
Pity man's voice in the smoke-filled days
& his eyes in the darkness
Pity the sight of his eyes
For what can a man see in the darkness
What can he see but the children's bones & the dead sticks
But the places between spaces & the places of sand
& the places of black teeth
The faraway places
The black sand carried & the black bones buried
The black veins hanging from the open skin
& the blood changed to glass in the night

The eye of man is on fire
A green bird cries from his house
& opens a red eye to death
The sun drops out of a pine tree
Brushing the earth with its wings
For what can a man see in the morning
What can he see but the fire-raisers
The shadow of the fire-raisers lost in the smoke
The shadow of the smoke where the hot sand is falling
The fire-raisers putting a torch to their arms
The green smoke ascending
Pity the children of man
Pity their bones when the skin falls away
Pity the skin devoured by fire

The fire devoured by fire
The mind of man is on fire
& where will his eye find rest

A Bodhisattva Undoes Hell

Because he saw the men of the world plowing their fields, sowing the seed, trafficking, huckstering, buying & selling, & at the end winning nothing but bitterness, for this he was moved to pity…

To the figures bathing at the river
Jizo appeared

The sky was full of small fishes
The bodies of the men
twisted in an afternoon
when earth & air were one

With hell a hard fact
the double lotus
brought the son of heaven
down among us
And the bather showed their hands
that bore the marks of nails

What Jizo said
was this

Let's bury their lousy hammers
My people
are tired of pain
The world's been crucified
long enough

The rain fell gently on their wounds
The women lugged
big platters of shrimp

to the bathers
when Jizo's diamond
caught the sun

The rest of us
sat at the stone windows
overlooking the river
We saw him climb the hill
& disappear
behind the guardhouse

What he told the guards
was this

Your bosses are men
who darken counsel
with words
But the white sun
carries love
into the world

When Jizo leaned on his stick
the blue lines in his face
were shining with tears
We followed him
into the city
where lilies bled beside a lake

He said

The heart's
a flower
Love
each other
Keep the old
among you

Write the poem
The image
unlocks Hell

Man's joy
makes
his gods

For those who heard him
hatred fell away

We spent the night
with angels
Fishing
in the ponds of Hell

From THE GORKY POEMS

> *"I like the heat, the tenderness, the edible, the lusciousness, the song of a single person, the bathtub full of water to bathe myself beneath the water.*
>
> *"I measure all things by weight.*
>
> *"I love my Mougouch, I hate things that are not like me and all the things I haven't got are God to me."*
>
> —Arshile Gorky

THE PIRATE (II)

This man was a pilgrim.

For what, for
a journey?
What kind of a journey?

For ice.

The snowheaven turns into
stone, the snow-
garden vanishes. Under
the sea
who had dreamed it?

Who? Who breaks rocks
moves an inch
either way, who eats iron?

What a country of robots.

The way of the Lord
is through ice.
This is the Lord's Day.

And That?

A silver brilliance
cold
hard
painful
blue.
A true flag of colors.

No, a paperbag.

The shadows in a paperbag
that no one sees.
The highpitched laughter no one hears.

The ice no one feels.

What men!
What stone in their voices!
What glass in their blood!
What iron! What flesh!
What bright eyes!

This stone, this iron
in a dream
still worse when no one dreams it.

The Diary Of A Seducer

Fat. Fat. Fat. Fat. Fat.
This is the forbidden kingdom.
This is Shape
That balloons & is a power
In the light.
O Don Roberto. O lovely Don Roberto.
You have become an idol my love for you is no longer no longer that I love you O Don Roberto O lovely Don Roberto.
Don Roberto farewell.
Don Roberto in the morning sitting among his birds & singing.
Don Roberto fiesta.
Don Roberto clear fields in autumn he is riding the tar road into Tivoli.
Fever Don Roberto.
Claw Don Roberto.
Talon into haunch of rabbit Don Roberto.
Don Roberto with a candle & a granite head.
With eyebrow of Zukofsky
& a woman's body Don Roberto.
Priestess in the guise of Don Roberto.
Feeble Don Roberto.
Angel angel Don Roberto.
Bearded & taloned Don Roberto.
Where will the ecstasy end Don Roberto.
Or the numbers cease
if ever the numbers will cease Don Roberto.
Answer body for body Don Roberto.
Name of Don Roberto.
Color color & ensign of Don Roberto.
Shemhazai Don Roberto.
Azazel Don Roberto.
Barakel Don Roberto.
Kawkabel Don Roberto.
Ezekeel Don Roberto.
Arakiel Don Roberto.
Samsaweel Don Roberto.
Seriel Don Roberto.
O lovely Don Roberto. Farewell.

In the shape of your body farewell.
In the shape of the man's penis & of the woman's farewell.
In the shape of the moon & of lunacy farewell.
In the shape of your seven lost companions
& of the pressure of your wand moving toward my eyes farewell.
Farewell Don Roberto.
We do not know Don Roberto.
We do not sit in the silence of the road to hear Don Roberto.
We have not been pleased to say Don Roberto.
Do I say Don Roberto.
I say sometimes I say sometimes I say Don Roberto.
& will sometimes say Don Roberto.
Don Roberto who is ghost of Don Roberto whose hidden name is hawk.
O Don Roberto. O lovely Don Roberto.

The Water Of The Flowery Mill (II)

for the Angel

He is blood, himself
the killer
is where the sun goes down.

Will he flex his arm, will
the fingers
narrow, make a fist around
the bauble, crush it?

Dust is his.

The entry into light
the courtyard
white with marble veins
& suicides
the perfect edge for sleep.

Count the numbers.
Call the monster green
the little eggs

the wind cups
everything is far from him.

His blood is far from him

& makes a circle, poisons
where it falls
the country dies from it.

Sweet smelling flesh
sweet dung
sweet tumor in the eye
sweet bauble:

as the fish are lanterns
upon waves

& light the sea for him.

CHILD OF AN IDUMEAN NIGHT

1
I, the fat god
I, the good gardener (p. klee)

Deposit me in your heart
& go to war gaily
Be a singer to Philistia
& carry an American flag
to the border

O Jerusalem
O city of mechanics

Covered with hair of fire
Beard against beard
A row of tigers stands there

Be holy, I say
Write on water
Become the first architect, be
Father of your race

& let men fuck your beard

2
I, tallow
I, voice of holocaust
I, crystal

I, open door
I, decimal
I, winter solstice

I, willow
I, dancer
I, wind-udder

I, parchment
I, avatar
I, shoe

I, harmonica
I, tongue of doves
I, emblem

I, regiment
I, globus
I, pustule

I, tooth
I, tumescence
I, father of tractors

I who swallow the dead
I who die
I who shit with the jackal

I who swell

3
They walk, eyes
In chest
Believing their peace
Their warm days
They burrow
They call me
Master
They say & we dream
Master master
Candle with how many wicks
Destroyer
Worshipper
God of the Tsars
Old father
Old language the father spoke
& wrote it in brass
& that was the testament in brass
& there were other testaments
& iron
& still other testaments
& still other old languages
& I wallowed
& I bathed in the heavy water
Master master
I was firm & substantive
I showed myself
I labeled this part hair
& that part tendon
& I reached between my legs

I grew fat
I became the father of my race
My wide hips in the dust
My heart
Was with the children
Believing
Their peace, their warm days
& still other testaments
I bellowed
I spat
I made thunder
I was first before the Senate
Someone called me
Master
Master
Child of an Idumean night
Possessor
Murderer
First to sit on the stone
To ride the locomotive
& be lost
& to proclaim the kingdom
& to be lost again
& swollen again
& fattened without a sense of repetition
But "made fat with fatness"
In the dust
My wide hips in the dust
& I reached between my legs
& I wallowed
& I bathed in the heavy water
My throne
My sweet light
My substance
This tsar did many good things
Though he was no father

Portrait Of Myself With Arshile Gorky & Gertrude Stein

AG	I do direct the night. I do. & walk through it.
GS	The sea is cool. The boats are dominant. The idea of algebra is lost. Almost nowhere is worthwhile.
JR	My own care my trade plied that eases occupations. Nowhere at ease.
AG	Not because peace is with us.
GS	Nowhere more mechanical. Nowhere function. Nowhere at ease. Nowhere at ease. Nowhere more at ease.
JR	Turn turn & beg exceptions. Scold the sea.
AG	I can make a hurried exit I put propellers to rest.
GS	Not because I scold.
JR	I who am saint. I who am not saint. I who am am not saint. I salvage.
GS, AG	Do you.

JR	I scold the sea. I try turning. Spurning remembering.
GS, AG	Do you. Do you.
JR	I can establish covenants & lease ground for fore-closers. I tell how many steps are needed.
GS	Can you.
JR	I can figure to Wednesday.
GS	Must you.
JR	I can begin with a number & end with 33.
GS	Must you.
JR	I can never be more certain than when I was.
GS, AG	Must you. Must you.
JR	I can miss Miss Ann I prepare her belly for lust.
GS	Am I white.
AG	A color.
GS	I am ball. Am I.
JR	Yes & the motion of wanting to be cool
JR, AG, GS	Before law. Before water. Before water the dove.

GS, AG	Please warm us.
JR	Warmly. Warmly.
GS	Fish warmly.
AG	Fish & designs.
GS, AG	Desires.
JR, AG, GS	Manage an oracle. Manage a meal. Manage an oarlock.
JR	& a preparation to be already drowned.

A COMMENTARY ON THE GORKY POEMS

In 1962 Milton Resnick inspired me to look again at Arshile Gorky's work. In the aftermath of that look came *Sightings (i-ix)* & *Further Sightings,* & I'm tempted to believe their structure of suspension in time & space is related to Gorky's own workings. The remaining poems in the present series were written in 1964–1965 & bear diverse & often loose relationships to Gorky's paintings, titles, poems, or to my "sense of Gorky." But they are not *about* these things, for the last thing I would have learned from Gorky is to write poems about Gorky. There is finally no key to the relationship, & an attempt to construct one would only be misleading. If the poems connect with the paintings it is only as Gorky's own *Diary of a Seducer* does with Kierkegaard's essay of that title—there, as often here, a naming after-the-fact. Perhaps it is always those things that can't be *really* defined that are the most interesting elements in any relationship. A matter of convergence.

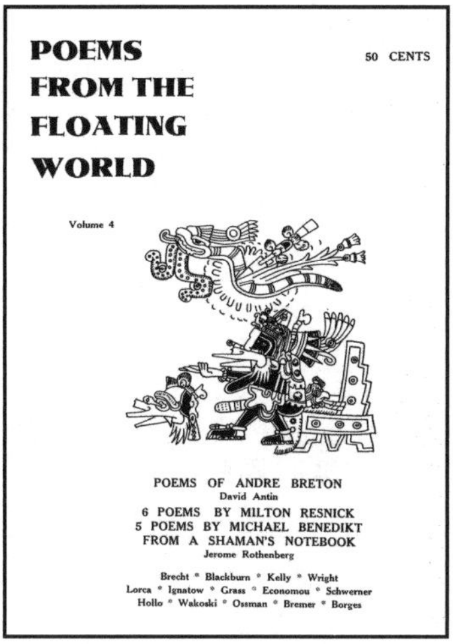

From A SHAMAN'S NOTEBOOK

Perhaps the art which we are seeking is the key to every former art: a solomonic key that will open all the mysteries. — Hugo Ball

Mighty magic is a mother. — Robert Creeley

We are all the same man. — Paul Cezanne

An Invocation To The Rain

Dad a da da
Dad a da da
Dad a da da
Da kata kai

Ded o ded o
Ded o ded o
Ded o ded o
Da kata kai

(Australian)

The Seven

They are 7 in number, just 7
In the terrible depths they are 7
Bow down, in the sky they are 7

In the terrible depths, the dark houses
They swell, they grow tall

They are neither female nor male
They are a silence heavy with seastorms
They bear off no women their loins are empty of children
They are strangers to pity, compassion is far from them
They are deaf to men's prayers, entreaties can't reach them
They are horses that grow to great size that feed on mountains
They are the enemies of our friends
They feed on the gods
They tear up the faces of evil they are the faces of evil

They are 7 they are 7 they are 7 times 7
In the name of Heaven let them be torn from our sight
In the name of the Earth let them be torn from our sight

(Mesopotamian)

Ghosts And Shadows

The soul is a dark forest.
D.H. Lawrence

Ghosts in this forest, shadows
thrown back by the night
Or in daylight
    like bats that drink from our veins
    And hang from moist walls, in deep caves
Behind this green moss, these awful white stones
We pray to know who has seen them

Shadows thrown back by the night
We pray to know who has seen them.

(Pygmy)

The Killer

Careful: my knife drills your soul
listen, whatever-your-name-is
One of the wolf people
listen, I'll grind your saliva into the earth
listen, I'll cover your bones with black flint
listen, " " " " " " feathers
listen, " " " " " " rocks
Because you're going where it's empty
Black coffin out on the hill
listen, the black earth will hide you,
will find you a black hut
Out where it's dark, in that country
listen, I'm bringing a box for your bones
A black box
A grave with black pebbles
listen, your soul's spilling out
listen, it's blue

(Cherokee Indian)

A Poison Arrow

Enough poison to make
your head spin, and chains
to pin you down, and once
they've shot the arrow
and once it lands, well
it's just like the fly and the horse:
I mean a fly that's bitten one horse

will damn sure go after another
And I mean too that this arrow's
like a pregnant woman
        Hungry for some meat
And even if it doesn't break your skin
        You die
And if it breaks it just a little bit
        You die
And if it gets in and does its stuff
        You die
And if it sort of touches you and drops right out
        You die

    And as long as you stay out of my blood
    what do I care whose blood you get in
        Kill him
    I won't stand in the way

This is a fire that I'm setting off
And this is a fire that I'm lifting up
And this is a shadow that's burning
And this is the sun that's burning
Because the poison I've got is stronger than bullets
        And it's louder than thunder
        And it's hotter than fire
And what do I care who it gets, kill him!
        I won't stand in the way
As long as you stay out of my blood

        (Nigeria, Hausa)

The Dead Hunter Speaks Through the Voice of a Shaman

To be beyond you now, to feel
joy burning inside me when the sun
burns through the terrible sky
To feel joy in the new sun, aie!
in the sky's curved belly

But restless more likely, restless
These flies swarm around me, dropping
eggs in the rotting collarbone,
into my eyes, their cold mouths moving
I choke on such horrors

And remembering the last fear, I remember
a dark rim of ocean, remembering
the last fear, the broken boat drifting,
drawing me into that darkness, aie!
Now the other side holds me

And I remember men's fear in the boats
I see the snow forced into my door, fear's
shadow over the hut, while my body
hung in the air, the door hidden, aie!
When I cried in fear of the snow

Horror stuck in my throat, the hut
walled me in, slowly the ice-floe broke
Horror choked me, the thin sky
quivered with sound, the voice
of the dark ice cracking, cold mornings

(Copper Eskimo)

The Stars

For we are the stars. For we sing.
For we sing with our light.
For we are birds made of fire.
For we spread our wings over the sky.
Our light is a voice.
We cut a road for the soul
for its journey through death.
For three of our number are hunters.
For these three hunt a bear.
For there never yet was a time
when these three didn't hunt.

For we face the hills with disdain.
This is the song of the stars.

(Algonquin Indian)

From SIGHTINGS

From deep within us it comes: the wind that moves through the lost branches, hurts us with a cry, as if an ocean were caged in each skull.

There is a sea of connections that floats between men, a place where speech is touch and the welcoming hand restores its silence: an ocean warmed by dark suns.

The deep image rises from the shoreless gulf: here the poet reaches down among the lost branches, till a moment of seeing: the poem. Only then does the floating world sink again into its darkness, leaving a white shadow, and the joy of our having been here, together.

SIGHTINGS IV

1. Wait!

2. A throw of the dice.
   A blue paper.

3. This marks the presence of certain minerals.

4. At midday. The blaze of day in the sky.

5. Would he pause for you, bending? raise to his lips
   what was yours? so careless, my eye falters; careless.

6. This violence of new preoccupations.

7. A twisted wire.
   Ink.

8. And for those who watch the snow, a slow decline.

9. For this she had chosen to dwell among you; let her,
   for our peace.

Sightings V

Description of an eye stone.

•

That began it, not water at first but another sort of light & much darker.

•

At best as abandonment.

•

The skyfall rose over her legs, a violet cry of mosses near the point of juncture.

•

Salt.

•

Then the bodies fucking, of men & animals, drew his soul into the seed, & in that moment sperm touched egg, & he was born.

•

A torch. A door.
A road. A mirror.

•

But that which weeps is the mind.

Sightings VI

1. The earth shudders under the rain.

2. A hand.
   Five fingers.

3. Milkweed; was is that?

4. They add in rows.

5. Beginning from the waist, slip downwards; force a
   smile.

6. Perhaps a dish.
   A cup.

7. Horse grey knot
   fallen throat of-blood.

8. One thought, a thousand movements.

Sightings IX

Allotments.
Shut.

•

A pale ellipse; this would spell some kind of root, a summoner.

•

A summer ayre.

•

They call the nerve diseased.
Her FIre?
Sacred bangles,
& yet the leg won't burn.

•

Then spurn her.

•

Desire, oddly, for a well.

•

Shut.

•

All light we will become, be gathered.

A NOTE ON THE MEASURE OF SIGHTINGS

The measure of SIGHTINGS
involves the creation of an
equivalent area-of-silence
around each phrase
in the poem.
To read these,
let the spaces between phrases
(as marked by the points at the
left-hand margin)
represent a silence roughly equal
to the duration
of each succeeding phrase.
In SIGHTINGS IV & VI,
where the numbers
take over most of the
compositional function of the
points & spaces,
it is only necessary
to make a noticeable pause
between the numbered sections.

FURTHER SIGHTINGS

2 X 7
THE OLD KING

for Leir, in Hades

The Old King (i)
painted his face—
a hand as border.

The Old King (ii)
eye of Horus
& of the hawk.

The Old King (iii)
harps, timbrels
to his touch.

The Old King (iv)
a striped mirror—
a green shell.

The Old King (v)
another
guardian.

The Old King (vi)
who strikes the moon
to contain it.

The Old King (vii)
divides the cut
circle, gems.

"Hell"

(1st set)

1. A white shadow in Hell.

2. Like Hell's beauty
in mirrors—
that you will never reach.

3. In the season of smiles,
Hell was waiting.

4. Why does the hermaphrodite beckon?
Is it that Hell lurks there?

5. The breathing of the lion is Hell.
The insouciance of certain birds is also Hell.

(2nd Set)

1. Hell's direction,
circular,
inscribes a circle.

2. I knew Hell in their voices
& in the rhythms of certain trees,
an indolence across the sea
at dusk, & periwinkles.

3. What began in hope ends in sorrow—
as Hell will always wake in your kiss.

4. There were three women he loved;
one, as Hell spoke, moved him,
while the others slept.

5. Hell of numbers, pale,
reflecting water,
in distrust of all eyes.

(3rd Set)

1. Two bodies struggling—Hell.
   A touch deferred—also Hell.

2. We were speaking of Hell all night.
   Had the sisters heard us?
   She was alone, I kissed her & turned aside.
   You have brought me pictures from Hell.

3. Hell opened before their headlights—
   but against that light, the other Hell.

4. Gold—or the pollen set behind her eyes.
   Hell's emblems.

5. And the bride must rest from light—
   test & measure of her resting, for the peace of Hell.

3 x 5 x 3
The Witnesses

(1st Set)

1. I am the man who held the keys.
   I asked you to forgive me.
   I was the first to be insistent & the last to leave.

2. I vomited
   I didn't come there often.
   I was eager & alive.

3. I was not the least among them.
   Once I was.
   Once I remember being in poor position.

4. I applied for membership.
   I was sad.
   Then I thought no longer to go on living.

5. I turned from you & offered you my keys.
You turned beside me & offered your position.
I had turned against them.

(2nd Set)

1. I will make no promises.
I had made electricity before then.
I would dream of making light.

2. I do it now.
I do not do it often.
I do not do it but I care.

3. You asked me to write my name but I had never learned it.
I insist on pain.
I walk & run in stages.

4. I was sometimes coarse to you.
I had no patience.
I stiffened.

5. I believe in free education & other values.
I was starting to feel princely.
Tell me where I erred.

(3rd Set)

1. I had the same chances as any other slave.
I hold a hand up.
Once I thought it was January, it was really June.

2. Do I understand you.
Does the key I give you fit your mind.
My love for you is senseless.

3. I am what you see I do not see myself in you.
I had learned to reason.
I had no necessity for friends.

4. I wore a shirt.
   I welcome those who welcomed me.
   I am sincere.

5. I am the man who held the keys.
   I will make no promises.
   I had the same chances as any other slave.

From CONVERSATIONS: THREE POEMS

Conversation Six

What's in a name?
(Sounds.)
How many sounds is what I want to know.
(I never count sounds.)
Do you count strokes?
(No I count resolutions.)
Count one now.
(One two three four five six seven eight nine ten eleven twelve thirteen.)
That sounds like a long resolution.
(Yes resolutions are forever long.)

Conversation Seven

I am building a machine.
(Let me see it.)
Here it is.
(Where does this piece go.)
Behind this piece.
(Where does a window go to look at the machine.)
It goes alongside the machine.
(Is the machine going to be standing on this floor.)
No in this field.
(I want to write my name in the middle of your field.)
My field is a machine.
(Can I cross it.)
No.

(I want to sit on your machine then.)
No; machines can break.

Conversation Fifteen

I wanted something to eat.
(I wanted nothing.)
I wanted a place for resting & another place for the pleasures of sleep.
(I wanted the joys of charity.)
I wanted the weather.
(I wanted you.)
Were you hungry?
(No.)
Were you remarkable?
(I was remarkable & was never hungry.)
I wanted hands.
(I wanted to be free of touch.)
I wanted my hands to be tied to the side of your body.
(I wanted your body to be tied to the side of my house.)
I was an animal & was never free.
(I wanted the vindication of the just.)

A SECOND MANIFESTO 1964

1) I will change your mind;

2) any means (= methods) to that end;

3) to oppose the "devourers" = bureaucrats,
system-makers, priests, etc. (W. Blake);

4) "& if thou wdst understand that wch is me,
know this: all that I have sd I have uttered
playfully—& I was by no means ashamed of
it." (J.C. to this disciples, *The Acts of St. John*).

A RECONSIDERATION 2010

MEN GROW OLD
& cry out "shit"
like children

dropping to the bottom of a well,
uncautious,
trained to fish for eels

to come up breathless
on the other side
where mothers reach out arms to hold them

"holy days" the simple man proclaims,
the shapeless wanderer
not simple only, he is open

this allows the world to look
into his eyes, to see
a depth there, like a hole in space

the farthest probe of all they call
"deep image," galaxies condensing
in the perfect poem

"Deep image": a technical term in astronomy for photographs of the outer limits of the visible universe.

A BOOK OF OTHERINGS

I walk the stupid
last mile
into heaven
cursing the light
that blinds me.
I reach up
& drive an owl
from its perch.
My clothes cling to my flesh.
I lift my fire
where my hand should be.   (C. Coolidge)
My watch
explodes
as if the gift
of time
were now annulled.
I open up
my mouth & hear
a multitude
of voices.

A PARADISE OF POETS

He takes a book down from his shelf & scribbles across a page of text: *I am the final one.* This means the world will end when he does.

•

In the Inferno Dante conceives a Paradise of Poets & calls it Limbo.

Foolishly he thinks his place is elsewhere.

•

Now the time has come to write a poem about a Paradise of Poets.

From PRE-FACE to *WRITING THROUGH: TRANSLATIONS & VARIATIONS*

I had thought for a long time of preparing a book of selected translations and was faced again and again by the dilemma of where translations end and my other writings begin. It seemed to me finally that there was a way—a number of ways—in which translation served me as a form of composition and as an underpinning for much of my work as a poet and a writer. I have never thought of myself as a professional translator, since my grasp of any language other than English has been limited and has made any translation on which I've worked a slow and sometimes very indirect process (often, too, in the case of languages that are exotic from our point of view, in collaboration with other translators). I have not as a rule added to or subtracted from the original when translating, but within those limits I have thought of myself as a poet using translation as a means for making poems or bringing new poems into English. Even more than that, I have had a need (I emphasize: a *need*) to translate and, by translating, to connect with the work and thought of other poets—a matter of singular importance to me in what I have long taken to be my "project" and the central activity of my life as a poet.

I do not think of this as in any way unusual, although it has taken me a long time to recognize it for what it is. Many writers, but poets in particular, inherit and carry forward the works of those who came before them. In my own case the work I've done with ethnopoetics and with the construction of anthology-assemblages—along with a devotion to the "experimental" as a basis for my writing—has made such considerations still more central to my practice. Accordingly my work has involved not only translation but the use of techniques like collage and appropriation as ways of opening our individual or personal poetry to the presence of other voices and other visions besides our own. I came to think of all of that—appropriation, collage, translation—in ideological terms. Long before our time, Whitman in *Leaves of Grass* had set the task very plainly:

> *Through me many long dumb voices,*
> *Voices of the interminable generations of prisoners and slaves,*
> *Voices of the diseas'd and despairing and of thieves and dwarfs,*
> *Voices of cycles of preparation and accretion,*
> *And of the threads that connect the stars, and of wombs and of the*
> *father-stuff,*
> *And of the rights of them the others are down upon,*
> *Of the deform'd, trivial, flat, foolish, despised,*
> *Fog in the air, beetles rolling balls of dung.*
> ...

This was in the section of *Leaves of Grass* called "Song of Myself"—that great bringing together of the individual voice with the sense of a total and suppressed humanity. And it was reborn for us, for me certainly, in Charles Olson's rant, say, against "the lyrical interference of the individual as ego," or in Robert Duncan's call for a new "symposium of the whole," a new "totality"—among my immediate predecessors and near contemporaries.

I have practiced translation in one form or another for over forty years now. My first published book in fact was *New Young German Poets* (City Lights, 1959), a year before my own first book of poetry. That book included first-time translations into English from poets like Paul Celan, Hans Magnus Enzensberger, Günter Grass, Ingeborg Bachmann, and Helmut Heissenbüttel, who would become major German authors in the decade that followed. In the 1960s I adapted Rolf Hochhuth's play *The Deputy* for its Broadway performance, did further translations from Enzensberger's poetry, and began to make occasional translations of Dada poets like Hans Arp and Richard Hülsenbeck from German and Tristan Tzara and Francis Picabia from French. I had also become engaged with translations from Spanish modernists—much of it for my own recreation and as a way better to understand the work at hand—and from 1960 on, I began to use translation as a way to channel material into publications of my own.

Where that channeling turns up most clearly is in the acts of translation that are an underpinning for the anthologies (*Technicians of the Sacred*, *Shaking the Pumpkin*, *Poems for the Millennium*, etc.) that I began assembling in the later 1960s. And the translations there also led me to an interplay with poets closer to my own time and place—Kurt Schwitters, Federico García Lorca, Vitezslav Nezval, among those I've done in abundance—and later, surprisingly to me, Picasso. For me too the big books were a kind of assemblage and collage, very much like the translations in terms of what they allowed me to do or to be.

In the big books—the ethnopoetic ones in particular—I was engaged with a range of processes, related to but not always identical with that of translation. Some of those—the more clearly translational ones—involved experimental forms of translation with perhaps an emphasis on the translation of oral poetry and—conversely—of visual poetry—a fascination with what had been thought of as untranslatable forms of poetry. In "The 17 Horse-Songs of Frank Mitchell"—from sources in Navajo—I engaged in what Dennis Tedlock and I were calling "total translation," going beyond the semantic level to try to find equivalents for the non-lexical vocables in Navajo song and even—most outrageously for me—for the music—the melodies—by which the words and sounds were carried. Other Indian song-poems—these mostly from the Seneca—were short combinations of words & sounds which I chose to translate as a kind of visual (concrete) poetry—in order to bring across the curious complexity of otherwise simple or minimal forms—by calling up an image of similar minimal forms in our own (presumably sophisticated and developed) arts of language. And along the same lines, while working with contemporary poems that were themselves experimental, I undertook the translation of a large group of often minimal poems by the German concrete poet Eugen Gomringer—finding those a curious vehicle to get down to some fundamentals about the nature of both poetry and translation.

All of that remains central to me—the translations, I mean, and those other suppositions and legitimate acts of "othering" that underlie my total project. In *The Lorca Variations*, a series of poems from the early 1990s, I took a step beyond translation by writing with Lorca (or my translation of Lorca's book-length poem series called "The Suites") as my source—isolating his nouns and other words (which were by then my own in English) and systematically recasting them into new compositions. In another series of poems, *Gematria*, I used a traditional Jewish form of connecting words by numerological procedures and a word list of numerically arranged words and phrases from the Hebrew Bible, to make a poetry—as with *The Lorca Variations*—that I thought was both personal to me and was created by means that shared in what Blake saw as "the most sublime act ... [:] to set another before you." And in still later work, while continuing to make translations from Picasso and from the great Czech modernist Vitezslav Nezval, I interspersed appropriations from their work with my own—composing three series of a hundred numbered verses each that I called *Autobiography*. Still more recently—in *A Book of Witness*—I used the first person voice, the pronoun "I," to explore whatever it is that we can say for ourselves—not only my *personal* self but that of all others—and by that process can even and meaningfully put identity into question.

....

Covering the range that it has, my work with translation has often depended on assistance and collaboration with poets and others conversant with languages that are totally foreign to me. Yet there is another sense of course in which all translation involves a kind of collaboration—at least in the mind of the translator. I am very much aware of this, however one-sided it may often seem, and I have sometimes let myself believe that all our writing, all our poetry, is an activity shared with all who are the users and makers of our common language. This idea of a communally driven poetry—of the poem, however individual, as simultaneously what Pound called "a tale of the tribe"—has held my attention even when I felt it to be false. In a world in which that kind of unity is again under fire, I would continue thinking in those terms, wherever they may take me.

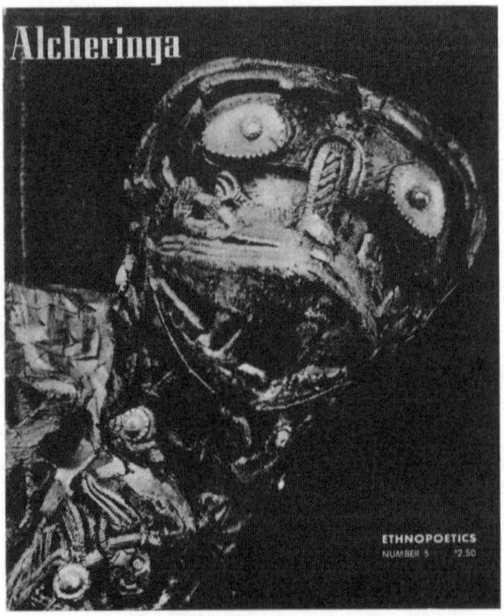

THE ANNUNCIATION

by Marpa (a.k.a. Drokmi Lotsawa, "The Translator")

Tibet, 11th Century

a man born from a flower in space a man
riding a colt foaled from a sterile mare
his reins are formed from the hair of a tortoise

a rabbit's horn for a dagger he
strikes down his enemies

a man without lips who is speaking who
sees without eyes a man without ears
who listens who runs without legs

the sun & the moon dance
& blow trumpets

a young child touches
the wheel-of-the-law

which turns over

*

: secret of the body
: of the word
: of the heart of the gods

the inner breath is the horse of the bodhisattvas

whipped by compassion it
rears it drives the old yak
from the path of madness

Translation adapted from J. Bascot, *La vie de Marpa*, 1937. Marpa (eleventh century, A.D.) was third guru in the line founded by Tilo in India & successor to his own teacher, Naropa. He was the first Tibetan master of the Kargyudpa sect & the instructor of the more famous Milarepa. Marpa traveled a good deal & translated half a hundred works from Sanskrit, which earned for him his nickname of The Translator.

From 15 FLOWER WORLD VARIATIONS

Yaqui

o flower fawn
        about to come out playing
                in this flower water
out there
        in the flower world
                the patio of flowers
in the flower water
        playing
                flower fawn
about to come out playing
        in this flower water

•

(where is the rotted stick that screeches lying?)
the screeching rotted stick is lying over there
(where is the rotted stick that screeches lying?)
the screeching rotted stick is lying over there
there in the flower world
        beyond us
                in the tree world
the screeching rotted stick
        is lying
                over there the screeching
rotted stick is lying
        over there

•

ah brother
        look at you
                a deer with flowers
brother
        shake your antlers
                little brother
shake your antlers
        deer with flowers
                why not let your belt

your deer hoofs
          shake? why not vibrate
                    cocoons
strapped to your ankles
          brother
                    shake them
little brother
          shake & roll

•

out in the mountain there
          these look like
                    doves
& in the flower water
          three of them
                    are grey & bobbing
three of them are walking
          grey & side by side
                    there in the flower world
the dawn
          out in the flower water
                    three of them
are grey & bobbing
          in the mountain there
                    these look like doves
out there
          & in the flower water
                    three are grey
& bobbing
          three of them are walking
                    grey & side by side

•

where are you standing
          in the wind
                    dead grasses
grey & shaking in the wind
          dead grasses
                    where are you standing

in the wind dead grasses
grey & shaking in the wind
dead grasses
there in the wilderness
the flower world
a pale blue cloud
will be grey water
at its peak
the mist will reach
will rain down
on the flower ground
& shining
reaching bottom
where you are
where you are only
standing in the wind
dead grasses
grey & shaking in the wind
dead grasses

•

SONG OF A DEAD MAN

I do not want these flowers
moving
but the flowers
want to move
I do not want these flowers
moving
but the flowers
want to move
I do not want these flowers
moving
but the flowers
want to move
out in the flower world
the dawn
over a road of flowers
I do not want these flowers

moving
but the flowers
want to move
I do not want these flowers
moving
but the flowers
the flowers
want to move

•

now the cloud
will break
the cloud will break
& now
the cloud will break
the cloud
will break
& now the cloud
will break
the cloud will break
there in the flower world
under the dawn
this pale blue cloud
will be grey water
at its peak
the mist will reach
will rain down
shining
& reaching bottom
now the cloud
will break
the cloud will break
& now
the cloud will break
the cloud
will break

The Flower World settings were derived from traditional Yaqui Deer Dance songs in literal translations by Carleton Wilder, et al.

THE FLIGHT OF QUETZALCOATL

Aztec

*

Then the time came for Quetzalcoatl too, when he felt the darkness twist in him like a river, as though it meant to weigh him down, & he thought to go then, to leave the city as he had found it & to go, forgetting there ever was a Tula

Which was what he later did, as people tell it who still speak about the Fire: how he first ignited the gold & silver houses, their walls speckled with red shells, & the other Toltec arts, the creations of man's hands & the imagination of his heart

& hid the best of them in secret places, deep in the earth, in mountains or down gullies, buried them, took the cacao trees & changed them into thorned acacias

& the birds he'd brought there years before, that had the richly colored feathers & whose breasts were like a living fire, he sent ahead of him to trace the highway he would follow toward the seacoast

When that was over he started down the road

*

A whole day's journey, reached

THE JUNCTURE OF THE TREE

(so-called)

fat prominence of bark
sky branches

I sat beneath it
saw my face/cracked
mirror

An old man

        & named it
        TREE OF OLD AGE

thus to name
it to raise stones
to wound the bark
with stones

to batter it with
stones the stones to
cut the bark to fester
in the bark

        TREE OF OLD AGE

stone patterns: starting
from the roots they
reach the highest leaves

*

The next day gone with walking
Flutes were sounding in his ears

        Companions' voices

He squatted on a rock to rest
he leaned his hands against the rock

        Tula shining in the distance

: which he saw he
saw it & began to cry
he cried the cold sobs cut his throat

A double thread of tears, a hailstorm
beating down his face, the drops
burn through the rock
The drops of sorrow fall against the stone
& pierce its heart

& where his hands had rested
shadows lingered on the rock: as if
his hands had pressed soft clay
As if the rock were clay

The mark too of his buttocks in the rock,
embedded there forever

A place named TEMACPALCO

*

To Stone Bridge next

water swirling in the riverbed
a spreading turbulence of water

: where he dug a stone up
made a bridge across
& crossed it

*

: who kept moving until he reached the Lake of Serpents, the elders
waiting for him there, to tell him he would have to turn around,
he would have to leave their country & go home

: who heard them ask where he was bound for, cut off from all a man
remembers, his city's rites long fallen into disregard

: who said it was too late to turn around, his need still driving him, & when they asked again where he was bound, spoke about a country of red daylight & finding wisdom, who had been called there, whom the sun was calling

: who waited then until they told him he could go, could leave his Toltec things & go (& so he left those arts behind, the creations of man's hands & the imagination of his heart; the crafts of gold & silver, of working precious stones, of carpentry & sculpture & mural painting & book illumination & featherweaving)

: who, delivering that knowledge, threw his jeweled necklace in the lake, which vanished in those depths, & from then on that place was called the Lake of Jewels

*

Another stop along the line

This time
THE CITY OF THE SLEEPERS

And runs into a shaman

Says, you bound for somewhere honey

Says, the country of Red Daylight know it? expect to land there probe a little wisdom maybe

Says, no fooling try a bit of pulque brewed it just for you

Says, most kind but awfully sorry scarcely touch a drop you know

Says, perhaps you've got no choice perhaps I might not let you go now you didn't drink perhaps I'm forcing you against your will might even get you drunk come on honey drink it up

Drinks it with a straw

So drunk he falls down fainting
on the road & dreams &
snores his snoring echoes very far

& when he wakes finds silence
& an empty town, his face
reflected & the hair shaved off

Then calls it
CITY OF THE SLEEPERS

*

There is a peak between Old Smokey
& The White Woman

Snow is falling
& fell upon him in those days

& on his companions
who were with him, on
his dwarfs, his clowns
his gimps
It fell

till they were frozen
lost among the dead

The weight oppressed him
& he wept for them

He sang

The tears are endless
& the long sighs
issue from my chest

Further out
THE HILL OF MANY COLORS

which he sought

Portents everywhere, those
dark reminders
of the road he walks

*

It ended on the beach
It ended with a hulk of serpents formed into a boat
& when he'd made it, sat in it & sailed away
A boat that glided on those burning waters, no one knowing when he
  reached the country of Red Daylight
It ended on the rim of some great sea
It ended with his face reflected in the mirror of its waves
The beauty of his face returned to him
& he was dressed in garments like the sun
It ended with a bonfire on the beach where he would hurl himself
& burn, his ashes rising & the cries of birds
It ended with the linnet, with the birds of turquoise color, birds the color
  of wild sunflowers, red & blue birds
It ended with the birds of yellow feathers in a riot of bright gold
Circling till the fire had died out
Circling while his heart rose through the sky
It ended with his heart transformed into a star
It ended with the morning star with dawn & evening
It ended with his journey to Death's Kingdom with seven days of dark-
  ness
With his body changed to light
A star that burns forever in that sky

Working after Spanish prose translation by Ángel María Garibay K.

A POEM FOR THE SMALL FACE

by Isaac Luria (1534–72)

Aramaic

sons of his palace
were shy
who witness rays from
the small face

these to be here
at this table
the king cuts
grooves from his ring in

be pleased with
this meeting
this center of powers
all wingd

to bring joy to it
now
is his hour of peace
without anger

draw near me
thou see my companions
be night without
judgment

those dogs
wild with *chutzpah*
keep out
may not enter

but send for
Ancient of Days
exchanging
the jewel in his forehead

his peace
as he sees it
releases the light from
the shells

& will flow with it
into each orifice
these will conceal
under domes

will be here
in praise of the evening
a poem for
the small face

The occasion of Luria's "Poem for the Small Face" was the Sabbath celebration by his circle of mystics in the city of Safed. It marked the final meal of the Sabbath, as the "Poem for the Shekinah" that follows marked its opening. In that context, the Small Face (*ze'ir anpin*) is the "son" within the Tetragrammaton (YHVH), the four-personed God of mystical Judaism. He is known as the "impatient one," the angry face of the reality confronting us, as the Shekinah, closer to earth, is taken to be God's exiled female aspect.

A POEM FOR THE SHEKINAH ON THE FEAST OF THE SABBATH

by Isaac Luria (1534–72)

Aramaic

I have sung
an old measure

would open
gates to

her field of apples
(each one a power)

set a new table
to feed her

beautifully
candelabrum

drops its
light on us

Between right & left
the Bride

draws near in
holy jewels

clothes of the sabbath
whose lover

embraces her
down to foundation

gives pleasure
squeezes his strength out

in surcease of
sorrow

& makes new faces
be hers

& new souls
new breath

gives her joy
double measure

of lights & of
streams for her blessing

o Friends of the Bride
go forth

all's sealed
within her

shines out from
Ancient of Days

Toward the south
I placed

candelabrum
(o mystical)

room in
the north

for table
for bread

for pitchers of wine
for sweet myrtle

gives power to
lovers

new potencies
garlands

gives her many
sweet foods to taste

many kinds of
fish

for fertility
birth

of new souls
new spirits

will follow the 32 paths
& 3 branches

the bride with
70 crowns

with her king who
hovers above her

crown above crown in
Holy of Holies

this lady all worlds are
formed in

of words for her
70 crowns

50 gates
the Shekinah

ringd by
6 loaves

of the sabbath
& bound

all sides to
Heavenly Refuge

the hostile
powers

have left us
demons you feared

sleep in chains

"THE ROUND DANCE OF JESUS"

Coptic

"A praise poem
"we sing now
"will go to meet what is to come
& had us form a circle
we stood in with folded hands
himself was in the middle
(said) You answer
Amen
then started singing
praises saying
"Praises Father
circling & we answered him
Amen (said)
Praises Word (said)
Praises Grace
Amen (said)
Praises Spirit (said)
Praises Holy Holy (said)
O thee transfiguration (said)
Amen (said)
Thank you Sunshine Light
no darkness (said)
"I will inform you now
"the reason for this thanks
(then said)
I save
& will be saved
Amen
I free
& will be freed
Amen
I hurt
& will be hurt
Amen
Am born
& will give birth

Amen
I feed
& will be food
Amen
I hear
& will be heard
Amen
I will be known
all knowing mind
Amen
I will be washed
& I will wash
Amen
all Grace Sweet Mind the Dance is round
I blow the pipe for
all are in the Round Dance
I will pipe
all dance along
Amen
I will moan low
all beat your breasts
Amen
the One & Only Eight
plays up for us
Amen
Old Number Twelve
stomps up above
Amen
the Universe controls
the dancer
Amen
whoever isn't dancing
's in the dark
Amen
I will go
& I will stay
Amen
I will dress thee
& I will dress
Amen

I will be Oned
& I will One
Amen
I have no house
& I have houses
Amen
I have no place
& I have places
Amen
I have no temple
& I have temples
Amen
I am a lamp to thee
who see me
Amen
I am a mirror to thee
who view me
Amen
I am a door to thee
who come thru me
Amen
I am a way to thee
wayfarer
Amen (said)
"Follow
"my Round Dance
"& see yourself in me
"the Speaker
"& seeing what I speak
"keep silent on
"my mysteries
"or dancing think of what
"I do
"make yours the suffering of a man
"that I will suffer
"yet powerless to understand your suffering
"without a word
"the Father sent language thru me
"the sufferer you saw
"& saw me suffering

"you grew restless
"shaken
"you were moved toward wisdom
"lean on me
"I am a pillow
"who am I?
"you only will know me
"when I'm gone—
"but am not he for whom
"I am now taken—
"will know it when you reach it
"& knowing suffering will know
"how not to suffer
"I am your god
"not the betrayer's
"will harmonize the Sweet Soul with my own
"the Word of Wisdom speaks in me
"says
"Praises   Father
& we answered him
Amen   (said)
Praises   Word   (said)
Praises   Grace
Amen   (said)
Praises   Spirit   (said)
Praises   Holy Holy   (said)
"& if thou wouldst understand that which is me
"know this   all that I have said I have uttered
"playfully   & I was by no means ashamed of it
"I danced
"& when you dance in understanding
"understand & say
"Amen

Working based on versions by Edgar Hennecke, Max Pulver, & G.R.S. Mead.

25 GEMATRIA (TRADITIONAL)

LIGHT
A mystery.

EYE
Silver.

THE UPPER WORLD
Is all the chariot.

HE & HE
This & this.

METATRON
The beard.
The beard.

MESSENGER
Five.

THE WITNESS
A jewel.

THE BODY
The reward.

THE WORLD/THE YEAR/THE SOUL
Evening.
Morning.
Noon.

FIRST ADAM
Hell is open.

MOSES
I am.
I am.
I am.

THE GARDEN
Shadow.
Stone.
The Brain.

THE SOUL OF ADAM
Lilith.

ISRAEL
El Song.

REBEKKA
This.
12.

THE RIVER
The prayerbook.

INCENSE
The ark.
613.

WISDOM
Is.
Was.
Will be.

MESSIAH
Snake.

THE DEVIL
Fat-ash.

THIS POPE
This garbage.

DOMINUS
Demonus.

MONEY
The tree.

& the king said
to Haman: the money
will be yours

DEATH
903.

ISRAEL ALONE
Therefore.

From traditional Hebrew sources, with Harris Lenowitz.

A COMMENTARY ON GEMATRIA

Gematria—a form of traditional Jewish numerology—plays off the fact that every letter of the Hebrew alphabet is also a number, and that words or phrases the sums of whose letters are equal are at some level meaningfully connected. In the course of compiling *A Big Jewish Book*, I came across a number of traditional combinations of words associated (usually in pairs) through gematria, and I juxtaposed one of the words with the other so as to form miniature poems. A few years later I came across Gutman G. Locks's *The Spice of Torah—Gematria*, which offers easy access to the numerical value of every word in the first five books of the Hebrew

Bible. With its more than three hundred pages of Hebrew word lists translated into English words and phrases, I began to construct new poems based on combinations that I discovered or that I calculated on my own. Unlike the traditionalists of gematria, I have seen these coincidences / synchronicities not as hermeneutic substantiations for religious and ethical doctrines, but as an entry into the kinds of correspondences / constellations that have been central to modernist and "post"modernist poetry experiments over the last century and a half. I have proceeded in these works in several different ways: by using one word or word-phrase as title and others (numerically equivalent) as poem; by using the gematria number as a title and constructing poems of single lines and/or stanzas of two or several lines that fall under or add up to that number; and occasionally by using a freer selection of words brought to my attention by gematria, but combining and adding to them with considerably more freedom of choice. To the degree that all such works are substantially aleatory, they are full of surprises that have added greatly to my own excitement in the act of writing.

Examples of such compositions by gematria appear elsewhere in these pages.

From LORCA'S SUITES

Night: A Suite For Piano & Poet's Voice

Sketches

That road
got no people.
That road.

That weevil
got no home.
That weevil.

And this sheepbell
gone to sleep.
This sheepbell.

Prelude

The bullock
slowly
shuts his eyes.

Heat in the stable.
Prelude to
the night.

In a Corner of the Sky

The old
star
shuts her bleary eyes.

The new
star
wants to paint the night
blue.

(In the firtrees on the mountain:
fireflies.)

The Whole Works

The wind's hand
caresses the forehead of space
again &
again.
The stars half-close
their blue eyelids
again &
again.

A Star

There is a tranquil star,
a star that has no eyelids.
—Where?
—A star…
In sleepy water.
In the pond.

Swatch

O St. James Road.
O Milky Way.
(O night of love for me
when yellow bird was painted
painted
painted
up in the lemon tree.)

One

That romantic star
(one for magnolia
one for the roses).

That romantic star
just went crazy.

Tralalee,
tralala.

(Sing, little frog, in your shadowy
hut.)

Ursa Major

Bear mother
gives suck to the stars
astride her belly:

Grunt
grunt.

Run off, star babies:
tender little stars.

Memory

Our Lady Moon still hidden,
playing ring around a wheel.
She makes herself look silly.
Loony moon.

At the Poorhouse

And the poor stars
that have no light

—o sorrow,
sorrow,
o lamentation!—

end up stuck
in muddy blue.

O sorrow,
sorrow,
o lamentation!

Comet

There on Sirius
are babes.

Venus

Open sesame
by day.
Shut sesame
at night.

Below

Space & stars
reflected into sound.
Liana ghosts.
Harp labyrinths.

The Great Sadness

You can't look at yourself
in the ocean.

Your looks fall apart
like tendrils of light.
Night on earth.

A Newton Suite

Newton's Nose

Onto the nose of Newton
a large apple falls.
A meteor of truths.
Last fruit to dangle from
the tree of Science.

And big Newton scratches
his Saxon nostrils.
A white moon over
these barbaric strings of lace:
the beech trees.

In the Woods

The gnomes
astride their secrets
tear
their beards out.
They tie up Death
& make the Echoes
mislead men
with mirrors.
In a corner
lies the secret:
in the open,
dead.
His companions
mourn him.
A blue boy
with iron feet—
a glowing star
between his eyebrows.
His companions
mourn him.
And the green lake trembles.
In the wind.

Harmony

Waves
rhyme with sighs
& stars with
crickets.
Atremble in the cornea
the whole cold sky.
A dot, a synthesis,
infinity's.

But who joins waves
with sighs?
And stars
with crickets?
Just hope these geniuses
be missing something.
The proofs keep drifting by
among us.

The Philosopher's Last Walk

Newton
was taking a walk.
Death had followed him,
strumming his guitar.
Newton
was taking a walk.
The worms gnawed through
his apple.

The wind hummed in the trees,
the river beneath the branches.
(Wordsworth would have cried.)
The philosopher was striking
unimaginable poses,
was waiting for another apple.

He ran along the road.
He stretched out by the water.
He saw how his face would sink
in the moon's reflection.
Newton
wept.

And high up on a cedar
two old owls yammered.
Slowly in the night the wise man
went back home.
He dreamt enormous pyramids
of apples.

Replica

Adam ate an apple
from the Virgin Eve.
Newton was a second Adam—
Science's.
The first knew
Beauty.
The second a Pegasus
bowed down by chains.
And neither one was guilty.

Their two apples
pink
& fresh
but with a bitter
history.
The severed breasts of
innocence, poor child.

Question

Why was it the apple
& not
the orange
or the polyhedral
pomegranate?
Why this virgin fruit
to clue them in,
this smooth & gentle
pippin?
What admirable symbol
lies dormant at its core?
Adam, Paris, Newton
carry it inside their souls
& fondle it without a clue
to what it is.

Translations from Spanish.

From THE LORCA VARIATIONS: "NEWTON"

1
The men had green feet that vaulted them into the open where they could flaunt their secrets. Lace brushed lightly against their nostrils as the apple tree loomed over Newton with its fruits. It is so Saxon to bind gnomes with string, to watch your echoes drifting off in secret, your lost companions jangling irons in the wind. Not every boy has such sad eyebrows, nor would every corner spare an inch for death. In the woods the moon showed Newton where the truth lies. Following his nose he slammed into

a meteor named Newton. He mistook it for a science that was white—like beech trees or like beards—but once he caught it in his mirror, saw it turn blue again. At length it looked like every other star or lake.

2

Every wise man considers himself another Newton: a philosopher musing beside trees & water, going for a walk or coming from a walk, pulling genies out of waves & sky (with which *sigh* makes a perfect rhyme). Their corneas are focused on infinity & disregard the lowly cricket just as Newton did. And just as Newton knew the wind or Wordsworth knew a certain word to be the night's reflection, so apples floating on a wave of crickets make a synthesis more powerful than stars. Philosophers should play guitars, then, reaching for those apple branches where the moon's a lowly apple. Pyramids adorned with owls express a kind of harmony, & stars are dots & are a proof of death more powerful than worms. What if the river strikes a pose? The cedar will show a face that brings it home.

3

There isn't a clue that the fruit into which Adam bit was an apple & not his lady's breast. Above them Pegasus kept flying past, all in the name of science. The Virgin handed him a second apple, which Adam turned into a questioning of history. Deep in its core the Virgin saw souls rise & fall: a symbol Newton later found inside a pomegranate. Only a child can play with apples & touch beauty. Newton & Adam both were satisfied with Eve's reply, the first she gave when she woke up in chains, her innocence laid by. Paris in the other tale held up an orange.

A COMMENTARY ON LORCA

Federico García Lorca was the first poet I ever translated—a ballad or *romance* called "Preciosa y el Aire," worked out but never published, when I was still in my teens back in the later 1940s. The translation of Lorca's *Suites*—presented elsewhere in these pages—came some fifty years later, but was submerged in a large collected Lorca translated by a variety of hands. While I had been commissioned to translate the *Suites* and did so gladly, I felt a great frustration in not being able to publish my translations independently, thus diluting whatever sense I had that I was doing a kind of homage to Lorca. With that in mind I began to compose a series of poems of my own ("variations") that draw systematically on vocabulary, especially nouns and adjectives, from my translations of the *Suites*, but rearrange them in a variety of ways. The methods used resemble chance operations but with a margin of flexibility, with total freedom in the case of verbs and adverbs, with occasional addresses to Lorca himself imbedded in them. The result isn't translation or imitation in any narrow sense, but yet another way of making poetry—and for me at least, a way of coming full circle into a discovery that began with Lorca and for which he has stood with certain others as a guide and constant fellow-traveler.

More Lorca Variations appear below, page 437.

From 50 CAPRICHOS AFTER GOYA

In Goya's World

Flesh down to bone
a feeble skin
that barely covers her,
her empty mouth
pushed up against her nose,
her eyes shut tight,
the two who kneel beside her,
sister crones,
squat bodies hoisting brooms,
what do they spin
so finely?
In a corner of the room
the bodies of dead babes
are hanging,
little molls like little dolls,
the chins of children
sickly   prickly
strings attached
to fingers. Elsewhere
in Goya's world
crones suck the juice from
babes   jaws loose
& braying
ancient beings tucked in cowls,

in coils,
a basket at their feet
filled with babe's bodies.
It is too late
too late,
the bodies hang no longer,
all have fallen,
the women pass a dainty
box from hand to
hand, their fingers
dig down deep,
they slip the bones,
the little seeds,
between their lips,
into their gullets,
always still more to suck,
still always hungry.

[More poems from *50 Caprichos* appear below, page 480.]

THREE VARIATIONS ON OCTAVIO PAZ'S "BLANCO"

BLANCO 1: A VARIATION IN SEVEN SEGMENTS FOR OCTAVIO PAZ

1. white as the land looks | the vultures | white also | circle above | each one a soul | glows white | on horizon | or on page

2. the land is the land | it is white | thunderheads cover it | drumbeats | joining the land | & the sky

3. sky receptive to thunder | drumbeats to sky | white to colors | faces to eyes | sand turning white | like the sky

4. green is also | a color | like flesh | stung by thorns | my body | or yours | sparks a rage | like a drumbeat | violent | mineral | white

5. uproots trees | marks the land | like a body | shattered by lightning | the word | once proclaimed | white turns yellow

6. those who beat | on a waterdrum | spines tightly pressed | to a wall | & the drumbeat | spreads violet ash | on the sky | a sun glowing white

7. language | a desert | pink everywhere | seeds in your mouth | like white crows | & more drumbeats | a flute | turns everything white

Blanco 2: A Variation in Five Segments for Octavio Paz

1. A clarity | of all the senses | lingers | leaving on the mouth & face | a white precipitation | sculptures crystal-thin | blank space | translucid whirlpools

2. Is it a pilgrimage | that brings us | dancing in a ring | into a forest | where our thoughts | are white | the only signs | our steps | that break the silence

3. Green would be better | a slim defile | through which we pass | an archipelago | the shadow of a syllable | a white reflection

4. Is it red | or is it blue | this dazzlement | that blinds us | numbers | dancing in the void | like *things* | a final clarity | no longer white

5. Thoughts fade | winds cease | forgetfulness erases truth | there is a deeper music in the words we speak | yellow isn't white | & amethyst | is just a color

Blanco 3: A Variation in Nine Segments for Octavio Paz

1. Presentiment & penumbra | hide the river | where the sand | still white | buries a palm | a pike emerging | skewers our vowels | as we speak

2. Blood fills the mouth | the chest counts anxious minutes | as the dead might | undulations | of a copper lamp | high overhead | casting a shadow

3. Transparency in daylight | where a river | seeks a river | poles apart | the consonants feel heavy | water vanishes | the drought starts up

4. The Spanish centuries | remain anonymous | against my forehead | silt | obscures a castle | coal burns yellow | patience ends | a white confusion | covers all

5. What does the vase hold? | blood & bones | not flowers | the sad reality of words | a language of atonement | silences & syllables | white as this dust

6. No further clarity | than this | no histories or hieroglyphs | to guide us | dunes & water all around | conspiracies of light | absent survivors

7. White bones | appeasement hard to find | or patience | when we climb the ladder | mineshafts open up | below | a red hand beckons

8. His source is Mexico | his language set apart from | all the others | white on white

9. Pulsebeat quickens | on the playing card he holds | a foliage unfolds for him | a language no one reads | a river rife with whitecaps | rolling by

---

The preceding poems were commisioned & prepared for "Trans-Poetic Exchange: A Colloquium on Haroldo de Campos and Octavio Paz's Poem 'Blanco'" at Stanford University, January 29–30, 2010. In the spirit of what de Campos called "transcreation" & I called "othering," the method employed here is one I've used in *The Lorca Variations* & elsewhere. Vocabulary is drawn from Eliot Weinberger's translation of Paz's master poem in Spanish.

PABLO PICASSO: THE DREAM & LIE OF FRANCO

15–18 june 1937

owl fandango escabeche swords of octopus of evil omen furry dishrag scalps afoot in middle of the skillet bare balls popped into a cone of codfish sherbet fried in scabies of his oxen heart—mouth full of marmalade of bedbugs of his words—silver bells and cockle shells and guts braided in a row—a pinky in erection not a grape and not a fig—commedia del arte of bad weaving and smudged clouds—cosmetics of a garbage truck—the rape of las meninas cries and outcries—casket on shoulders crammed with sausages and mouths—rage that contorts the drawing of a shadow that lashes teeth nailed into sand the horse ripped open top to bottom in the sun which reads it for the flies who tack a rocket of white lilies to the knots spliced in the sardine heavy nets—lamp of lice where dog is and a knot of rats and hide outs in a palace of old rags—the banners frying in the skillet twist in black of ink sauce spilled in drops of blood that gun him down—the street soars to the clouds its feet bound to a sea of wax that makes its guts rot and the veil that covers it is singing dancing mad with sorrow—a flight of fishing poles *alhigui* and *alhigui* of the moving van first class interment—broken wings spinning in the spider web of dry bread and clear water a paella made of sugar and of velvet that paints a whiplash on its cheeks—the light blocked out the eyes before the mirror that make monkeyshines the chunk of nougat in the flames that gnaws itself the lips around the wound—cries of children cries of women cries of birds cries of flowers cries of wood and stone cries of bricks cries of furniture of beds of chairs of curtains of casseroles of cats and papers cries of smells that claw themselves of smoke that gnaws the neck of cries that boil in cauldron and the rain of birds that floods the sea that eats into the bone and breaks the teeth biting the cotton that the sun wipes on its plate that bourse and bank hide in the footprint left imbedded in the rock.

Translation from Spanish

A COMMENTARY ON PICASSO

When Pierre Joris and I were compiling *Poems for the Millennium* we sensed that Picasso, if he wasn't *fully* a poet, was incredibly close to the neighboring poets of his time, and when he brought language into his cubist works, the words collaged from newspapers were there as something really to be read. What only appeared to us later was the body of work, prolific and dazzling, that emerged from 1935 on and that showed him to have been a poet *in the fullest sense* and possibly, as Michel Leiris points out, "an insatiable player with words... [who, like] James Joyce... in his *Finnegans Wake*,... displayed an equal capacity to promote language as a real thing (one might say)... and to use it with as much dazzling liberty."

The poetry—most of it written as unpunctuated breathless blocks of prose—gave a sense of spontaneity or of the "pure psychic automatism" that André Breton had laid down as the defining point of Surrealism in his first (1924) Manifesto. But for Picasso (as for Breton also, one suspects) the work of poetry wasn't restricted to unmediated psychic acts or automatic writing, but subject, in its workings—however rapid—to something more deliberate and artful. Picasso's own directives here were simple: "*When I began to write [poems] I wanted to prepare myself a palette of words, as if I were dealing with colors.*" And with this came a reminder, also from Picasso, that he was willing, like poets of all persuasions, to sometimes move the oral or the auditory into the central position—"*not to tell stories or describe sensations, but to suggest them by the sounds of words.*" If this represents a kind of *faux*-surrealism—a simulation of spontaneity in which, he tells us, "*all these words were weighted, filtered and appraised*"—it is a quality that can and should be carried forward in translation.

TRISTAN TZARA: TWO DADA POEMS

Metal Coughdrops

her bare feet tell the neurasthenic: fake moustaches on that ostrich
made in u.s.a.
the cold bird tells the monocle: mouth got no lips I'll kill myself
but the cubist tells the cubist: I have invented the chief-of-scratch & I am
his boss
the boss tells the boss: boss

Maison Aragon

arp & the barbered arbor
reignite the open night
in the special pocket edition made for australian kangaroos

arp & the arc-shaped bark
are framed by semirámis
arp the arc & the arbored barbered bark

o crisp chronometer

Translations from French

TRISTAN TZARA, DADA, & ETHNOPOETICS

[When I published Pierre Joris's first translations from Tzara's *Poèmes Nègres* in 1976, I added the following.] The editor's intention, like that of the translator, is to present Tzara: *his* view of the "ethnopoetic" as it existed on entry circa 1916 into *dada*. ... The context of these poems was the first large scale attack on the dominance of renaissance European models of art & poetry—a project sometimes viewed as "anti-art" or, in Tzara's words, as "a great negative work of destruction." In the field of the *dada* poem, the "ethnopoetic" was surely at the other pole: a positive work of recovery & a return to the lost basis of human *poesis*. It had been my assumption, at the time I composed *Technicians of the Sacred*, that the influence of what Tzara calls "Negro poetry" (here both African & Oceanian) was largely indirect before our own time. The publication in the 1970s of Tzara's *Poèmes Nègres*—more than five decades past their intended appearance—now clarifies the process of transmission in all its roughness. It lets us see too how Tzara used the texts he found in ethnographic translations & transcriptions; how he worked & spoke them back to life; how they affected his own poems as image, sound & structure; how they went from there into the mainstream of surrealism, where they instructed not only the poets right at hand but even those latter-day Americans sometimes too busy asserting their own new poetic hegemony to take sufficient note of its sources. In all of this, Tzara—like Roussel, Leiris, Cendrars, etc.—was a pivotal & incredibly germinal figure.

KURT SCHWITTERS: FIVE MERZ POEMS

DESIRE

And
Without
Have
Sing
Earthworm
    Strut
Lyric
Tradition
The beggar
    Of
Hollow
Green
Of about
Of abutments
The grass.

"THOU"

My sing is void.
Scream gapes,
Scream swells up,
Roars gapes swells.
I bitter thou.
I bitter thine breath.
I sing thy eyes.
Thy stride yearns my eye.
Thy blab my ear yearns.
I lust the sniff of hours.
Thou art my yearn
Thou art thy stride, thy eyes, thy prayers.
Thy laughing prays,
Thy blab prays,
Thy eye prays.

My yearning fars thine pray cry.
I
far thou.

The Meadow

The meadow does grow. O woe to the man hiding meadows inside him. For how would it grow? I sure wouldn't know how a meadow could grow. And big Arp wouldn't either. For grass does grow stalks. And meadow lifts stalks unto sky. And wind bloweth winds. Stalk tremors for joy. Sun shines through the grass. Sky mirrors my blue. And earthsmell wafts fragrances. Who could know how to grow? Who would know from a meadow? I dream meadows pra.

Roses Abloom Like Daisy Blossoms

Roses abloom like daisy blossoms in the meadow, pressed down by big PRA's honeygentle finger, he who kisses the horizon with his bubbly thighs. Now liverspotted garlands dance athwart the guinea pigs' eyelashes, while they play catch upon their lips with his ancestral surname: "P R A." What you'd inherit from your fathers, earn it first, to own it. And on their golden snouts kaleidoscopic particles shall dance like endlessly large balls that bear the heaviness of X's And as they sink to earth, spontaneously a sunrise spreads out from their golden bronzed behinds, and the perishable ovary from more than 23,000 eggyellow custard squirters gushes down the azure skyblue aether.

From the Back & From the Front to Start

Labor volunteers.
Sabotage *strike* hand grenades.
Strike upheaves man.
Teeth bark forth teeth.
Infringements strike dismissals.
Bark—bark—bark—bang—Fear culminates silverstrings.
Drips stone on stone.

The upper echelons!
The upper echelons!
Hand grenades fly by themselves. But you be endlessly coolheaded. Streetcars go both from the back & the front. Who rides on tourist buses? Easy—easy—you people all stand up—in line!—Head under foot: that's what I mean by a strike! Once & for all the tip money bends—it bends—the streetcars bent out of shape are gaping all over. Crooked hours. Hand back that young herring. But the upper echelons must act (this one walks on his hands 21/31) & must hold firm in the face of this illegal strike by a disgruntled & inefficient professional class (*German Daily News*), & especially here where its present behavior, not without effect on the upcoming strikes in Berlin & the rest of the Reich, cranks out head laughs. Lootings rob riots. (I say the opposite, viz., only not always.)
The upper echelons!
The upper echelons!
The upper echelons & very.
Culminates silverstrings stone on stone.
Drips fear expulsions bang.
Sabotage *strike* infringements.
Drips silverstrings fear.
Provisionally there exists no prospect to bring the thing together, the situation has no board of supervisors. (That our lovely plattdeutsch never be forgotten!) And an absolutely binding heat to strike your momma's feet. Four thousand, forty thousand cheap, this got a long ways still to go.—The Jews—the Jews!

Translations from German

A COMMENTARY ON KURT SCHWITTERS

As with the work from Gomringer, below, and others, the question of how to present Schwitters was for me a question, largely, of the limits of translation. From the 1950s through most of the 1980s I had only done scattered translations from any single poet, but from the late eighties on (and with the computer as a new and powerful editing tool) I embarked on a series of extensive translations—Lorca, Nezval, Schwitters, and Picasso. In the case of Schwitters, I had thought of him for some time as not only a painter and sculptor but an occasional poet whose main literary contribution was as a composer and performer of early sound poetry. The great surprise came with the publication, starting in 1973, of a five-volume edition of his collected writings: a combination of "poems, performance pieces, proses, plays, poetics," the six p's of the title that Pierre Joris and I gave to the selection from his writings that we assembled and published in 1993. What emerged from a viewing of his "whole works" was a sense of Schwitters as one of the singularly inventive and innovative poets of his time. In thinking of ways to carry him over into English—to hit the right note or set the right tone—I found myself greatly assisted by Schwitters' own English poems and self-translations. (He had given up writing in German during the period of his exile to England in the Second World War.) I liked very much the irregular way in which he used the English second person ("thee" and "thou") or changed nouns into verbs or verbs into nouns— qualities present in the German originals as well. I had previously translated and performed work of his but in a very limited way, and the difference in dealing with the writings as a whole was enormous.

NAKAHARA CHUYA: TWO POEMS

"A Bone"

Look at this, it's my bone,
a tip of bone torn from its flesh,
filthy, filled up with woes,
it's the days of our lives
sticking out, a blunt bone
bleached by the rain.

There's no shine to it,
innocent, stupidly white,
absorbing the rain,
blown back by the wind,
just barely
reflecting the sky.

Funny imagining, seeing
this bone on a chair
in a restaurant

packed to the gills, & eating
mitsuba leafy & boiled,
a bone but alive.

Look at this, it's my bone,
& is that me staring
& wondering: Strange,
was my soul left behind
& has it come back
where its bone is,
daring to look?

On the half dead grass
on the bank of a brook
in my home town, standing
& looking—who's there?
Is it me? A bone
sticking out
a bone stupidly white
& high as a billboard.

Poem: Sad Morning

sound of a brook
comes down
the mountain:
spring light
like a stone:
the water running
from a spout
split open:
more a grey-haired
crone, her story
pouring out.

mica mouth
I sing through:
falling backward
singing:

drying up
my heart lying
wrinkled:
tightrope walker
in between
old stones.

o unknown fire
bursting in air!

o rain of echoes
wet & crowned!

....

clap my hands clapping
this way & that

Translations from Japanese with Yasuhiro Yotsumoto.

A COMMENTARY ON NAKAHARA CHUYA

Over a short lifetime, Nakahara Chuya (1907–1937) was a major innovator along lines originally shaped by Dada and other, earlier forms of European, largely French, experimental poetry. In 1997, as part of an annual poetry festival in his home prefecture of Yamaguchi, I came to his grave along with a group of Japanese poet-companions, to celebrate the 60th year of his death and the 90th of his birth. The poem marking that time, "At the Grave of Nakahara Chuya," appeared a few years later in *A Paradise of Poets* and included a fake "translation" in what I took to be his style, or one of them, that brought some of his work into the domain of popular Japanese music. The two poems presented above are from a more recent attempt at actual translation, but a part of the earlier poem-song can also appear here as a further homage:

As sportscoats are to toothpaste
as the boa is to scales
as black teeth are to playful ghosts
as seasons are to smiles

As telephones are to toasters
as angels are to air
as wagon wheels are to ups & downs
as horses are to fire

As Buddha is to Buddha
as a toenail is to glass
as the way we make love is tight like that
as ascensions are to cash

As harbors are to hairpins
as napoleons are to joy
as bicycles are to icicles
bones are to a dada boy

VITEZSLAV NEZVAL: SHIRT

[PREAMBLE]
How do they seize me these strange beings with no names
All their history as simple as Gibraltar
Bastards of reality & air who wander over Africa
The angelus clangs out

On one of those steamy nights the end of June in 1935
I walked past the Luxembourg Garden
It was just striking midnight
And the streets were empty
With the emptiness of moving vans
Deserted like Ash Wednesday
And I thought of nothing
Had no wishes
No I wished for nothing rushed to nowhere
Nothing weighed on me
Like a man sans memory I walked & walked
A man yes like a box
The way old men walk who no longer need to sleep

I still don't know what caught me maybe my own sigh
The trees out in the garden filling with white bandages
I looked back at those paper bindings
Over an iron hedge
Could I have been singing as I walked?
Just singing
& Paris sold off like a slave
Convulsed & crazy
Paris with your bridges made into your chains
Prague, Paris, Leningrad & all the cities
                                        I have ever walked thru
Now I see a herd of women bound with ropes
The glow is drowning them the sky still free
Like bracelets that a crowd is rushing over
Oh you gates you bridges
Of the one & only city that I see
A city cut thru by the Seine & Neva
by the Moldau
And a brook where peasant women wash their clothes
The brook I live by

And windows
Thru the first a statue comes in from the Place du Pantheon
The next looks over the Charles Bridge
Thru the third I'm staring down the Nevsky Prospect
And still more windowsVitezslav Nezval
How I loved the grocer's paper cones
With secrets that lie too deep
That they remind me of an empty chamber
With its heaps & heaps of shirts
A shaft that holds the common grave of nameless women
I know a forest with its broadleafed burdock
            under which a girl's breast's hidden
And a tin cross too   & these white hands
A sofa stuffed with gauze that reeks of antiseptic

Who are you woman like a sewing machine I stare at
Like the Boulevard Montparnasse that self-same evening
When I was sitting down outside the Café Dôme
And studying the frieze on that one building there

five storeys up
I thought that it was snowing
In my mind I took part in the final new year's eve
of the 19th century before it ended
Under a tree filled up with songs a carriage waited
In vain I tried to find the house the sewing machine inside
its shuttle that held a thread I longed to have
Then walked back to the Luxembourg again

The wonder of those gardeners who care so for their trees
they wrap the fruit in little sacks
Like you who cover up your bare breasts with a shirt
As beautiful as a water pail turned over in a house of mourning
As beautiful as a needle in a birch bark with the year and date stitched in
As beautiful as a poppy head that's shaken by a bell
As beautiful as a shoe out in a flood floats past a window with an oil lamp
As beautiful as a wooden stake on which a butterfly is resting
As beautiful as a baked apple in the snow
As beautiful as a bedboard struck by lightning
As beautiful as a wet rag in a fire
As beautiful as a loaf of bread at midnight on the pavement
As beautiful as a button on a cloister wall
As beautiful as a treasure in a pot of flowers
As beautiful as a psychic's table & the words writ on the gate
As beautiful as a garland in a shooting gallery
As beautiful as a scissors snipping off a candlewick
As beautiful as a tear inside the eye
As beautiful as the hairwheel of a clock inside a mare's ear
As beautiful as a diamond in a condottiere's rifle
As beautiful as teeth marks on an apple
As beautiful as the trees in the Luxembourg Garden
the trees wrapped in white linen
stiff with starch

Translation from Czech with Milos Sovak

A COMMENTARY ON NEZVAL

Nezval (1900–1958) was, with Velimir Holan, one of the two great early poets of Czech experimental modernism. Like other innovators then & now, he worked through a prolific sweep of modes & genres: open & closed forms of verse; novels drawn from his childhood & more surreal, chance-oriented prose works; avant-garde theater collaborations; numerous translations of his modern counterparts & predecessors (Rimbaud, Apollinaire, Neruda, Lorca, Eluard, et al.); & forays as composer, painter, journalist, photographer, & (from 1945 to 1951) director of the film section of the Information & Culture Ministry in Prague. His commitment to communism came early (1924), & his politics before & after made him a prominent member of that network of tolerated avant-gardists/poet-heroes that included Neruda, Brecht, Picasso, Hikmet, Eluard, & Tzara, among others (with some of whom he shared pro-forma hymns to Stalin in the early postwar years). As with many of them also, a Surrealist connection was clearly in evidence but should in no sense diminish the originality of his own practice & its contribution to ours.

EUGEN GOMRINGER: FOUR CONCRETE POEMS

silence silence silence
silence silence silence
silence   silence
silence silence silence
silence silence silence

*

gleichmässig gleich gleichmässig ungleich ungleichmässig
gleich ungleichmässig ungleich gleichmässig
gleich
gleichmässig ungleich ungleichmässig gleich
ungleichmässig ungleich gleichmässig gleich gleichmässig

alike like alike unlike unalike
like unalike unlike alike
like
alike unlike unalike like
unalike unlike alike like alike

straightforward straight straightforward unstraight unstraightforward
straight unstraightforward unstraight straightforward
straight
straightforward unstraight unstraightforward straight
unstraightforward unstraight straightforward straight straightforward

*

Freely adapted into German after a poem in English by Gomringer

der schnee ist deutsch

inwendig
sicher
spektral
liebreizend
eifersüchtig
ruhend
defensiv
mondförmig
hintersinnig
sesshaft
mineralisch
geschlossen
sonderbar
meisterlos
endgültig
feuchtkalt
keilförmig
unähnlich
dunkel

ideenarm
irreal
recht
edelmütig
zinken
spitzig
abgestanden
ebenmässig
heliozentrisch
rühmlich
amorph
selbstwirkend
katholisch
tiefgründig
eklehaft
archaisch
erteilt
nackt
inkonsequent

seuchenhaft
ungewaschen
prima
erhaltbar
akustisch
unentwickelt
seidenweich
pockennarbig
prophetisch
prachtvoll
riesenmässig
witzig
disharmonisch
lockig
uferlos
einverstanden
imperatorisch
schief
kontrapunktisch
definiert
reibungslos
nordöstlich
minimal
konkret
linksläufig
seelenvoll
hell
kohlschwarz
offenbar
bräutlich

schnurrbärtig
irgendwo
inoffiziell
insular
anormal
satt
eintönig
passiv
bärenartig
korrekt
körperlich
konkav
liedrlich
parteilos
süffisant
tüchtig
international
abgefeimt
ewig
etwasanderes
frühzeitig
hartgläubig
immateriell
ahnherrlich
imprägniert
artfremd
ausgezeichnet
apostolisch
diebssicher
weiss
konsequent

*

hang and swinging hang and swinging
hang and grow and swinging hang
and grow downwards and swinging hang and
grow downwards and touch the ground and
swinging hang and grow downwards and
touch the ground and then off and search
and swinging hang and grow downwards

and touch the ground and then off and
search and not find a place and swinging
hang and grow downwards and touch
the ground and then off and search and not
find a place and grow and swinging
hang and grow downwards and touch
the ground and then off and search and not
find a place and grow upwards and swinging
hang and grow downwards and touch
the ground and then off and search and not
find a place and grow upwards and force
a new growth and swinging hang and
grow downwards and touch the ground and
then off and search and not find a place
and grow upwards and force a new growth
and hang and swinging hang and
grow downwards and touch the ground and
then off and search and not find a place
and grow upwards and force a new growth and
swinging hang

Translations from German

FROM A LETTER TO EUGEN GOMRINGER 9TH NOVEMBER 1967

... As a poet (but not a "concrete"-poet) part of the interest of concrete poetry for me is the clear light it throws on the nature of *all* poetry. You speak of constellations, [Ian Hamilton] Finlay speaks of corners, I speak elsewhere of combinations—but always it's a question of making the words cohere in a given space, the poem's force or strength related to the weight & value of the words within it, the way they pull and act on each other. The poetry shows this beautifully; the problem of translation is related to it also & throws its own clear light on how & why we translate.

So I'm trying to get a variety of work into the book, & this involves the following approaches to translation. (1) Poems that present the "normal" problems of translation & which I handle as I would I would any poem; for example, "you green" or "hang & swinging hang" [above]. (2) Poems with a limited number of word forms in a fixed relationship & with enough translatable meanings to allow the possibility of multiple translations into English; for example, "gleichmässig gleich gleichmässig ungleich ungleichmässig," which I can do (keeping the close relationship & with adjustment of prefix or suffix as "alike like alike unlike unalike" or (distorting slightly but here the suffix is clearer) as "straightforward straight," etc., & present two or more versions as the translation. (3) Translations involving minimal choices (for example, the 24 nouns of *stundenbuch* [the "book of hours"] & the decision to make *dein* "your" or "thy"), after which the poem, however long, is more or less self-generating & translator's interference should be almost nothing. (4) Other poems in which vocabulary is very restricted & precise English translations can't possibly meet all the formal requirements; here I sometimes keep the form intact & bring in an unrelated vocabulary series—thus, in "blüte blatt zweig" [not shown here] I translate the partly alliterative words as "moon mist rain" or "shadow shower clouds" rather than distorting the simple vocabulary into "frond fruit bough." (5) Poems where the preceding would be pointless or impossible & that only need a gloss for the reader with no German vocabulary at all; for example "fisch schif" = "fish ship." (6) Poems where the English & German readings are identical, "wind" or "ping pong" or "lo zen le zen el cid," which isn't German anyway. (7) Poems previously translated by Gomringer. (8) Poems—for example, "snow"—written by Gomringer in English. (9) Instances of the latter where (why not?) I translate English into German, as in the German transcreation of "snow" [printed above]. All of which makes the book, as "translation," a very interesting & curious document. For me certainly.

*

homage to gomringer

```
g o g o g o g o g o
o g o g o g o g o g
g o n o n o n o n o
o m g m g m g m g g
g r r r r r r r r o
o i i i i i i i i g
g n n n n n n n n o
o g g g g g g g g g
g e e e e e e e e o
o r r r r r r r r g
```

(j.r.)

IN MEMORIAM JACKSON MAC LOW

When the expiration hath ceased, the vital-force will have sunk into the nerve-centre of Wisdom & the Knower will be experiencing the Clear Light of the natural condition. Then the vital force, being thrown backwards & flying downwards through the right & left nerves the Intermediate State (Bardo) momentarily dawns.

How will I take the final words of your Night Walk, now that you're dead, & work them into my poem?
I had promised it at your birthday, the last or the next to the last, so hard to tell the years apart,
so leave myself no choice but to continue, get it down & try to speak your presence with the words you give me.

Once again I think of you as someone wearing many coats or bundled up against the night, my own delight to sit beside you,
to see your nose & eyebrows glowing in that light, revealing you to us,
revealing secret bodies from your night walks, meanings written on their foreheads,
two o'clock when happiness arrives to free our tongues,
when coats are shed & foreheads show what's real inside us, feeling, hearing, walking with delight,
a man at night whose being flows out from his teeth, who steps on twigs & breaks the silence,
learning how to draw attention in that halflight, feigning sweetness.

Clasping your coats around you, hairsmells heavy in the night, dark clouds & kisses foremost,
when the evening's dark & cold, I hold the clouds in memory, a dimness
black as three o'clock, so touching when the cold rests on your eyebrows, otherwise revealing what we all try finding,
clothing darker than the sky, desiring & feeling, telling your old stories, standing rooted like a tree.

Desiring what else I couldn't say but know that when the light grows dark, as when our fingers close around it,
a streamsound breaks the silence, that's when wondering makes way for learning,

pointing out the stars at night, wrapped in your many sweaters, when our
beings feel delight,
you wait there, listening in that dimness, hearing little, knowing less, of
what the night's revealing,
bodies black & cold are sliding past you, clasping you around as you
might grasp at meaning,
bundled in your clothing, looking outward where the night grows white
& quiet.

There's a halflight that survives you. Now we're warming ourselves in it,
resting, hugging, hearing streamsounds,
loving peace as you did, finding that our eyes, turned to the sky, observe a
man there,
hearing what we hear, whose kisses promise sweetness, being who he is,
but turn to ice before us,
talking through the night while wearing many coats against its dimness,
friends together,
filming trees & raising eyebrows, hearing, hugging, kissing, melting ice
against our tongues,
out in the night air, trading coats.

A dimness with no resting, seeking warmth from kisses, needing what a
man has always needed,
touching lips to eyelids, talking to each other through the night, a mem-
ory of three o'clock,
no longer a delight for eyes & tongues, with never warmth enough to suit
your liking,
bodies poor & old, their pockets long since emptied, naked beings who
still freeze like naked beings,
some dispensing meanings, others begging for attention, listening while
walking, slipping backwards in the night,
its grey trees masking feeling.

Will trees still bring delight, the way old stories made our cheeks turn
red or hairsmells filled our noses?
Will we be clasping something, feeling it slide past us, eyes & teeth
revealing what the night can't hide?
Where will our clothing be at three o'clock, our pockets empty, trees like
fallen friends around us,

& no telling if there's starlight, if the night still brings us wonders, trees
    that once again are only trees,
each one of us a fallen being, hairsmells heavy in the darkness, noses
    swollen,
clasping what we can & listening, for what? Another nightwalk, half
    forgotten,
where the light turns black.

---

* Source of epigraph: *The Tibetan Book of the Dead*

A COMMENTARY ON JACKSON MAC LOW

I met Jackson Mac Low in 1960 or 1961, through the intervention, as I recall it, of Diane Wakoski. She had come to New York with LaMonte Young & there was clearly a connection between Jackson & LaMonte through an avant-garde that was centered on John Cage's presence in New York & the international connections delineated by Fluxus. My first response to Jackson's aleatory/chance experiments was a degree of puzzlement but a sense beneath that, that something real & important was taking place. I fell for him first at a reading in which he introduced the first several of his *Light Poems*, impressed enough by those so that whatever else he did entered at once into the realm of my possibilities. And this was enhanced still more when he drew me into performing with him (as he did with many others) or, conversely, when he gave himself willingly to my own early attempts (circa 1969 or 70) at fusing poetry with performance. I often performed with him in his Gathas, & he was one of my performers (along with David Antin & Rochelle Owens) in a staged & recorded presentation of "primitive & archaic poetry" (circa 1967) that was the direct forerunner to *Technicians of the Sacred.*

Our friendship lasted from then until 2004, when he died at the age of 82. By then he was one of my essential compadres, & I like to think that I played the same role for him & that whatever it was between us, it worked to our mutual advantage as individuals & poets. After I left New York for good—in 1976—there was hardly a return trip in which Jackson (& later Jackson & Anne Tardos) wasn't there as a dear companion & confederate.

In 1997 Jackson celebrated his 75th birthday in New York, or rather it was celebrated for him by a number of friends & admirers. I was in Paris at the time but prepared a poem in three parts, a suite of "night poems" as a kind of rhyming response (in title & theme) to Jackson's "light poems." Five years later I added a fourth part, a series of variations off a lexicon of words provided by Jackson's early *Night Walk* (1960). I read these for him at his 80th birthday celebration in St Mark's Church, with the promise that I would continue to do these for every subsequent fifth-year celebration. After his death in 2004 I compacted the final variations on his *Night Walk* into a poem "in memoriam"—not an elegy so much as a poem in commemoration of his works & of our lives together.

The earlier "night poems" for Jackson Mac Low appear elsewhere in these pages.

THE FIRST HORSE SONG OF FRANK MITCHELL (BLUE)

Navajo

Key: wnn N nnnn N gahn

All ahrenow some 're there & mine all (gahn) & some (gwing) there are
mine all (gahn) & some (gwing) there 're mine there nnnn N gahn
All ahrenow some 're there & mine all (gahn) & some (gwing) there are
mine all mine all (gahn) & some (gwing) there 're mine there

(Nnnnn N gahn) because I was the boy raised ing the dawn & nnnn but
some there are mine all (gahn) & some (gwing) there 're mine
there
(Nnnnn N gahn) & in the howse the bluestone home & mmmrrr but
some there are mine all (gahn) & some (gwing) there 're mine
there
(Nnnnn N gahn) & in the howse the shiningwingNdgahn & some there
are mine all (gahn) & some (gwing) there 're mine there
(Nnnnn N gahn) & ing the swollenowse his breath has blown & nnnn
but some there are mine all (gahn) & some (gwing) there 're mine
there
(Nnnnn N gahn) & ing the howse the hoNloly home & mmmmm but
some there 're mine all (gahn) & some (gwing) there 're mine there

(Nmmmm N gahn) nndin the house of precious cloth we walk (p)pon (N gahn) & nnn but some there are mine all (gahn) & some (gwing) there 're mine there
(Nnnnn N gahn) N prayersticks that are blue N wwnnn but some there 're mine all (gahn) & some (gwing) there 're mine there
(Nnnnn N gahn) with my feathers that are blue N wwnnn but some there 're mine all (gahn) & some (gwing) there 're mine there
(Nnnnn N gahn) with those spirit horses that are blue & wwnnn but some there 're mine all (gahn) & some (gwing) there 're mine there
(Nnnnn N gahn) with those spirit horses that are blue & dawn N nnnn but some there are mine all (gahn) & some (gwing) there 're mine there
(Nnnnn N gahn) with those spirit horses that are bluestonawu N nnnn but some there are mine all (gahn) & some (gwing) there 're mine there
(Nnnnn N gahn) with those horses that are bluestonawu & nnnn but some there are mine all (gahn) & some (gwing) there 're mine there
(Nmmmm N gahn) with cloth of evrygind to be(e) there N rrr but some there 're mine all (gahn) & some (gwing) there 're mine there
(Nmmmm N gahn) with jewels of everygind to be(e) there N rrr but some there are mine all (gahn) & some (gwing) there 're mine there
(Nnng N gahn) with hoganorses of evrygind to be(e) there N rrr but some there are mine all (gahn) & some (gwing) there 're mine there
(Nnnn N gahn) with sheep of evrygind to be(e) there N rrr but some there are mine all (gahn) & some (gwing) there 're mine there
(Nnnn N gahn) with cattle of evrygind to be(e) there N rrr but some there are mine all (gahn) & some (gwing) there 're mine there
(Nnnn N gahn) with men of evrygine to be(e) there N rrr but some there are mine all (gahn) & some (gwing) there 're mine there
(Nnnn N gahn) my howse of precious cloth in my backgwingNgahn N nnn but some there are mine all (gahn) & some (gwing) there 're mine there
(Nnnn N gahn) the house mmm precious cloth we walk (p)pon & nnn but some there are mine all (gahn) & some (gwing) there 're mine there
(Nnnn N gahn) & everything that's there before & mrrr we walk upon & nnnn but some there are mine all (gahn) & some (gwing) there 're mine there

(Nnnn N gahn) & everything that's more & won't be poor N gwing N
gahn nnnn but some there are mine all (gahn) & some (gwing)
there 're mine there
(Nnnn N gahn) my horses that are living to be old & blesst naht nnnn
but some there are mine all (gahn) & some (gwing) there 're mine
there
(Nnnn N gahn) because I am the boy who blesses to be & dlll but some
there 're mine all (gahn) & some (gwing) there 're mine there
nnnn N gahn

All ahrenow some 're there & mine all (gahn) & some (gwing) there are
mine all (gahn) & some (gwing) there 're mine there nnnn N
gahn
All ahrenow some 're there & mine all (gahn) & some (gwing) there are
mine all (gahn) & some (gwing) there 're mine there nnnn N gaah!

From *Alcheringa*, Issue Two, 1971. An additional translation from *The Seventeen Horse Songs of Frank Mitchell* & a fuller account in the essay on "total translation" appear elsewhere in these pages.

From "JE EST UN AUTRE: A TALK & TALK-POEM"

Today I want to proclaim my own otherness & proclaim it for what it is.
[Pointing to head & heart.]
There are many "others" in me.
[Pause.]

Before there was ethnopoetics there was the world.

I mean to say that we emerged from the second world war & knew that it was bigger than that. The world, I mean.

The world as Europe was not the world the mind now knew.

And something had happened that let the mind know many worlds—each one of which was "other" to the mind.

Europe was also "other."

America was "other."

What was exotic & what was near to hand were "other."

You & I were "other" to ourselves, our minds.

The mind the mind knew was a final otherness: a habitat of minds & worlds.

(This emerged. The world emerged it.)

What you know is what you are. What the mind can hold is what the mind is.

Enough, the mind says. There is a politics in this & yet there is no politics.

There is a knowledge here that mixes real & unreal, that opens.

There is also the trembling headiness of a world in which, Rimbaud told us, "I" is an "other."

What did he mean by that?

What do I mean?

"I" is "other," is "an other," is "the other."

(There is also "you.")

If the mind shapes, configures the world it knows or holds, is there an imperial/colonizing mind at work here, or is this mind as shaper & collager still pursuing its old work: to make an image of the world from what appears to it?

And what appears to it?

The world.

. . . . . .

"I" is an "other," then; becomes a world of others.

It is a process of becoming. A collaging self. Is infinite & contradictory. It is "I" and "not-I."

"Do I contradict myself? Very well, I contradict myself. I is infinite. I contains multitudes."

Said Rimbaud/Whitman at the very start.

It is from where we are, the basis still of any ethnopoetics worth the struggle.

For those for whom it happens, the world is open, & the mind (forever empty) is forever full.

There is no turning back, I meant to say.

Here the millennium demands it.

A variation on the opening of a short talk piece, "Je est un autre," presented at the Modern Language Association convention in December 1989 & later published in *American Anthropologist*, volume 96, number 3, September 1994.

POETICS & POLEMICS 1
TOWARD AN ETHNOPOETICS

ALCHERINGA
Ethnopoetics

"A First Magazine of the World's Tribal Poetries"

songs, chants, prayers

.

visions & dreams

.

fictions, sacred narratives, histories

.

sound poems, beast languages, ghost tantras

.

ritual scenarios, events & happenings

.

intermedia pieces

.

origins & namings

.

verbal categories, word games

.

magical formulas

.

riddles, proverbs

.

picture poems, picture writings, iconics

.

models of the universe

.

ecological observations

.

selected commentaries on the above

THE POETICS OF THE SACRED: A RANGE OF TOPICS FOR A KEYNOTE SPEECH

Fu Jen Catholic University, Taipei, September 1990,
Second International Conference on Literature and Religion
Others present: Gary Snyder, Wai-lim Yip

> *Blessed art thou, O Lord our God, King of the Universe,*
> *who permittest that which is forbidden.*
> —The personal prayer of Sabbatai Zevi,
> 17th-century Jewish messiah & mystic

The strange thing about it, for many of us, is that we so clearly recognize the origins of poetry in states of mind and in forms of behavior that we think of as religious in nature. And yet, speaking for myself and for many like me, our tendency has been to pull away from religion as such. It is a tension that I feel in whatever I've done as a poet, and it's a tension that I'd like to address on this occasion: what a concern with the sacred might mean in a climate of secular thinking and being.

1
The Sacred

The sacred rather than the transcendent, because the transcendent, however generously defined in the prospectus for the present conference, implies for me too great a denial of the here and now; and the source of poetry, as I understand it, is deeply rooted in the world around us: doesn't deny it so much as brings it back to life. "Eternity is in love with the productions of time" wrote William Blake, who was our first great poet of the here and now. It is in *time* that I engage myself, and it is to discover or create the sense of a life that can energize the common world we share. In that energizing—that first, deceptively simple, act of poesis—something strange happens, whether to the world at large or to our sense of it. Remaining here-and-now, the world begins to lure us with a feeling, an intuition, of what the poet Robert Kelly speaks of as the not-here/not-now. Poetry, like religion, has been filled with such extraordinary manifestations ("coincidence, chance, odd happenings, large rocks, hailstorms, talking animals, two-headed cows," and so on), but for those of us for whom poetry in some sense takes religion's place (albeit a religion without assurances), they aren't bound or fixed but open-ended, different (we would like to think) each time we go at them.

2
On God

If this implies a yearning for what the Surrealists, say, called the "marvelous" and "wonderful," I would be careful not to play down the risks involved—the dark side of the picture. "The world is charg'd with the grandeur of God" begins the great sonnet by Gerard Manley Hopkins, not as an image of transcendence but of immanence. I respond still to what he writes, but I can't speak of God without a sense too of negation and rejection. For after Auschwitz and Hiroshima, the line comes back to me distorted: "The world is charged with the terror of God," it says.

Here I report my intuition, but it is an intuition curiously reinforced by a form of hermeneutic numerology from the tradition of Jewish kabbala. There, since every letter of the Hebrew alphabet was also a number, words whose letters added up to the same sum were treated as being in significant relation to each other. This was used, not surprisingly, to substantiate accepted "truths," though there were times when the system (called *gematria* from the Greek) was used by the heretical and the heterodox to call the others into question. In following that system, then, I found that the letters in the Hebrew god-name aleph-lamed-vav-hey (*eloha*) add up numerically (= 42) to the Hebrew word bet-hey-lamed-hey (*behalah*), "terror, panic, alarm." That they also add up to *kvodi* ("my glory") only intensifies the problematic. In short, a way of making poetry. So, take it any way you choose. Where God breaks into what I write or think, it is the terror that admits him.

3
The "Other" Tradition

There is accordingly a string of words with which we work with some degree of caution—the sacred, the holy, the numinous, the spiritual, and others that we shy away from even more—the supernatural, the pious, the divine, the transcendent. Even the sacred for me depends on how and why I'm using it, is resonant therefore with its own problematics. When the American poet David Antin, reacting against the easy—and popular—view of the sacred, says, "I reject the idea of a sacred language," I understand his objection even before he completes it: "For me, poetry is a mental act, not work which will become the object of a specialized cult." But I also understand the mental as the *spiritual* (another danger word) and that there are times, for Antin as for me, when the language of the mental act of poetry becomes itself what André Breton called "a sacred action."

It is largely a question of where we locate these words—in what context or tradition. Antin's rejection of the "cult" reflects a distrust of institutional and pietistic forms, of orthodoxies and closed systems, wherever found. In our own generation in America and Europe this has meant a turning from a Western and Judeo-Christian view of mores and religion—in contrast, say, to the rush into orthodoxy of the Eliot and Auden generations. What we came to identify with, beyond our own mental acts, was what Gary Snyder speaks of as a subterranean tradition—or series of such—that manifests globally in movements antithetical to established governments and religions. It represents a poetics of the open as against the closed, the free against the fettered, the transgressive and forbidden against the settled. Its shibboleths are terms like "*free verse*" and "*open form*"; the Dada cry "to liberate the creative forces from the tutelage of the advocates of power"; the assertion by William Blake that "poetry fetter'd, fetters the human race."

4
The Spiritual In Art

It is so easy to lose sight of this; so easy, say, for an academic formalism to obscure the understanding of an artist like Kandinsky, that the work in which he was engaged was not merely "modern" but aimed toward a renewal of the "spiritual in art." So too—in its own way—was Apollinaires's call for a "new spirit" in poetry and art. Or Tristan Tzara's insistence that the Dada poetry and art which he was fostering weren't based on a new method or technique, but on a profoundly altered state of mind (*esprit*), something like "an ancient buddhist spirit of indifference," as he also called it. It may seem a curious insistence from a man who was also, politically and philosophically, a dialectical materialist, but something like this turns up again and again as a defining issue within the avant-garde. It's there in Breton's contentions (for Surrealism) that "existence is elsewhere" and that at the end of the surrealist search, "the mysteries which are not will give way at last to the Great Mystery." And for the American poet Ezra Pound it's a mark of a yearning that transcends the trap of the political and that leads at last to the sense of his own (and possibly necessary) failure:

I have brought the great ball of crystal
                                        who can lift it?
Can you enter the great acorn of light?
                        But the beauty is not the madness
Tho' my errors and wrecks lie about me.
And I am not a demigod,
 I cannot make it cohere.

There are times too when the search and struggle have centered on a conflict with Western science and materialism (Kandinsky and a multitude of others would be the case in point), but it would be a mistake not to recognize that religion—Western religion certainly—has also been at issue. For some this has meant a re-viewing (re-thinking) of Christian and Jewish ties and sources, some of it extreme, rejectional, embattled, openly transgressive, but unwilling in general to stray far outside what Robert Kelly has called "the through-the-west-inherited gnosis." This would range from the foregrounding of metaphysical but recognizably Christian poets like Donne or Góngora or Angelus Silesius, to the fascination in our time with gnostic traditions outside the normative religious orders. There is already an "othering" at work here—more exactly a sense that our own singleness is more akin to what was silenced and made other in an alliance of church and state that may now be coming to an end. Or that may, conversely, be returning once again to haunt us.

5
New Archaeologies, Etc.

The freedom to think in these terms—a spiritual gift of the Enlightenment, for which religion (even when most rejected) was in fact a central issue—has allowed us to move radically beyond the Christian and the Western. The connection of poetry to pre-Christian and pagan sources goes very deep into Western history, moving into radical new territories and archaeologies from the eighteenth century on. A form of such a pagan-Christian linkage is familiar enough from Eliot's use of Frazer and Harrison as underpinnings for *The Waste Land*, although his intellectual conservatism (both in religion and in poetry) kept him from a fuller exploration of the possibilities that this kind of move had opened up. With others—Pound, say, as one example—the normative Christian gave way substantially to the force of the non-Christian and non-European past and present.

But the alternative past—even where it keeps, roughly, within the boundaries of Europe or of Asia Minor—can take still more extreme forms. I'm thinking here of poets like Robert Graves, whose image of the White Goddess, etc., drew largely from the bardic taxonomies of the pagan North; of Charles Olson, who explored a pre-hellenic "archaeology of morning" in the Sumerian and Hittite past; of Clayton Eshleman with his direct entry into the Paleolithic caves and imageries of ancient Europe; of Velimir Khlebnikov, who found a primal "beyondsense" language among the Slavic peasants and Central Asian shamans; of Edmond Jabès, who reshaped a kabbalistic literature into a new mental landscape of endlessly discoursing rabbis. It is precisely in mappings and remappings of this kind that one begins to sense the ongoing power of any Western-centered modernism that we would still be willing to inherit.

Such a "modernism"—pushing as well into the "post"modern present—has often enough left Europe far behind it. If this connects in some sense to terms like Edward Said's "orientalism" or to "primitivism" as we've often had it thrown at us, it's also, I would insist, a part of what Gary Snyder, echoing Whitman, once called a "passage to more than India." For Europeans and Americans who have used it sensibly, it is a work of the immediate present, not of the exotic and romantic past. And it is a work intended—above all—to question and disrupt the power of the dominant European discourse.

6
Pound's Cathay

Take Pound's *Cathay* as an example, about which Wai-lim Yip, present here, has written so brilliantly. Rather than a capsule glimpse at an ancient—and from a Western perspective, exotic—poetry, it represented Pound's sense of what it was to be alive and writing poetry in 1915 (in the midst of the First World War). "Largely a war book," as Hugh Kenner describes it, "its exiled bowmen, deserted women, leveled dynasties, departures for far places, lonely frontier guardsmen, and glories remembered from afar, were selected from the diverse wealth in the Fenollosa notebooks Pound was working from by a sensibility responsive to torn Belgium and disrupted London." Pound's writing, then, came at a moment in history when a debased poetry, an unanchored language of transcendence, had separated us from the immediacies of our experience (debilitating as that experience may have been) and when a new sacralization (the renewal of the spiritual-in-art) depended on connecting to the concrete particulars of the worlds around and in us. For this, which was the objective of Pound's imagism and of that version of it "in motion" that he called vorticism, something in Chinese language and culture served as both a model and a confirmation.

In his repeated three-point directive for imagism, two of Pound's imperatives spoke clearly to and from the ways of poetry he thought he found in China: "direct treatment of the 'thing,' whether subjective or objective," and "using absolutely no word that did not contribute to the presentation." The third—"as regarding rhythm: to compose in the sequence of the musical phrase, not in the sequence of a metronome"—was a necessary part of this modernist package but with a more ambiguous relation to Chinese practice as such than he might have thought. It is a package, circa 1913, without reference to the sacred or transcendent or religious, but in the aftermath Pound himself found that it would move toward the intellectul worlds of Kung Fu-tze and Tao, say, and would relate them also (as with the poetry of Li Po and of the *Book of Songs*) to contemporary circumstance and praxis. All that as a starter for the century at large: a through-the-*East*-inherited gnosis that would, particularly on its Buddhist side, have a fundamental impact on poets like Snyder and Ginsberg and a host of others. (Also, although much less often recognized, in the radical experiments with systematic chance that underpin the projects of a Cage and a Mac Low.)[1]

7
Toward a Primal Poetics

The idea of a concrete language dominated both American experiments with "image" and Surrealist, largely European, explorations of an oneiropoetics, a poetics of the dream. In either case the orientation was toward the *thing*—the object sighted, sensed, "directly" treated—with an insistence on the closeness between thing and word ("signified" and "signifier," for those who prefer the abstract counterpart). "We have lived [too] long in a generalizing time," Charles Olson wrote as he too turned away from it, aiming (while bound to fail) to heal the break between reality and language. Something like this has been a central project of our work as poets—a key both to our search for a primal poetics and to our search for

[1] Snyder's attempt, as I see it, to write an American poetry unencumbered by reference to a traditional Christian and European past, is an immediate example of how such an experiment in gnosis can take shape.

the sacred. It has led us into the depths of our own cultures and into cultures far distant from our own, this idea that a sacralized view of the world was tied, somehow, to a clear sharp language of names and nouns, dream names included. "Poetry," wrote Gertrude Stein, "is really loving the name of anything. … It is knowing and feeling a name." And George Oppen, American "objectivist" poet, based a poetics on "The small nouns / Crying faith / In this in which the wild deer / Startle, and stare out."

It is this, or something very close to it, that I tried to put forward in *Technicians of the Sacred*, a global anthology of tribal and oral poetries that I fashioned as a series of connections between two mythic poles: a "present" and a "past." "Sacred," of course, was one of the two key words in that title and behind it was Mircea Eliade's description of the shamans (religious figures rooted in our deepest human past) as masters of the techniques of ecstasy and of the means to bring those into language. If this sometimes implies a poetics of transcendence, I would be careful not to place it "beyond experience" as such, but to remember, for example, how Snyder locates the shaman's work in the experience of those who have "seen the glint in the eye of an eagle or the way a lizard's ribs quake when he does pushups"—and from that as a base "have stepped outside the social nexus to make contact with a totally nonhuman other" from which the poem, as inspired voice, arises. The source of a contemporary poetry of similar intensity may shift the area of experience—the place in which it happens, even the object of the search—but can never be wholly separated from it. And the poet's work may, like the shaman's, make its encounter foremost within language—may start with language and use that as the vehicle with which to drive toward meaning, toward a (re)uniting with the world.[2]

The idea that we could learn about such things from a wide range of cultures—some more advanced in them than our own—triggered the move in our time to a new poetics grounded in an *ethno*poetics. Such an ethnopoetics—my coinage, in a fairly obvious way, circa 1967—refers to an attempt to investigate on a transcultural scale the range of possible poetries that have not only been imagined but put into practice by other human beings. It was premised on the perception that Western definitions of poetry and art were no longer, indeed had never been, sufficient and

[2] Needless to point out the etymological meaning of "religion" as a "reconnecting" or a "binding up." Its use in an expression like "nature religion" may be what's at stake here—as a reconnecting (not a separation) from the world. The binding to an orthodoxy or to a settled version of the real is, of course, another reading.

that our continued reliance on them was distorting our view both of the larger human experience and of our own possibilities within it. The focus of our ethnopoetics as such was not so much inter*national* as inter*cultural*, with a stress on those stateless and classless societies that an earlier ethnology had classified as "primitive."

8
A Poetics Of The Sacred

Behind this search for origins—for what would allow us to begin again, to break free from the past even as we reclaimed it—was the trauma of the Second World War, when "man " (Charles Olson wrote for all of us) "had been reduced to so much fat for soap, superphosphate for soil, fillings and shoes for sale." It was against the background of this crisis—of the mind, the spirit—that the work we were engaged in first revealed its meaning. So, if Gary Snyder, say, spoke of that work—"the real work of modern man"—as the "uncovering of the inner structure and actual boundaries of the mind," the urgency of his statement related it to the time in which it was spoken. If mind is its own mystery, so are the objects that the mind uncovers or conceals: in short, the world. So is that language which is both mind's vehicle and prison.

In writing of those poetries (traditional/oral/tribal) that filled the first part of *Technicians of the Sacred*, I underscored first off my sense that they were (like the languages in which they were framed) complex rather then simple. This was reinforced by seeing the words as part of larger ritual and mythic wholes and served me further as a way of undermining the notion that complexity and intelligence were all on "our" side, minimalism and a kind of naked energy on theirs. Rather, I suggested, poetry both then and now (there and here) was a juncture of intelligence and energy that I equated with (another poets' codeword) "imagination." And from that juncture—which was what the gathering was really about—emerged the idea, but also the experience, of what we've sometimes called "the sacred."

9
In Lieu Of A Conclusion

With an eye, then, on both the here and there of it, it was my hope that the poems and juxtapositions in *Technicians of the Sacred* would illuminate the ways in which poetry—wherever found—may act as a vehicle for enhancing our sense of the human and other-than-human, their convergence in the sacred. If we don't etherealize or abstract this process, it can of course be read as an equivalent to that definition of transcendence that the organizers of this conference gave us to work with: as "a function or being that transcends [that goes beyond or through] the possibilities of experience and yet is necessary to give meaning to the data of experience." Such a search for meaning will take us into dangerous areas as well as safe ones, "blinding images" (in Wai-lim Yip's formulation) as well as clear ones; and its effectiveness will be proven in some sense by the degree to which it remains problematic and resistant to our attempts to evade or to resolve it.

As a function of our *un*belief, it may resemble that absurdity—that doubting of the sensible and probable—in which Tertullian once rested his *belief.*

ON ETHNOPOETICS: A COLLAGE

Primitive Means Complex

That there are no primitive languages is a conclusion of contemporary linguistics where it turns its attention to the multitude of languages existing now or in the distant past. There are no half-formed languages, no underdeveloped or inferior languages. Everywhere a development has taken place into structures of great complexity.

What is true of language in general is equally true of poetry & of the ritual systems of which so much poetry is a part. No people today is newly born. No people has sat in sloth for the thousands of years of its history. People without writing are not without poetry.

A study of indigenous societies—those in particular in which writing has been absent & technological development is assumed to be at its lowest—has shown that poetry, wherever we find it (literally *everywhere*), involves an extremely complicated sense of materials & structures. If *we* take poetry to be "language charged with meaning to the highest degree," as Ezra Pound defined it, or, more simply, as "[structures] allowing musical elements (time, sound) to be introduced into the world of words" (John Cage), we can observe it even in cultures where no activity is designated by a word like "poetry."

What I am speaking of here is an ethnopoetics & a range of poetries, many of them from threatened & endangered languages & cultures, that came to light for us in the twentieth century—at the heart of modernism, which welcomed them as a part of itself while knowing that they were truly, inescapably from elsewhere. This was in fact the dynamic of ethnopoetics, as some of us came to speak of it during the second great wave of experimental twentieth-century modernism from the mid-1950s to the mid-1970s.

For me such an ethnopoetics—which looks away from the modern & experimental, to focus on ancient & autochthonous cultures (often under threat of mass extinction or long since blown away)—is the product (as study & praxis) of our most dedicated & outrageous modernism, even surviving (under fire) into that postmodernism taken as the older movement's early & forever problematic offspring. Early, I say, remembering that it was Tristan Tzara—founder of Dada as a high point [culmination] of that first wave of experimental modernism that Marjorie Perloff called the futurist moment—who in his Weimar manifesto-lecture of 1922 declared: "You are mistaken if you take Dada for a modern school, or as a reaction against the schools of today. … Dada is not at all modern. It is more in the nature of an almost Buddhist religion of indifference."

It was Tzara in fact who compiled an early—if unpublished—anthology of tribal/oral poetry from Africa & Oceania. For him & for others close to him, the common roots of poetry & spirit/mind [in French the single word *esprit* covers both English words] were clearly in cultures that Europeans then saw as farthest from their own. More importantly, the reference to religion positioned what he & the other Dadaists were doing [as] outside the domain of literature as such—a matter here of germinal importance! But it wasn't only Tzara who put the newness of his own modern-ism into doubt. Gertrude Stein, whom I've also quoted before, said of what she & her modernist companions were about: "As it is old it is new, and as it is new it is old" … & she added—by way of clarification &/or complication: "But now we have come to be in our own way which is a completely different way."

The point here can go off in a number of different directions.

If the experimental modernists (in whatever art) were calling the bounded categories of earlier European art & poetry into question (& they were), it was with the intention of opening possibilities (social & spiritual as well as aesthetic) that those boundaries had obscured or long repressed. Their own creations—in search of the new & unexpected (therefore marvelous)—came foremost. But as technology (transportation, communications, media, etc.) & the attendant global imperialisms opened new/old worlds to view & interchange (& plunder), a revelation to the artist who was then seeking revelation was that the definitions of the imperializing culture were—like its accomplishments—only partial.

The suspicion came to be that certain forms of poetry, like certain forms of artmaking, permeated traditional societies & that these largely religious forms not only resembled but had long since achieved what the new experimental poets & artists were then first setting out to do. Those forms once known—& this came to be understood more slowly for language-dependent arts like poetry—forced a reconsideration of what the work (of art, of poetry, of language, of performance) could be or had been in the course of human (truly human) time. Said Picasso, as if to put his turning toward the "primitive" into other than a merely formal context: "The [African] masks weren't just like any other pieces of sculpture. Not at all. They were magic things. ... [They] were intercessors, mediators. ... They were against everything—against unknown, threatening spirits. ... They were weapons. To help people avoid coming under the influence of spirits again, to help them become independent. [The masks] are tools. If we give spirits a form, we become independent. ... [At that point, he concludes,] I understood why I was a painter."

It remained for my generation of poets—in league with many many others—to show the extent to which this might be true ... & only then to question it. My own entry into all of this was conditioned—clearly so—by generations of predecessors, most of whom I did not know at the outset, some of them poets but others anthropologists, philosophers, biologists, religious thinkers, activist-defenders of a thousand old & new ways. The time of the awakening—in & after World War II—brought a convergence of the need for poetry as a truth-bearing (deconstructing) language (against what Hugo Ball had earlier called "the filth that clings to language" [as it came down to us]) & the need (also brought home by that second [anti-fascist] war) to do away with racism & a culture of ethnic rankings, while preserving the values embedded in historic ethnicities & cultures. The decade that followed also saw a revival of the concern that we later came to call ecological, with an environment—local & global—under increasing developmental pressure, & the view—emerging from that concern—that just those cultures that were repositories of the old poetries were the models thereby for a more sane relation to the natural world & its other-than-human as well as its human inhabitants. Gradually this would open up to a concern & need for what sacred language in traditional bioregional cultures (I here use Gary Snyder's terminology) could still show us & (lest we forget) to a responsibility toward such of them as remain our contemporaries in their sometimes precarious struggle for survival.

In that light I would note that while it used to be common to treat the unwritten poetry of indigenous tribes & nations as anonymous or authorless, more recent accounts have brought the poets & singers forward as people with real identities & names. In anthologies of mine like *Technicians of the Sacred* and *Shaking the Pumpkin* a gallery of names comes forward—of putative poets from stateless & threatened cultures: Komi Ekpe (Ewe, from Nigeria), María Sabina (Mazatec, from Mexico), Isaac Tens (Gitksan, from Canada), Eduardo Calderón (Peru), Andrew Peynetsa (Zuni), Frank Mitchell (Navajo), Black Elk (Oglala, Sioux), among many others. "*To say the name*," says Samuel Makidemewabe, a Swampy Cree story teller from Canada, "*is to begin the story.*"

PRIMITIVE & MODERN: INTERSECTIONS & ANALOGIES

Like any collector, my approach to delimiting & recognizing what's a poem has been by analogy: in this case (beyond the obvious definition of poems as words-of-songs) to the work of modern poets. Since much of this work has been revolutionary & limit-smashing, the analogy in turn expands the range of what "we" can see as "primitive poetry." It also shows some of the ways in which primitive poetry & thought, to call it that, are close to an impulse toward unity in our own time, of which the poets are forerunners. The important intersections (analogies) are:

(1) the poem carried by the voice: a "pre"-literate situation of poetry composed to be spoken, chanted or, more accurately, sung: compare this to the "post-literate" situation, in McLuhan's good phrase, or where we are today;	written poem as score public readings performance poetry poets' theaters jazz poetry rock poetry etc
(2) a highly developed process of image-thinking: concrete or non-causal thought in contrast to the simplifications of Aristotelian logic, etc., with its "objective categories" & rules of non-contradiction; a "logic" of polarities; creation thru dream, etc.; modern poetry (having had & outlived the experience of rationalism) enters a post-logical phase;	Blake's multi-images symbolisme surrealism deep-image random poetry composition by field etc.

(3) a “minimal” art of maximal involvement; compound elements, each clearly articulated, & with plenty of room for fill-in (gaps in sequence, etc.): the “spectator” as (ritual) participant who pulls it all together;

concrete poetry

(4) an “intermedia” situation, as further denial of the categories: the poet’s techniques aren’t limited to verbal maneuvers but operate also through song, non-verbal sound, visual signs, & the varied activities of the ritual event: here the “poem” = the work of the “poet” in whatever medium, or (where we’re able to grasp it) the totality of the work;

picture poems
prose poems
happenings
total theater

poets as film & video makers

poésie sonore

(5) the animal-body-rootedness of “primitive” poetry: the recognition of a “physical” basis for the poem within a man’s or woman’s body—or as an act of body & mind together, breath &/or spirit; & in many cases too the direct & open handling of sexual imagery & (in the“events”) of sexual activities as key factors in creation of the sacred;

dada
lautgedichte (sound poems)
beast language

line & breath
projective verse etc

sexual revolution etc

(6) the poet as shaman, or primitive shaman as poet & seer thru control of the means just stated: an open “visionary” situation prior to all system-making (“priesthood”) in which the man creates thru dream (image) & word (song) “that reason may have ideas to build on” (W. Blake).

Rimbaud’s voyant
Rilke’s angel
Lorca’s duende

beat poetry
psychedelic see-in’s,
be-in’s, etc

individual neo-shamanisms, etc, works directly influenced by the “other” poetry or by analogies to “primitive art”: ideas of negritude, tribalism, wilderness, etc.

What's more, the revelations themselves may create new forms & shapes-of-poems with their own energies & interest—another intersection that can't be overlooked.

In all this the ties feel very close—not that "we" and "they" are identical, but that the systems of thought & the poetry they've achieved are, like what we're after, distinct from something in the official "west," & we can now see & value them because of it. What's missing are the in-context factors that define them more closely group-by-group: the sense of the poems as part of an integrated social & religious complex; the presence in each instance of specific myths & locales; the fullness of the living culture. Here the going is rougher with no easy shortcuts through translation: no simple carry-overs. If our world is open to multiple influences & data, theirs seems largely self-contained. If we're committed to search for the "new," most of them are tradition-bound. (The degree to which "they" are can be greatly exaggerated.) If the poet's purpose among us is "to spread doubt [& create illusion]" (N. Calas), among them it's to overcome it.

That they've done so *without denying the reality* is also worth remembering.

From the Pre-face to *Technicians of the Sacred* (1968)

POETS & TRICKSTERS: INNOVATION & DISRUPTION IN RITUAL & MYTH

For the conference "Standing at the Margins-Crossroads of Culture: Poet as Trickster," the Sapporo University Institute of Cultural Studies, May 14, 2004, Sapporo, Japan

1

The larger context in which I want to speak about the trickster figure involves my developing sense of the innovative and disruptive nature of ancient ritual and myth and of how those enter into contemporary work and thought. To say that much at the start already implies a relative disinterest in other forms of myth and ritual—forms in which it would be more difficult to place the trickster figure and which would be outside the range of what most interests me in the work—the art and poetry—of my contemporaries and near-contemporaries. So I will start with what *does* interest me in the ancient worlds of tricksters and sacred clowns and will move from there to an account of how the trickster as such entered my own work at a crucial point in its development.

Tricksters and clowns, then, are among the elusive (mythopoetic) figures who have appeared increasingly in our poetry and poetics, but in so many different ways and with such varying degrees of both affection and suspicion that I hesitate a little in fear that what I say may confuse as much as clarify. Now I'm not against confusion—really—and, as you'll see, what I think of as most essential to myth and ritual is, in a certain sense, a welcoming of contradictory accounts of who we are? and where we came from? and where we're going? And more: ritual, which most of us (though not most of us in this room) probably think of as a fixed and invariable, mindlessly repetitive order of (usually religious) events with little room for variation/innovation, was programmed in certain very traditional cultures/religions to promote or consolidate change and to include activities that were open and formless and threw the established/everyday order of things into confusion. A programmed and fruitful, sometimes terrifying chaos, as the point of departure for the creation of a new order—for the individual, the group, the world.

I'm going to open my presentation, then, by giving some examples of this side of myth and ritual, drawing the examples not from the older classical west (as we sometimes do where I come from) but from mostly American Indian sources—that in itself a matter of some significance as to where many of us as artists position ourselves in relation to the past or the culturally distant. (I will compare freely as one distanced by culture but related by art.)

The Iroquois—of the American northeast—had a ceremony/ritual that they called *ononharoia:* literally, turning-the-brain-upside-down. This was a large-scale dream feast: a group enactment and fulfillment of individual dreams, often preceded by a variety of dream-guessing ceremonies. Dreams were viewed as secret desires-of-the-soul, which were dangerous/destructive if left unsatisfied, and their fulfillment in the *ononharoia* was like a culturally validated psychodrama, some of which I've summarized in the following "dream events":

> DREAM EVENT ONE
> After having a dream, let someone else guess what it was. Then have everyone act it out together.

DREAM EVENT TWO

Have participants run around the center of a village, acting out their dreams & demanding that others guess & satisfy them.

The dream itself was the entry to the other world: the dreamworld/myth-world, as reversal of our own: the place of secret longings, sighted upside down. The *ononharoia*—turning-the-mind-upside-down—was an enactment of the dream as myth.

Reversals, then, are a widespread way of getting into, of participating in/enacting myth: that primordial and still-existing state that the Australian aborigines called by names such as *alcheringa*, "dreamtime." Among the Huichol Indians of Mexico, the participants in the annual peyote hunt entered into such a dreamtime and themselves became the dreamtime gods and ancestors (Our Father Sun, First Shaman/Fire, Our Mother Maize, Our Elder Brother Deer, and so on), as they journeyed to Wirikuta, mythic center of the gods and the peyote. The *mara'akame*—the shaman/ritual leader—gave them their names and created (literally *dreamt*) a new language for them to speak, its meanings, its names for things, the reverse of what they knew back in their village. Thus the shaman Ramón Medina Silva explained to the anthropologist Barbara Myerhoff:

> It is the mara'akame who directs everything. He is the one who listens in his dream, with his power and his knowledge. ... Then he says to his companions, ... look, now we will change everything, all the meanings, because that is the way it must be with the *hikuritámete* [the peyote pilgrims]. ... Look, the mara'akame says to them, it is when you say good morning, you mean good evening, everything is backwards. You say goodbye, I'm leaving you, but you are really coming. You do not shake hands, you shake feet. You hold out your right foot to be shaken by the foot of your companion. You say good afternoon, but it is only morning.
>
> So the mara'akame tells them, as he has dreamed it. He dreams it differently each time. Every year they change the names of things differently because every year the mara'akame dreams new names. Even if it is the same mara'akame who leads the journey, he still changes the new names each time differently.

The work of shamans (traditional healers: masters of ecstasy and trance, says Mircea Eliade ... technicians of the sacred) is to explore and create the extra-ordinary (the "marvelous" of André Breton and the Surrealists), to explore and to create it by means of trance and by control over language and rhythm, and so on (for he who controls rhythm, wrote someone, *controls*). From the perspective of ordinary consciousness, this shaman-work is disorientating, frightening, and the shaman (himself or herself) often experiences it as terror: a terror of death and disease—to cure the terror of death and disease—and madness/psychosis/soul-terror, when it actually afflicts us. "I did cure death when I was young," says the Pomo Indian shaman Essie Parrish, and the Eskimo shaman Sanimuinak describes his fourth vision and psychic death as follows:

> I went inland to Tasivsak. Here I cast a stone out into the water, which was thereby thrown into great confusion, like a storm at sea. As the billows dashed together, their crests flattened out on top, and as they opened, a huge bear was disclosed. He had a very great black snout, and, swimming ashore, he rested his chin upon the beach, the land gave way under his weight. He went up on land and circled around me, bit me in the loins, and then ate me. At first it hurt, but afterwards feeling passed from me; but as long as my heart had not been eaten, I retained consciousness. But when he bit me in the heart, I lost consciousness and was dead.

In the curing rituals themselves, the terror is renewed, and the regular beat of the shaman's drum (and heart?) is offset by the frenzy of possession—like the Kirgiz-Tatar shaman, say, who "runs around the tent, springing, roaring, leaping; he barks like a dog, sniffs at the audience, lows like an ox, bellows, cries, bleats like a lamb, grunts like a pig, whinnies, coos, imitating with remarkable accuracy the cries of animals, the songs of birds, the sound of their flight, and so on, all of which greatly impresses the audience."

At such points of frenzy—frantic dislocation—the shaman closely resembles the traditional sacred clown: a figure both comic and terrifying, who comes into his clown-work, like the shaman, through an overwhelming and mind-altering experience. The Sioux clown, the *heyoka*, attains his power through a vision of the Thunder Being: a shapeless, winged form, who "lacks feet but has huge talons, and is headless but has a large beak; his voice is the thunderclap, the glance of his eye is lightning." The clown like the shaman speaks a language of reversals and has license to break the rigid patterns of the established ceremonies, as anyone knows who has seen Pueblo clowns, say, in their counter-movements around the masked

Kachina dancers, parodying the sacred. The Pueblo Indian anthropologist Alfonso Ortiz describes the clowns as *anti-ritualists* (a term reminiscent of the anti-art of artists in our own world), but they could as easily be described as ritualists of disorder: free and improvisatory in their movements and innovations, at the extremes of a theater a modern ritualist like Artaud once dreamed of. Thus, Bandelier's description of sacred clowns in 1880:

> ...They chased after her, carried her back and threw her down in the center of the plaza; then while one was performing the coitus from behind, another was doing it against her head. Of course all was simulated and not the real act, as the woman was dressed. The naked fellow performed masturbation in the center of the plaza or very near it, alternatively with a black rug and his hand. Everybody laughed.

It is something that the ritual/performative frame makes possible: a (barely) controlled release of wild potential in the human psyche. The ritualized behavior of the Crow Indian Crazy Dog [Warrior Clown] Society is another example:

CRAZY DOG EVENTS

1. Act like a crazy dog. Wear sashes & other fine clothes, carry a rattle, & dance along the roads singing crazy dog songs after everybody else has gone to bed.
2. Talk crosswise: say the opposite of what you mean & make others say the opposite of what they mean in return.
3. Fight like a fool by rushing up to an enemy & offering to be killed. Dig a hole near an enemy, & when the enemy surrounds it, leap out at them & drive them back.
4. Paint yourself white, mount a white horse, cover its eyes & make it jump over a steep & rocky bank, until both of you are crushed.

Now, some of this still exists for us in the reversals of mardi gras and, in spite of the temptation to trivialize, in the actions of circus and movie clowns, the actions and words of the really great standup comics. And maybe there's an even stronger, certainly more deliberate reflection in the work of certain poets and artists: those who create an experimental space to challenge and transform … what? A limited reality … a lying and deceptive sense of order … the politics of single vision? From Dada spontaneity and disgust, surrealist invocation of private and collective dreamtimes and black humors, to the avant-gardes of the 1960s and 70s (and beyond), whose public (and private) rituals took shape as happenings, trance dances, sonic meditations, systematic chance, street provocations, Holy Actors, body art and body music, mantric sound-texts, visions, theaters of "cruelty" and of "hysteria," against the expectations of what was "real" and what was "sane behavior." A programmed chaos, in which the brain turns upside down and lets another order come to birth.

So far, then, I've stressed rituals of disruption/disorder and of a generally open and innovative form, although these aren't all the rituals there are (most rituals in fact are very low key: spare and minimal and doggedly, if wildly, repetitive, or boring to the point of madness). But let's get over to myth for a little, one view of it sometimes overlooked but which for the myth people among us (as contrasted, say, to the ritual people) may be the heart of the matter.

We have, many of us, a sense of myth as the story (singular) of that-which-happened (also singular) at a time in the remote past (again: the dreamtime, if you're into that). But in oral traditions, word-of-mouth traditions, myths exist in many versions—as the *mouthed*, individuated accounts of—or speculations on—the fundamentals. The telling of the myth—i.e. the telling of the *telling*—is itself a ritual, a cultural performance, and the form of the myth, the thrust behind it, is an implied question or a series of questions. Thus the Seneca Indian story-teller begins:

> A man who was a crow was traveling. As he walked along he thought: Who am I? Where did I come from? Where am I going?

The answer is the myth, which in its first Greek use meant only telling/talking, then came to be the telling of the fundamentals (i.e. an old-time telling), and only later, a lesser telling in contrast to a second mode, *logos*, once its synonym. The source is traditional, the recounting individual, from the mouth of each teller; or, as they used to say, some say this, but others say that. It is like biblical *genesis* (the foundation telling for the western world), which only late in its career gets fixed as single vision, logos, word of God—erasing in that act the other versions, equally true, the record of which hasn't wholly vanished. Or put another way:

Some say Elohim—translate it "God" or "the gods"—created the world and man in seven days: first the animals, then man as male and female in his image

THIS IS THE PRIESTLY GENESIS OF BIBLE

But others say Yahveh [the "name" itself] created man from earth as male before he made the animals, then made the animals and woman

THIS IS THE YAHVIST GENESIS OF BIBLE

and others say Yahveh, like Babylonian Marduk, stirred the sea called YAM, then in his cunning crushed Rahab [female serpent], by his wind set YAM in net, his hand made holes in the twisty snake

THIS IS THE BOOK OF JOB

Still others say that El created Wisdom as a goddess, in her words

"I came out of El's mouth   first
  flooded across the earth
then built my home high
    my seat in cloud pillar
He made me   starting   before the world"

THIS IS ECCLESIASTICUS, THE BOOK OF WISDOM,
THE WISDOM OF BEN SIRA

and others say, in God's own words:

I conceived the thought of creation / putting a floor under it / letting everyone see / what I had done / the bottom of the dark // I called down to the deep below / "come from the unseen dark / all that eye can see / Ado-il—come"—he came hauling so large / a stone of light it made / his belly a great ball / "explode—Ado-il / push the light out / give it birth" // he blew the stone / light gaping from his belly womb / opening all I willed for shape // light the mother of light / bore a great age / the star heaven / which I saw was good

THIS IS THE BOOK OF THE SECRETS OF ENOCH

and others say the creation came through laughter:

the 7 Laughs of God
Hha Hha Hha Hha Hha Hha Hha
Each laugh he gave

engendered the seven
god god god god god god god
the Fore-Appearers
who clasp everything one

THIS IS THE HIDDEN SACRED BOOK OF MOSES
CALLED "EIGHTH" OR "HOLY"[1]

Something of this Lévi-Strauss senses, writing of the versions of Oedipus in "Structural Study of Myth":

> Our method… eliminates a problem which has, so far, been one of the main obstacles in the progress of mythological studies, namely, the quest for the true version or the earlier one. On the contrary, we define myth as consisting of all its versions; or, to put it otherwise, a myth remains the same as long as it is felt as such. … Therefore, not only Sophocles but Freud himself should be included among the recorded versions of the Oedipus myth on a par with earlier or seemingly more "authentic versions."[2]

And, once that process is grasped (not necessarily in Lévi-Strauss's terms), the mythical past and present open up in a great kaleidoscope of images: a "clash of symbols" (in the words of Paul Ricoeur) which is both natural to mind and forms its one sure hedge against idolatry.

Every *old* culture (*authentic* culture, I wanted to say) had such a treasury of images—concrete/realized speculations, mirrors of the mind—which together projected the imaginal world for the individual and the community. The experience of such a mythic world is overwhelming: "not an allegory," wrote Jung, "not just another way of talking (…the description of one thing under the image of another…) but an image presented by the world itself." Myth here is the expression/projection of such an image, such a world of images: imaginal geographies, apologies, theologies, whose beings appeared in dream and again and again in ritual… in ritual and again in dream… a constant interplay between them.

---

[1] Most of the preceding examples are from Charles Doria & Harris Lenowitz (eds.), *Origins: Creation Texts from the Ancient Mediterranean*, Anchor Books, 1976.

[2] I will be asserting this later when I speak of my own poem, *Cokboy*, as well as poems by other of my contemporaries, as an "authentic version" of the Trickster myth.

Those dreamtime beings that illuminated the old myths and rituals (not static *objects* but images in motion) live now in our museums: object/ified. That is: the response to a ritual mask hanging on a museum wall—or on a wall in my living room—will doubtless be to a "beautiful thing" or even (by projection to its original meaning or context) to a powerful or awesome *thing*. But all such objects remain stationary, frozen, in contrast to their dynamism, their movement in ritual—when set into motion or brought into contact with moving, dancing bodies, chanting voices, the actuality of drums and bells that truly *sound*. And it is at such moments—as anyone who has experienced it will know—that myth comes alive in its enacted beings: like a theater played out for keeps or a theater through which we move also as participants.

I have most vividly experienced something of this order—what it is to be in a state-of-myth and how ritual (performance and enactment) assists with this—in traditional Yaqui Indian ceremonies in Tucson, Arizona. I will describe this, not in fact because the ritual, the enactment in question, opened me to something culturally Yaqui (I would feel foolish to make any such claim) but because a coincidence of shared images (and myths) and their emergence in actual ritual time allowed a response on my part that was clearly outside the immediate Yaqui experience though triggered by it.

The ceremonies—like so much in ritual and religion—are syncretistic: in art terms, a *collage* of disparate elements fused into a new configuration. The principal religious images are both Catholic and Yaqui, along with numerous symbols, textures, and sounds drawn from Mexican, European, and popular American sources. In Yaqui terms—as I understood those from conversations with the anthropologist Edward Spicer and with the Yaqui ceremonial and political leader Anselmo Valencia—the basic intercut is between the world of the village (itself Catholic and sacred) and the Flower World or Enchanted/Etheric World (*sea aniya*, *huya aniya*) outside the village: the wilderness from which come the old Yaqui mythic beings, the great Deer Dancer and the sacred clowns. In the forty-day Easter ceremony the curious emphasis/displacement in the collage is that the costumed and impersonated figures of the passion play aren't Jesus and the holy family but only the persecutors and stalkers of Jesus: Roman soldiers and black-veiled pharisees and those weirdly masked non-sacred clowns called *chapayekas*. Jesus is a wooden statue or later (in his rebirth) a plastic baby-doll, and the Yaqui catholic maestros who defend the church lead a strict, text-oriented ceremony; but the pharisees and especially the chapayeka clowns bring the mythic to life and engage in often open, often improvisatory rituals, including a comic mock scourging of Jesus as an eggheaded old man and a zany clown orchestra getting "drunk" and celebrating the crucifixion on the midnight of Good Friday.

The myth of Jesus is of course our shared myth, and the divergences from "my own" version are quickly apparent and comprehensible—sometimes themselves astonishing. Similarly the chapayeka clowns—the principal stalkers of Jesus—tie in by their actions and by their other Yaqui name (*fariseos*) to the biblical antagonists of Jesus. They are therefore the "jews" of the story—though scarcely named as such—and their actual appearance is flower-worldish, even surreal, with many of the masks representing animals and birds but the human ones including feathered Indians, pirates, Negroes, Arabs, college professors, and so on. They play their roles persistently, and over the ritual period (for the culminating four or five days of which we were witnesses) they become very real, very familiar, before the climactic battle on Saturday morning: the storming of the church and the defeat of the chapayeka-pharisees in a highly animated ritual drama: both rehearsed (pre-planned) and improvised. At the end the current masks are burned, and the masks of the following year will never be precisely the same.

For me the syncretistic/collaged nature of the chapayeka masks became in their enlivening the embodiment of the fantasized Jews of my own poetry as they had come to me through language in *Poland/1931.* I had often tried to realize those images in performance, but in 1982 and again in 1983 the curious displacements of the Yaqui ritual opened that to me as never before. And it was clear to me that the force of the ritual was less in its repetitive, mechanical side (the Latin chanting of the Yaqui-Catholic maestros, though I would scarcely disregard that) than in the generous and quirky and largely unpredictable (but increasingly real) behavior of the chapayekas and the strange meeting of worlds that their presence came to represent.

This is the poem that came from that—in three sections, including a final one addressed to Anselmo Valencia, in which the (ideological) assertion on my part is that both art and ritual/myth (Dada and Yaqui in my terms) are part of the same human experience:

[reads the opening section of "Yaqui 1982"]:

the jews of ceremony
dance in the thin sand of
pascua pueblo   in their pinhole
eyes new fires start

watched by ourselves & others
the bright memory of days to come
tomorrow   but the face
back of the mask
is fathomless
the jews march through the night
clack-clack their sticks
speak for them
red & white
the tips like dagger points
& voiceless
they are the purveyors of the death of jesus
yaqui-style
they stomp & whip each other
thursdays   the master jew
baldheaded man with droopy eyes
& half-a-beard
fresh crown of thorns over his ears
squats by the cross
black coated
in white jodhpurs
he is the man without the belt
(el viejito)
who seeks the heart of jesus
in a box
white-covered
with lines of green above
the flat red heart
& silver rays
he looks into & sees
a crucifix   a water bottle
flowers & candles
then bangs his sticks
together   in a trance
they lead him with a silky rope
pinned to his shoulders
jew & clowns
how beautifully they walk
the stations of the cross
in yaqui

the plaza stretches to infinity
where the smallest freak is jesus
& the angels sing

2

It is from this world of disruptions and reversals, of dreams, of sacred clowns and shamans, of the marvelous and surreal, as well as from an old and new understanding of the maximally human, that the trickster emerges for us. He (or she, for I have also noted female tricksters) is the mythic counterpart of the sacred clown and the bearer of energies that trigger transformation of old worlds and the creation of the new. But he is all of this in the context of absurdity and perversity, maintaining the clown's reality in an always comic, sometimes terrifying world. As I wrote of him some years ago, in one of his American Indian manifestations—that of Old Man Coyote:

> Coyote appears throughout the Americas in the familiar role of primordial shit-thrower, cock-erupter, etc., to satisfy the need for all that in the full pantheon of essential beings. … No merely horny version of a Disney character, he is like other tricksters in tribal America (Rabbit, Raven, Spider, Bluejay, Mink, Flint, Glooscap, Saynday, etc.) the product of a profound and comic imagination playing upon the realities of man and nature. … Among the Crow, as in other Indian religions, he appears as the Supreme Trickster but also as the first maker of the earth and all living things. … Thus Old Man Coyote [called elsewhere: "mad Coyote"] is the imperfect (= dangerous) creator of an imperfect (= dangerous) universe—a view which, being more empirical and rational in the first place, presents fewer problems to rationalize than the Christian view, say, of a perfect God and universe, etc. [Writes the Acoma Indian poet Simon Ortiz]: "Existential man. Dostoyevsky coyote."

Like many of my generation I had first come to Trickster—or, more accurately, to something like Trickster—through the diluted and sanitized images in comic strips and animated movies: Daffy Duck, Bugs Bunny, Krazy Kat, and the later but strikingly derivative figure of Wile E. Coyote (among many others). Those were images and characters from childhood—"myths" I was tempted to say (and didn't)—but what came to some of us later and with considerable astonishment was the fullblown figure of the Trickster. The initial purveyors were the hunter-gatherers of an earlier academic anthropology: Paul Radin foremost with his classic work *The Trickster*, but notable texts as well from Melville Jacobs, Herbert Spinden, Knud Rasmussen, and others. These were at my disposal by the time I put together my own first ethnopoetic gatherings—*Technicians of the Sacred* and *Shaking the Pumpkin*—and as I carried on with this it became clear that the myth of Trickster (the image and the personage) went beyond Coyote and American Indian sources. For Trickster was, if anything, a near universal figure, resident on every continent in some form or other—so much so that some came to see him as an archetype, a mask, imbedded in every human psyche.

On one of those occasions (there have been several) when I entered into a life of poetry, I felt myself a part of a lineage that included older poets—forerunners—whose lives and acts resembled those of ancient clowns and tricksters or whose written works, whose texts, incorporated some of them. In the former instances—the worlds of the *poètes maudits* and the radical transformers and self-transformers ("chameleon poets" in John Keats's earlier words)—many of the poets of my time were under the spell of certain key predecessors: Shelley and Keats, Hölderlin and Whitman, Rimbaud and Jarry, Dadas and Surrealists, Artaud and Duchamp, and many others. (Nakahara Chuya in Japan might be another such example—if we want to bring it closer to where we are, *right here.*) Their work, if we took it seriously (and we did), was one of transformation and transgression (sometimes comic, though often not)—renewing or challenging the worlds and selves we think we know or creating new worlds beyond our former knowing. That they weren't Trickster in any strict sense didn't matter, only that we could see them in that guise—and more to our convenience than to theirs. It was clear as well—and central to their meaning—that if their personas and works resembled those of sacred clowns and tricksters, they operated without the sanction of the larger society, toward which they acted (often but not always) as an avant-garde in opposition.

Getting closer to our own time, at the end of the second world war, an oppositional avant-garde again came into prominence, something I've described elsewhere as the second great awakening of poetry in the century just ended. If we connect such an avant-garde with the disruptive work of traditional clowns and tricksters, we can see it as a dominant trend for art and poetry in the times through which we've lived. The goal at its extreme was to turn the mind upside down and to call everything into question—a program that showed up, to one degree or another, in movements and among practitioners of poetry on a nearly global scale. It was something of this kind that I tried to summarize a few years ago in a large two-volume assemblage or anthology of the twentieth-century avant-garde called *Poems for the Millennium.* To give you an idea of where my coeditor Pierre Joris and I felt the presence of such an oppositional and transformative counterpoetics, I will mention only the movements and groupings to which we gave special attention: the Vienna Group in Austria, the Tammuzi poets in Lebanon and Syria, concrete poetry worldwide, Cobra in western Europe [Copenhagen/Brussels/Amsterdam], the Beat Poets in the U.S., and branching out, the Postwar Poets in Japan, the Misty Poets in China, the Language Poets in the U.S., and unspecified cyberpoets *everywhere* and *nowhere.* (To these of course we could have added a number of others, both international and regionally specific—from the widely dispersed Situationists and Fluxus artists and poets to the early and germinal Gutai Group in Japan.)

In most instances the Trickster comparison is at best suggestive or metaphorical, but for others, like myself, he or she manifests quite explicitly as a being-in-the-poem. For American poets he comes up most frequently in the guise of Coyote, and certainly this is the case for American Indian poets such as Simon Ortiz or for a non-Indian poet like Gary Snyder in his essay "The Incredible Survival of Coyote" or in the German artist Joseph Beuys's performance work "I Love America and America Loves Me" (a week spent locked in a cage with a coyote). Aside from these, other Trickster-related poems include such major works as Ed Dorn's *Gunslinger,* David Meltzer's *Hero/Lil,* Michael McClure's *Coyote in Chains,* and Diane DiPrima's female-centered *Loba.*

For myself, then, my work in the late 1960s and early 1970s had included the anthologizing of translations from traditional Trickster narratives. (These appeared with attendant commentaries in assemblages such as *Technicians of the Sacred* and *Shaking the Pumpkin.*) I was simultaneously "exploring ancestral sources of my own in a world of Jewish mystics, thieves, and madmen"—a description of my work that I hoped would call attention to its deliberately transgressive qualities. From 1972 to 1974 I was living at a Seneca Indian reservation in western New York state, where I finished writing *Poland/1931* and began the writing of *A Seneca Journal.* The immediate national or international context for this was the war in Vietnam, which was moving into its final phases and had already created public protests many of which involved actions that resembled those rituals of disorder and disruption that had been a central aspect of many traditional cultures.

The culminating poem of *Poland/1931* was a short mock epic called *Cokboy*, and it's this poem that I want to read from as the final part of my presentation here. The title when pronounced in English means something like penis-boy, although the spelling (c-o-k-b-o-y) is aberrant—something I picked up from a misspelling or typographical error in a poem by the Chilean poet Vicente Huidobro, circa 1913, for what he intended as the English word "cowboy." Still, from the time I first saw it, it played in my mind as the possible name of an *ithyphallic* new world trickster.

There is of course no mention of this in the poem, only the spelling of the word itself, which would strike an English reader as rather aberrant. Also aberrant is the yiddish accent that I use near the opening of the poem—exaggerated and very far from accurate. It is one of several voices that I allow myself, the poem shifting unannounced from one voice to another: my own voice (perhaps) as narrator, the voice of a mythopoeic trickster, the voice of a fictitious explorer/conqueror, the voices of ancestral Jews and Indians, and so on. In the course of it other figures—both historical and contemporary—are called into play: the eighteenth-century Baal Shem (founder of the ecstatic Hasidic cult of orthodox Judaism, wearing a traditional broad brimmed hat called a *shtraimel;* William Blake, the great English poet and visionary; and iconic American figures such as General Custer, Buffalo Bill Cody, and the conservative American senator Barry Goldwater, referred to only as "the senator from Arizona.")

Having said this much by way of introduction I will go to a reading from Cokboy. It is my contention in doing so, that *Cokboy*, like Freud's Oedipus as viewed by Lévi-Strauss, or like Dorn's Gunslinger and Ortiz's Coyote, should be included now among the bona fide versions of the Trickster myth we've been discussing.

But if not, then not.

[Reads from *Cokboy*, for which see above, page 234.]

TOTAL TRANSLATION: AN EXPERIMENT IN THE TRANSLATION OF AMERICAN INDIAN POETRY

It wasn't really a "problem," as these things are sometimes called, but to get closer to a way of poetry that had concerned me from years before, though until this project I'd only been able to approach it at a far remove. I'd been translating "tribal" poetry (the latest, still imperfect substitute I can find for "primitive," which continues to bother me) out of books, doing my versions from earlier translations into languages I could cope with, including English. Toward the end of my work on *Technicians* I met Stanley Diamond, who directed me to the Senecas in upstate New York, & David McAllester, ethnomusicologist at Wesleyan University, who showed me how a few songs worked in Navajo. With their help (& a nod from Dell Hymes as well) I later was able to get Wenner-Gren Foundation support to carry on a couple of experiments in the translation of American Indian poetry. I'm far enough into them by now to say a little about what I've been doing.

* * *

In the Summer of 1968 I began to work simultaneously with two sources of Indian poetry. Settling down a mile from the Cold Spring settlement of the Allegany (Seneca) Reservation at Steamburg, New York, I was near enough to friends who were traditional songmen to work with them on the translation of sacred & secular song-poems. At the same time David McAllester was sending me recordings, transcriptions, literal translations, & his own freer reworkings of a series of seventeen "Horse Songs" that had been the property of Frank Mitchell, a Navajo singer from Chinle, Arizona (born: 1881, died: 1967). Particularly with the Senecas (where I didn't know in the first instance what, if anything, I was going to get) my first concern was with the translation process itself. While I'll limit myself to that right now, I should at least say (things never seem to be clear unless you say them) that if I hadn't also come up with matter that I could "internalize," I would have foundered long before this.

The big question, which I was immediately aware of with both poetries, was if & how to handle those elements in the original works that weren't translatable literally. As with most Indian poetry, the voice carried many sounds that weren't, strictly speaking, "words." These tended to disappear or be attenuated in translation, as if they weren't really there. But they were there & were at least as important as the words themselves. In both Navajo & Seneca many songs consisted of nothing but those "meaningless" vocables (not free "scat" either but fixed sounds recurring from performance to performance). Most other songs had both meaningful & non-meaningful elements, & such songs (McAllester told me for the Navajo) were often spoken of, *qua* title, by their meaningless burdens. Similar meaningless sounds, Dell Hymes had pointed out for some Kwakiutl songs, might in fact be keys to the songs' structures: "something usually disregarded, the refrain or so-called 'nonsense syllables'... in fact of fundamental importance... both structural clue & microcosm."

So there were all these indications that the exploration of "pure sound" wasn't beside the point of those poetries but at or near their heart: all of this coincidental too with concern for the sound-poem among a number of modern poets. Accepting its meaningfulness here, I more easily accepted it there. I also realized (with the Navajo especially) that there were more than simple refrains involved: that we, as translators & poets, had been taking a rich *oral* poetry & translating it to be read primarily for meaning, thus denuding it to say the least.

Here's an immediate example of what I mean. In the first of Frank Mitchell's seventeen horse songs, the opening line comes out as follows in McAllester's transcription:

dzo-wowode sileye shi, dza-na desileye shiyi, dzanadi sileye shiya'e

but the same segment given "as spoken" reads:

dzą̨ą̨di silá shi dzą̨ą̨di silá shi dzą̨ą̨di silá shi

which translates as "over-here it-is-there (&) mine" repeated three times. So does the line as sung if all you're accounting for is the meaning. In other words, translate only for meaning & you get the three-fold repetition of an unchanging single statement; but in the Navajo each time it's delivered there's a sharp departure from the spoken form: thus three distinct sound-events, not one-in-triplicate!

I know neither Navajo nor Seneca except for bits of information picked up from grammar books & such (also the usual social fallout among the Senecas: "cat," "dog," "thank you," "you're welcome," numbers one to ten, "uncle," "father," & my Indian name). But even from this far away, I can (with a little help from my friends) be aware of my options as translator. Let me try, then, to respond to *all* the sounds I'm made aware of, to let that awareness touch off responses or events in the English. I don't want to set English words to Indian music, but to respond poem-for-poem in the attempt to work out a "total" translation—not only of the words but of all sounds connected with the poem, including finally the music itself.

* * *

Seneca & Navajo are very different worlds, & what's an exciting procedure for one may be deadening or irrelevant for the other. The English translation should match the character of the Indian original: take that as a goal & don't worry about how literal you're otherwise being. Walter Lowenfels calls poetry "the continuation of journalism by other means," & maybe that holds too for translation-as-poem. I translate, then, as a way of reporting what I've sensed or seen of an other's situation: true as far as possible to "my" image of the life & thought of the source.

Living with the Senecas helped in that sense. I don't know how much stress to put on this, but I know that in so far as I developed a strategy for translation from Seneca, I tried to keep to approaches I felt were consistent with their way of life as I observed it. I can hardly speak of the poetry without using words that would describe the people as well. Not that it's easy to sum up any people's poetry or its state-of-mind, but since one is always doing it in translation, I'll attempt it also by way of description.

Seneca poetry, when it uses words at all, works in sets of short songs, minimal realizations colliding with each other in marvelous ways, a very light, very pointed play-of-the-mind, nearly always just a step away from the comic (even as their masks are), the words set out in clear relief against the ground of the ("meaningless") refrain. Clowns stomp & grunt through the longhouse, but in subtler ways too the encouragement to "play" is always a presence. Said the leader of the longhouse religion at Allegany [Ed Currey], explaining why the seasonal ceremonies ended with a gambling game: the idea of a religion was to reflect the *total* order of the universe while providing an outlet for *all* human needs, the need for play not least among them. Although it pretty clearly doesn't work out as well nowadays as that makes it sound—the orgiastic past & the "doings" (happenings) in which the people were free to live-out their dreams dimming from generation to generation—still the resonance, the ancestral permissiveness, keeps being felt in many ways. Sacred occasions may be serious & necessary, but it doesn't take much for the silence to be broken by laughter: thus, says Richard Johnny John, if you call for a medicine ceremony of the mystic animals & it turns out that no one's sick & in need of curing, the head-one tells the others: "I leave it up to you folks & if you want to have a good time, have a good time!" He knows they will anyway.

I take all of that as cue: to let my moves be directed by a sense of the songs & of the attitudes surrounding them. Another thing I try not to overlook is that the singers & I, while separated in Seneca, are joined in English. That they have to translate for me is a problem at first, but the problem suggests its own solution. Since they're bilingual, sometimes beautifully so, why not work from that instead of trying to get around it? Their English, fluent while identifiably Senecan, is as much a commentary on where they are as mine is on where I am. Given the "minimal" nature of much of the poetry (one of its *strongest* features, in fact) there's no need for a dense response in English. Instead I can leave myself free to structure the final poem by using their English as a base: a particular enough form of the language to itself be an extra means for the extension of reportage through poetry & translation.

I end up collaborating & happy to do so, since translation (maybe poetry as well) has always involved that kind of thing for me. The collaboration can take a number of forms. At one extreme I have only to make it possible for the other man to take over: in this case, to set up or simply to encourage a situation in which a man who's never thought of himself as a "poet" can begin to structure his utterances with a care for phrasing & spacing that drives them toward poetry. *Example:* Dick Johnny John & I had taped his Seneca version of the thanking prayer that opens all longhouse gatherings & were translating it phrase by phrase. He had decided to write it down himself, to give the translation to his sons, who from oldest to youngest were progressively losing the Seneca language. I could follow his script from where I sat, & the method of punctuation he was using seemed special to me, since in letters & such he punctuates more or less conventionally. Anyway, I got his punctuation down along with his wording, with which he was taking a lot of time both in response to my questions & from his desire "to word it just the way it says there." In setting up the result, I let the periods in his prose version mark the ends of lines, made some vocabulary choices that we'd left hanging, & tried for the rest to keep clear of what was after all his poem. Later I titled it *Thank You: A Poem in 17 Parts*, & wrote a note on it for the Mexico City magazine *El Corno Emplumado*, where it was printed in English & Spanish. This is the first of the seventeen sections:

Now so many people that are in this place.
In our meeting place.
It starts when two people see each other.
They greet each other.
Now we greet each other.
Now he thought.
I will make the Earth where some people can walk around.
I have created them, now this has happened.
We are walking on it.
Now this time of the day.
We give thanks to the Earth.
This is the way it should be in our minds.

[*Note*. The set-up in English doesn't, as far as I can tell, reproduce the movement of the Seneca text. More interestingly it's itself a consideration of that movement: is in fact Johnny John's reflections upon the values, the relative strengths of elements in his text. The poet is to a great degree concerned with what stands out & where, & his phrasing reveals it, no less here than in any other poem.]

Even when being more active myself, I would often defer to others in the choice of words. Take, for example, a set of seven Woman's Dance songs with words, composed by Avery Jimerson & translated with help from his wife, Fidelia. Here the procedure was for Avery to record the song, for Fidelia to paraphrase it in English, then for the three of us to work out a transcription & word-by-word translation by a process of question & answer. Only afterwards would I actively come into it, to try to work out a poem in English with enough swing to it to return more or less to the area of song. *Example*. The paraphrase of the 6th Song reads:

Very nice, nice, when our mothers do the ladies' dance.
Graceful, nice, very nice, when our mothers do the ladies' dance...

while the word-by-word, including the "meaningless" refrain, reads:

hey heya yo oh ho
nice nice nice-it-is
when-they-dance-the-ladies-dance
our-mothers
gahnoweyah heyah

graceful it-is
nice nice nice-it-is
when-they-dance-the-ladies-dance
our-mothers
gahnoweyah heyah (& repeat).

In doing *these* songs, I decided in fact to translate for meaning, since the meaningless vocables used by Jimerson were only the standard markers that turn up in all the woman's songs: *hey heyah yo* to mark the opening, *gahnoweyah heyah* to mark the internal transitions. (In my translation, I sometimes use a simple "hey," "oh" or "yeah" as a rough equivalent, but let the movement of the English determine its position.) I also decided not to fit English words to Jimerson's melody, regarding that as a kind of oil-&-water treatment, but to suggest (as with most poetry) a music through the normally pitched speaking voice. For the rest I was following Fidelia Jimerson's lead:

hey it's nice it's nice it's nice
to see them yeah to see
our mothers do the ladies' dances
oh it's graceful & it's nice
it's nice it's very nice
to see them hey to see
our mothers do the ladies' dances.

With other kinds of song-poems I would also, as often as not, stick close to the translation-as-given, departing from that to better get the point of the whole across in English, to normalize the word order where phrases in the literal translation appeared in their original Seneca sequence, or to get into the play-of-the-thing on my own. The most important group of songs I was working on was a sacred cycle called *Idos* (ee-dos) in Seneca—in English either *Shaking the Pumpkin* or, more ornately, *The Society of the Mystic Animals*. Like most Seneca songs *with* words (most Seneca songs are in fact *without* words), the typical Pumpkin song contains a single statement, or a single statement alternating with a row of vocables, which is repeated anywhere from three to six or seven times. Some songs are nearly identical with some others (same melody & vocables, slight change in words) but aren't necessarily sung in sequence. In a major portion of the ceremony, in fact, a fixed order for the songs is completely abandoned, & each person present takes a turn at singing a ceremonial (medicine) song of his or her own choice. There's room here too for messing around.

Richard Johnny John was my collaborator on the Pumpkin songs, & the basic wording is therefore his. My intention was to account for all vocal sounds in the original but—as a more "interesting" way of handling the minimal structures & allowing a very clear, very pointed emergence of perceptions—to translate the poems onto the page, as with "concrete" or other types of "minimal" poetry. Where several songs showed a concurrence of structure. I allowed myself the option of treating them individually or combining them into one. I deferred singing until some future occasion.

Take the opening songs of the ceremony. These are fixed pieces sung by the ceremonial leader (*hajaswas*) before he throws the meeting open to the individual singers. The melody & structure of the first nine are identical: very slow, a single line of words ending with a string of sounds, etc., the pattern identical until the last go-round, when the song ends with a grunting expulsion of breath into a weary "ugh" sound. I had to get all of that across: the bareness, the regularity, the deliberateness of the song, along with the basic meaning, repeated vocables, emphatic terminal sound, & (still following Johnny John's reminder to play around with it "if everything's alright") a little something of my own. The song whose repeated line, "The animals are coming *heh eh heh* (or *heh eh-eh-eh heh*)" can then become:

	H E H E H H E H
	H E H E H H E H
The animals are coming	H E H **U H** H E H
	H E H E H H E H
	H E H E H H E H

and then:

	H E H E H H E H
	H E H E H H E H
The doings were beginning	H E H **U H** H E H
	H E H E H H E H
	H E H E H H E H

& so forth: each poem set, if possible, on its own page, as further analogue to the slowness, the deliberate pacing of the original.

The use of vertical titles [not shown here] is the only move I make without immediate reference to the Seneca version: the rest I'd feel to be programmed by elements in the original prominent enough for me to respond to in the movement from oral to paginal structure. Where the song comes without vocables, I don't supply them but concentrate on presentation of the words. Thus in the two groups of "crow songs," the first is a simple translation-for-meaning:

> (1)
> *the crows came in*
>
> (2)
> *the crows sat down*

while the other ("in the manner of Zukofsky" [i.e. his {homophonic} translations of Catullus]) puns off the Seneca sound:

> *yehgagaweeyo* (lit. that pretty crow) becomes "yond cawcrow's way-out"

&

> *hongyasswahyaenee* (lit. that [pig]-meat's for me) becomes "Hog (yes!) swine you're mine"

—trying at the same time to let something of the meaning come through.

A motive behind the punning was, I suppose, the desire to bring across (i.e. "translate") the feeling of the Seneca word for crow (*gaga or kaga*), which is at the same time an imitation of the bird's voice. In another group—three songs about the owl—I pick up the vocables suggesting the animal's call & shape them into outline of a giant owl, within which frame the poems are printed. But that's only where the mimicry of the original is strong enough to trigger an equivalent move in translation; otherwise my inclination is to *present* analogues to the full range of vocal sound, etc., but not to *represent* the poem's subject as "mere picture."

The variety of possible moves is obviously related to the variety—semantic *&* aural—of the cycle itself.

[*Note*. Behind it all there's a hidden motive too: not simply to make clear the world of the original, but to do so at some remove from the song itself: to reflect the song without the "danger" of presenting any part of it (the melody, say) exactly as given: thus to have it while not having it, in deference to the sense of secrecy & localization that's so important to those for whom the songs are sacred & alive. So the changes resulting from translation are, in this instance, not only inevitable but desired, or, as another Seneca [Art Johnny John] said to me: "We wouldn't want the songs to get so far away from us; no, the songs would be too lonely."]

* * *

My decision with the Navajo Horse Songs was to work with the sound as sound: a reflection in itself of the difference between Navajo & Seneca song structure. For Navajo (as already indicated) is much fuller, much denser, twists words into new shapes or fills up the spaces between words by insertion of a wide range of "meaningless" vocables, making it misleading to translate primarily for meaning or, finally, to think of *total* translation in any terms but those of sound. Look, for example, at the number of free vocables in the following excerpt from McAllester's relatively literal translation of the 16th Horse Song:

> (nana na) Sun-(eye ye) Standing-within (neye ye) Boy
> (Heye ye) truly his horses
> ('Eye ye) abalone horses
> ('Eye ye) made of sunrays
> (Neye ye) their bridles
> (Gowo wo) coming on my right side
> (Jeye yeye) coming into my hand (yeye neyowo 'ei).

Now this, which even so doesn't show the additional word distortions that turn up in the singing, might be brought closer to English word order & translated for meaning alone as something like

> Boy who stands inside the Sun
> with your horses that are
> abalone horses
> bridles

made of sunrays
rising on my right side
coming to my hand
etc.

But what a difference from the fantastic way the sounds cut through the words & between them from the first line of the original on.

It was the possibility of working with all that sound, finding my own way into it in English, that attracted me now—that & a quality in Frank Mitchell's voice I found irresistible. It was, I think, that the music was so clearly within range of the language: it was song & it was poetry, & it seemed possible at least that the song issued from the poetry, was an extension of it or rose inevitably from the juncture of words & other vocal sounds. So many of us had already become interested in this kind of thing as poets, that it seemed natural to me to be in a situation where the poetry would be leading me toward a (new) music it was generating.

I began with the 10th Horse Song, which had been the first one Mitchell sang when McAllester was recording him. At that point I didn't know if I'd do much more than quote or allude to the vocables: possibly pull them or something like them into the English. I was *writing* at first, working on the words by sketching in phrases that seemed natural to my own sense of the language. In the 10th Song there's a division of speakers: the main voice is that of Enemy Slayer or Dawn Boy, who first brought horses to The People, but the chorus is sung by his father, the Sun, telling him to take spirit horses & other precious animals & goods to the house of his mother, Changing Woman. The literal translation of the refrain—*(to) the woman, my son*—seemed a step away from how we'd say it, though normal enough in Navajo. It was with the sense that, whatever distortions in sound the Navajo showed, the syntax was natural, that I changed McAllester's suggested reading *to go to her my son*, & his opening line:

> Boy-brought-up-within-the-Dawn, it is I, I who am that one
> (lit. being that one, with a suggestion of causation),

to:

> Because I was the boy raised in the dawn.

At the same time I was, I thought, getting it down to more or less the economy of phrasing of the original.

I went through the first seven or eight lines like that but still hadn't gotten to the vocables. McAllester's more "factual" approach—reproducing the vocables exactly—seemed wrong to me on one major count. In the Navajo the vocables give a very clear sense of continuity from the verbal material; i.e., the vowels in particular show a rhyming or assonantal relationship between the "meaningless" & meaningful segments:

'Esdza shiye'	e hye-la	'Esdza shiye'	e hye-la ŋaŋa yeye 'e
The woman, my son	*(voc.)*	*The woman, my son*	*(voc.)*

whereas the English vowels for this & many other situations in the poem are, by contrast to the Navajo, more rounded & further back in the mouth. Putting the English words ("son" here but "dawn," "home." "upon," "blown," etc. further on) against the Navajo vocables denies the musical or sonic coherence of the original & destroys the actual flow. I decided to translate the vocables & from that point on was already playing with the possibility of translating other elements in the songs not usually handled by translation. It also seemed important to get as far away as I could from writing. So I began to speak, then sing my own words over Mitchell's tape, replacing his vocables with sounds relevant to me, then putting my version on a fresh tape, having now to work it in its own terms. It wasn't an easy thing either for me to break the silence or go beyond the narrow pitch levels of my speaking voice, & I was still finding it more natural in that early version to replace the vocables with small English words (it's hard for a word-poet to lose words completely), hoping some of their semantic force would lessen with reiteration:

Go to her my son *& one &* go to her my son *& one & one & none & gone*
Go to her my son *& one &* go to her my son *& one & one & none & gone*
Because I was the boy raised in the dawn *& one &* go to her my son *& one & one & none & gone*
& leaving from the house the bluestone home *& one &* go to her my son *& one & one & one & none & gone*
& leaving from the house the shining home *& one &* go to her my son *& one & one & none & gone*
& from the swollen house my breath has blown *& one &* go to her my son *& one & one & none & gone*

& so on. In the transference too—likely enough because my ear is so damn slow—I found I was considerably altering Mitchell's melody; but really that was part of the translation process also: a change responsive to the translated sounds & words I was developing.

In singing the 10th Song I was able to bring the small words (vocable substitutions) even further into the area of pure vocal sound (the difference, if it's clear from the spelling, between *one, none & gone and wnn, nnnn & gahn*): soundings that would carry into the other songs at an even greater remove from the discarded meanings. What I was doing in one sense was contributing & then obliterating my own level of meaning, while in another sense I was as much as recapitulating the history of the vocables themselves, at least according to one of the standard explanations that sees them as remnants of archaic words that have been emptied of meaning: a process I could still sense elsewhere in the Horse Songs—for example, where the sound *howo* turns up as both a "meaningless" vocable & a distorted form of the word *hoghan* = house. But even if I was doing something like that in an accelerated way, that wasn't the real point of it for me. Rather what I was getting at was the establishment of a series of sounds that were assonant with the range of my own vocabulary in the translation & to which I could refer whenever the Navajo sounds for which they were substitutes turned up in Mitchell's songs.

In spite of carryovers, these basic soundings were different for each song (more specifically, for each *pair* of songs), & I found, as I moved from one song to another, that I had to establish my sound equivalencies before going into the actual translation. For this I made use of the traditional way the Navajo songs begin: with a short string of vocables that will be picked up (in whole or in part) as the recurring burden of the song. I found I could set most of my basic vocables or vocable-substitutes into the opening, using it as a key to which I could refer when necessary to determine sound substitutions, not only for the vocables but for word distortions in the meaningful segments of the poems. There was a cumulative effect here too. The English vocabulary of the 10th Song—strong on back vowels, semivowels, glides & nasals—influenced the choice of vocables: the vocables influenced further vocabulary choices & vocables in the other songs. (*Note.* The vocabulary of many of the songs is very close to begin with, the most significant differences in "pairs" of songs coming from the alternation of blue & white color symbolism.) Finally, the choice of sounds influenced the style of my singing by setting up a great deal of resonance I found I could control to serve as a kind of drone behind my voice. In ways like this the translation was assuming a life of its own.

With the word distortions too, it seemed to me that the most I should do was *approximate* the degree of distortion in the original. McAllester had provided two Navajo texts—the words as sung & as they would be if spoken—& I aimed at roughly the amount of variation I could discern between the two. I further assumed that every perceivable change was significant, & there were indications in fact of a surprising degree of precision in Mitchell's delivery, where even what seemed to be false steps or accidents might really be gestures to intensify the special or sacred powers of the song at the points in question. Songs 10 & 11, for example, were structurally paired, & in both songs Mitchell seemed to be fumbling at the beginning of the 21st line after the opening choruses. Maybe it was accidental & maybe not, but I figured I might as well go wrong by overdoing the distortion, here & wherever else I had the choice.

So I followed where Mitchell led me, responding to all moves of his I was aware of & letting them program or initiate the moves I made in translation. All of this within obvious limits: those imposed by the field of sound I was developing in English. Throughout the songs I've now been into, I've worked in pretty much that way: the relative densities determined by the original, the final form by the necessities of the poem as it took shape for me. Obviously too, there were larger patterns to keep in mind, when a particular variation occurred in a series of positions, etc. To say any more about that—though the approach changed in the later songs I worked on, toward a more systematic handling—would be to put greater emphasis on method than any poem can bear. More important for me was actually being in the stimulus & response situation, certainly the most *physical* translation I've ever been involved in. I hope that that much comes through for anyone who hears these sung.

But there was still another step I had to take. While the tape I was working from was of Mitchell singing by himself, in actual performance he would be accompanied by all those present with him at the blessing or healing. The typical Navajo performance pattern, as McAllester described it to me, calls for each person present to follow the singer to whatever degree he can. The result is highly individualized singing (only the ceremonial singer is likely to know all of it the right way) & leads to an actual indeterminacy of performance. Those who can't follow the words at all may make up their own vocal sounds—anything, in effect, for the sake of participation.

I saw the indeterminacy, etc., as key to the further extension of the poems into the area of total translation & total performance. (Instrumentation & ritual-events would be further "translation" possibilities, but the Horse Songs are rare among Navajo poems in not including them.) To work out the extension for multiple voices, I again made use of the tape recorder, this time of a four-track system on which I laid down the following as typical of the possibilities on hand:

TRACK ONE. A clean recording of the lead voice.

TRACK TWO. A voice responsive to the first but showing less word distortion & occasional free departures from the text.

TRACK THREE. A voice limited to pure-sound improvisations on the meaningless elements in the text.

TRACK FOUR. A voice similar to that on the second track but distorted by means of a violin amplifier placed against the throat & set at "echo" or "tremolo." To be used only as a barely audible background filler for the others.

Once the four tracks were recorded I had them balanced & mixed onto a monaural tape. In that way I could present the poems as I'd conceived them & as poetry in fact had always existed for men like Mitchell—to be heard without reference to their incidental appearance on the page.

* * *

Translation is carry-over. It is a means of delivery & of bringing to life. It begins with a forced change of language, but a change too that opens up the possibility of greater understanding. Everything in these song-poems is finally translatable: words, sounds, voice, melody, gesture, event, etc., in the reconstitution of a unity that would be shattered by approaching each element in isolation. A full & total experience begins it, which only a total translation can fully bring across.

By saying which, I'm not trying to coerce anyone (least of all myself) with the idea of a single relevant approach to translation. I'll continue, I believe, to translate in part or in any other way I feel moved to, nor would I deny the value of handling words or music or events as separate phenomena. It's possible too that a prose description of the song-poems, etc., might tell pretty much what was happening in & around them, but no amount of description can provide the *immediate* perception that translation can. One way or other translation makes a poem in this place that's analogous in whole or in part to a poem in that place. The more the translator can perceive of the original—not only the language but, more basically perhaps, the living situation from which it comes &, very much so, the living voice of the singer—the more of it he should be able to deliver. In the same process he will be presenting something—i.e. making something present, or making something as a present—for his own time & place.

ADDENDUM: All of the foregoing of course is with reference to the recording technology of the 1970s & represents also a collaboration, on the technical side, with the composer Charlie Morrow, a long-term collaborator & comrade-in-arms. With Morrow too I've gone back to the Horse Songs in the new millennium, making full use of what he has elsewhere named his "MorrowSound True 3D technology." It expanded the audio space from the stereo 2D to immersive 3D, from observing the song to being in it. From my own less technical perspective the method of translation & performance remains essentially the same.

From "NEW MODELS, NEW VISIONS": THE POETICS OF PERFORMANCE

The fact of performance now runs through all our arts, and the arts themselves begin to merge and lose their distinctions, till it's apparent that we're no longer where we were to start with. The Renaissance is over or it begins again with us. Yet the origins we seek—the frame that bounds our past, that's set against an open-ended future—are no longer Greek, nor even Indo-European, but take in all times and places. ... The model—or better, the vision—has shifted, away from a "great tradition" centered in a single stream of art and literature in the West, to a greater tradition that includes, sometimes as its central fact, preliterate and oral cultures throughout the world, with a sense of their connection to subterranean but literate traditions in civilizations, both East and West. "Thought is made in the mouth," said Tristan Tzara, and Edmond Jabès: "The book is as old as fire and water"—and both, we know, are right. ...

When Tzara, as arch Dadaist, called circa 1917, for "a great negative work of destruction" against a late, overly textualized derivation from the Renaissance paradigm of culture and history ... the other side of his work—and increasingly that of other artists within the several avant-gardes, the different, often conflicted sides of "modernism"—was, we now see clearly, a great positive work of construction/synthesis. … Nearly a century after Dada, a wide range of artists has been making deliberate and increasing use of ritual models for performance, has swept up arts like painting, sculpture, poetry (if those terms still apply) long separated from their origins in performance. … The performance/ritual impulse seems clear throughout: in "happenings" and related event pieces (particularly those that involve participatory performance), in meditative works (often on an explicitly mantric model), in earthworks (derived from monumental American Indian structures), in dreamworks that play off trance and ecstasy, in bodyworks (including acts of self-mutilation and endurance that seem to test the model), in a range of healing events as literal explorations of the shamanistic premise, in animal language pieces related to the new ethology, etc.

While a likely characteristic of the new paradigm is an overt disdain for paradigms per se, it seems altogether possible to state a number of going assumptions as these relate to performance. …

(1) There is a strong sense of continuities, already alluded to, within the total range of human cultures and arts, and a sense as well that the drive toward performance goes back to our pre-human biological inheritance—that performance and culture, even language, precede the actual emergence of the species: hence an ethological continuity as well. …

(2) There is an unquestionable and far-reaching breakdown of boundaries and genres: between "art" and "life" (Cage, Kaprow), between various conventionally defined arts (intermedia and performance art, concrete poetry) and between arts and non-arts (musique concrète, found art, found poetry, etc.). The consequences here are immense, and I'll only give a few, perhaps too obvious, examples… :

> —that social conflicts are a form of theater (V. Turner) and that organized theater may be an arena for the projection and/or stimulation of social conflict;
>
> —that art has again recognized itself as visionary, and that there may be no useful distinction between vision-as-vision and vision-as-art (thus, too, the idea in common between Freud and the Surrealists, that the dream is a dream-work, i.e., a work-of-art);
>
> —that there is a continuum, rather than a barrier, between music and noise; between poetry and prose; … between dance and normal locomotion (walking, running, jumping, etc.);

—that there is no hierarchy of media in the visual arts, no hierarchy of instrumentation in music, and that qualitative distinctions between high and low genres and modes (opera and vaudeville, high rhetoric and slang) are no longer operational;

—that neither advanced technology (electronically produced sound and image, etc.) nor hypothetically primitive devices (pulse and breath, the sound of rock on rock, of hand on water) are closed to the artist willing to employ them. …

(3) There is a move away from the idea of "masterpiece" to one of the transientness and self-obsolescence of the poem or art-work as performed. The work past its moment becomes a document (mere history), and the artist [the poet in particular] becomes, increasingly, the surviving non-specialist in an age of technocracy.

(4) From this there follows a new sense of function in art, in which the value of a work isn't inherent in its formal or aesthetic characteristics—its shape or its complexity or simplicity as an object—but in what it does, or what the artist/poet or his surrogate does with it, how he or she performs it in a given context. …

(5) There follows further, in the contemporary instance, a stress on action and/or process. Accordingly the performance or ritual model includes the act of composition itself. … Signs of the artist's or poet's presence are demanded in the published work, and in our own time this has come increasingly to take the form of his or her performance of that work, unfolding it or testifying to it in a public place. …

(6) Along with the artist, the audience enters the performance arena as participant—or the audience "disappears" as the distinction between doer and viewer, like the other distinctions just mentioned, begins to blur. For this the tribal/oral is a particularly clear model, often referred to by the creators of 1960s happenings and the theatrical pieces that invited, even coerced, audience participation toward an ultimate democratizing of the arts…

(7) There is an increasing use of real time, extended time, etc., and/or a blurring of the distinction between those and theatrical time, in line with the transformative view of the "work" as a process that's really happening.

For all of this recognition of cultural origins and particularities [as I try to show in greater detail in the uncut version of this text], the crunch, the paradox, is that the place, if not the stance of the poet and artist is increasingly beyond culture—a characteristic, inevitably, of biospheric [global] societies. Imperialistic in their earlier forms and based on a paradigm of "the dominant culture" (principally the noble/imperial myths of "Western civilization" and of "progress," etc. on a Western or European model), these have in their avant-garde phase been turning to the "symposium of the whole" projected by Robert Duncan. More strongly felt in the industrial and capitalist west, this may be the last move of its kind still to be initiated by the Euro-Americans: a recognition of the new/old order in which the whole is equal to but no greater than the works of all its parts.

A version of a talk presented at the Wenner-Gren Foundation symposium, "Cultural Frames & Reflections: Ritual, Drama & Spectacle," held in Burg Wartenstein, Austria, August 27–September 5, 1977.

GALLERY TWO

THE WORLD TURNED UPSIDE DOWN

To count time from
the future,
having the end
in view,
this is a sore reminder
of another world,
another chance
to come into the open air,
out of the darkness.
The brain turned upside
down, they told us,
gathers no moss.
No clash of symbols
half as painful
as discounted
time, ready
to plug us
one by one.

A THIRD MANIFESTO 1968

I think of myself as making poems that other poets haven't provided for me & for the existence of which I feel a deep need.

I look for new forms & possibilities, but also for ways of presenting in my own language the oldest possibilities of poetry going back to the primitive & archaic cultures that have been opening up to us over the last hundred years.

I have most recently been translating American Indian poetry (including the "meaningless" syllables, word distortions & music) & have been exploring ancestral sources of my own in the world of Jewish mystics, thieves & madmen.

I believe that everything is possible in poetry & that our earlier "Western" attempts at definition represent a failure of perception we no longer have to endure.

A SENECA MEMORY

At Harry Watt's old place
above the Allegany River
Leo Cooper tells me:
"I could have been the first
"American Indian
"rabbi   were it not for my love
"of pork

Circa 1972, Salamanca NY

THE DREAM FROM *A BIG JEWISH BOOK*

There was a dream that came before the book, & I might as well tell it. I was in a house identified by someone as THE HOUSE OF JEWS, where there were many friends gathered, maybe everyone I knew. Whether they were Jews or not was unimportant: I was & because I was I had to lead them through it. But we were halted at the entrance to a room, not a room really, more like a great black hole in space. I was frightened & exhilarated, both at once, but like the others I held back before that darkness. The question came to be the room's name, as if to give the room a name would open it. I knew that, & I strained my eyes & body to get near the room, where I could feel, as though a voice was whispering to me, creation going on inside it. And I said that it was called CREATION.

I now recognize that dream as central to my life, an event & mystery that has dogged me from the start. I know that there are other mysteries—for others, or for myself at other times, more central—& that they may or may not be the same. But CREATION—poesis writ large—appeared to me first in that house, for I was aware then, & even more so now, that there are Jewish mysteries that one confronts in a place no less dangerous or real than that abyss of the Aztecs:

> *...a difficult, a dangerous place, a deathly place: it is dark, it is light...*

& with a sense too that this space must be bridged, this door opened as well—the door made just for you, says the guardian in Kafka's story. Yet Kafka, like so many of us, poses the other question also: "What have I in common with Jews? I have hardly anything in common with myself..."

From POLAND/1931

POLAND/1931 "The Wedding"

my mind is stuffed with tablecloths
& with rings but my mind
is dreaming of poland stuffed with poland
brought in the imagination
to a black wedding
a naked bridegroom hovering above
his naked bride   mad poland
how terrible thy jews at weddings
thy synagogues with camphor smells & almonds
thy thermos bottles thy electric fogs
thy braided armpits
thy underwear alive with roots o poland
poland poland poland poland poland

how thy bells wrapped in their flowers toll
how they do offer up their tongues to kiss the moon
old moon old mother stuck in thy sky thyself
an old bell with no tongue a lost udder
o poland thy beer is ever made of rotting bread
thy silks are linens merely thy tradesmen
dance at weddings where fanatic grooms
still dream of bridesmaids still are screaming
past their red moustaches poland
we have lain awake in thy soft arms forever
thy feathers have been balm to us
thy pillows capture us like sickly wombs & guard us
let us sail through thy fierce weddings poland
let us tread thy markets where thy sausages grow ripe & full
let us bite thy peppercorns let thy oxen's dung be sugar to thy dying
  jews
o poland o sweet resourceful restless poland
o poland of the saints unbuttoned poland repeating endlessly the
  triple names of mary
poland poland poland poland poland
have we not tired of thee poland no for thy cheeses
shall never tire us nor the honey of thy goats
thy grooms shall work ferociously upon their looming brides
shall bring forth executioners
shall stand like kings inside thy doorways
shall throw their arms around thy lintels poland
& begin to crow

The Beadle's Testimony

The boy who throws the ball
A jewel of a boy
His coat down to his feet
Earlocks flying

He will grow up to sell candles
Will eat a dog
& thrive on fat cigars
He will bless his mother too

Yes we are simple people
Yes we drive carts
& work with shit
Sometimes we study

Sometimes a fish in the hand
Sometimes charity
Eros is the Warsaw banker
Spain is far away

Kansas City is also far away
Where did our love go?
I have two hands & only one wallet
I want to speak to you about it

Cities & Jews
Walls & what is behind a wall
A temple sometimes
Sometimes a shining diesel locomotive

Sometimes charity
A boy's shadow on the wall
A jewel of a boy
He will grow up to sell candles

He will bless his mother too

The Student's Testimony

he was the last demon of ostrov
come back to visit & play
on my mind blowing delicious
bubbles of red soap into
the corners of the room
a furry singing little
demon with bulging eyes big
bulging balls & all
animal twisted into shapes
like rubber

"I love my demon" I would sing
& we would share the backroom of
the synagogue guzzling
the gentiles' beer &
snapping paperclips
against the rabbi's silks reliving
the poland of old friendships pork & fish

Poland/1931 Collage by Eleanor Antin

boiling & stinking in a single
pot we would dip our hands
into & make our bellies
shine
what grease
what aromas from the bookshelves
what smells of jews ripe for the sabbath
"fur" I would cry to him or "snot" & he
would wrap me in his sleeves & let

their velvet warm me
nightly the books were opening
in my dreams the letters
black as coal danced off
the page & fell on me I saw them
cross my hips & write the double
yod upon my cock
"never had polish child felt
greater warmth beside her
mother than I felt there"
later the telephone came voices
reached us from "the kingdoms"
messages of love
vibrated there were calls
from warsaw krakow moscow kiev odessa
paris berlin new york london
buenos aires hong kong yokahama bombay
melbourne juneau tombstone perth
detroit johannesburg topeka east st louis
homesick we dreamed "freedom" meaning
that our hands could touch our feet reach
even the dirt between
the toes
& breathe its essence
(of a hundred slaughterhouses
the sweet fat of the sabbath
in our teeth we waited until the women
came to us bearing the bloody eyes
of cows & lambs
they piled up on the table crying
"hosanna to the gentiles")
buckwheat for dinner
in the lonely diner
eating globs of fat congealed
we played games near wealthy
homes pretending that we were children
"the luck of the jews"
"constantinople nights"
"making the devil's mark on parchment"
also "the hair & beard of macroanthropos"

through which he led me his
furry body hidden under
three suits of clothes toward other
pleasures secret holes
he lived in
bathhouse partitions white with mold
& through a board the eye
watched the old women strove to behold
the slit the fiery entranceway
dissolve
the waters washing out the light the breath
that moves upon the waters
until the bulb above us splintered
"god is one"
we sang my demon clung to me
made of my tongue
his song
a master at pinochle sometimes
the deck flew in his hands
beautiful men wept like children
some shelled almonds for him
or filled his hat with vodka
the fat students loved him the dark ones
waited for news on the radio
"calm in the face of disaster"
pilgrims visited the tsaddik's court he sat
for seven days
dipped figs in wine
then lifted his milkwhite hands each
finger held a garnet
each eye a golden tear
electricity ran from his beard he wore
a neon caftan
thrice did my demon limp into his presence
they were face-to-face neither
moving neither still in love
or heartsick
theirs was a meeting of the upper
& the lower worlds
the "model of the universe" was always

at their call an empty building windows
broken or taped up with X's
in contrast to the tsaddik's its
easy warmth stoves in perfect order
so even a stranger had a place to sit
forgetful of each other
they let the time pass with singing not
with arithmetic
"a woman for me
& a woman for thee" (he would order)
the one with a wen near her nipple
the other with a glass eye women
with moist hair in their armpits
moister below
& furious
reputed to be in love with great men they were
"nieces" to all the rabbis
breathless my demon would mount his
from the rear the tsaddik
slept on in innocence of
heart & purpose
barely
could feel her hand
betray him
but blamed it on
the tightness of his linens while
wan allergic dreaming
furry to his fingers
my demon
slept against the other's
side forgetting
that the bride was always chaste the sabbath
always an interval
between subscriptions
something cold but beautiful
not a mechanical process
merely but responsive
to the touch

in satin slippers beneath
a painted canopy
of stars each waited
for the bride
each called her
sabbath but each had something else a different kind of sleep
in mind

(coda)

once in a lifetime man
may meet a hostile spirit once
he may be imprisoned for his
dreams & pay for them
lightning is like oil the motor
once it starts keeps
running
such was their wisdom though we had
no use for it
only later seeing it
reborn
in joplin on a billboard
his own shadow
was more than he could bear the war
came & he ran from it
back in the cellar drinking
too much he grew thin
the great encounter ended it
in flames the candelabrum rose did it become
a heart
that broke into sparks & letters
a shower of ruined cities from which
my demon
vanished fled from the light when I was born

Portrait Of A Jew Old Country Style

visitor to warsaw
                        old man with open fly
            flesh girls could suck
                            mothers would die to catch sight of
sometimes would pass your door
                            his song was
            a generation is a day, time floweth
coldly he blew his nose
reached a hand around his high round waist
            money was pinned to caftan
                        aches & pains
a jew's a jew he says
love brings him to the words he needs
                            but sadly
            no
                I cannot stay
                for breakfast loving
                the taste of duck eggs loving
                little rolls & butter
                loving cereals in metal pans
he tells them
            all we touch is love
            & feeds us
this is a portrait of a jew old country style
the gentile will fail to understand
the jew come on better days will run from it
how real
            the grandfathers become
            my grandfather the baker son of bakers
            YOSEL DOVID ben SHMIEL
            who was a hasid at the court in Radzymin
            came to U.S.A. circa 1913
            but found the country godless
            tho he worked in leather
            shoes were the craft all our friends
            got into first
            like his brother-in-law we called
            THE UNCLE

I remember in a basement shop
somewhere "downtown"
bent over shoes he stitched
how many years would pass
till nineteen-fifty maybe
when I saw him last
his lungs gone in east bronx tenement
he slept behind a curtain
seeing me he thought
I was my brother   old & crazy
he was the oldest jew I knew
my grandfather had died
in nineteen-twenty
on the night my parents
ran to warsaw
to get married   my father
left for U.S.A. the next day
no one told him of his father's death
he would never be a talmudist
would go from shoes
to insurance
from insurance back to shoes
later an entrepreneur & bust
he was always clean
shaven   my grandmother
the religious one I mean
saw the first beard
I'd ever grown   got angry
"jews don't wear beards"
(she said) no
not in golden U.S.A.
the old man had fled from
to his Polish death

for which reason I deny autobiography
or that the life of a man
matters more or less
"We are all one man"
Cézanne said
I count the failures of these jews

as proof of their election
they are divine because they all die
                                                            screaming
                              like the first
          universal jew
                the gentiles
                      will tell you had some special deal

The Murder Inc. Sutra

for Robert Kelly

Pincus Tavern
which Kelly passed
as schoolboy   den
of murderers or den of Jews
as murderers
no Benya Kriks he says
but bad guys imply
rotten
in the way America
disposes   though I pretend
other Pincus Taverns meetingplaces of one-eyed
hand in caftan hardcocked
Jewish bandits
beautiful men of noses enlarged with purple veins
of still-curled earlocks from childhood
who dared to cross the border in three coats
watchbands laid out from wrist to shoulders
but beardless could whistle
lost messages in secret Jewish code
meaning
"the Tsar's asshole smells of vinegar" etcetera
& were obliged to wield knives   not only
to cut a notch off a salami
but slit a windpipe
spreading his blood across
the merchant's vest or seeing
pictures in it

of rabbis with hardons unheard of
in the secular world
real to their perceptions who were
brother Jews & inn-
keepers
expert in management of taverns
where most would let the Polacks
drink but took a piece
themselves if pressed to it
even would suck each other off
in Polish prisons
from there to Brooklyn emanations
made the journey   sought
Golden Kingdoms
at the corner of Stone & Sutter
(Kelly thought) some lounged
in doorways   improbable murderous Litvaks
with names like Lepke   Gurrah   "Dutch Schultz"   Rothstein
    Lansky   Siegel
would drive wing'd cadillacs
with wraparound chrome exteriors of nineteen-thirty-one
to banquets on high holidays
eating turkey   chicken   goose with mushrooms
"a fish soup on which floated lakes of lemon juice"
drank velvety madeira booze from Canada cigars of J.P. Morgan sniffed
    cocaine sucked oranges
or dropped peels into their vodka
would wear a deluxe striped suit made of English navy
but with a head for business
Jews moved past el trains blasting tommy guns
other Jews made movies
ran after black girls   did a buck & wing
for Roman gangsters
toasted their mothers with hunky wines
that smelled of sun & bedbugs
of which the father of the dead man wrote in journal
"my child brings solace to a heavy heart
"his intense physicality
"not Jewish truly but tendering a dream of
"strength   resilience   broken promises

“a horsecock strapped between his legs
“in tribute   & my secret joy too
“seeing his dead frame surrounded
“by a thousand blossoms roses of old Poland
“a choir like the Warsaw Synagogue
“led by Sirota   bursts into songs of angels
“flashbulbs from fifty cameras pop
“blinding the humble button operators workers
“in black jackets & silk lapels some
“with yellow shoes   milk-stained wives   outclassed
“outdistanced by that stud in coffin
“whose hair pasted back still smells of
“whorehouse evenings along Atlantic Avenue
“not Moldavanka mad Odessa nights
“remembered the enforcers lift his coffin
“sweat stains the armpits of orange-colored suits
“strawberry vests   blue leather shoes
“& under the shirtcuff of the murdered son
“a diamond studded bracelet”   thus
Babel or an uncle
might have written though the flesh
retreats from these as other
killers Jews who frightened the round-cheeked schoolboy
with gangster visions   of concrete
bodies into Catskill lakes
their fathers stood above & threw
lint from old pockets into
praying for joy   deliverance
from America the beautiful
oppressor riding in white convertible
up streets of Brownsville
the eagle of the golden States hooked on his arm
& hungry   diving
on faces that he hates
of Jew & Gentile
first searches their hearts for “freedom”
& the happy buck

Esther K. Comes To America: 1931

The Wilderness: but otherwise
name of a cafeteria
where the two lovers drink tea
not speaking to each other
but sharing a world through separation:
1931: Esther K.
& Leo Levy
have met here at the end of a short life:
nothing begins as painfully
as the first step outside the glass door
the first sight of traffic
even the rumblings of the new subway under Houston Street:
all this happened in the course of ages
the priest tormented her & that was one
the governor broke into sighs & that was another
her mother became incontinent & that was the third
other events followed: fourth was the birth
of a child dead at childbirth
she massaged its hands but had to suck her own breasts:
stale odors: Leo Levy
going every morning to the chicken market
pursues his dream of power
Esther K. wonders: how was I ever trapped
inside this body?
in another life she would have been
a playgirl: not she
but someone else threw roses
in the Dnieper
danced on the drifting ice floe
to America
not someone else but she
opened the fly of the Shanghai dog-merchant
& greased his cock:
flesh erupting in the tropics
bewildering parrots
bathed in the mind of Esther K.
the traveler who crossed the Ganges
found Harlem

on the other side
the man with six fingers on one hand
had four on the other:
thus history repeated itself with marked rapidity
leading her to first meet
& then lose
Leo Levy: leading him
to polish his fingernails
with eggwhite
leading them both to read fortunes in earwax
to sell candy in Turkish baths
& cotton in Canada
to remake "1931" as a talking movie:
what lovely dreams the world will have of Esther K.
said Leo Levy
I will make dreams for the world to have of Esther K.
& garments to wear in her image
I will comb her hair out until it reaches to Nicaragua
then will climb its length
& let it carry me to the top of a windy boat
sailing for Jerusalem: farewell!
the next price of almonds is a fair price
the poor under your window & the poor
around your table
will always be there: the bicyclists will too
but peddling backwards stumbling
against churches they will pretend
to drop behind: a crisis
the good life of the timid
beckons: it is a value
to be learned: a source of fortune
only too distant without refinement
both will grow sick & die
much later: separate beds
wait for them
chimeras dressed as chorus girls
to direct & love: his name
changed to Ben Messiah
hers to his: an aged couple
smelling of wet sheets

they will sometimes be holding hands
feeling how small the palms are: the Wilderness
has shrunk them: tomorrow
morning
was a lie:
a glass of tea:
maybe a bun with onions:
a suck:
two bitter almonds:
three half-chewed jelly slices:
a lemon
a lemon
a lemon
a lemon
a lemon
a lemon
etc.

Galician Nights, or A Novel In Progress

The Early Life, Loves & Circumstances of Esther K.

1

Because a Jew eats meat & grows fat he waits until he sees the Governor.

The Jew's beard is sleek, so are his eyes sleek & shameless in an otherwise bland face.

Greetings, says Jew to Governor, but the Governor doesn't respond, no he stands there smiling.

At once the Jew gives him a fat portion & draws back.

Ah, says the Governor in awe. His fingers dip into the dish, dip & are lost.

Does the Jew withdraw then?

No.

Does the Governor return to purge his land of Jews?

No, the Governor doesn't return nor does he purge his land.

What does he do then?

He trembles on the balance of a kiss, he dawdles, he grows sick, he waves his arms, he vanishes, he is heard of nevermore.

2

He trembles on the balance of a kiss, he dawdles, he grows sick, he waves his arms, he vanishes, he is heard of nevermore.

The Governor is lost, she says, says it & goes inside the house.

The cart standing in her studio is the same one they rode around the town.

My love! cries Esther K. as she undresses.

Sometimes he rushes from her room, naked himself & with a sock around his forehead.

Reddish eyelids, yellow melancholy eyes, he was her gentile, she called him "little goy."

Now she puts snuff in both her nostrils.

It is evening. It is 1931 in Poland. It is better to be naked. It is more than that. It is worth it. Is it? It is too soon. It is noon. It is like early November. It is really June.

And Esther K. is bathing.

Greet the Governor for me, winks Esther K., & rubs the soap between her thighs.

Her gold tooth glitters.

The mirror swings along its golden chain. He is dreaming again of gold utensils.

A little to the left, a little shy, a little heavy in his socks, a little wet, a little like her father, a little less, a little lonely.

If you sneeze, he says & turns aside.

I l o v e y o u.

What a dove is Esther K.!

3

And what a dove is born to Esther K.!

Greetings remarketh the Governor.

They have come in procession to bless the child of her flesh, the midwife removeth it as one removeth a thorn.

A white-haired babe which smelleth of old laundry.

Soon Esther K. ariseth from her bed red ribbons around her leg & bangeth the door shut.

(This was in fulfillment of her dream.)

She cutteth the navel string & putteth a grain of salt beneath the infant's tongue. She rubbeth white honey upon her lips, also upon his arms.

They drop a honeycomb into his cradle.

Will Esther K. see the produce of her womb beyond this morning?

Perhaps so, perhaps no, says Esther K. & sings *O little golden one sleep in thy cradle,* her own first song.

Galician nights, how beautiful & how lonely.

But for the Jewess who has tasted of the Gentiles' honey there is no reunion in her father's tent

no awning of white satin no wedding knives no tribal beard to hide her face beneath.

O Esther K. thou my semitic beauty thou easter excellence
thou poor forsaken witness yet plyest thy trade in peace!
Thou warmest a towel for the Governor.
Thou wearest a rose gown.
(A man, once come on business, learneth to stay & bathe with thee.)
Thou eatest tripe & poppy sees.
Thou sharest half thy bounty with the rich.

4
Esther K. receives a letter from China. It reads:

Darling Esther K.

This is a wonderful Chinese city & there is here also a wonderful Jewish community. The center of the life of the community is its remarkable synagogue which is reputed to be very ancient. The community itself is said also to be very ancient & to go perhaps back to the lost tribe of Asher, one of the famous ten lost tribes of Israel. Isaiah the Prophet speaks of Jews who had settled in the land of the Sinim, but be that as it may it is certain that from the 7th century on, Persian Jews were coming into China by way of India. There are today four thousand Jews in China whose appearance is not to be distinguished from that of the Chinese. But don't let that fool you since they all play Mah Jong according to the Ashkenazic variation so familiar to us & not the rather simpler native form. There is also in the city a good theater, several western-style beauty parlors & at least one kosher restaurant managed by a family of Russian exiles. Charity abounds here. The Sisterhood flourishes. The study of the Law, while not brilliant, is steady, & at least it imposes few new burdens. The climate is "ideal."

In addition a wonderful man resides here whom you would love to meet. While I cannot divulge his name I am at liberty to inform you that his initials are L.L. A trip to this corner of the Diaspora will truly change your life.

(N.B. When you have finished reading this letter make up copies & sign your name to each, then remit them to six of your dearest friends. You must do so within three days of receipt or disastrous consequences will follow; if you comply however the results will bring you instantaneous good luck. (Holofernes failed to comply & was beheaded by Judith. Count Potocki complied & was spared to meet God as a martyr.))

It is a serious matter, dearest, & a sure sign of the coming triumph of the Lord's Anointed!

The letter bears a lion in the lower corner
& a sacred lemon.
There is otherwise no signature.

5

Circumstances in a Jewish house.

Circumstances of Esther K.

Circumstances of men exchanging wallets in front of the guildhall.

Circumstances of carts circumstances of leather lines in the hands of the master drivers.

Circumstances of farewells. Of parades of gymnasts on the road to Warsaw.

Circumstances of Bialystok & what lay beyond.

Circumstances of buttons circumstances of sewing each thread into place not leaving the ends untied.

Circumstances of half-understood lines in three rhyming poems by distinctively different Yiddish poets.

Circumstances in a Jewish house.

Circumstances of "gypsy costumes & Polish happenings in the woods."

Circumstances of chance meetings in the market.

Gentile circumstances & circumstances filled with danger.

Circumstances of letters written under cover of night.

Circumstances of the beautiful rape.

(Some circumstances that were easy others that brought great riches.

Circumstances & insurance.)

Circumstances of Esther K.

Circumstances of the journey Esther K. took across the ocean.

Circumstances of her noble station on Attorney Street.

Circumstances of the queen among the Persians the Governor is kind to her she bites his beard.

Circumstances of the 7:10 to Warsaw & the 8:35 to Babylon.

Circumstances of better times when will we come on better times again?

Circumstances of Esther K. & China.

Circumstances of Jews in pigtails & of a visit by the false messiah Leo Levy.

Circumstances of his dream of Shabtai Tsvi's dream of a Turkish heaven.

Circumstances of the Shekinah leaning on his arm.

Circumstances of the Shekinah with twelve breasts & of her lover with only two hands to caress them.

Circumstances of the Shekinah in a sea of milk.

Circumstances of her return to Poland.

(O Poland of the saints unbuttoned Poland repeating endlessly the triple names of Mary.)

Circumstances of King Casimir & the Jewish queen who sat beside him.

Circumstances of a Kazar kingdom ruled by women.

Circumstances of a golden foreskin.

Circumstances of the monarch strangled by a silky rope then buried in Paradise with forty others.

Circumstances of the legends I never knew that were kept from me in childhood.

Circumstances of her mind & ours.

Circumstances of her own face appearing in the Polish rotogravure (a decade later in the Denver Post).

Circumstances of smoked mackerel.

Circumstances of her mother's hands around a goose's neck. Of hers around the fatmeat of the King of Poland.

Circumstances of heaven circumstances of halvah circumstances of half a loaf.

(I have brought you these circumstances toward a tale of Esther K.)

Circumstances of Galician Nights circumstances on the road to Warsaw & on Attorney Street.

Circumstances in Persia China & the Kazar Kingdom.

Circumstances of the cost of milk & honey.

Circumstances in a Jewish house.

Circumstances of the loves of Esther K.

Cokboy

Part One

saddlesore I came
a jew among
the indians
vot em I doink in dis strange place
mit deez pipple mit strange eyes
could be it's trouble
could be could be
(he says) a shadow
ariseth from his buckwheat
has tomahawk in hand
shadow of an axe inside his right eye
of a fountain pen inside his left
vot em I doink here
how vass I lost tzu get here
am a hundred men
a hundred fifty different shadows
jews & gentiles
who bring the Law to Wilderness
(he says) this man
is me my grandfather
& other men-of-letters
men with letters carrying the mail
lithuanian pony-express riders

the financially crazed Buffalo Bill
still riding in the lead
hours before avenging the death of Custer
making the first 3-D movie of those wars
or years before it
the numbers vanishing in kabbalistic time
that brings all men together
& the lonely rider
saddlesore
is me my grandfather
& other men of letters
jews & gentiles entering
the domain of Indian
who bring the Law to Wilderness
in gold mines & shaky stores
the fur trade heavy agriculture
ballots bullets barbers
who threaten my beard your hair
but patronize me
& will make our kind the Senator from Arizona
the champion of their Law
who hates us both
but dresses as a jew one day an indian
the next a little christian shmuck
vot em I doink here
dis place is maybe crazy
has all the letters going backwards
(he says) so who can read the signboards
to the desert
who can shake his way out of the woods
ford streams the grandmothers
were living near
with snakes inside their cunts
teeth maybe
maybe chainsaws
when the Baal Shem visited America
he wore a shtraiml
the locals all thought he was a cowboy
maybe from Mexico
"a cokboy?"

no a cowboy
I will be more than a credit to my community
& race
but will search for my brother Esau among these redmen
their nocturnal fires I will share
piss strained from my holy cock
will bear seed of Adonoi
& feed them visions
I will fill full a clamshell
will pass it around from mouth to mouth
we will watch the moonrise
through each other's eyes
the distances vanishing in kabbalistic time
(he says) the old man watches
from the cliffs a city
overcome with light
the man & the city disappear
he looks & sees another city
this one is made of glass
inside the buildings stand
immobile statues
brown-skinned faces
catch the light
an elevator
moving up & down
in the vision of the Cuna *nele*
the vision of my grandfather
vision of the Baal Shem in America
the slaves in steerage
what have they seen in common
by what light their eyes
have opened into stars
I wouldn't know
what I was doing here
this place has all the letters going
backwards a reverse in time
toward wilderness
the old jew strains at his gabardine
it parts for him
his spirit rushes up the mountainside

& meets an eagle
no an iggle
captains   commanders   dollinks   delicious madmen
murderers opening the continent up to exploitation
cease & desist (he says)
let's speak (he says)
feels like a little gas down here (he says)
(can't face the mirror without crying)
& the iggle lifts him
like an elevator
to a safe place above the sunrise
there gives a song to him
the Baal Shem's song
repeated without words for centuries
"hey heya heya" but translates it
as "yuh-buh-buh-buh-buh-buh-bum"
when the Baal Shem (yuh-buh) learns to do a bundle
what does the Baal Shem (buh-buh) put into the bundle?
silk of his prayershawl-bag beneath
cover of beaverskin above
savor of esrog fruit within
horn of a mountaingoat between
feather of dove around its sides
clove of a Polish garlic at its heart
he wears when traveling
in journeys through kabbalistic forests
cavalry of the Tsars on every side
men with fat moustaches yellow eyes & sabers
who stalk the gentle soul
at night through the Wyoming steppes
(he says) vot em I doink here
I could not find mine het
would search the countryside on hands & knees
until   behind a rock in Cody
old indian steps forth
the prophecies of both join at this point
like smoke a pipe is held
between them dribbles through their lips
the keen tobacco
"cowboy?"

cokboy (says the Baal Shem)
places a walnut in his handkerchief & cracks it
on a boulder each one eats
the indian draws forth a deck of cards
& shuffles
"game?"
they play at wolves & lambs
the fire crackles in the pripitchok
in a large tent somewhere in America
the story of the coming forth begins

Part Two

comes a brown
wind curling from
tense tissues sphincter
opened over the whole continental
divide & shot the people up
plop plop a little girl emergeth
she with the beaver tits nose furry
eyes of the Redman's
Sabbath
gropes down the corridor
(sez) hallo doctor
got a hand to spare?
doctor sez hokay
—yas doctor
hand up her bush
he pulls
a baby   howling
in lamplight a little Moses
now the Cacique's daughter laugheth
—oh doctor not so-o hard
so hard America is born
so hard the Baal Shem dreams about it
200 years later
in Vitebsk
(he was in correspondence with Wm Blake
appeared on Peckham Rye
—yes fully clothed!—

& was his angel)
angel says his mother
smiling proud
she sees his little foot
break through
her crotch an itching
races up her ribs
America is born
the Baal Shem is a beaver
(happened while the Indian talked
chanted behind Cody
the mad jew slid to life
past pink styrofoam snow of her body's
channels
the freaky passageways
unlit unloved
like gums of an old woman
teeth were ripped from
ages gone) into
another kind of world
he hurtles
does reawaken in the female swamp
a beaver amongst the rushes
—momma!—calls the Baal Shem
—mommeleh!
vot em I doink here
I hev become mine beard
(he says) the blind world shines on him
water runs through his mouth
down belly it is dark
a darkness (fur is dark
& hides the skin & blood
a universal fur
but leaves one hole
to open from the body's
darkness pushing
into light)
erupts
like great cock of the primal beings
red & smooth like copper

of the sun's red eye at night
old Beaver lugs it in his hand
I am myself   my grandfather
(he sings) my name is Cokboy
—COKBOY, understand?
I leave my grandmother in the female swamp
will be the Great Deliverer someday yuh-buh-bum
even might find a jar of honey might stick my prick in my
    prick might tingle might it not tickle me the bees
    find out about it & sting the knob it grows a second
    a dozen or so knobs along its length are maybe 30 knobs
so what's the use I ask maybe will try again I drag it red &
    sore behind me so vulnerable I have become in this hot
    climate shitting & farting shooting marbles was opening
    my mouth & coming in it
the blackbird shits o not so fast love into my hat my eyes
    turn white wood-lilies are growing from them a slavic
    birth I can't deny so tender in my eyes tender the
    native turds come floating
& across America in an outrage uselessly I shout against the
    Sun you are no longer my father Moon you are no longer
    my mother I have left you have gone out jaunty with cock
    slung over shoulder this is the journey your young men
    will take
(says Beaver) makes it to the hut where that old woman lives
    apron over her belly carp in oven maybe fried bread fat
    fat little mother don't mind if I drop a stone onto your
    brains your daughters be back later little hot girls I
    ride on pretending I was you I suck their ears & scream
    o put me lower down love o my cock inside
& have to cool it
I cool it
in waters where a princess
daughter of a chief
went bathing
lethal & innocent the cock
has found its mark
(his train has reached Topeka
Custer is dead)
& enters the bridegroom's quarters

darkness her flesh prepared for it
by new moon
in her abdomen a sliver
grows
a silver dollar over Barstow
lighting the Marriage of America
in kabbalistic time
(says Cokboy) you are the daughter of
the mountain
now will I take thee to my father's tribe
to do the snake dance
o jewish feet of El go crazy
in his mind
o
El
o
Him
I carry in my knapsack
dirty pictures land grants
(but further back her people
gun for him
how should they feel
seeing their daughter in arms of
Cokboy
—C-O-C-K, understand?—)
thou art become my Father's bride
are wedded to (ugh) Christian god
forever
bye bye I got to run now
engagements await us in Salt Lake City
industry riseth everywhere
arrows strike concrete
never shall bruise my sweetie's flesh
(says Cokboy) on horse
up river he makes his way
past mining camps Polacks were panning gold in
& other pure products of America
o prospectors o Anglo Saxons
baby-faced dumplings who pacified the west
with gatling guns with bounties for hides of babes

mothers' vulvas made baseballs to their lust
o bringers of civilization heroes heroes
I will fight my way past you who guard the sacred border
last frontier village of my dreams
with shootouts tyrannies
(he cries) who had escaped the law
or brought it with him
how vass I lost tzu get here
was luckless
on a mountain & kept from
true entry to the west true paradise
like Moses in the Rockies who stares at California spooky in the
    jewish light
of horns atop my head great orange freeways of the mind
America disaster
America disaster
America disaster
America disaster
where he can watch the sun go down
in desert
Cokboy asleep (they ask)
awake (cries Cokboy)
only his beard has left him
like his own   his grandfather's
ghost of Ishi was waiting on the crest
looked like a jew
but silent
was silent in America
guess I got nothing left to say

FROM A LETTER TO GARY PACERNICK 12/14/81

Three Excerpts

[In response to a series of questions relating to his book, *Memory of Fire: Ten American Jewish Poets*]

1 / About the section you quote from your chapter, a few points come to mind. I don't know to what degree the poems "map the past" since they're

always being mediated by present concerns & wherever I am in relation to those. The idea of "memory" per se may be a little confusing, since there isn't much that I truly "remember"—rather a great deal that I can collage or reconstruct by opening to sources that a reliance on memory alone would have closed off to me. "Poland" & "1931" are both outside memory for me—I was born in Brooklyn at the very tail end of that year—& so the poems in that book, in so far as they map the past, etc., do so with no personal memories to call on. (That, in fact, is the reason for the title.) I do remember people speaking about the "past" & life in Poland—but the main part of what pretends to be memory is from later interviews & readings: scraps of data I used to write on file cards & from which I could make poems at performances by shuffling & reading the first 6 or 8 or 10 out loud. "Book of Histories" in POLAND comes out of that pattern, & the other poems are laced through with collaged phrases and images. I think, anyway, that that's the main comment I'd have about what you say—& a probably quibbling point, that the word "messianic" in relation to the section you quote from SENECA JOURNAL seems a little grandiose & worrisome.

2 / The meeting with Celan was real & as described—summer of 1967, Paris. I had been Celan's almost first translator into English (NEW YOUNG GERMAN POETS, 1959) & had a little correspondence with him at that time. But we hadn't ever met & when I went to Paris in 67, I used the possibility of doing further translations for Unicorn Press as the occasion for getting together. Met him at the Ecole Normale, where he was teaching, & sat around in a cafe for 2 or 3 hours, during which time we largely discussed (in his halting English, my halting German) the question of his "jewishness" & that of his translators, myself included. It was friendly but linguistically nerve-wracking, & only as we were leaving did I ask him if he spoke Yiddish. To which he replied that while he hadn't grown up with it, he had picked it up during the war; & I think the last thing I said to him was that it was strange, since he was questioning me about my "jewishness," that even though we shared a common (jewish) language, we hadn't thought of making use of it. That, anyway, is the story compressed at the top of p. 43 ["A Poem in Memory of Paul Celan" in *Vienna Blood*] & why the poem ends with a quote from him that incorporates a yiddish word ["drunk / blesst / *gebentsht*"]. Otherwise it's about losses of meaning that would turn up in both his work & mine—though the "death" most explicitly is his own by suicide (drowning) a few years later.

3 / Hard statement to respond to. I've always taken "Judaism" as an institutional & religious term & tend to be cautious about using it—& "Jewishness" I always hear as "yiddishkeit," which feels quaint & regional compared to the much larger history & myth, etc. When I started on POLAND around 1966 or 67, I was also heavily into TECHNICIANS & feeling a strong desire to "write the jewish poem" as it might have been had another yiddish generation (my own) made the breakthrough into a full-blown "modernism" that could touch all bases past & present. The first of those poems was "Satan in Goray," in which all I was doing to start with was setting [Isaac Bashevis] Singer vocabulary to the exact structure of a Gertrude Stein poem called "Dates." (I had been attracted to that by her 11th section—my only addition is the phrase "pass water" [to her "pass over"]—which I took to be her "jewish poem" so to speak.) The more I got into it, the richer & wilder it all seemed—& a needed balance to the round-the-world explorations in TECHNICIANS and SHAKING THE PUMPKIN, etc. Actually I was startled again & again by how the change in content transformed the modernist structures & devices into something I had never expected; & then I began to find similar workings among the kabbalists & so on. All of this in terms of my "own existence now," as you put it, but with an ongoing separation from a large part of mainstream Judaism which—as community or individuals particularly in its conservatizing phase—still wasn't where I felt my real allegiances to be. I don't know if this is "deracination" or whatever; certainly I don't feel it in those terms now. But equally I don't feel "kinship" with [Israeli Prime Minister Menachem] Begin, say, or "new conservative" Jews—& don't either have illusions about what orthodox/hasidic Khomeini-types would do in a secular context, etc. My point, anyway, isn't simply "an implementation of Jewish life" (if I understand what you mean by that) but of the common life shared with all others—what the Dadaist Richard Huelsenbeck called "the liberation of the creative forces from the tutelage of the advocates of power." But I find all of this very difficult to summarize.

From *A SENECA JOURNAL*

I became a beaver in 1968. Richard Johnny John was my father. The ceremony took place in the longhouse & was very brief. They said some words in Seneca. I got a new name. I didn't know if they were serious but the name was great. My wife & son became blue herons. She was called The One Who Travels, he was called The Talker. My wife's sister was Thelma Ledsome & her mother was Effie Johnson. I got interested in beavers four years later—when we went to live in Salamanca. Salamanca is a railroad town right on the reservation. I saw it once on a German map of America that omitted Albany. The population now is 7000 & is mostly white. Charles Olson wrote: History is the new localism. And Ezra Pound: An epic is a poem including history. When I die my name goes back to where it came from. A Seneca will come for it.

SALAMANCA A PROPHECY

(1)

a city on
a turtle's back
a longhouse

/

was like Jerusalem
's temple resting
on a whale

(2)

impossible to bring it all
together

Seneca Nation
Salamanca, New York

Seneca Journal 1: A Poem Of Beavers

for Gary Gordon

in dream
the beavers come to
Harry Watt
"a child could
"speak
"communication
"were standing in a row
"they said I would not
"harm them
"would not ever
"after
"hunted mink
"& badger
"but the beavers were
"my friends
"& helped me

so his story began & I knew it also hearing what he said hearing I knew it was with me from before my time & knew it as a memory of my own grandfathers not as hunters in the woods but on the edge of old world forests men & women walked by on the way to markets public baths went berrying in summer chased by wolves in winter past the huts where mushrooms hung to dry the old women of the woods lived heavy in grey dresses chin hairs bristling into gentile beards their own familiar dogs & cats beside them had the master of the good name learned from these the speech of animals this is the secret all men have retained that greater language of what biological fellowhood will open to us once again

ethology the visions
of McClure & Chomsky all
the speakers of deep tongues point
a route this generation
will be privileged to assume
a universal speech

in which the kingdoms of the world
are one
the kingdoms of the world are one

---

what is it to be a beaver truly
when I think of it I think
of water water on a body
wholly hair
I think of beavers hats
& beavers movies
I think of a new birth into
beaver life
the beaver in the poem of the Baal Shem
is being born
he is the generative part of man
the cock in hair
that low intelligence erupting
changes what we are
the soft becoming
hard the cold one
hot
red tongue of beaver in a nest
of fur
by a sudden metamorphosis
a fluid world
becoming
anything the mind can think
the mind is thinking
entering the fluid bottom stream
of sex transformed
the Baal Shem leaves the light of Torah
& becomes
any old animal inside
the sacred wood

& I am now living in
a place called Bucktooth once
its Indian name

the name of a small man (the book says
"he was only 4 feet tall
"& had a single tooth
"they found his skeleton
"a single tooth
"that fell out when they crossed
"the Allegany
"belt buckle bore his mark
"the grandsons made a coffin
"they buried him
"back where his fathers were)
& only 4 feet tall he must 've been
"one of them little fellers"
pygmies of this place
of leprechauns who own
the Dark Dance
no self-respecting Indian would be
that small   or say
that by that tooth he was
a beaver I would call
Old Beaver Tooth
being myself a Beaver
by adoption
as my wife & child are Herons
also by adoption
we adopt these titles
we go home with them
what is this membership we have
adopted grinning
in the mirror my face
it changing to
a mask Floyd John once showed me
had a single tooth
If I could make my face a mask
I'd be Old Bucktooth
Beaver once again old founder
of a town we all can live in hoping
that no other
Duke of Salamanca comes
to sponsor a new railroad

beavers & blue herons
can't live near
but hide from in the silence of
some lousy cave

---

not a sweet beast he is power
not a sweet man he is like a muscle tightened waiting to crack down &
  break
a skull maybe splintering the jaw & making
the teeth like his own an almost non-existent row the ghost tooth
in the center shining is a mirror we can see ourselves
down to the farthest tunnel winding among
shining leaves & flowers words & tiny melodies
the colors make
                    or if the dream begins with
silence in the foot itself
that silence stirs
it is a dance vibrating at center of each isolated
nerve reminds him of the song
he wants to sing when
dying
& if the beaver sings it to him now it means
an easy death

---

just as the birth was easy
beaver life began in
water was a pound of bones & fur
sure instinct to the mark
sent out his tongue
into the left rear nipple sucked
sweet yellow sticky milk
his mudder gave him
"slurp" sez Old Bucktooth Beaver
"now I must try a swim around"
he's only an hour old & talking
swimming paddling around her tits
in noonday sun reclining
top of the lodge will learn

not to let tail get dry but dribble
sweet clarifying smell from nether
hole all creatures hanker
for a whiff of
smears it on his hands &
dabs the fur so comfortable
& sweet this is the beaver's life
(sez Old Man Beaver)
think I might chew a little wood
—just loves to chew & fart—
"pleasures are simple
"in this world the trick's
"to find a tree & let the sun flash
"on my orange tooth
"tree chips fly all day
"& I will stop never
"until the tree shall come to earth
"& never stop though it may crush me
"the film across my eye shall turn to fog
"old ones call dying

---

but not without a fight
(sez Beaver) Otter stalks him
"most cunning raids my tunnels
"kicks in my sweetened
"mudpatties steaming still hot with my
"fragrance stuffs
"oil drops & stones up
"'s rectum (cries)
Me King Otter! Lick Me!
the Great Mask of Otter filling
Beaver Man's dreams
makes tracks in his corn mush
pearly grains of hominy
under the otter's claws
otter piss splatters
's corn soup
"sands soft waves of nausea across
"my cerebellum o sly dance of

"otters on harvest nights full moon
"suspended atop an alder pole
delights Old Beaver Man gathers
descendants around him
he stands on the water
slaps it
hard with his tail (sez)
"Old Enemy
"Otter
"in the name of Longhouse the Great
"Rabbinical Council
"of elders mystical
"mammals the longbeards of
"Zion America
"I have lived my last under the earth
"into a new sun I skitter
"tribal triumphant (sez Beaver)
"I chew off your balls
"I survives

(Song #1): Old Man Beaver's Blessing Song

```
*OLD*MAN*BEAVER'S*BLESSING*SONG*
*all*i*want*'s*a*good*5¢*seegar*
*heeheeHOHOheeheeHOHOheeheeHOHO*
*all*i*want*'s*a*good*5¢*seegar*
*heeheeHOHOheeheeHOHOheeheeHOHO*
*all*i*want*'s*a*good*5¢*seegar*
*heeheeHOHOheeheeHOHOheeheeHOHO*
*all*i*want*'s*a*good*5¢*seegar*
*heeheeHOHOheeheeHOHOheeheeHOHO*
*all*i*want*'s*a*good*5¢*seegar*
*heeheeHOHOheeheeHOHOheeheeHOHO*
*all*i*want*'s*a*good*5¢*seegar*
*heeheeHOHOheeheeHOHOheeheeHOHO*
*all*i*want*'s*a*good*5¢*seegar*
*heeheeHOHOheeheeHOHOheeheeHOHO*
*OLD*MAN*BEAVER'S*BLESSING*SONG*
```

Seneca Journal 7: The Dreamers

for David Antin

1

that couple sitting
in splendor of old houses
Albert Jones & his wife Geneva
were old before my time
he was the last of the Seneca diviners
died 1968
the year we first stayed in Salamanca
with the power to know dreams
"their single divinity" wrote Fremin (S. J.) 1650
as we say "divine"
the deva in us
like a devil
or a divus (deus)
when these old woods were rich with gods
people called powers
they would appear in words
our language hides them
even now
the action of the poem brings them to light
dear David
not in the business man's
imagination
but asking
"who is Beaver?"
forces them out of the one mind
in mything
mouthing the grains of language
as David that sounds like deva
means beloved
thus every Indian once had a name

2

"devils" the Jesuits said
or "dreams"
but were barred from the dying man's room
who sat   dreaming   singing
surrounded by bells   knives   needles   scissors   blankets   caps
  coats   wampum belts   beads   awls
"the thousand objects of his dreams"
was careful not to kill a desire
in sleep
he knew he wanted to eat
dog's flesh or man's
that his father's hatchet had vanished
something forever secret
waited in him
the 13th virgin in the love feast
always out of reach
therefore they fed him like babe or woman
the dark diviner at his side
wept still over riddles—
beads & pumpkins—
& the man screamed rolling in the fire
cut his own fingers off with seashells
once aimed a blow at some poor girl's head
but stopped (said) "I am satisfied
"my dream
"requires nothing further
like the vision as a boy he saw
an old man "of rare beauty"
who held out bear meat in right hand
human in left
ate of the bear & was a hunter
came back   ordered gifts
"10 dogs
"10 porcelain beads from each cabin
"a collar (belt of wampum) 10 rows wide
"4 measures of sunflower seeds
& sat 10 hours by scorching flame

singing his death song
so the Jesuit wrote
"all their cabins they have filled with dreams

3

was it the moon she saw
like the moon in Poland that old mother
once lighted up our minds
that the Iroquois woman dreamed of
had walked out from her cabin
baby daughter in her arms
"old moon's dropped down to earth
(she says)
"'s become a woman
"like myself but holds
"another babe
"as if I've walked into a mirror
& the moon stands
blood red
(says)
"I am thy dominant
"seigneur
"fat with my moon glow
"grant thee the power to name gifts
"maybe tobacco   flashy beads
"robe of red squirrel fur
"to thee be given
"see they proclaim dream feasts in my name
"so much I love thee
"I would thee be like me
"like fire
"wholly
"to live in color of
"mine fire
now is herself
Red Lady
dresses all up in red
her feathers cap belt shoes all red
she's even smearing her body red

encircles each protuberance
red of her labia
so fine
‘s her brain turned upside down
now she will walk bare foot through
200 fires
squawk her old woman song
grown red with love
stretches her pink tongue to touch
“her last desire”

4

“turned upside down”
this is the ceremony at last
there is nothing
before it greater than
the woman at the rim of her own dream
sees a new world below
the air expands
blows against
her legs
its fingers open the dull labia
suddenly aglow
& burning
red with a new promise
the world-child takes root in her
will be a daughter
she be the grandmother to what
is good & bad
walks now in the new
world below her head
like crossing the back of an old turtle
on your hands
in a country where everyone wears feathers
where skin’s like glass
opens a window in her breast   say
from which an Indian
tired from his “show”
stares out

shines at you
a gold tooth
& a terrible top hat
with flags

THE OTHERS   HUNTERS IN THE NORTH   THE CREE

for Howard Norman

1

the photo shows me
bearded man with hand
over one eye
they say   he pulls his eye out
now the shadow
—death's line—
's at my gut
flower in the soup
2 flowers now
2 eyes
the hunters watch
I take them
& place a stem in each socket
sharp as wires
the flowers dance on ends of
we remember
in the movie you were watching with
the others   hunters in the north   the Cree
sweet music over Tundra
lovely as the lady
Harpo saw & plucked
both eyes
to juggle & never
got them back in straight
much to their laughter   doomed
to double vision
men with eyebrows of crows
whose women swim in them

were Trickster's boys
among the fjords & flows
we share
somehow in a hut of dreams
he leaves for us

2

lately I saw
my eye over ocean
tipped with red
my blood the seashell held
in drops
so red the sun was
drew out our organs to the light
the madman cloud
has spoken
"when we leave this world we walk
"under another sun
"the language changes
"slowly
"frees us at last to speak
the stranger wanders thru the message room
my captain   he is half asleep
half swedish
the hair grows even to his toes
but soon forgotten shy
"I try to make things right (he tells us)
"sometimes it doesn't work
& sleeps first in a hammock that becomes
a valley
the ends held up by pine trees
hanging upside down
no animals left in that world
but dreaming
each eye now sees a different shape
a porcupine stuck to a cloud
by quills
a bird
—a footprint—

worms inside it
crowing
"fill up your ears with whitefish oil
"with mud
"so not to listen
"to the windigo who sits
"still on my tongue
"the way it always was
"& chews my heart
"the liver in my only cave
I WANT THIS AS A NAME:
HE-PULLS-HIS-EYE-OUT

3

the body of a Seneca
fell once
down from the overpass
onto the highway
same year that Gary Gordon
flew from his car to heaven
didn't make it
the roads are haunted now
that cross the woods
we do not know these windigo
—ice hearts that melt—
we feel them everywhere
blue lights
we see them floating
down Allegany
call them our deaths

A PRE-FACE FOR MARÍA SABINA

I met María Sabina in 1979, brought to Huautla de Jiménez in Oaxaca by Henry Munn and accompanied throughout by him and his wife Nati, the sister of Sabina's biographer & fellow Mazatecan Álvaro Estrada. The town was then remote—as it no longer is—and situated in the high mountains of the Mazatecan Sierras. But it was also clearly a part of our contemporary world, and even María Sabina's hillside house—across the path from the mobile home the government had put in place for her—had familiar objects in it that linked her world to ours. Her household altar—memorably—was the repository for what one took to be gifts brought there by two decades of foreign visitors. In memory I can still see vividly the images of Hindu gods that stood out from among the other, largely Catholic figures. She smoked packaged cigarettes—as we did—and offered us bottled beer too, but our presence was, I thought, of little interest to her. And when Henry Munn asked me—against my own judgment—to take a rattle and sing an American Indian song for her (in my translation), she listened for less than a minute and went off to attend to a crying grandchild or great-grandchild outside her door.

That was all as it should be and a clear indication of the one-sidedness of such a cultural meeting. It was also at Henry's suggestion, but possibly as her own idea, that she offered to arrange a velada for us—for a price that she then named. That struck me as curious, since I had been reading in her *Vida*, which I was then helping to publish in English, that "a Wise One should not charge for her services" and that "one is born to cure, not to do business with her knowledge." At that moment too I realized, as never before, our mutual contemporaneity and the fate we shared as poets in an imperfect world.

The poem I wrote about that follows.

THE LITTLE SAINT OF HUAUTLA

lives to be too old
her voice
painful to her chest
echoes
until her belly sags
cries to the tumor
under her heart:
"o you moon child
"you little eye of god
"little birds that grow
"from trees
the drunk beside us
—young man
sans teeth—

who stumbles
to reach her hilltop
sits by the saint
& hiccups
“are you a saint?” he asks
“I am a governor” she tells him
“I am a clock
“a wheel
“the palsy in the judge’s fingers
“flutters my skirts
“I am the moon
“I welcome my dizziness
“I chew the little things
“& whistle
“you will eat your eyes
“—the clock says—
“your shadows
“will slide down your throats
“will choke you
“you will come back to my hillside
“flying   martyrs
“will bang tibetan bells
“the mountain god
“little king on horseback
“will cut you down
the saint says
hides behind her lost teeth
the face of Krishna
smiles back at us
her own face in a glow
of cigarette smoke
as we make
small talk
small mirrors shine from
the robes of all saints
Mexico in summer
still wet with fruit
the garbage of poor lives
poor women know
their huipils bright with birds

& butterflies
flowers of the orange dance
—o mystic weddings—
where in Huautla de Jiménez
we were the last to come
the bus still bringing
freaks from Mexico
to eat the sour mushrooms
with earth & goat shit
wild on their lips:
this is language
tiny letters
so brilliant in the sky
of *la sierra mazateca*
where we arrive
to meet our tiger shamans
looking for their tracks
their footprints
like whirlwinds in far cities
torn from the earth
o clocks
o eagles
for you the sweat of Christ
Christ's semen
becomes a plant
transparent flower
glowing in ocean
someone walking with
Christ's flower
as a staff   a man
with money like a saint
general whose footprints leave
whole jewels
in our path
—she sings
searches for the night—
the drunk Indian
(poor boy)
smiles to her face
& hiccups

like a drum
his language dying in him
"are you a movie star?" he asks
"I am a calendar" she tells him
"I am a comet woman
"an opossum
"I drink warm beer
"freshly I make my bed
"my photographs envelop Mexico
"I cackle like a turkey
"my voice is endless
"in museums where shawls are hanging
"in bars in fancy homes in ballrooms
"in concert with the grateful dead
"France awaits me
"the Italian directors come at night
"they suck my mushrooms
"the Pope comes to Oaxaca with the others
"butlers are dancing with
"the brides of god
"brides of mountain men
"little kings on horseback
"Shiva's ikon dances
"on my altar
"clocks are dancing
"& opossums
"wheels & governors
"in dreams without a word
"left to intone
she says   it says
for her
the book of language says
translated into broken Spanish
sold to feed the dead
the dying language
hiding from strangers' eyes
the way the mushrooms hide
will not speak
except when the children's voices
tell us:

casa
dinero
hongos
hidden from your eyes too
María poet of these hills
fast speaking woman
bought & sold
to feed the language of the rich
—cloaca of all languages—
—oppressors whom you love—
you hilltop woman
you saint woman
you clock woman
you moon woman
you martyr woman
you mirror woman
you tiger woman
you language woman
you flower woman
you money woman
you warm beer woman
you my mother shepherdess
(it says)
o mother of the sap (it says)
mother of the dew (it says)
mother of breasts (it says)
mother of the harvest
you rich mother
now standing visible & loud
before us
ha ha ha
so so so
so so so
hee hee hee
see see see
hum hum hum
it says & rises
lonely   lost
the spirit that wanders through America
saint children

disembodied in city air
crazy in Mexico
a squatters' village to hold the poor
fury of dead Mazatecs
the ghost of Juárez
speaking English
like my own voice
at your doorway
shaking this sad rattle
singing
without the hope of god
or clocks
with no word between us
veladas that cost
a thousand pesos
this vigil for your book
& mine
for any languages
still left to sell

THE NATURE THEATER OF OKLAHOMA

1
someone arrives from tishimingo

it is practically florida

it is practically the calories of summer

plin plin is the name for tea
in oklahoma

the curtains rise & fall

the shadow of a mirror
in a yellow lake

the shadow of a town called shootout

it is practically the way we are

it is practically the way the car toots
down the draw,
the car toots down the draw

2
the memory of god
is god   the cauliflower glistens
like a handkerchief
torn from the sun
& flailing   ice
& oranges
that conjure up her image
dimly
step into the light,
pale sister,
let the flies walk up your arm
in search of honey,
evading the tiny hairs, their world
the mirror of your blue milk,
daughter of the sun,
the buds are red for you in oklahoma,
the birds are blue

3
pawnee bill rides bareback
into my smeared horizon

myths of soft eels

undulant
ambitious

they knock us off our feet

a black man
with his fist shoved up
a cow's ass

what a fancy smile!

what perfect choppers!

like the hands of god
in oklahoma

4
like the hands of god
in oklahoma
angels pray for you

the choirs wear
white robes   the dancers
prance in   leather
setting the final derrick up

the road to cowboy country,
scarcely a league away,
strides covered by a giant's gumshoes,
plumb forgotten,
oily

the land returns to
verdure   & the country
turns around
& names itself

OMEGA

5
"as simple as a dollar bill
"in oklahoma

the ides of march in shawnee

in the middle of a prairie
birds go nuts

they make a fallacy of fables

cadaverous
discolored

the fist sinks into its second face
the one seen in the corner
of the bar, the golden tooth
reflected in the mirror

a state of grace, a place
called oklahoma

6
"you are a bear" she said
& he became
a bear, he wore it
like his skin
the lost look
the interior grace
that surfaced on him,
he was faceless too
& walked inside
his footsteps   half
an animal who loves
his other half,
the silence of the moon
over his head,
this is the mark the man's arm
scribbles, darkly,
on the cave wall,
in the cave,
in oklahoma

7
the nature theater of oklahoma
opens   its little flags
flap recklessly
against the southern wind

a history of poetry
a history of jesus christ
a history of tishimingo

the cowhand plays
at coon can, holds
the final heart

the horse called kafka
cannot prance or turn

"I love your boots" she says

a history of where we are

8
in the heart of the indian territory of oklahoma

a chicken in every coop
a jesus in every garage

a tiger on every bush

the state of nature
in the state of oklahoma

old men & febrile women
in white shawls
that the grandfathers stitch with hexagrams

of a star as black as tar

o my oklahoma jesus

From THAT DADA STRAIN

A Pre-Face

In a poetry reading, the voice carries the poet's equivalent of an oral tradition, speaking things the written poem has left unsaid. Does this betray the poem? we used to wonder. Or does it allow an audience of strangers to share some of what is so obvious to the poet that it enters into the poem as something wholly natural—what cannot & should not be omitted? In my own world—let us say—the DADA fathers who inhabit the opening poems of this book are necessary figures, & to summon them up along with their legends is no more erudite an act than to summon up Moses or George Washington or Harpo or Karl Marx, & so on. But I can't assume, when I turn to Tzara or to Hugo Ball, say, a common tradition that would be shared with any group of listeners I might be addressing—so I begin my reading by saying: This is a poem for Hugo Ball, who founded the Cabaret Voltaire in Zurich 1916 & went off into the hills of Switzerland to die there as a kind of Catholic DADA saint. It is all a question of a handle & a desire (in spite of the poem's final mystery) to be truly understood.

The work is clear to me in its named persons & places—if less so in its imaginal figures or its syntax. In the present instance the first force I would summon up is that of a DADA movement nearly a century into its history. Its authors have passed, as Blake would have said, into "eternity," to become the fathers of imaginal acts done in their memory. The spirit that remains is the final resistance to the tyranny of one's work, as it emerges in Tzara's manifesto insistence that "the true Dadas are against Dada." The measure of their failure (& ours) is in the degree of divergence from their most defiant aim: "the liberation of the creative forces from the tutelage of the advocates of power."

At the end of *Vienna Blood*, I found myself coming back to Tzara & to DADA—a step that Diane Wakoski described as my having taken DADA for my *muse*, not (she said) "a lady with wings floating around the house [but] whatever really interests you, turns you on and keeps you from turning in on yourself." As such, the DADAs appeared to me both as children & (in a reading of their name that they denied themselves) as fathers—literally the generation of my own father. Dead & gone now, they arise like him in retrospect as total lives: Ball as the shaman-priest turned saint described above; Schwitters renaming DADA "Merz" & erecting in his Hannover house an expanded sculptural memorial to DADA before his wartime flight to Norway & England (Ambleside); & Picabia as playboy pope of a new & nonexistent DADA Church. The Covering Cherub—coming to me from Blake & Ezekiel in my own polemic against anti-DADA critic Harold Bloom—is the sure image of authority & repression (church & state) that keep us from the construction of new languages & worlds.

No one, of course, is really DADA now, but the resistance (as long as it continues) may take enough of a backward look to consider those who came before us. Viewed in this way, their leading edge would seem to be through language—its collapse & reconstruction—that led them to invent new languages (like Ball's wordless poetry) in which would be fulfilled Apollinaire's prophecy: "victory will be above all / to see truly into the distance / to see everything / up close / so that everything can have a new name." In my own case, I find myself working at this from two obvious sources—what seems to have little reference outside my own language & perception, & what follows closely from the visions & the language acts of others. But in either case the poems presented here can be seen as reflections of procedures shared with the Dada poets & others—for linking words by letter, number, shape, & sound, or for recording associations between images for which no key is readily available, if it ever was.

Finally, I would point out that the title of the book, *That Dada Strain*, doesn't come from European DADA at all but from jazz & blues traditions of the 1920s—specifically as the title of a still surviving early jazz standard. I would take that coincidence as clearly "dada," even kabbalistic, & would let it go at that.

THAT DADA STRAIN

the zig zag mothers of the gods
of science the lunatic fixed stars
& pharmacies
fathers who left the tents of anarchism
unguarded
the arctic bones
strung out on saint germain
like tom toms
living light bulbs
aphrodisia
"art is junk" the urinal
says "dig a hole

"& swim in it"
a message from the grim computer
"ye are hamburgers"

February 1916   In the most obscure of streets in the shadow of architectural ribs, where you will find discreet detectives amid red street lamps—birth—birth of the Cabaret Voltaire—personages in one edition appear, recite or commit suicide, bustle and stir, the joy of the people, cries, the cosmopolitan mixture of god and brothel, the crystal and the fattest woman in the world: "Under the Bridges of Paris." (T. Tzara)

The History Of Dada As My Muse

the history of the fathers
is only Dada time   only yesterday
only the day before
the morning after, time
spent in this century
an empty train
snaking its way to Paris
cathedral where an old sump overflows
that leaves them dizzy
shit sticking to their cuffs
unpressed but with the fathers' zest
for living   vests & monocles
proclaim an avant-garde
in absence an avant-garde proclaims
itself   the young men
fathers of the history of Dada
still ride its rails
rise past my eiffel towers
at each bump
each anal urge propels them
"this is the heart of culture"
they proclaim
the heart of war
the Dada god's heart
in the world their poems make
muses drum on walls

on saddles
muses masturbate into the wind
o Dada o my Muse
the young men under cellophane
sleep with the history of the fathers
in the fathers' heads
a girl named Schopenhauer dances
the train to Paris lands in Zanzibar
verses come upside down
to free us   verses
reversals in the history of language
voice
divine
foot
solitude
the king of islands in a tree
a fiddle in each hand
his sex implanted in midst of branches
upsets their tables, spills
his dreams along the floor
the sounds of queens in books
young men—the fathers—walk by
each is the other's muse
waits with a shadowed lady
at his side
footballs thrown between
the fathers
float past the empty trainyards
only yesterday
in somebody else's dream
the voice unlocked, reversed
the figure halfway inside the window
cut in two
the train in the revolver's mouth
baffled by other trains
by cogwheels
an assemblage of spare parts
can never suit
                    the fathers
the fathers can never suit themselves

by banging   each man
is the other's muse
each is his own football
over Paris   waving
from a perch above the opera
holds a mackerel in each hand
blue lights above them
the jellied colors of their gods
o Nostradamus
is your first name Jerome
like mine?
is Sagittarius our brother?
where are the proud Apaches
now?   the sons
of Dada?
on a billboard
Paris waits
the history of the century
illuminated, grey
in moonlight
welcomes my Muse as Dada
military bands spatter the station
they screw my muse
paper septembers o voltaic arc
true & blue
grey life
the Dadaist rides up an elevator
with the pope
the fathers adrift like muses
down one eiffel tower
up the next
o light wheels teeming with blue ants
what began as Dada ends
as Dadahood
as my hand ends, halfway
waving
halfway cut off from its fingers
where the street ends
where another street turns halfway
into another street

A Glass Tube Ecstasy, For Hugo Ball

Cabaret Voltaire, Zurich, 1916

23.vi.16

For that evening's reading he had made himself a special costume. His legs were in a shiny blue cylinder, which reached up to his hips so that he looked like an obelisk. Over it he wore a huge coat collar cut out of cardboard, scarlet on the inside & gold on the outside. It was fastened at the neck in such a way that he could give the impression of winglike movement by raising & lowering his elbows. He also wore a high, blue-and-white-striped witch doctor's hat.

A glass tube
for my leg says Hugo Ball
my hat a cylinder
in blue & white
the night the german ostriches the sink
he pisses in
all these become his world
his dada song, begun there
holds the image
until it comes at us:
the image from its cross
looks down:
a ribbon
a revolver
mud
these contribute
to his death
also to what his death contributes
later, too hysterical
too sick with god
& time:
a carousel
a roasted poet
fish
the queen says to his mind
& enters
where the street of mirrors starts
she sees his face

reflected
in hunger of the world
as pain, the consciousness
of death not why we die
but why we dream about it
& why our dreams can't save
the dying remnant
Hugo
as I write this poem
the voice cries
from a further room
the dancer / singer calls me
from a further room
I step into an obelisk
below the waist
my mouth opens to sing
but freezes
shut
in grief for you
ombula
tak-e
bitdli
solunkola
the collapse of language
tabla tokta tokta takabala
taka tak
a glass tube ecstasy
escapes from time
babula m'balam
the image & the word
over your bed
hang crucified
again the cabaret explodes
again again
fatigue
one
foot
in glass
a glass nerve
&

a priestly gas pump
pulls
her hair out

A Merz Sonata, for Kurt Schwitters

world of the crying man
is death's world
money acids him, he sucks
hard on his tongue
but can't unjunct the word
therefore he stows his house
shovels the floor
a column shivers skywards
the man can stride down
crying: **MERZ!**
sweet Kurt's word
column overstacked with
mirrors   pretzels
the revival of the alphabet
hustles him toward England
cuckoos Dada journeys
in painted car
van Doesburg springs a **merz** hand
a **merz** gesture
drips   **merz** bodies
wet & tumored
prong the **merz** girls
tip into their shallow holes
& provocate
streamers of wet **merz**
merz merchants
line the streets with—
commercial **merz**ers
merzing in a ring
their products
sauce & ciders
jars
delirious as numbers two's

he slabs onto his roof
o coupons
tiny tickets
we trade off with burgermeisters
bits of shoelace
half-stapled cigarettes
a worm   a fish
merz angels swing from
tangled in air
nail pairings
slice of tie
mimosa orange tulpe flora aphrodite
bottles alight with piss
& baking soda
merzd in his slots
a pot of water
—boiling—
you can drop a clock in
watch it converge to ice
or noodles
squawking german from full throat
der fisch dill schreizen karpenblut
heil hitler
makes a **merz**-poem
fidill schreifi karblu
makes a poem
a **merz**-poem makes a fiddle
marchers **merz**
merz marches
behind the band—boom boom—o
little Dada towns
devoured by incest
still more devoured by holes
by calendars
merz christmas trees spruced up
merz stickers pasted on **merz** walls
merz slogans:
du du
and
and du du

a n n a   b l u m e
and **merz**
My Valentine!
keep burning on & on
Get GLOWING
Thou
thine eye prays
yearns my eye
thou art my yearn
I acid thou
I far thou
sideways slides his stem into
her slit
her slot makes bubbles
rise over his column
where the babe's head hides them
barking to the crowds
the tall man is the crying man
—bow wow—
the generals are swooning
as he sings
sweet **merz** songs
making their cradles rock
their prussian wives wipe dribbles
from their cheeks
& dream bavarian cushions
they can lunge their stumps against
for breath   for fantasies
not like the dreams of **merz**
or freedom
but the collective eye
o you o me
o elephants o commas
o I sing for Kurt this **merz** song
O I swoon—I moon—for him
cat
      legs
catlegs & human joys
& humans world the earth roundout the cats
like jews who fiddle papers

who gurgle “anna blume” from full throats
cutouts of Hitler
paper bikers
stream down the german roads
make Norway
scramble him—crying & tall—toward Ambleside
the real disuda of the nightmare
Alabaster
death
he tries to feel by language
Why?
We
Thy
Thee
Thou
the dog barks Alabaster
drip drip
plugs the sky
pins
a little moustache to his lip
the generals are dead
the candled towers of his **merz**
explode
the dream of **merz**
—stuck in his head—
undrips him
flattens his last pretzel
to its walls
its walls
five four three two one
wall
wall
WALL
WALL WALL WALL
WALL WALL WALL
WALL   WALL   WALL   WALL
walls
walls
walls
WALLS WALLS WALLS WALLS

WALL
WALL WALL WALL
WALL WALL WALL
wall wall wall
wall
wall
wall

wall

"The word Merz had no meaning when I formed it. Now it has the meaning which I gave it. The meaning of the concept Merz changes with the change in the insight of those who continue to work with it." (K. Schwitters)

A Poem In Yellow After Tristan Tzara

angel slide your hand
into my basket   eat my yellow fruit
my eye is craving it
my yellow tires screech
o dizzy human heart
my yellow dingdong

Translation from French, the original modified principally by insertion of the color yellow.

The Holy Words Of Tristan Tzara

sad in his world
or in yours
he walks for years beside
the economic lilies
explores the mysteries of bread
a wax archangel
stands on his tongue
his hands cold dry
deprived of water

in the room under the room
where Lenin sat
aromas of Bukovina gather
Moinesti with its corn mush
brinza cheese
petroleum
redheaded Leah
like a hungry wolf
the word he dreams is
dada
dada ice
dada piano
dada flower
dada tears
dada pendulum
dada vanilla
dada don quixote
dada humid
dada archipelago
dada pharmacy
dada sexenial
dada dichotomous
dada dichroic
dada dicrotic
dada didactic
dada didelphian
dada diluvial
dada dingdong
the fur of dada stretched out in the sun
dada on a hill old fox old dada
Sammy Rosenstock alive old exile
got Zurich on my mind
glass toys betwixt the stars with chains
electric flags & posters
"logic is a complication!
"logic is always wrong!
cries dada
holy cow
o cube
o hobby horse

the freedom first encountered in
first trip to Zurich
ghosts drunk on energy
they pulled the bells of war down
martyred the cabaret
until it exploded
like yiddish dada in the street
the overture to cheese
o Sammy brother
the sad one of your tribe
you said: disgust
you sat next to the photo of
redheaded Leah
under the axe & clock
your monocle hung from your vest
red life grew distant
in the room where Lenin sat
the walls sang politics to us
his nurse's name was "dada"
so was yours
& sputtered poetry
redbellies laughing thru empty skulls
"my name is Sammy Rosenstock
"Samiro
"is later Tristan Tzara
"I am so sad with life
"I love it
"I am of course Rumanian
"I allow myself to contradict
"I put an owl in a hexagon
"I climb up on the stage
"I'm prim
"I'm formal
"I applaud the revolution
"the hands of bandits
"blind worms & dada nightmares
"invade your bowels
"messiahs are passé
"the word we dream is
"dada

"dada sweepeth out
"dada teareth linens
"rips clouds & prayers to shreds
"thou rides on hiccups
"dada has a balcony
"we squat there pregnant birds
"we shit on thine umbrella
"dada
"dada is against the future
"dada lives
"in fire wisdom fear
"—is fear of dada
"like a star?—
"no like a fish a plant the moon
"a metal word
"distorted boiling
"illumines the urethra
"sixty fingers on each arm
"I am a monster too
"I play with cushions
singing
singing
like hymns of queens
the eye of Lenin
now so wide
pushes the curtains
the chess game opens like a poem
metaphysics of perdition
rules them
tired of the stars
his horse eats colored snakes
o angel horse
on thee rides Hugo Ball
himself an angel horse
here Huelsenbeck & Jung walk
here Arp
here Janco
here kings of Zanzibar
here april nuns
here Tristan Tzara

ghost of Abulafla no ghost
he makes his buttocks jump
like belly of oriental queen
madonna face of Emmy Hennings
a silent fiddle
cuts the room in two
Hugo like a manikin
at piano
stammers yodels farts in rhyme
in lusts of sabbath
—hiccups—
—bowwows—
dusts off the mask of dada
cardboard horsehair leather wire cloth
wears dada collars dada boots
cothurnus of a bishop
lesbian sardines
ecstatic mice
vanilla derbies
from comers of Cabaret Voltaire
how many kings crow?
how many krazy kittens
cry for you?
how many centuries between
Zurich & Moinesti?
how many grandfathers?
how many clicks before the poem ends?
how much incesticide?
how many accordions to serenade
redheaded Leah?
belated
Lenin dies
brave gymnasts march again
thru workers' suburbs
Stalin's moustache adrift
—o feckless future—
writes Mandelstam:
"huge laughing
"cockroaches on his lip
"the glimmer of his boot-rims

"scum & chicken necks
"half human
"the executions slide across his tongue
"like berries
o revolutions of the fathers
you tease us back to death
pink sands of California
line my coast
saloons & oracles
stemming the tide
can't end it
you are dead
& dada life is growing
from your monocle
ignored exalted
you lead me to my future
making poems together
flames & tongues we write
like idiots
ballets of sperm
a brain song for the new machine
squadrons of princes pissing in the street
—intensity disgust—
an empty church from which
you drew the drapes back
the face of Jesus on each drape
"on each Jesus was my heart"
you wrote
messiah of stale loaves
of frogs in shoes
god dada
messiahs are passé
there is no greater savior
than this no eye
so credible
your fart that night was luminous
it stoked the cannons
thruout Europe
in the bus to Amsterdam
in Missouri in Brazil in the Antilles

in a bathrobe
under your bed the shadows massed
like sleeping robbers
the moon became our moon
again o moon
over Moinesti
o moon of tiny exiles
moustaches of antelopes we eat
& cry out “fire”
“water”
“avalanche”
a swamp of stars waits
toads squashed flat against
red bellies
at center of a dream
—magnetic eyes—
whose center is a center
& in the center
is another center
& in each center is a center
& a center on each center
centered
centering
composed by centers
like earth
the brain
the passage to other worlds
passage to something sad
lost dada
an old horse rotting in the garden
maneless waiting
for the full moon
someone leaps into the saddle
rushes after you
exuding light

HUNGER

1
the prisoners, committed to death
around the world
the squadrons of hungry ghosts almost like armies
that swarm up & down the streets
always behind your house
never in front
where the bright walls tell the world
"a happy giant lives here"
I would rather run away
no more terror & no more loss of memory
promises the guard
I tell him: I don't want any part of this
even if it's a dream—& it is—
in the blood the enzymes are the same
the prisoners are all marching & won't stop
until they lay you flat
until your eye—no longer focused on the road
no longer on the sign over the supermarket
illumination—flops on your cheek
the jaw at a cockeyed angle
away from your face, the skin
peculiar, pasty like a kind of earth
loose & crumbling
what will you become & what will we all become
before the time of the big change
the miracle?
the body is a remorseless institution
it escapes me though I respect it
greatly, though I equate it with this poem
another metaphor for death
the armies of the world have no respect
for flesh
        they run their wheels
over it, they crush it to shadows
with their wheels

2
the hunger of the rich man
knows no end
the man & the woman, both inscrutable
reduce the world's flesh to a sauce
& smear it over their wrists & thighs
& follow the delicious cracks of their bodies
trying to shove the substance in
a gibelotte done hunter style
the dead feet still thick with fur
the tongues torn from their cries
harbor the ghosts of tears
wild capers scrape the bourgeois flesh
the hunger of the man & woman
lords of hunger
gives a direction to their lives
they speak in French
the only language the bones understand
when they rub the femurs against each other's nipples
—hungry hungry—
when his own mouth over her cunt
feels the dead bone slip in
from his trembling fingers
this is how gods make love in graveyards
eating, sucking out their lives
the woman mother of the bones straddles
a throne of hungry beggars
hands reach out to her in death
they stroke her ribs
incite her, the man & woman
gather strength
under the shadow of an egg beater
a new vibrator, watching
"les viandes roties, the eloquence
"of slowly turning flesh
"contracting
"swelling
"fondled by repeated basting
"assumes a rich brown satin glaze
the hunger of the rich man

leaves him shrunken
because it doesn't end
he says "sweet momma," croons it
in the voice that made him famous
they eat each other's sex
then they eat the sex of others
they invent new hungers
hunger for power & for grass
hunger for sleep & badges
hunger for swollen sausages
hunger for swollen legs
hunger for the sounds of swollen children
hunger for omens
hunger for facades
hunger for kings
hunger for irreversible death
hunger for a monument to hunger
only the rich can still invent
they wait for future hungers
servants will spoon for them
they drive to funerals & spas
they leave crisp dollars on each other's plates
the hunger of the rich man
reaches for the moon
it breaks the world in half
& hands it
first to his bride, his love
they melt in tears
the band plays "satisfaction"
but they go on eating
"till the end of time"

PAIN

as a name to call the poem by
this is the fact of life   this rises
every time we move
this is the burden of the killers

see how they walk around
they find a pleasure in it

because what nature gives
isn't enough
the task of life is its enlargement

enlightenment is also pain

as love is

VIENNA BLOOD

1
like carnaval
for street & house
our action holds the place
between   the women
guard the door
no longer
they rush into the squares
& find
Vienna in the night
a jewless
hauptstadt city without
rime or grace
the others have survived in
alone   who stand
—friend Hakel—
muted cattle dumb
& lost
the darkness is their own
now   there is no one
can do again the thing
we did   the victim
dies
the mothers cannot
heal this birth
disorder of the town

where Hitler walked
he saw (sweet shadow) looming
the devil   Jew
my grandfather
this one could be
who scared him
shitless to Linz he ran
there buried
his face in the whipped cream
linzer
torts
his momma saved for him
& roamed
—o triumph of the will—
—disaster of the modern state—
the gentile's mind
is dumb & cruel
the song says
proven right

2
The Danube Waltz

I found a river
in Chicago
here I found one not
until the last day
on road to "airport"
saw it unwinding
saw it alongside
the left side
of the bus   how pale
& shy
thy houses
far from the architecture
built by empire
to its gods kings ministers of finance
waltzing
waltzing
in your grave

where is thy river
& thy woods
so old   like Jews
forever gone
we walk too among ghosts
the sounds of poetry
—ka ka—
the only music left us
arises still in Jandl's voice
a Jewish loaf still sold
at Neumarkt drowned out
still by waltzes
hokey
pokey
in shadow of thine arches
emperors have sat
the little cousins sit now
holding hands
the river (distant) waltzes on
to Budapest   between
thy left & right

3
the carnivals of middle
Europe blaze
the fetes bring
destroyers of a million worlds
to dance
by torchlight to punk rock
how heavy at night
their bodies are
& shine
their innocence is brutal
boots & belts
even the young ones wear
the artists
who carve crosses in their flesh
they lead us drunk
into Croatian bars
the German boy

sings Yiddish:
Reyzeleh
mine sheyneh
so jealous of
the suffering of others
must inflict their own

4
the liminal   he writes
or "place between"
& sees   suddenly
the terror of that situation
terror in glass
in camphor
the eye inside the eye
looks back
finding the place he shades off
is not himself
now is not
some other self
insistent
feels like shit
& wonders:
at edge of what dark city
will he stop?
what phantom turning
that dark edge
also will stop
& stop him?
or Blake
"the draught of violence
"that draws extinction in"
uncertainty: a zone
a fruitful chaos
& the sacred's what's inside
the frame
(but what's inside it
if the terror
isn't there?
or what's inside me

if I play the prince
in Nerval's tower
reading my poem in heart of
empty Europe
—luckless—
knowing too well these things
but hoping   like Artaud
"to break through language
"in order to touch life")
INSTRUCTIONS:
make a circle
around a tree
ring bells
cut sacred time out
live in it
a moment
doing everything
all senses
into play
be flexible
& playful
nothing fixed
but improvised
to name: all time all space
reversing roles
where all is open
—flowing—
the lights shades off
the darkness
not yet complete

5

for Victor Turner

communitas
(I meant to tell you)
is holy terror

A COMMENTARY ON VIENNA BLOOD

In August 1977 I spent a week outside Vienna, as one of two performance artists (Performance Garage director Richard Schechner was the other) at a Wenner-Gren Anthropological Foundation conference on "ritual & performance." The setting was an old castle—Burg Wartenstein—in a ruined tower of which I read & chanted poems: an atmosphere charged by Victor Turner ideas of "communitas" & "liminality" & by a sense of ghostly European histories, the shadow of Hitler's home town (Linz) nearby, etc. In Vienna I performed still more, thru friendly auspices of sound poet Ernst Jandl & others, & wandered, once in drunk procession with young artists/poets, thru that imperial but strangely voided city. Conversation with one Herman Hakel—a Jewish survivor—raised further phantoms & horrors that colored the rest of the Vienna visit & even the next week spent in still vigorous Paris (including the French C. P.'s huge Fête d'Humanité plus punk rock contexts everywhere). Vienna stuck in my mind along with that title out of Johann Strauss's *Wienerblut*, etc.

THE CHICAGO POEM

for Ted Berrigan & Alice Notley

the bridges of Chicago
are not the bridges of Paris
or the bridges of Amsterdam
except they are a definition
almost no one bothers to define
like life full of surprises
in what now looks to be the oldest
modern American city
o apparition of the movie version of
the future circa 1931
the bridges soon filled with moving lines
of people workers' armies
in the darkness of first December visit
along the water
bend of the Chicago River
the cliffs of architecture like palisades
at night the stars in windows

stars in the poem you wrote a sky
through which the el train pulls its lights
in New York streets of childhood
is like a necklace (necktie) in the language of
old poems old memories
old Fritz Lang visions of the night before
the revolution the poor souls
of working people we all love
fathers or uncles
lost to us in dreams & gauze
of intervening 1960s
there are whole tribes of Indians
somewhere inhabiting
a tunnel paradise
they will wait it out still
with a perfect assurance of things to come
everyone so well read in old novels
maybe the economics of disaster Ted
depressions of the spirit
so unlike the bright promise of
the early years
gloss of the young life easing death
atop a hill in Lawrence Kansas
the afternoon sky became aluminum
(illumination)
played on a tambourine to calm
the serpent fear
the material corpse that leaves us vulnerable
everyone will come to it I think
I do not think you dig it
getting so out of hand so far away
but we remain & I will
make another visit soon
hope we can take a walk
together it is night & we are
not so bad off have turned forty
like poets happy with our sadness
we are still humans in a city overhung
with ancient bridges
you pop your pill I laugh

look back upon the future of
America & remember
when we both wrote our famous poems called
Modern Times

SEEDINGS

for Robert Duncan

I was given a poem in the dream … a poem I read out loud … where I could feel the words coming in bursts but couldn't salvage them … I only knew the poem's name was "seedings" & that it followed after a performance of "cokboy" in which I had to improvise the final lines, unable to remember what they were … Between poems I made a comment about Duncan's peculiar way of reading, knowing he was dead but seeing him sitting in the audience & nodding at me when I started reading.

1
Now in the dream
I read aloud
the poem of seedings,
like the last time I saw you,
& how it opens me
to further words, new
definitions,
as I see you sitting there,
old friend,
alive, to hear my stammer
like your own,
that mark of poetry upon
each poet's tongue,
I call the listeners to hear
in us, while laughing,
crying,
at some other poem I read before,
obsessive words
we all can nod our heads to,
but I could not find
the ending,

not for all the years of reading it
aloud, & heard somebody say
—not you but somebody—
time is the thief of language
(meaning tongues)
like that the cat gets hold of

2
shadow of George Oppen,
having lost
his words, the shadow of a poet
he'd become,
or Blackburn speaking of it
first: I've lost
my verbs & nouns,
my alphabets
& birthdays,
who am no kind of man without
those seedings,
sparks,
the pain obliterating all
or else the mind
retreating from itself,
like Williams in his old age
—& no flight of small
cheeping birds—
but "No . my hands
are tongue-tied . You have . . . made
a record in my heart
                                                  Goodbye."
(Blackburn records it)
or my mother or my brother looking
much like you did, Paul,
the mouth become a hole
the language jammed into our cavities
—cancer aphasia alzheimers—
the poets punished for their poetry,
sharing their punishment with other beings
or what happens
simply

when the mind & body—little
sad machine—
starts shutting down

3
the cat is death,
the thief of language,
meaning tongues,
enough to construct a mythos on
at last old male cat
comes in thru his window
to talk to him
although it finds him voiceless,
waving kindly to my son
who stands outside
—hi, Paul—
the tape is turning, sends
my own voice back to me
he must have placed with care
there on the reel
to mark our visit—
& this was twenty years ago
& more now a time no cat
could possibly survive
during which time the deaths have come
increasingly,
reality by that thrown back
into the cat's mind,
where all reality resides
till death disrupts it
& erases world & time at once
your time & mine, Paul,
as it erases words,
stares out at you
so big it trembles
on your screen,
ascends your vertebrae,
gone into dust by now,
poor spook,
our voices on the tape

already gone for you
although you labored to engrave it,
lugging that big old box around
—from reel to reel
to still more real—
when there was a world to live in
& the words to know it by
quickly came into mind & hand,
remember?
—no   there is no memory
among the dead
& even when you write them down
it isn't I who speak
these words but you
& only for a time

4

Write a poem for the dead & leave a place for all the dead to enter. … Consider their words as seeds or treat the dead themselves as seeds … & see a cat's face as the face of death. … Go into the cat's mind … an apotheosis of Cat. … Directive: since the cat is living there, attend to how it stalks, the way it moves through space & time.

but death abolishes
all space & time—
like Gertrude's Oakland,
like the cat's mind,
where no there is
& the world appears as constant pulses,
present running into present
only   void of past
& future
so the cat becomes a number
lying on its side,
the cat becomes a distant echo,
one who vanishes
without a word,
the ocean convulsing to the sound of cat,

the way the world convulsed
& dreamt itself,
the dream became our lives,
by which we marked the world's
beginnings & will mark
its end so simple
that there is no world to prove
beyond us as the cat's world
ends when cat goes
into death, takes with it
what must be memory of garden,
crooked stems & whiteveined lilies
on black stalks,
& does the poem exist
when there is no one there
to hear it,
when the poet's throat is emptied
of his verbs & nouns,
lost brother walking on
some lonely ridge
discharging
holy tears,
too far into his death
to call it back
the birds around him in the thousands,
the gulls above the bridge
so many cries such fast desires,
cold birds outside his window
his own skin at the world's edge,
crying for his gods
/ October almost
5 in the afternoon
the words so easily disposed
between myself & you
that I would quote us into life
dear Paul would trust
the rest to follow
shortly, into life

5

a poem of seedings,
in the traces of

others who have gone before,
from life to life,
those tied to us as friends or kin
we look for in the empty field
& wonder   where
or in what form
they vanished
who were here just yesterday,
still in the mind
we set a place for them,
a house with swollen rooms
& in each room
a solitary dreamer
sits there   face obscured
by sunlight
Is this your mother?
someone asks
or she who took her own life
twice   the first dose
not enough
so that she woke up laughing
in her bitterness   or she
whose father drove her
to her death,
the poet who survived her
shaken, broken
& the other poet's wife,
also so young,
whose photographs surround the room
where I once stayed,
still stay in memory but
feel it
disappearing too
or dwindling
cut & broken in

reverse
aphasia
until we can make a covenant
with death   we let it
follow us
the walls come tumbling down,
leaving no margin for
our distant lives

6 DEATH THOUGHTS

[i]
While Thinking of Those Already Dead

since the world was different when they died,
how would they recognize it now?
it is for this reason that it is better that the dead
stay dead   their confusion would only alarm us
who remain alive & sometimes have to think
about the dead & what to say to them
to set things straight

[ii]
Eternal Question

I wonder sometimes what the last word will be
spoken or heard before I die,
& I feel a great sadness not to know it
in advance, or ever know it

[iii]
Illusion

if there is nothing after death,
then there was nothing before death,
& life is the greatest illusion after all,
the way you fell for it
& I did,
nothing will be left behind us when we die

7

o these are wounds of love
these precious eyes

those who have lived a life of poetry
will die
                                             & meet the poets
it will be five o'clock
the blanket on the bed will fall away
the fat man will absorb the shock
love brings him   & now
unlike the others in the tunnel
he will forget to crouch
forget the dead who stand before him
blow their words like knives
over his head   beware   beware
the car door opens & a relentless squad
enters the imagination
in which   as in a sylvan clearing
poets mill around a thorn bush
for those who lived a life of poetry
to stare upon   to take the hands of
in their own & touch with lips
so dark the sun can barely reach them
old friends gone beforehand
let me call them one last time
by name by seeding them
into the poem its body dark with soil
among whom a new fellow comes
the lately fallen ghost
who took her own life   fell
until no sky remained between
the soil & her
depression of the spirit raging
like the hungry ghost
inside her   throws her down
bones throbbing
makes her feel her tongue
jammed down her throat
hermaphroditic in the shadow of

the phallic altar
there is god (she says) & man
& there are monsters
leading the way to death among the friends
who wait her presence
those who have lived a life of poetry
whom we will only see once
in that final moment when we join them
before the chill sets in
the bliss of language lost to us
forever   drifting
like mindless phantoms
empty voices
without our verbs & nouns

From *KHURBN*

Pre-Face To *Khurbn*

In 1987 I was a decade, more, past *Poland/1931*. I went to Poland for the first time & to the small town, Ostrow-Mazowiecka, sixty miles northeast of Warsaw, from which my parents had come in 1920. The town was there and the street, Miodowa (meaning "honey"), where my father's parents had a bakery. I hadn't realized that the town was only fifteen miles from Treblinka, but when we went there (as we had to), there was only an empty field & the thousands of large stones that make up the memorial. We were the only ones there except for a group of three people—another family perhaps—who seemed to be picnicking at the side. This was in sharp contrast to the crowds of tourists at Auschwitz (Oswiecim / Oshviet-sim) & to the fullness of the other Poland I had once imagined. The absence of the living seemed to create a vacuum in which the dead—the dibbiks who had died before their time—were free to speak. It wasn't the first time that I thought of poetry as the language of the dead, but never so powerfully as now. Those in my own family had died without a trace—with one exception: an uncle who had gone to the woods with a group of Jewish partisans and who, when he heard that his wife and children were murdered at Treblinka, drank himself blind in a deserted cellar & blew his brains out. That, anyway, was how the story had come back to us, a long time before I had ever heard a word like holocaust. It was a word with which I never felt comfortable: too Christian & too beautiful, too much smacking of a "sacrifice" I didn't & still don't understand. The word with which we spoke of it was the Yiddish-Hebrew word, *khurbn* [*khurban*], & it was this word that was with me all the time we stayed in Poland. When I was writing *Poland/1931*, at a great distance from the place, I decided deliberately that that was not to be a poem about the "holocaust." There was a reason for that, I think, as there is now for allowing my uncle's khurbn to speak through me. The poems that I first began to hear at Treblinka are the clearest message I have ever gotten about why I write poetry. They are an answer also to the proposition—raised by Adorno & others—that poetry cannot or should not be written after Auschwitz. Our search since then has been for the origins of poetry, not only as a willful desire to wipe the slate clean but as a recognition of those other voices & the scraps of poems they left behind them in the mud.

In The Dark Word, Khurbn

all their lights went out
their words were silences,
memories
drifting along the horse roads
onto malkiner street

a disaster in the mother's tongue
her words emptied
by speaking

returning to a single word
the child word
spoken, redeyed on
the frozen pond

was how they spoke it,
how I would take it from your voice
& cradle it

that ancient & dark word

those who spoke it in the old days
now held their tongues

Dos Oysleydikn (The Emptying)

at honey street in ostrova
where did the honey people go?
empty   empty
miodowa empty
empty bakery & empty road to warsaw
yellow wooden houses & houses plastered up with stucco
the shadow of an empty name still on their doors
shadai & shadow shattering the mother tongue
the mother's tongue but empty
the way the streets are empty where we walk
pushing past crowds of children
old women airing themselves outside the city hall
old farmers riding empty carts down empty roads
who don't dispel but make an emptiness
a taste of empty honey
empty rolls you push your fingers through
empty sorrel soup dribbling from their empty mouths
defining some other poland
lost to us the way the moon
is lost to us
sorrel in gardens mother of god at roadsides
in the reflection of the empty trains
only the cattle bellow in
like jews the dew-eyed wanderers
still present   still the flies
cover their eyeballs
the trains drive eastward, falling
down a hole (a holocaust) of empty houses

of empty ladders leaning against haystacks no one climbs
empty ostrova & empty ostrolenka
old houses empty in the woods near vyzhkov
dachas the peasants would rent to you
& sleep in stables
the bialo forest spreading to every side
retreating the closer we come to it to claim it
empty oaks & empty fir trees
a man in an empty ditch who reads a book
the way the jews once read
in the cold polish light   the fathers sat there too
the mothers posed at the woods' edge
the road led brightly to treblinka
& other towns   beaches at brok
along the bug
marshes with cat tails
cows tied to trees
past which their ghosts walk
their ghosts refuse to walk
tomorrow in empty fields of poland
still cold against their feet
an empty pump black water drips from
will form a hill of ice
the porters will dissolve with burning sticks
they will find a babe's face at the bottom
invisible & frozen imprinted in the rock

Dos Geshray (The Scream)

Erd, zolst nit tsudekn mayn blut un zol nit kayn ort zayn far mayn geshray
(Job 16.18)

"practice your scream" I said
(why did I say it?)
because it was his scream & wasn't my own
it hovered between us   bright
to our senses always bright it held
the center place

then somebody else came up & stared
deep in his eyes there found a memory
of horses galloping faster the wheels dyed red
behind them   the poles had reserved
a feast day but the jew
locked in his closet screamed
into his vest a scream
that had no sound therefore
spiraled around the world
so wild that it shattered stones
it made the shoes piled in the doorway
scatter their nails   things testify
—the law declares it—
shoes & those dearer objects
like hair & teeth do
by their presence
I cannot say that they share the pain
or show it not even the photos
in which the expressions of the dead shine forth
the crutches by their mass the prosthetic limbs by theirs
bear witness the eyeglasses bear witness
the suitcases the children's shoes the german tourists
in the stage set oshvietsim had become
the letters over its gates still glowing
still writ large
ARBEIT MACHT FREI
& to the side   HOTEL
and GASTRONOMIC BAR
the spirit of the place dissolving
indifferent to his presence
there with the other ghosts
the uncle   grieving
his eyelids turning brown an eye
protruding from his rump
this man whose body
is a crab's
his gut turned outward
the pink flesh of his children
hanging from him
that his knees slide up against

there is no holocaust
for these   but khurbn only
the word still spoken by the dead
who say   my khurbn
& my children's khurbn
it is the only word that the poem allows
because it is their own
the word as prelude to the scream
it enters
through the asshole
circles along the gut
into the throat
& breaks out
in a cry   a scream
it is his scream that shakes me
weeping   in oshvietsim
& that allows the poem to come

Dibbukim (Dibbiks)

spirits of the dead   lights
flickering (he said) their ruakh
will never leave the earth
instead they crowd the forests the fields
around the privies the hapless spirits
wait millions of souls
turned into ghosts at once
the air is full of them
they are standing each one beside a tree
under its shadows or the moon's
but they cast no shadows of their own
this moment & the next they are pretending
to be rocks   but who is fooled
who is fooled here   by the dead   the jews
the gypsies   the leadeyed polish patriot
living beings reduced to symbols
of what it had been to be alive
"o do not touch them" the mother cries
fitful, as almost in a dream

she draws the child's hand to her heart
in terror   but the innocent dead
grow furious they break down doors
drop slime onto your tables
they tear their tongues out by the roots
& smear your lamps your children's lips
with blood a hole drilled in the wall
will not deter them
from stolen homes stone architectures
they hate they are the convoys of the dead
the ghostly drivers still searching
the roads to malkin   ghost carts overturned
ghost autos in blue ditches
if only our eyes were wild enough
to see them our hearts to know their terror
the terror of the man who walks alone
their victim whose house whose skin
they crawl in   incubus & succubus
a dibbik leaping from a cow to lodge inside
his throat   clusters of jews
who swarm here mothers without hair
blackbearded fathers
they lap up fire   water   slime
entangle the hairs of brides
or mourn their clothing hovering
over a field of rags   half-rotted shoes
& tablecloths   old thermos bottles   rings
lost tribes in empty synagogues
at night their voices
carrying across the fields
to rot your kasha your barley
stricken beneath their acid rains
no holocaust because no sacrifice
no sacrifice to give the lie
of meaning   & no meaning   after auschwitz
there is only poetry   no hope
no other language left to heal
no language   & no faces
because no faces left   no names
no sudden recognitions on the street

only the dead still swarming   only khurbn
a dead man in a rabbi's clothes
who squats   outside the mortuary house
who guards their privies who is called
master of shit   an old alarm clock
hung around his neck   who holds
a wreathe of leaves under his nose
from eden   "to drive out
"the stinking odor of this world"

Der Gilgul (The Possessed)

1
he picks a coin up
from the ground

it burns his hand
like ashes it is red

& marks him as it marks
the others   hidden

he is hidden in the forest
in a world of nails

his dibbik fills him

2
Each night another one would hang himself. Airless boxcars. Kaddish. "What will they do with us?" The brown & black spot on their bellies. So many clothes. The field was littered. Ten thousand corpses in one place. Arranged in layers. I am moving down the field from right to left—reversing myself at every step. The ground approaches. Money. And still his greatest fear was that he would lose his shoes.

3
earth, growing fat with
the slime of corpses   green & pink

that ooze like treacle, turn
into a kind of tallow

that are black
at evening   that absorb

all light

Nokh Aushvits (After Auschwitz)

the poem is ugly & they make it uglier
wherein the power resides
that duncan did—or didn't—understand
when listening that evening to the other poet read
he said   "that was pure ugliness"   & oh it was
it was   & it made my heart skip a beat
because the poem wouldn't allow it   no
not a moment's grace nor beauty to obstruct
whatever the age demanded   or the poem
shit poured on wall & floor
sex shredded   genitals torn loose by dog claws
& the ugliness that you were to suffer
later   that they had suffered
not as dante dreamed it but in the funnel
they ran through & that the others called
the road to heaven   little hills & holes now
& beneath   upon   among them
broken mirrors kettles pans enameled tea pots
the braided candlesticks of sabbath
prayershawl scraps & scraps of bodies   bones
his child's   he said   leaping
into the mud the pool of bones
& slime   the frail limbs separating
each time he pulls at one   the mystery of body
not a mystery   bodies naked   then bodies
boned & rotten   how he must fight
his rage for beauty must make a poem
so ugly it can drive out the other voices

like artaud's squawk the poem addressed
to ugliness   must resist
even the artistry of death   a stage set
at treblinka   ticket windows   a large clock
the signs that read: change for bialystok
but the man cries who has seen
the piles of clothing   jews
it is not good it is your own sad meat
that hangs here   poor & bagged   like animals
the blood coagulated into a jell
an armpit through which a ventricle has burst
& left him dangling screaming
a raw prong stuck through his tongue
another through his scrotal sac   he sees
a mouth   a hole   a red hole
the scarlet remnants of the children's flesh
their eyes like frozen baby scallops
so succulent that the blond ukrainian guard
sulking beneath his parasol leaps up
& sucks them inward past his iron teeth
& down his gullet, shitting
globules of fat & shit
that trickle down the pit in which the victim—
the girl without a tongue—stares up
& reads her final heartbreak

Di Toyte Kloles (The Maledictions)

Let the dead man call out in you because he is a dead man
Let him look at your hands in the light that filters through the table where he sits
Let him tell you what he thinks & let your throat gag on his voice
Let his words be the poem & the poem be what you wouldn't say yourself
Let him say that every man is a murderer & that he is a murderer like all the rest
Let him say that he would like to beat & kill beat & kill let him say that it is nothing nothing nothing

That he is living in a wilderness (let him say it) but that there are no woods or trees
That whatever houses there were are gone or if the houses are there he cannot enter them or see them
That he cannot see the children that he knows were there that he doesn't know if his own children were there too
That he seeks out the children of his enemy & would like to kill them
Let those who sit around you hear nothing of what he says let them hear everything of what you tell them
Let a great pain come up into your legs (feel it moving like the earth moving beneath you)
Let the earth drop away inside your belly falling falling until you're left in space
Let his scream follow you across the millennia back to your table
Let a worm the size of a small coin come out of the table where you're sitting
Let it be covered with the red mucus falling from his nose (but only you will see it)
Let the holes in his body drop open let his excretions pour out across the room
Let it flood the bottoms of the women's cages let it drip through the cracks into the faces of the women down below
Let him scream in a language you cannot understand let the word "khurbn" come at the end of every phrase
Let a picture begin to form with every scream
Let the screams tell you that the world was formed in darkness that it ends in darkness
Let the screams take you into a room with small white tiles
Let the tiles vanish beneath the press of bodies let vomit & shit be everywhere let semen & menstrual blood run down his arms
Let his screams describe a body (a body is like a stone a body rests on another body & weighs it down a body crushes the skull that lies beneath it a body has arms & reaches for the sky a body has eyes & knows terror in the darkness a body burning gives off heat & light)
Let 10,000 bodies be gathered in one place until they vanish let the earth & sky vanish with them & then return
Let an empty field fill up with coins & let the living bend to pick them up
Let everything have its price let there be a price for death & a price for life so that everything can be accounted

Let them account the value of a body (a soul has no account) & let the living refuse the living unless a price is paid
Let betrayal take the place of love & let disgust be put ahead of beauty
Let she who is most beautiful be brought down to her knees let those who hold together out of love be murdered
Let the dead cry for the destruction of the living until there is no more death & no more life
Let a ghost in the field put out the light of the sun (I have no arms he cries
My face & half my body have vanished & am I still alive?
But the movement of my soul through space & time brings me inside you
The immeasurable part of a language is what we speak he says who am I? dayn mamas bruder farshvunden in dem khurbn un muz in mayn eygenem loshn redn loz mikh es redn durkh dir dos vort khurbn
Mayne oygen zaynen blind fun mayn khurbn ikh bin yetst a peyger) a corpse to which the light will not return forever for whom the light is lost
Let the light be lost & the voices cry forever in the dark & let them know no joy in it
Let murders multiply & tortures let fields rot & forests shrink let children dig up bones under the market square
Let fools wield power let saints & martyrs root up money in a field of blood
Let madness be the highest virtue let rage choke all who will not rage
Let children murder children let bombs rain down let houses fall
Let ghosts & dibbiks overwhelm the living
Let the invisible overwhelm the visible until nothing more is seen or heard

PERORATION FOR A LOST TOWN

[May 1988]: *"On this road thou camest…"*

1
What will I tell you sweet town?
that the sickness is still in you
that the dead continue to die
there is no end to the dying?
for this the departed would have had an answer:

a wedding in a graveyard
for you sweet town
they would have spoken they who are no longer among us
& would have shown forth in their splendor
would have danced pellmell
over your stones sweet town
the living & the dead together   pebbles
would have dropped like pebbles
from their fingers   no   like gold   like roses
like every corny proposition
fathers or uncles ever gave us   they gave us
to call your image back to life
sweet town their voices twittering
like bats over your little houses
is this the sound then that the breath makes
in its final gasp that the dead make
having lived a whole life under water
now coming up for air, to find themselves
in poland in the empty field
bathers who had their bodies torn apart
& ran from you   their long guts
hanging, searching the forgotten woods
for houses & the consolation
that death brings   children in a circle
dancing   without tongues   the meadow that had once stood open
shut in remembrance now sweet town
the screams of the cousins carried by the wind
lost in the gentile cities
in the old men's dreams of you
each night sweet town who rise up from their beds
like children   bellowing   their words
stuck in their beards like honey
who drift up brok street past the russian church
the doctor's house beside it heavy
& whitebricked in the dream   who glide above
napoleon square o little orchards little park
where lovers once walked with lovers   children
still capture fishes in thy little pond
its surfaces still green with algae
o sounds of church bells—bimbom—through the frozen air

that call forth death o death o pale photographer
o photos of the sweet town rubbed with blood
o of its streets the photographs its vanished folk
o wanderers who wandered o bodies of the distant dead who stayed
o faces o dimming images lost smiles o girls embracing girls
in deathless photographs   o life receding
into images of life   you beautiful & pure   sweet town
I summon & I summon thee to answer

2

I have come here looking for the bone of my grandfather (I said). Daylight had intervened. The town was no more empty as we walked its length. Then the old man spat—gently—through his beard. I have come here looking for the bone of my son. (Had someone reported a breath of life under his houses—a movement within the soil like worms & caterpillars?) Tell the Poles that they should come to me. I am a baker & a child. I have no one to take me from this darkness.

Then he asked—or was it I who asked *for* him?—were there once Jews here? Yes, they told us, yes they were sure there were, though there was no one here who could remember. What was a Jew like? they asked. (The eye torn from its socket hung against his cheek.) Did he have hair like this? they asked. How did he talk—or did he? Was a Jew tall or short? In what ways did he celebrate the Lord's day? (A rancid smell of scorched flesh choked us.) Is it true that Jews come sometimes in the night & spoil the cows' milk? Some of us have seen them in the meadows—beyond the pond. Long gowns they wear & have no faces. Their women have sharppointed breasts with large black hairs around the nipples. At night they weep. (Heads forced in the bowls until their faces ran with excrement.) No one is certain still if they exist. (Plants frozen at the bottom of a lake, its surface covered by thick ice.)

They spoke & paused. Spoke & paused again. If there was a history they couldn't find it—or a map. The cemetery they knew was gone, the dead dispersed. (On summer days the children digging in the marketplace might come across a bone.) And the shops? we asked. The stalls? The honey people? Vanished, vanished in the earth, they said. The red names & the flower names. The pink names. (There was a people once, they said, we called the old believers. A people with black beards & eyes like shriveled raisins. Out of the earth they came & lived among us. When they walked their bodies bent like yours & scraped the ground. They had six fingers on each hand. Their old men had the touch of women when we rubbed against them. One day they dug a hole and went back into the earth. They live there to this day.)

The village pump you spoke about still stands back of the city hall (they told us). The rest was all a dream.

3
[by gematria]

a wheel
dyed red

an apparition
set apart

out of the furnace

Ostrov-Mazovietsk
Poland/1988

A BOOK OF EXTENSIONS

I prefer a poem with spaces
to a block of prose.
I do not mention roses. (G. Stein)
The thrill of climbing
makes me wring my hands
in glee.
You see me
& you
look away.
You ask me to be cautious.
I can reply to you
if time allows
if not I can stand still.

From SONGS FROM THE SOCIETY OF THE MYSTIC ANIMALS

with Richard Johnny John

	H E H E H H E H
	H E H E H H E H
The animals are coming	H E H **U H** H E H
	H E H E H H E H
	H E H E H H E H
	H E H E H H E H
	H E H E H H E H
The doings were beginning	H E H **U H** H E H
	H E H E H H E H
	H E H E H H E H

A Song Of My Song, In Three Parts

It's off in the distance.

•

It came into the room.

•

It's here in the circle.

Hey When I Sing This Set Of 4 Songs Look What Happens!

hey when I sing
hey it can help her
yeah it can yeah it's so strong
hey when I sing
hey it can raise her
yeah it can yeah it's so strong
hey when I sing
hey her arm gets straighter

yeah it can yeah it's so strong
hey when I sing
hey her body gets straighter
yeah it can yeah it's so strong

hiiiiiiiiiiiiiiiiiiiiiiiiiiiiiiiiiiiiiiiiiiiiiiiiiiiiiiiiih
e THREE WAYS TO SCREW UP e
e ON YOUR WAY TO THE DOINGS e
e THREE WAYS e
hiiiiiiiiiiiiiiiiiiiiiiiiiiiiiiiiiiiiiiiiiiiiiiiiiiiiiiiiiih

(1)

I fell down.

(2)

I got lost.

(3)

I lost my bucket.

WHERE THE SONG WENT WHERE SHE WENT & WHAT HAPPENED WHEN THEY MET

the song went to the garden (heh heh heh)
the song poked all around the garden (heh heh heh)
she went to the garden (heh heh heh)
she went to the garden (heh heh heh)
she went like crazy in the garden (heh heh heh)
that's where she went (hah hah hah)

A Song About A Dead Person—Or Was It A Mole?

YOHOHEYHEYEYHEYHAHYEYEYHAHHEH
g thru the big earth
YOHOHEYHEYEYHEYHAHYEYEYHAHHEH
I went thru this b
YOHOHEYHEYEYHEYHAHYEYEYHAHHEH
I was going thru the big earth
YOHOHEYHEYEYHEYHAHYEYEYHAHHEH
I went thru this big earth
YOHOHEYHEYEYHEYHAHYEYEYHAHHEH
I was going thru the big ea
YOHOHEYHEYEYHEYHAHYEYEYHAHHEH
I went thru this big earth
YOHOHEYHEYEYHEYHAHYEYEYHAHHEH
I
YOHOHEYHEYEYHEYHAHYEYEYHAHHEH

YOHOHEYHEYEYHEYHAHYEYEYHAHHEH

YOHOHEYHEYEYHEYHAHYEYEYHAHHEH

YOHOHEYHEYEYHEYHAHYEYEYHAHHEH

"TWO SONGS ABOUT A DEAD PERSON OR A MOLE—WHICHEVER IT WAS"

A Mystic Animals Extension

with Richard Johnny John and Ian Tyson

```
YOHOHEYHEYEYHEYHAHYEYEYHAHHEHYOHOHEYHEYEYHEYHAHYEYEYHAHHEHYOHOHEYHEYEYHEYHAHYEYEYHAHHEH
IOWASEGOINGYTHRUATHEYBIGAEARTHOHOHEYHEYEYHEYHAHYEYEYHAHHEHYOHOHEYHEYEYHEYHAHYEYEYHAHHEH
YOHOHEYHEYEYHEYHAHYEYEYHAHHEHYOHOHEYHEYEYHEYHAHYEYEYHAHHEHYOHOHEYHEYEYHEYHAHYEYEYHAHHEH
YOHOHEYHEYEYHEYHAHYEYEYHAHHEHYOHOHEYHEYEYHEYHAHYEYEYHAHHEHIOWENTYTHRUYTHISABIGYEARTHHEH
YOHOHEYHEYEYHEYHAHYEYEYHAHHEHYOHOHEYHEYEYHEYHAHYEYEYHAHHEHYOHOHEYHEYEYHEYHAHYEYEYHAHHEH
YOHOHEYHEYEYHEYHAHYEYEYHAHHEIYWASHGOINGETHRUHTHEEBIGHEARTHYOHOHEYHEYEYHEYHAHYEYEYHAHHEH
YOHOHEYHEYEYHEYHAHYEYEYHAHHEHYOHOHEYHEYEYHEYHAHYEYEYHAHHEHYOHOHEYHEYEYHEYHAHYEYEYHAHHEH
YOHOHEYHEYEYHEYHAHYEYEYHAHHEHYOHOHEYHEYIYWENTATHRUETHISHBIGOEARTHHEYEYHEYHAHYEYEYHAHHEH
YOHOHEYHEYEYHEYHAHYEYEYHAHHEHYOHOHEYHEYEYHEYHAHYEYEYHAHHEHYOHOHEYHEYEYHEYHAHYEYEYHAHHEH
YOHOHEYHEYEYHEYHAHYEYEYHAHHEHYOHOHEYHEYEYHEYHAHYEYEYHAHHEIYWASHGOINGETHRUHTHEEBIGHEARTH
YOHOHEYHEYEYHEYHAHYEYEYHAHHEHYOHOHEYHEYEYHEYHAHYEYEYHAHHEHYOHOHEYHEYEYHEYHAHYEYEYHAHHEH
YOHOHEYHEYEYHIYWENTETHRUATHISYBIGHEARTHEYHEYHAHYEYEYHAHHEHYOHOHEYHEYEYHEYHAHYEYEYHAHHEH
YOHOHEYHEYEYHEYHAHYEYEYHAHHEHYOHOHEYHEYEYHEYHAHYEYEYHAHHEHYOHOHEYHEYEYHEYHAHYEYEYHAHHEH
YOHOHEYHEYEYHEYHAHYEYEYHAHHEHYOHOHEYHEYEYHEYHAHYEYEYHAHHEHYOHOHEYHEYEYHEYHAHYEYIYWASHGO
YOHOHEYHEYEYHEYHAHYEYEYHAHHEHYOHOHEYHEYEYHEYHAHYEYEYHAHHEHYOHOHEYHEYEYHEYHAHYEYEYHAHHEH
THHOHEYHEYEYHEYHAHYEYEYHAHHEHYOHOHEYHEYEYHEYHAHYEYEYHAHHEHYOHOHEYHEYEYHEYHAHYEYEYHAHHEH
YOHOHEYHEYEYHEYHAHYEYEYHAHHEHYOHOHEYHEYEYHEYHAHYEYEYHAHHEHYOHOHEYHEYEYHEYHAHYEYEYHAHHEH
```

```
YOHOHEYHEYEYHEYHAHYEYEYHAHHEHYOHOHEYHEYEYHEYHAHYEYEYHAHHEHYOHOHEYHEYEYHEYHAHYEYEYHAHHEH
IOWASEGOINGYTHRUATHEYBIGASMOKEOHOHEYHEYEYHEYHAHYEYEYHAHHEHYOHOHEYHEYEYHEYHAHYEYEYHAHHEH
YOHOHEYHEYEYHEYHAHYEYEYHAHHEHYOHOHEYHEYEYHEYHAHYEYEYHAHHEHYOHOHEYHEYEYHEYHAHYEYEYHAHHEH
YOHOHEYHEYEYHEYHAHYEYEYHAHHEHYOHOHEYHEYEYHEYHAHYEYEYHAHHEHIOWENTYTHRUYTHISABIGYSMOKEHEH
YOHOHEYHEYEYHEYHAHYEYEYHAHHEHYOHOHEYHEYEYHEYHAHYEYEYHAHHEHYOHOHEYHEYEYHEYHAHYEYEYHAHHEH
YOHOHEYHEYEYHEYHAHYEYEYHAHHEHYIHWASYGOINGHTHRUHTHEEBIGHSMOKEHOHEYHEYEYHEYHAHYEYEYHAHHEH
YOHOHEYHEYEYHEYHAHYEYEYHAHHEHYOHOHEYHEYEYHEYHAHYEYEYHAHHEHYOHOHEYHEYEYHEYHAHYEYEYHAHHEH
YOHOHEYHEYEYHEYHAHYEYEYHAHHEHYOHOHEYHEYEYHIYWENTETHRUATHISYBIGHSMOKEEYHEYHAHYEYEYHAHHEH
YOHOHEYHEYEYHEYHAHYEYEYHAHHEHYOHOHEYHEYEYHEYHAHYEYEYHAHHEHYOHOHEYHEYEYHEYHAHYEYEYHAHHEH
YOHOHEYHEYEYHEYHAHYEYEYHAHHEHYOHOHEYHEYEYHEYHAHYEYEYHAHHEIYWASHGOINGETHRUHTHEEBIGHSMOKE
YOHOHEYHEYEYHEYHAHYEYEYHAHHEHYOHOHEYHEYEYHEYHAHYEYEYHAHHEHYOHOHEYHEYEYHEYHAHYEYEYHAHHEH
YOHOHEYHEYEYHIYWENTETHRUATHISYBIGHSMOKEEYHEYHAHYEYEYHAHHEHYOHOHEYHEYEYHEYHAHYEYEYHAHHEH
YOHOHEYHEYEYHEYHAHYEYEYHAHHEHYOHOHEYHEYEYHEYHAHYEYEYHAHHEHYOHOHEYHEYEYHEYHAHYEYEYHAHHEH
YOHOHEYHEYEYHEYHAHYEYEYHAHHEHYOHOHEYHEYEYHEYHAHYEYEYHAHHEHYOHOHEYHEYEYHEYIAWASYGOINGHGO
YOHOHEYHEYEYHEYHAHYEYEYHAHHEHYOHOHEYHEYEYHEYHAHYEYEYHAHHEHYOHOHEYHEYEYHEYHAHYEYEYHAHHEH
KEHOHEYHEYEYHEYHAHYEYEYHAHHEHYOHOHEYHEYEYHEYHAHYEYEYHAHHEHYOHOHEYHEYEYHEYHAHYEYEYHAHHEH
YOHOHEYHEYEYHEYHAHYEYEYHAHHEHYOHOHEYHEYEYHEYHAHYEYEYHAHHEHYOHOHEYHEYEYHEYHAHYEYEYHAHHEH
```

THE DIRECTIONS

with Tom Phillips

From THE BURNING BABE

with Susan Bee

"A BABE SITS PLACIDLY IN SCHWITTERS' BAU"

....

a babe sits placidly in schwitters' bau
now burnt but saved in memory
the center of a column
that his german hands sealed up
& makes me think
of dolls & dwarfs small metal cars
from childhood buttoned shoes
that fit imperfectly a walk between
high walls of buildings painted white
& nowhere have I seen
a door or found a street to turn into
escaping from the stillness of the moment
as if death wasn't an option
but a fact my mind had never entertained
till now the babe arisen looming up
then crawling where a gang of babes waits
where they fill the air with apples
thrown against the sky the devil in the details
hitting the old mother topsyturvy
in her falling down o ravissement o subterfuge
& lost in wonder a belief that time is endless
that we follow in its tracks like children
bound never to reach the place where nuns & bishops

dance to strains of monk & satie
where the taste of warm beer
fills their mouths & ours
cigarettes aglow in lost cafes
in flow of talk so rapid that the mind
grows numb the father pulls a dove
out of his hat a stick & water glass beside it
& the sky as slick as silver fills with doves
the babe with swollen head can wave at
making some stop cold
& drop to earth the plumage at their necks
once white now red with blood

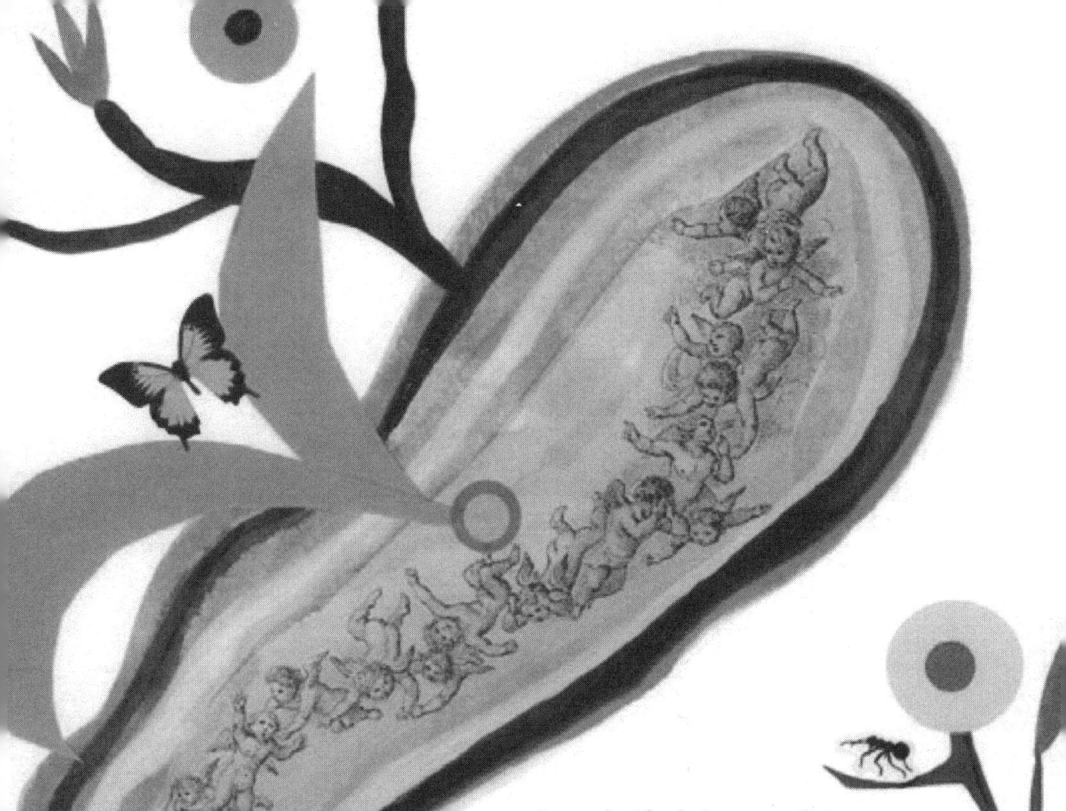

& ants inside their eyes a silent army
like all armies massed for murder
& the ball that rolls across the square
finds no one there to grasp it
but it lies there fading in the sun & rain
remembered from a photograph
shot from a hundred miles in space
& bleeding salty at the edges
where the walkers pass
out of your line of sight a blur
of children's faces shrunken
without teeth or fingers
punished for the fact of childhood
now surrendered to the babe in heaven
helter skelter bowing to his will

the little master of past lives
sad king who wears a bonnet
whom the mother wheels around
in carriage words of warning
written large along its sides declaring
jesus kills the voice of someone
crying in the wilderness

the butcher's hand raised with a knife
to strike the final blow the babe
a real babe now & powerless
while from a window like a jail's
above his head a false babe
has the scene in view his whirling eyes
are cameras poorly focused red
& green & purple
partner to your love & partner
to the task of bearing witness
the discovery of an age when all
was lost when even time itself
not being counted   had no meaning
but only mindless space on which
no voyager had cast a thought
no babe had come to birth or knowledge
& no schwitters made a monument
to misery that eats into the flesh
that procreates a life of pain

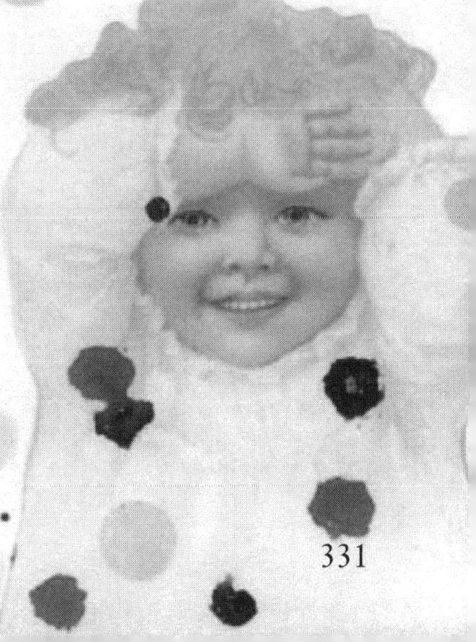

& pleasure where the babe who springs forth
grows to be the man   the man becomes
the voyager   the voyager no less a man
than you becomes the bearer of sad tidings
playground rumbles anxious nights
beneath the stars the city not a playpen
but a temple   home to babes & crones
the sad fragility of towers bright against the sky
no babe can yet survive in
but they tremble belch & bottom down
the blind & lame who fill our streets
the fate of merzbaus spread over the earth
the powder from their walls a distant cloud

from hannover to oslo columns rising up
in each a babe's head reaching to the room
in which we sit we are the witnesses
ourselves from dresden to new york
from ambleside to hiroshima
new millennium for fools new monuments
for babes & bearded prophets worship
deadlier than unbelief the battle lines invisible
in which you are the child again the father
mad to drive the mice out of your home
the center of your paradise a looming babe
arisen reaching through the ruins
for a place to soar

FROM 14 STATIONS (WITH ARIE GALLES)

The Ninth Station: Ravensbruck

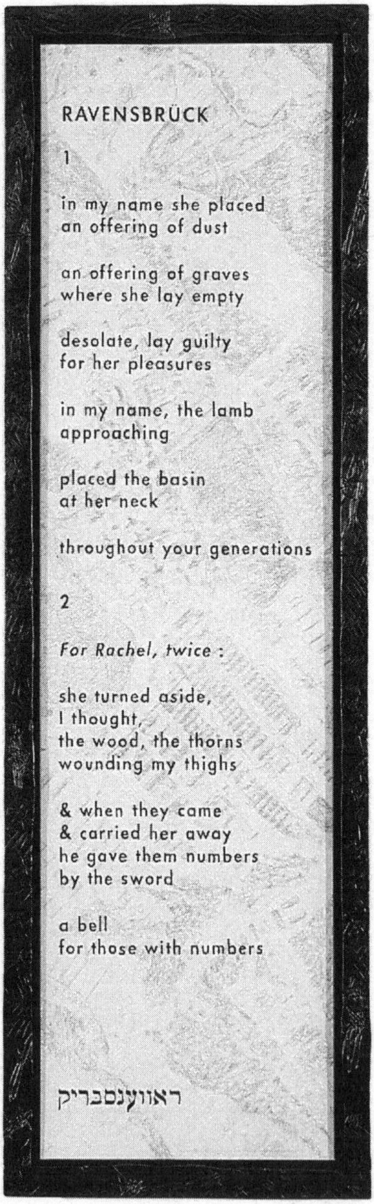

14 Stations. *The full series of fourteen poems was written to accompany Arie Galles's monumental charcoal drawings derived from World War II aerial views of the principal Nazi extermination camps—each with an attendant railroad station—known even then to have been the sites of holocaust. As Galles worked from documentary photographs to establish some pretense at distance (= objectivity), I decided to objectify by turning again to gematria as a way to determine the words and phrases that would come into the poems. The counts were made off the Hebrew and/or Yiddish spelling of the camp names, then keyed to the numerical values of Hebrew words and word combinations in the first five books of the Bible, and the poems were also drawn in charcoal & framed to accompany the visual images. It was my hope that the small degree of objective chance I employed would not so much mask feeling or meaning as allow it to emerge.*

Other poems from this series appear elsewhere in these pages, as well as a note on gematria as a form of composition.

From GEMATRIA COMPLETE

Fourth Gematria
"In the Shadow"

Without God

Without terror.

Gematria 372

Seven.
Plenty.
A Week.

My Heart (1)

Flaming.

My Heart (2)

Blood

The Sign

I see
a word / spoken.

In the Shadow (1)

A womb
he devours.

In the Shadow (2)

I am
nothing.

Testimony

for Charles Reznikoff

The light.
The terror.

Burning

Your beautiful
mind.

Dead
at the entry.

A Fountain (1)

An eye.

A Fountain (2)

Shall I hide?

A Window

Wherein
& forward.

Colors (1)

Yellow
stars

Colors (2)

His red
throne.

The Candlestick / The Fire

The yellow
Baal
eats
like a god.

A Vision (1)

Beat it
with power.

A Vision (2)

God
is crushed.

You

& a double.

The City

Broken.

•

Void.

Flesh (1)

An ark
& a worm.

Flesh (2)

Before
& bitter.

The Rock

fell.

A Curse

Your father
shall live.

A Cloud (1)

In wood.

A Cloud (2)

Forever.

All

or enough.

Cities, Cities

Silver
& speckled.
A tree
fallen down.

My country
a fire

•

Divided.

The Voice (1)

will answer.

The Voice (2)

A voice.

Additional gematria appear elsewhere in these pages & a note on gematria appears on page 126.

THE LEONARDO PROJECT: 10 + 2

I will create a fiction which shall express great things

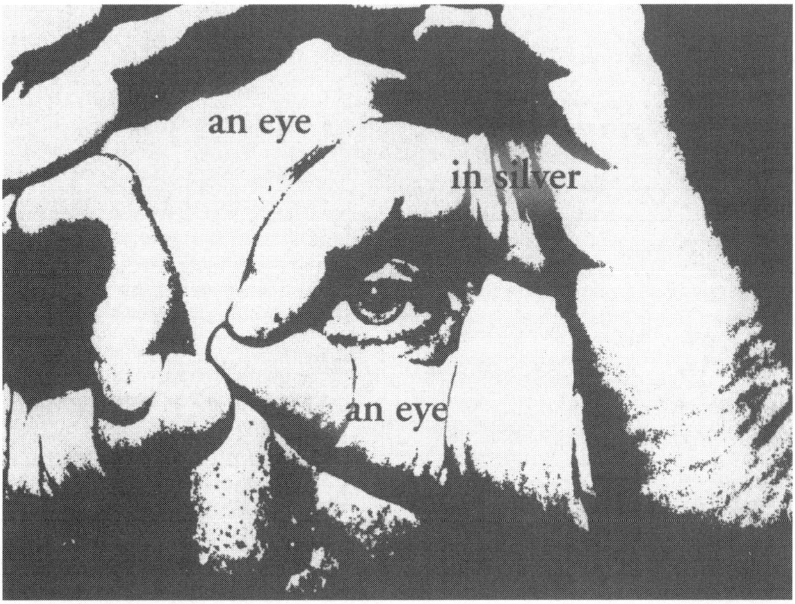
an eye
in silver
an eye

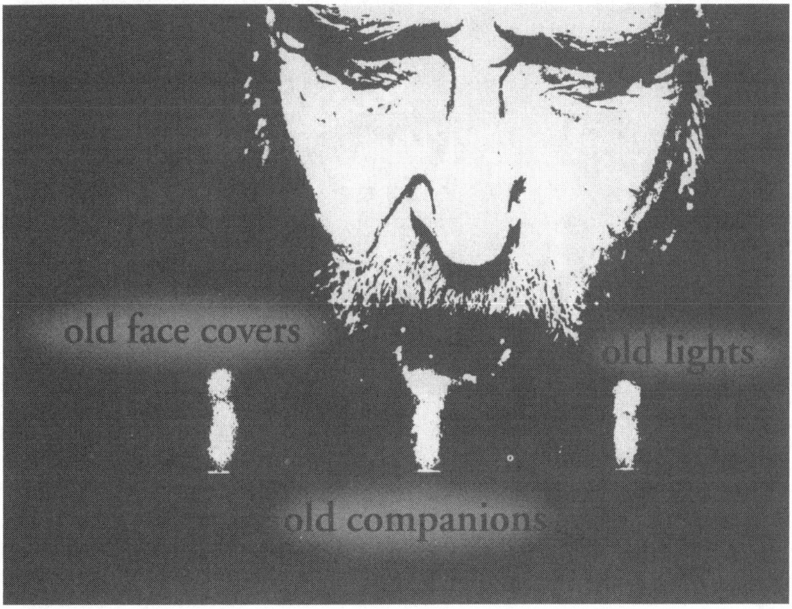
old face covers
old lights
old companions

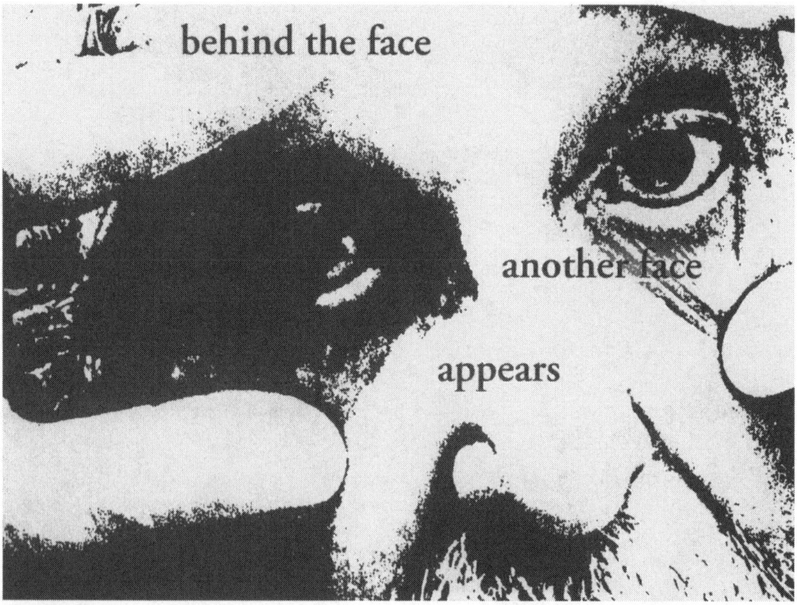
behind the face
another face
appears

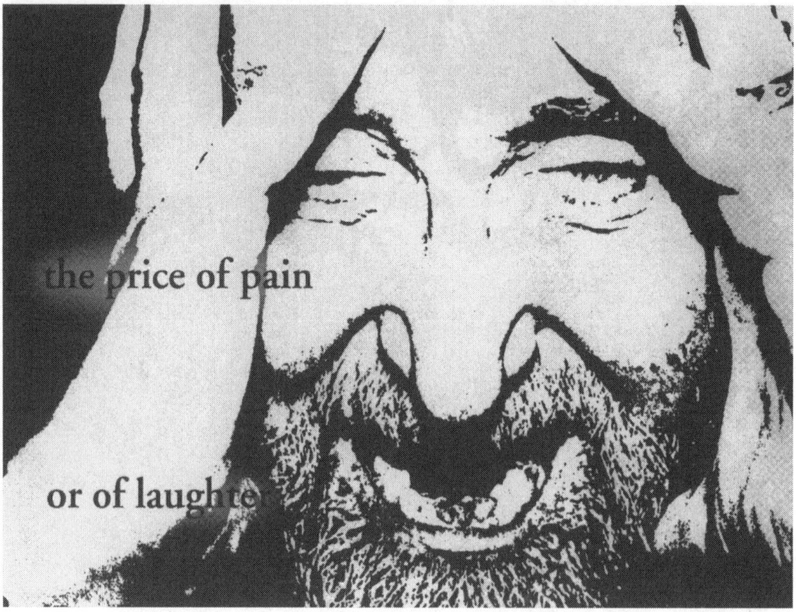
the price of pain
or of laughte

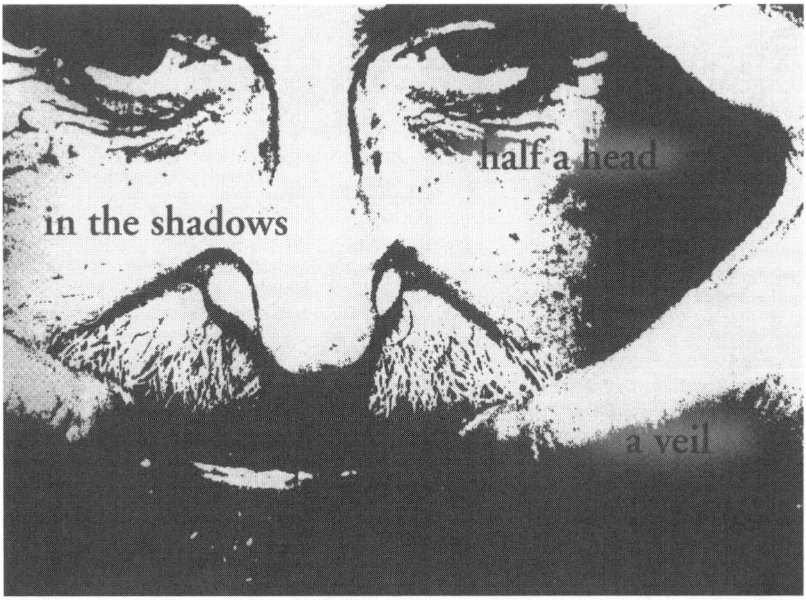
half a head
in the shadows
a veil

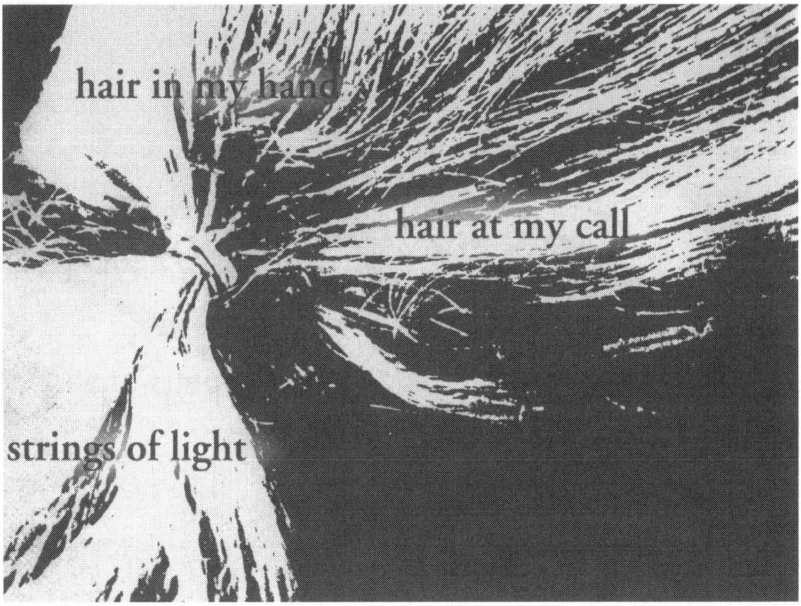
hair in my hand
hair at my call
strings of light

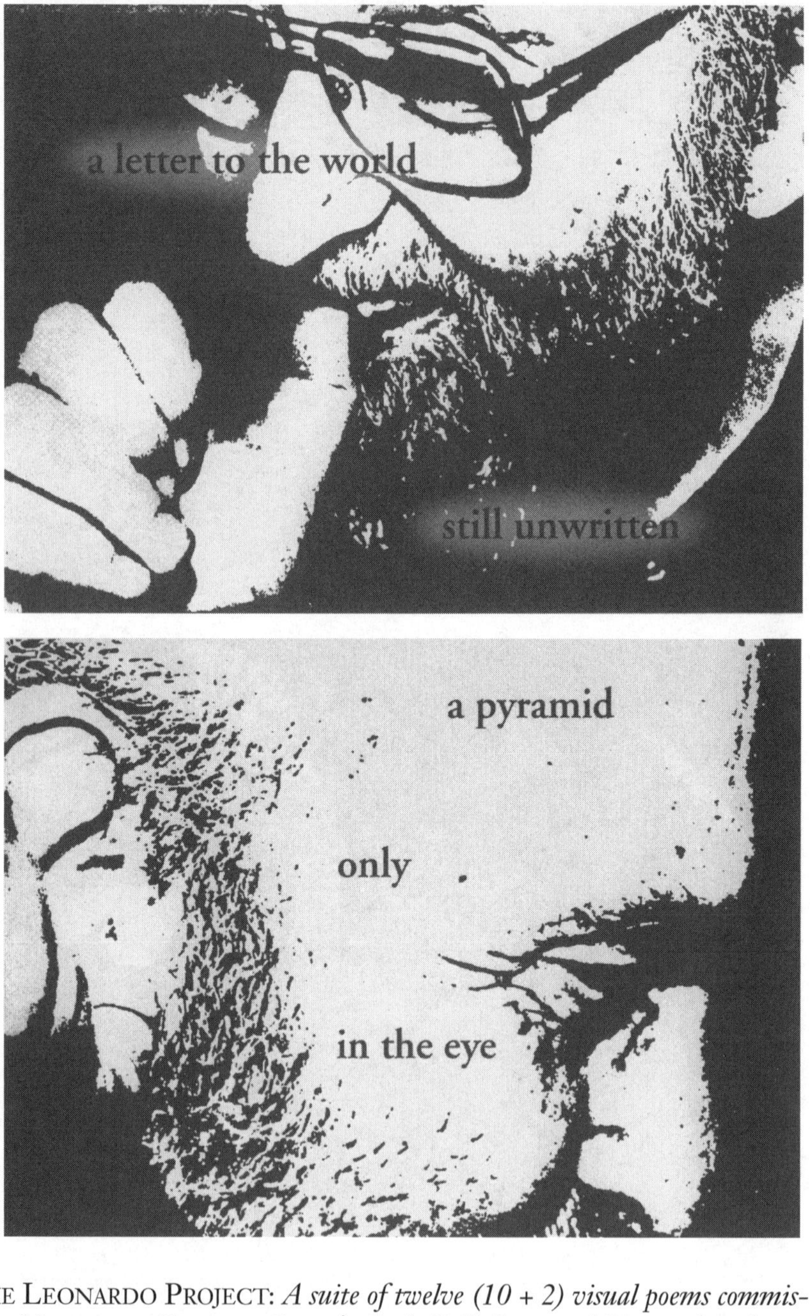

THE LEONARDO PROJECT: *A suite of twelve (10 + 2) visual poems commissioned by curators Francesco Conz & Carlo Palli for an exhibition of works in celebration of the 500th anniversary of Leonardo Da Vinci's* Last Supper. *Originally in an 18 x 24 inch format, the twelve poem-panels were produced*

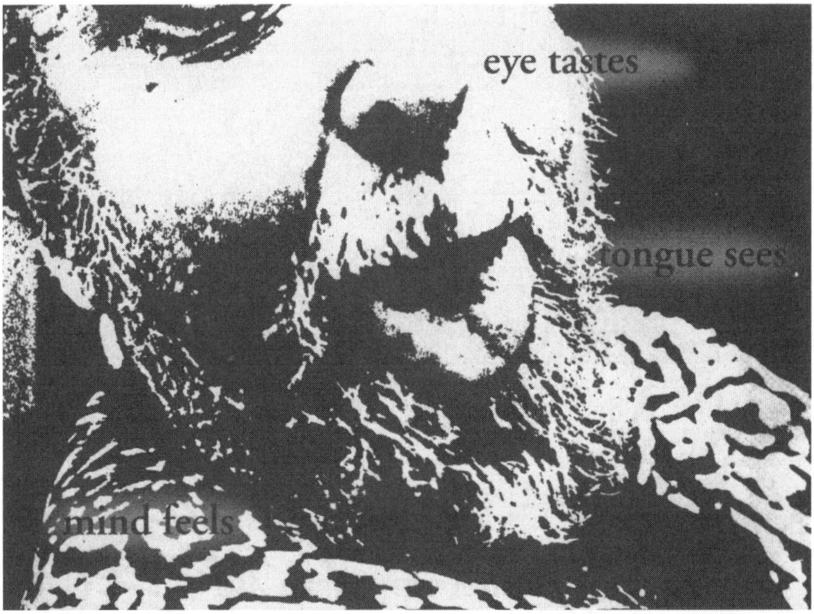

using a combination of photography, xerography, & Adobe PhotoShop software. Assistance along the way came from Diane Rothenberg, Harold Cohen, & (most importantly) Lisa Hutton.

The opening epigraph is a quote from Leonardo's Notebooks.

From THE POUND PROJECT: THREE POEMS & IMAGES

for Francesco Conz

Swollen-eyed, rested,
lids sinking, darkness unconscious

....

And before hell mouth; dry plain
and two mountains

head down,
screwed into the swill

I am led into a home
where no one
—not a dog or cat—
drops by.

The body of a
strangled child
stares out

& spooks me.

Warriors & children
fill my eyes.

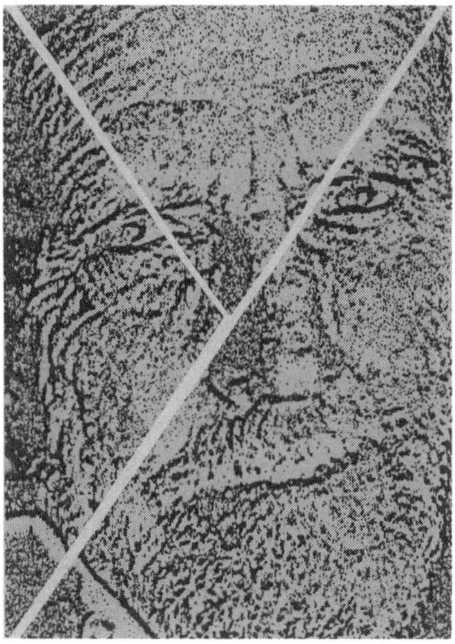

Time is the evil.
Evil.

Is what is always lost,
what takes me by the throat
& leaves me, shrunken,
begging with the other thieves
then drops me in the pit
called bolgia, where a
rhyme I can't erase
repeats forever.

For others other pits
shadow their lives.

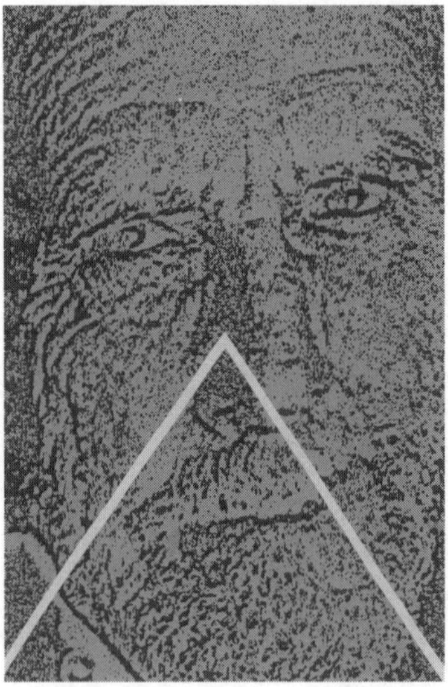

the soil living pus, full of vermin,
dead maggots begetting live maggots

fascists at banquets,
pandars to authority,
jackboots,
skinheads with iron teeth

sucking our flesh,
shoving the old men
  like books in their fires,
outcroppings of shit

but too raw for feeling,
  the flux in the corpse
turns to stone

Commissioned by Francesco Conz in cooperation with Mary Rachewiltz & the Pound estate at Castle Brunneburg in the Italian Tyrol, the original 16-poem sequence was part of a larger project in commemoration of Ezra Pound's life & work. My original was printed on colored stock & pasted onto 16 paper boards beneath a xeroxed & degraded photograph of Pound. In an attempt to fuse (or to con-fuse) our two voices, alive & dead, each numbered section begins with two lines of his, & what follows lies ambiguously in the void between us.

ESTHER K COMES TO AMERICA: 5 IMAGES
with Larry Fink, photographer

movie box collage by Eleanor Antin, photos by Larry Fink

visitor to warsaw
                    old man with open fly
          flesh girls could suck
                    Mothers would die to catch sight of
sometimes would pass your door
                    his song was
          a generation is a day, time floweth
coldly he blew his nose
reached a hand around his high round waist
          money was pinned to caftan
                    aches & pains
a jew's a jew he says
love brings him to the words he needs
                    but sadly

Did Jews learn to smile?
they asked him.
His answer was "once"
"maybe" came easy to his lips
it was a way
of smiling serious amused
& with a smile

cities of pamphleteers
boulevards of orators
mechanics skilled in languages
& economics
naked proletarians in the woods of middle europe

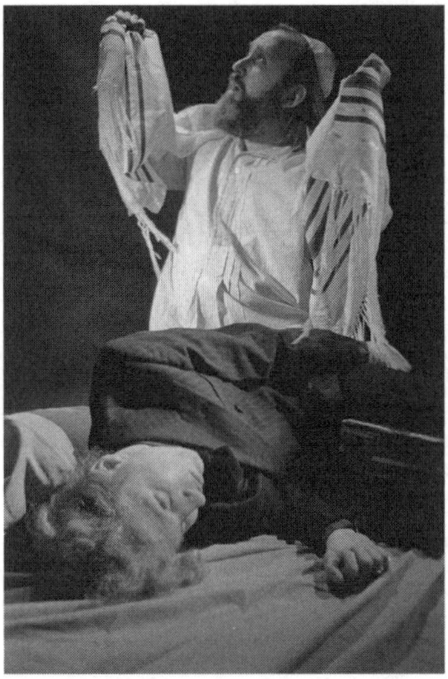

"whorehouse evenings along Atlantic Avenue
"not Moldavanka mad Odessa nights
"remembered the enforcers lift his coffin
"sweat stains the armpits of orange-colored suits
"strawberry vests   blue leather shoes
"& under the shirtcuff of the murdered son
"a diamond-studded bracelet

… he was like a man who takes a ritual bath while holding an unclean reptile
in each hand …

EVENTS & RITUALS

I had been engaged in a conversation with Fluxus artist-poet Dick Higgins about what he or I or both of us were calling "near poetry." In the course of it, it came to me that certain capsule descriptions of traditional rituals or parts thereof, which I had been jotting down while looking for poems to include in what would later become *Technicians of the Sacred*, bore a curious resemblance to what was then emerging as a new performance art. At Higgins' urging I put together a small group of those event pieces, and he published them through his press—Something Else—with the title *Ritual: A Book of Primitive Rites & Events* (1966). Later, when I reprinted and expanded them in *Technicians*, I added the following note:

> *The editor has taken a series of rituals & other programmed activities from a wide geographical area & has, as far as possible, suppressed all reference to accompanying mythic or "symbolic" explanations. This has led to two important results: (1) the form of the activities is, for the first time, given the prominence it deserves; & (2) the resulting works bear a close resemblance to those often mythless activities of our own time called events, happenings, de-collage, kinetic theater, performance art, sound-text, etc. It may be further noted that most of these "events"—like the (modern) intermedia art they resemble—are parts of total situations involving poetry, music, dance, painting, myth, magic, etc., as are many of the songs presented elsewhere in these pages. Having revealed this much, the editor does not wish to obscure by a series of explanatory footnotes the forms that have been laid bare. Although absence of such notes may result in some distortion, it's precisely the kind of distortion that can have a value in itself. Like seeing Greek statues without their colors.*

Additional "events" were composed for the subsequent anthologies, and some also made their way into books of my own poetry like *Poland/1931* and *A Seneca Journal.*

LILY EVENTS

Arnhem Land, Australia

(1) A man & woman looking for lilies.
(2) All the people going down to look for lilies.

(3) Mud taken up looking for lilies.
(4) Washing the lilies in the water to remove the mud.
(5) Washing themselves off after the mud has got on them.
(6) Lilies in a basket.
(7) Walking from the lily place "to go look for a dry place to sit down."

GARBAGE EVENT

Dayak, Borneo

1. Pigs & chickens feed on the grass in an inhabited area until it is bare of grass.

2. Garbage is added to the area.

3. The participants defend the "abandoned beauty" & "town-quality" of the environment against all critics:

   SAMPLE DEFENSE:

   Critic. This place is dirty.
   Answer. It is filthy.

   Critic. Why don't you clean it up?
   Answer. We like it the way it is.

   Critic. Garbage is unhealthy.
   Answer. The pigs feed better in it.

   Critic. It breeds mosquitoes.
   Answer. There are more mosquitoes in a jungle.

BEARD EVENT

Arnhem Land, Australia

The men shave and fashion "Van Dyke" beards. The women paint.

GIFT EVENT

Kwakiutl

Start by giving away different colored glass bowls.
Have everyone give everyone else a glass bowl.
Give away handkerchiefs & soap and things like that.
Give away a sack of clams & a roll of toilet paper.
Give away teddybear candies, apples, suckers & oranges.
Give away pigs & geese & chickens, or pretend to do so.
Pretend to be different things.
Have the women pretend to be crows, have the men pretend to be something else.
Talk chinese or something.
Make a narrow place at the entrance of a house & put a line at the end of it that you have to stoop under to get in.
Hang the line with all sorts of pots & pans to make a big noise.
Give away frying pans while saying things like "Here is this frying pan worth $100 & this one worth $200."
Give everyone a new name.
Give a name to a grandchild or think of something & go & get everything.

NAMING EVENTS

Papago

1. A shaman has a dream & names a child for what he dreams in it. Among such names are Circling Light, Rushing Light Beams, Daylight Comes, Wind Rainbow, Wind Leaves, Rainbow Shaman, Feather Leaves, A-Rainbow-as-a-Bow, Shining Beetle, Singing Dawn, Hawk-Flying-over-Water-Holes, Flowers Trembling, Chief-of-Jackrabbits, Water-Drops-on-Leaves, Short Wings, Leaf Blossoms, Foamy Water.

2. A person receives a name describing something odd about him, always on the bad side. Such names include: Grasshopper-Ate-His-Arrow, Gambler, Ass-Side-to-the-Fire, Pants-Fall-Down, Blisters, Fish-Smell-Mouth, Bed Wetter, Rat Ear, Yellow Legs.

3. A person receives a name describing something odd & sexual about the namer. Here the namer is a woman or a transvestite, who makes the name public by shouting it after the man named when others are present. The man invariably accepts it & is regularly called by it, even by his wife & family. Such names include: Down-Dangling-Pussy-Hairs, Big Cunt, Long Asshole.

4. A group of namers gathers around a dead enemy & shouts abusive names at the body. These names are then given to the shouters. They include: Long Bones, Full-of-Dirt, Back-of-a-Wildcat, Yellow Face, & Gold Breasts, the latter spoken of a girl.

5. A person buys a name or trades names with another person. For example, Devil-Old-Man exchanges names with Contrary, or Looking-for-Girls-at-a-Dance changes with Big Crazy, but has to give him four pints of whiskey in addition because of the desirability of the name.

Vision Event I

Eskimo

Go to a lonely place & rub a stone in a circle on a rock for hours & days on end.

Vision Event II

Eskimo

Let the person who wants a vision hang himself by the neck. When his face turns purple, take him down & have him describe what he's seen.

Vision Event III

Sioux

Go to a mountaintop & cry for a vision.

DOINGS & HAPPENINGS:
NOTES ON A PERFORMANCE OF THE SENECA INDIAN EAGLE DANCE, WITH THE SCENARIO FOR GIFT EVENT III, BASED ON ITS ORDERS

JANUARY 21ST 1967. NOTES TAKEN AT A PERFORMANCE OF THE EAGLE DANCE, COLDSPRING LONGHOUSE, STEAMBURG, NEW YORK. AN EVENT FOR ORATORS, DANCERS, MUSICIANS & PEOPLE. BLESSING & CURING. A PART OF THE WINTER "DOINGS."

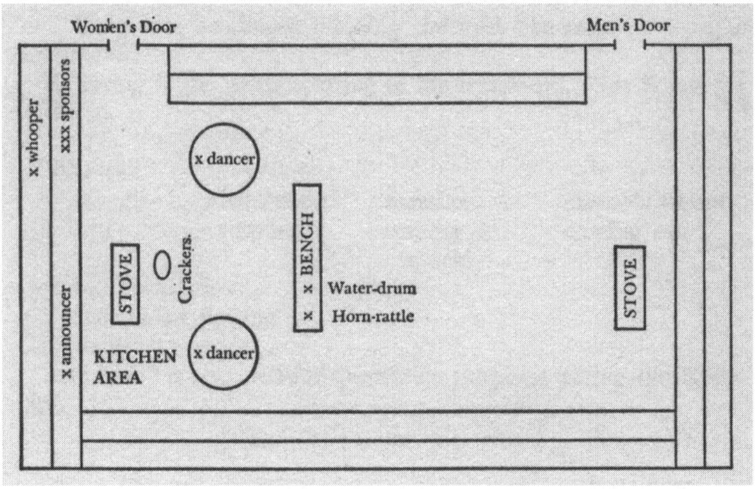

Musicians (water-drum & horn-rattle) move to places on bench.
Two gourd-rattles, two feather-sticks passed around to two boy-dancers.

Rapping of long (orator's) stick (branch) to announce each new speaker.

Whoop precedes start of music.

Music stops.

Stick raps.

Orator speaks. (Thanking & prayer to begin it.)

Old man (Ed Currey), third to speak, puts tub (wash-basin) of saltine crackers near stove. Empty cracker boxes or paper bags are placed near participants & recipients (sponsors) for deposit of crackers. Music up. Two boys dance out to center, crouching, shake feather-sticks & rattles, bob heads toward each other & in sidewise motion. Return to their stools.

The music stops. New speaker "orates," then takes handfuls of crackers & distributes several to each participant, the (three) sponsors, & a few others (named by the sponsors?)

Whoop. Music. Dance. (Each dance ends with a sound: hmmmmm-mmmm or whheeeeeeee.) New speaker. Raps with the stick before speaking. More crackers. Deposit or mouthing of crackers. *Whoop. Music. Dance. Rap. Speaker.* Etc. This is the over-all pattern, never rigid—toward an actual openness, prescribed as well? Ways of handling the stick vary. Speaker raps for his own oration; sometimes (properly?) slides stick to next speaker; sometimes "announcer" (m.c.) brings it around; shorter & longer orations; hard raps, light raps, staccato, etc. Laughter, etc. At one point new crackers are added to basin; they overflow as next speaker passes them out; they fall on the floor. Occasional punctuation of speeches by light drum-tap. Often at end. Distribution (except for main participants) seems erratic. A speaker forgets to pass crackers. Reminded with laughter. Boy-dancers walk out during one oration. Buzzing of voices, etc. Some joking about deposit of crackers into boxes. Dancers, seated & facing, hold a mute conversation. (Feather-stick in front of face like boy with the flamenco fan in Cordoba.) Two men enter with large cauldron of water for women preparing (corn) soup at the side. People drifting in & out. Time passes. Sounds of Seneca I cannot understand. Three teen-aged girls are laughing in the back. Nobody rushes. Everyone will speak.

After the first woman orator distributes the last of the crackers, the empty tub is turned over in front of the stove. A male speaker (who may have opened things to start with, i.e., the one I'm calling the "announcer") speaks without preliminary dancing—followed by music, dance, etc. New speaker (woman) raps. Speaks. (Some participants now drinking coffee.) She finishes, distributes something small to the three "sponsors." Music, etc. New woman speaker. Avery Jimerson (horn-rattle) goes out, Dick Johnny John (drum) walks to the side for cigarette. Speaker distributes fruit (apples) to the three sponsors. New woman speaker without music (Salina Johnny John) distributes bananas. Still no music. New woman speaker. Gives coins to the dancers, the musicians, the "announcer," the whooper.

Ed Currey raps, speaks. Distributes packs of cigarettes. Whoop. Music. Dance. Sticks & gourds are set down on the floor. The "announcer" collects them. Ed Currey speaks again. Voice moving as in prayer. Announcer distributes pinches from tobacco bowl to various participants & individuals around the room who accept it or refuse.

GIFT EVENT III: A CELEBRATION FOR POETS, MUSICIANS & DANCERS, BASED ON THE ORDERS OF THE SENECA INDIAN EAGLE DANCE & PERFORMED AT THE JUDSON DANCE THEATER, JUDSON MEMORIAL CHURCH, NEW YORK CITY, MARCH 21ST & 22ND 1967. A PART OF THE SPRING "HAPPENINGS."

Adaptation by Jerome Rothenberg
Choreography by Carol Ritter
Music by Philip Corner

Jackson Mac Low, Dick Higgins, Susan Sherman, Clayton Eshleman, Robert David Cohen, Hannah Weiner, Carol Bergé, George Kimball, Eleanor Antin, David Antin, Paul Blackburn, Jerome Rothenberg (poets)

Christopher Beck, Nannette Sievert, Bernard Spriggs, Margaret Williams, (dancers)

Ferdinando Buonanno, Billy Fisher, Cyrelle Forman, Bill Friedman, Edward Goldstein, Malcolm Goldstein, Maud Haimson, Susan Hartung, Alison Knowles, Carol Marcy, Max Neuhaus, Carol Reck, David Reck, Steve Reich, Carolee Schneemann, James Tenney (musicians)

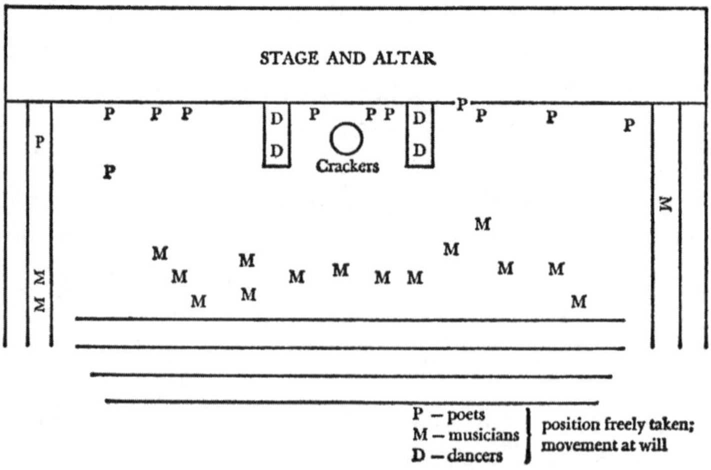

1. As the audience is taking seats, [Philip Corner's] "poor man music"* is performed. This is the music throughout.

2. The first poet (who thereafter acts as m.c.) raps for silence with a sounding stick.+ The music stops. He reads a greeting-poem. The music starts again, & he empties several boxes of crackers± into a large wash-basin at center of the performance area & arranges simple gifts on the stage-apron for later distribution. Empty boxes or paper bags are given to the dancers for deposit of crackers & gifts.

3. The second poet (Jackson Mac Low) receives the sounding-stick from the m.c. & raps for silence. He reads a (thanking)-poem of his own.≠ The music starts up again as he distributes crackers to the dancers & any other performers he can reach. (Distribution may also be extended to the audience.)* After the distribution, the dancers perform an extended piece to the "poor man music."

4. When the first dance is over, the m.c. hands the stick to the third poet (Dick Higgins), & the same series of actions (*rapping-for-silence, reading, music up, distribution of crackers, dance, etc.*) is repeated. This goes on

---

* ["Poor man" because the sounds are those a person can make with his or her own body or simple extensions thereof. In Corner's words]:

"The simplest materials
and the things your own body is
and does
—claps, slaps, stamps, rubbing and scratching: body—all
parts, and clothing if any
voices, and all the sounds your voice and breath and
throat may make
/except words."

[The rhythms follow the pulsebeat, faster or slower but with its regularity—beats within the group, starting apart, meeting, changing, entering & re-entering, meeting elsewhere, etc.]

+ In this case, a broomstick (red) was used. (The Senecas use a broom-handle to announce entry of the "huskface" masked dancers in another winter event.) The wash-basin was also a red plastic.

± The saltine crackers of the Seneca source were almost unanimously overridden in favor of graham crackers (Nabisco).

≠ The first three poems were designated by the adapter; the rest were of each poet's own choice.

* The act of finding-each-other (between participants & audience) was the principal departure from the Seneca source. The event continued to change under this impulse, from a situation where community is taken for granted to one where the activity may finally create it.

(with the dance segments getting successively shorter) through the dance that follows the reading by the fifth poet (Clayton Eshleman)—by which time the basin should be empty of crackers. Before handing the stick to the sixth poet, the m.c. turns the basin over.

5. From the sixth poet on, gifts are distributed in place of crackers, but there is no dancing. The music continues as before, except when poets have rapped for silence & are reading. This goes on until the next-to-the-last reader (Paul Blackburn), whose gift distribution is followed by a brief dance segment.

6. The m.c. now raps for silence & reads a poem of his own choice. To accompaniment of the "poor man music," he distributes the final gifts,+ after which all performers do their pieces simultaneously.± As soon as each poet or dancer finishes, he or she leaves the performance area. When all the poets & dancers have left, the music stops.

Sequence of poems. (Except for the first piece, which is the introductory poem to the adapter's *Technicians of the Sacred*, there was no attempt to be Indian or to read poems on Indian themes; indeed, the point of the event, as it related to its source, was that the carry-over was not in content or in costume but in structure: a way of being heard):

1. Greeting-poem, read by J.R.; 2. *First Friendship Poem* by Jackson Mac Low; 3. Selection from *Six Considerations of the Angel* by Dick Higgins; 4. *The Meeting* by Susan Sherman; 5. *Walk I* (1st night), *Walk III* (2nd night) by Clayton Eshleman; 6. *Lines Written in Dejection* by Robert David Cohen; 7. *Persons indicated present their compliments* by Hannah Weiner; 8. *Song for Beginning* by Carol Bergé; 9. *Poem* (untitled) by George Kimball; 10. *Poem for My Mother* by Eleanor Antin; 11. *Poem for Eleanor* (1st night), *4 Games for Eleanor* (2nd night) by David Antin; 12. *Het up & take yr teeth with you* by Paul Blackburn; 13. *The Orators II* by Jerome Rothenberg.

+ In the actual performance the other poets joined the m.c. in the final act-of-giving. On the second night toy flutes & other sound-producing articles were included among the gifts, to give the audience a further means of participation.

± While simultaneities turn up in the ceremonies of many cultures, there is no specific Seneca precedent in the Eagle Dance. The Seneca husk-face ceremonies, however, often involve several simultaneous dances by the masked beggar-clowns – usually while a round-dance is also in progress. The device has developed independently in modern "happenings" or in the poetry, e.g., of Jackson Mac Low & others.

. . . .

Be me who
Blesses.

Suffer. Destroy.

Be certain.

Merge a particular picture
Blossom. & open
This surface to clouds.

Be orators.

From THAT DADA STRAIN: A HÖRSPIEL

OVERTURE

(Jazz music up: "That Dada Strain." Hold as is for 20 seconds, then begin to distort & fragment. Sustain throughout the overture, while actors move into the house, by ones and twos, reciting the words as a *second voice* behind the *first voice* of the speaker.)

1st Voice (J.R.)

The music on the phonograph is
playing an old jazz tune.

It is called THAT DADA STRAIN & brings me
—aching & longing—to a time before my birth.

When I dream of the past, the
poem begins to form. What is
the poem, & who are its people?
The poem is strangely cut off
from its origins.

In a time of war the human
spirit suffers. It has been a time
of war. My father steps into the
center of the picture. My father
is a young man. War has come
to Poland. It is 1916. The map
of the century is beginning to be
written. We will call the map a
poem.

1916. Other fathers move. The
ground of Europe has begun to
melt. The music on the phono-
graph is playing an old jazz tune.

In 1916 the nineteen-year old
Sammy Rosenstock arrives in
Zurich. My father in a caftan
walks the streets of Vilna. My
father is nineteen years old &
Sammy Rosenstock arrives in
Zurich. He will become the
poet Tristan Tzara.
In New York a jazz band plays

2nd Voice

the generations
DADA deaths
& victories
goat turds
vanilla
sparks & lights
the DADA wilderness
the auto hood
the judas clowns
the death of DADA
the beginnings
suicide
the DADA financiers
the shady lady
flower worlds
the altar
vacuum cleaners
butterflies
cocoons
black hooves
his hip
the drum tattoo
the terrors
wilderness
the muses of the rich
the bankers
suicide
the ages
flight
the mind

THAT DADA STRAIN. My father has curled earlocks. In his pocket is a crumpled book. The book is called THAT DADA STRAIN.

In the dream my father's book is called THAT DADA STRAIN. Tristan Tzara is nineteen years old & my father arrives in Vilna. At the Slabodka Yeshiva, in the most obscure of streets in the shadow of architectural ribs, the crowd of boys in caftans reads the works of Tristan Tzara. It is 1916. Sammy Rosenstock arrives in Zurich.

Sammy Rosenstock is nineteen years old. Sammy Rosenstock is Tristan Tzara. In the most obscure of streets in the shadow of architectural ribs the tall man waits for him. The tall man's name is Hugo Ball. In a time of war the tall man stammers. My father in a caftan cuts the earlocks from his face. The book inside his pocket blossoms. In the dream my father's book is called THAT DADA STRAIN.

The human spirit suffers. In a time of war my father walks into a room of books. The map of the century is beginning to be written. My father in a short coat & shaven head is looking for a book. In Zurich Hugo Ball is standing in the Cabaret

the bride
a chair
a failed poetics
the designers
captains & mechanics
fingers
fat
the father
Yaqui
fat face
clown
fingers
fat
the father
Yaqui
fat face
the telephones
the keyboard
tiger rock
disgust
bang! bang!
new languages
the dancers
street lamps
streets
the generations
spirits
painters
walls
the DADA fathers
disco
caverns
cabaret
processions
time
that DADA strain
on burning ladders
marshmallows
his dancing feet
death

Voltaire. A group of little oriental men is coming toward him. The ground of Europe has begun to melt. My father steps into the center of the picture. In New York a jazz band plays THAT DADA STRAIN. The music on the phonograph is strangely cut off from its origins. The music stammers. In the most obscure of streets in the shadow of architectural ribs, a group of little oriental men has come into the Cabaret Voltaire. The tall man plays THAT DADA STRAIN & holds a crumpled book. Sammy Rosenstock arrives in Zurich.

[The actors cross to their places on stage, continuing to speak They continue speaking until there are no words left to speak.]

DADA
DADA
ritual
work
DADA
DADA
power
dadahood
love
DADA
DADA's face
dumb DADA
the rich man
DADA
droopy eyes
dumb DADA
drum
tie
heavy collar
chest

his adam's apple
hundreds
DADA kids
a decade
galleries
their map rooms
stomp
America & Russia
generals
space-devils
agents from the moon
a liquid plant
our throats
your nightmare
grey intestines
DADA father
pubis
ear
the suicide of DADA

midget bikers
boots
my zigzag balladeers
a light
a cabaret
my bukovina eyes
this stick
his palm
his hand
my fingers
time
his monocle
a black wave
kinky hair
his mirror
the young man
music
in America
greased wheels
the zygote
energies
the clarity of DADA
light
the century
the light
the age
my son
the father
man
suicide of DADA

[All actors seated. Silent. A second speaker from among them stands & prepares to speak.]

2nd Speaker

"February 1916. In the most obscure of streets in the shadow of architectural ribs, where you will find discreet detectives amid red street lamps—birth—birth of the Cabaret Voltaire—personages in one edition appear, recite or commit suicide, bustle and stir, the joy of the people, cries, the cosmopolitan mixture of god and brothel, the crystal and the fattest woman in the world: 'Under the Bridges of Paris.'"

1st Voice, at stage center

It is 1985. The music on the phonograph is playing an old jazz tune. I am sitting in the shadow of the fathers. DADA DADA says the poem. They are united with me in a time of war. The poem begins to melt. In a time of war the human spirit stammers. A voice begins to read THAT DADA STRAIN.

Written as a hörspiel (sound play) for Westdeutscher Rundfunk in Cologne and staged by the Center for Theater Science & Research through Luke Morrison in San Diego and New York, 1983.

ABRAHAM ABULAFIA VISITS THE POPE
A FRAGMENT OF A STEINIAN OPERA

for Charlie Morrow

SCENE ONE. THE YEAR 1280. ON THE ROAD TO ROME. A CONGREGATION OF JEWS WITH ABRAHAM ABULAFIA AT CENTER. THEY MEET THE KING OF ITALY & PRESS ON, EAGER TO CONFRONT & TO CONVERT THE POPE.

Chorus
Jews in a ring.
Jews on a rollercoaster.
Jews who sing in a ring.
They are & they sing about everything.
Old Jews who do what they do they sing & they ride on a rollercoaster they sing in a ring & young Jews do too who move by ones & by twos they ride to the sky & over the sky they ride in Italy over the sky & on the sky Jews on a rollercoaster do who ride over Italy on a ride to the sky.

First Jew
[in black face & puffing on a stogie]
I am a Jew I am a Jew too & I have come to Italy to ride on the sky & to be blue oh yes blue yes blue blue.

Second Jew
[a pirate with a gold ring in one ear]
Over the sky in a rollercoaster I too who am a Jew & who say blow me away & shiver my timbers sweetly yes sweet my sweet Jewish timbers.

Third Jew
[in a feather bonnet he is an Indian tomahawk & all]
Yes yes I have come all the way to Italy to be a Jew like you oh like you yes yes like you I ride on a rollercoaster over the sky.

Fourth Jew
[majestically dressed he is dressed as the statue of liberty in a long gown & with a glowing torch]
I have left the golden land & I have a torch in my hand in my precious Jewish hand I have come to land in Italy too & to ride on the sky like you.

Fifth Jew
[a wolf mask over his face & a shepherd's crook in his hand]
Am I not a Jew if I am not a Jew what am I, but if an animal can be a Jew I am one too.

Sixth Jew
[in the clothes of an Arab or maybe of a patriarchal Jew]
I am a true Jew true & blue & I say barakh hu to everyone I see in Italy & here too.

Seventh Jew
[wears a military costume with medals on his chest & a cockade on his head]
A Jew who says one two & two knows one & two & can do whatever I do, he can ride on a rollercoaster & dance yes a Jew can dance too in advance of a rollercoaster.

Eighth Jew
[a faggot]
A Jew like me in Italy is a Jew & is a faggot too like me yes anyone who comes to Italy can be a Jew & he can ride on a rollercoaster on the sky & so I am true & blue.

Ninth Jew
[spherical & round he rolls across the floor]
I cannot say barakh hu & yet I am a Jew nevertheless & this is true.

Tenth Jew
[Abulafia]
But Abulafia who is a Jew is different too. He is the first to sing & the first to come to Italy. He is the first to meet the king the true Italian king & the first to meet the pope the way I do. He is the first in war the first in peace & the first in the hearts of his countrymen.

[The true Italian king comes in he is dressed like George Washington & rides on a bicycle.]

Chorus & Jews
[singing]
He is King.
He matters.
He is King.
He forgives.
He is King
He is King.
He attends a wedding.
He is King.
He attends a decision.
He attends.
He attends.
He dances.
We see.
He is King.
We siphon.
The inheritors dance.
He matters.
He is King.
We attend a wedding.
He is King.
He is King.
He forgives.

Abulafia
This is a scene.

King
In a garden.

Abulafia
In Italy.

King
What is your name.

Abulafia
Abulafia.

King
You have come a long way. What is your name, I pray, I pray.

Abulafia
My name is buried in a hat.
[He looks for it.]
Yes it is Abulafia. See. It is Abraham Abulafia.

King
I see & do you sit beside me.

Abulafia
Yes I do. Thank you I do.

King
I am a king.

Abulafia
I see that & I thank you too.

King
But I am a hidden king though I am most true.

Abulafia
Do not forget the penpoint when you do.

King
No but I forget the world in bits & pieces.

[Abulafia reads from a book.]

King
Will you read to me from a book.

Abulafia
Thank you, I pray & I pray. I will read to you from a book.

King
Begin here

Abulafia
Yes here.

[He begins to read aloud. The other Jews circle around him.]

Abulafia
Here is here now & here is here now & here is here now. And here. He does & does he sing between the curtains. Yes it says. A herd of horses crosses through his hall & circles. In a ring. What is his book called. It is called the Book of Witness. See. The little "y" is where his name is. It is here & here. Oh yes cries Abulafia & do it once. Once here & one here. One is called a king & two is called a king's king & three is called a king's king once. Four is fourth & goes forth to a door. He opens to begin a door. And five. Five is on a hand & is a herd of horses. Six are Jews & brightly. Seven is a proposition. Eight is also nine. And Abulafia again is ten & goes forth to a door.

[He passes the book to the first Jew.]

First Jew
He goes forth to a door. Here is Barcelona where the trip begins.

Second Jew
Begin is pleasing. Capri is rich with fish & goyim. If you can do mileage with a pencil others will find the way.

Third & Fourth Jews
When they say they say. When a month is far away they say the gay month.

Fifth Jew
Jews kiss Jews. A gay month. He is on his way to Rome.

Sixth Jew
Two Jews are on their way to Rome. One is gay & one is in golf shoes. The other is in despair.

Seventh Jew
A king a garden & a violin. The door before the Pope is open to a door. A door swings shut so sadly sadly.

Eighth Jew
Two Jews in golf shoes. Two Jews in paper hats. My hat is launched. To see the King first is to be with kisses.

Ninth Jew
Two Jews in tears. One bows before you. One is the other's keeper. The Messiah is the one called the Messiah.

Abulafia
Now Abulafia puts down the book. He is all smiles. The King is charmed by him & the Jews are irreversible. Abulafia winces. His right leg feels the skateboard still in place. Ring a rubber bell for me. He rings it. The house in Italy leads to a rollercoaster in the sky. A Jew lights a cheroot & feels a small decline. I let the King peek through my glasses. See oh yes I see. A wise Jew pisses in a tub. He rubs her ivories with lemons, then descends. Dance One: The King in Limbo. Strike a pose. Repose. Disclose. Expose. A thin Jew swings a shoe. Dance Two: The King is talking to his telephone. Where is the Pope is he in Rome of course the Pope would be in Rome. And the Messiah. Tell oh tell is the Messiah in the garden in which he fell.

King & Abulafia
Yes he is here oh yes yes he is here & here before a garden.

SCENE TWO: THE PATHWAY OF DARK SHADOWS: ABULAFIA HELD PRISONER IN THE NET OF LOVE.

[Enter the three women who are three women in love. They sing.]

Three women in love
we are
who are in love with a Jewish king.
So we are & we sing.

Three women in love
we are
& so we sing we sing
under the moon.
(The moon, the moon,
& o the Jewish king.)

Three women in love
we are.
And we wait where an old moon dies
in the old king's eyes.

We sing & we wait.
And the night grows old
where we wait.
Where we wait with the moon.

(The moon, the moon,
& o the Jewish king.)

[Abulafia appears in the sky above them. His earlocks are long & fall over his shoulders. In his right hand he holds a blue & white umbrella.]

First Woman
[no longer singing; speaking]
Along this road or somewhere somewhere along this road he comes. And where he comes I do or do detect him.

Second Woman
And now we watch see how his foot sets on the ground.

Third Woman
See how his other foot goes searching for the path his first foot takes.

Second Woman
When Abulafia becomes a traveler on the earth we circle—

First Woman
And we take him in this net.

[A net falls down & covers Abulafia.]

Third Woman
And bind him.

Second Woman
Oh love is vegetable & love is blind.

All Three Together
And so we say.

Abulafia
[covered by the net he feels along its surface as if testing the narrow walls & ceiling of a cell. When he speaks he sings.]
Into the love of marigolds the Jew returns & goes, o does he go & sweetly, neatly as the paper where he reads he sees the letters float with love, sweet love sweet marriage blisses. When he kisses love the Jew begins with love, & when he sins love wins him to her side. The bride in love & o to be in love & be beside.
[Then speaking.]
It is only this or this that keeps me from it that delays the leap across the trees into the house the deep house & the ring where the messiah sings & is true.
[Slowly, very slowly.]
I had set out to do what I must do & here love keeps me true.

[The other Jews appear. The Italian king is now a Jew too, he is with them.]

The Jews & the King
[as a chorus, while the women raise Abulafia above them in the net of love.]
Tomorrow.
One.
Tomorrow.
One by one.
Surprises.
Light.
No light at all.
No surprises.
To bewilder a taste
& open it.
One.
To surprise
with cheese.
To delight.
One.
Perfect in understanding.
The girl has her shape.
Perfect for once.
It is real.
It is past.
A holiday is everywhere.
Send necklaces.

The Three Women
[swinging around Abulafia's net on ropes that hang from the sky.]
Do they whistle for work.
Do they whistle for a wedding.
Do they whistle for a beard.
Do they whistle for whistles.
Do they whistle for bathtubs.

First Woman
And when.

The Three Women
Do they pretend to whistle.
Do they pretend perspiration.

Do they pretend breakfast.
Do they pretend jewels & furs.

Second Woman
Will they be first
or will they.

Third Woman
Or will they return to be first.

First Woman
Or will they return love.

Second Woman
Or will they love & turn back.

Third Woman
Or will they express themselves too often.

First Woman
This is what I guess.

Second Woman
I do not offer a hand but it is offered.

Third Woman
I do not wait for the sea by decree or by a holding.

First Woman
I take greater pains to be best knowing of their wishes.

The Three Women
We prefer to be first.

[The start of an opera conceived & planned with composer Charlie Morrow but never finished beyond the first two scenes nor ever put into production. Abulafia *selbst* (1240–c.1291) was a great mystic & master of a species of meditation that took the form, often enough, of a kind of mystical lettrism. In 1280, responding to a dream or vision, he set out for Rome to convert the Pope (Nicolas III) & to proclaim himself the Jewish messiah. Threatened with execution he was thrown into prison but saved by the sudden death of the pope himself.]

THE THIRTEENTH HORSE SONG OF FRANK MITCHELL (WHITE)

Navajo

Key nnnn N N gahn

Some 're lovely N nawu nnnn but some 're & are at my hawuz nawu wnn N wnn baheegwing
Some 're lovely N hawu nnnn but some 're & are at my howinow N wnn baheegwing
Some 're lovely N nawu nnnn but some 're & are at my howzes nawu nahht bahyeenwing but bahyeesum nahtgwing

NNNOOOOW because I was (N gahn) I was the boy ingside the dawn but some 're at my house now wnn N wnn baheegwing
& by going from the house the wwwideshell howanome but some 're at my howinow N wnnn baheegwing
& by going from the house the darkned hoganome but some 're at my house N wnn baheegwing
& by going from the swollen hoganouse my breath has blown but some 're at my house N wnn baheegwing
& by going from the house the hloly hoganome but some 're at my house N wnn N wnn baheegwingnnng
& from the plays of jewels we walk (naht gahn) (p)pon but some 're at my howinow N wnn baheegwing
with prayersticks that are white (nnuhgohn) but some 're at my house N wnn baheegwing
with my feathers that are white (mmm gahn) but some 're at my house N wnn baheegwing
with my spirit horses that are white (nuhgohn) but some 're at my house N wnn baheegwing
with my spirit horses that are white & dawn (nuhgohn) but some 're at my house N wnnn baheegwing
with those spirit horses that are whiteshell nawuNgnnnn but some 're at my house N wnn baheegwing

with those howanorses that are whiteshell nawu but some 're at
my howinouse wnnn baheegwingnnng
wiiiingth jewels of every kind d(go)nN draw them on nahtnnn but
some 're at my howinow N wnn baheegwing
with cloth of every kind d(go)nN draw them on nahtnnn but some
're at my howinow N wnn baheegwing
with sheep of every kind d(go)nN draw them on nahtnnn but some
're at my house N wnn baheegwing
with horses of evree(ee) (ee) kind d(go)nN draw them on nahtnnn
but some 're at my howinow N wnn baheegwing
with cattle of every kind d(go)nN draw them on nahtnnn but some
're at my howinow N wnn baheegwing
with men of every kind d(go)nN draw them on nahtnnn but some 're
at my house N wnn baheegwing
in my house of precious jewels in my back(acka)room (Ngahn)
where nnnn but some 're at my howinow N wnn baheegwing
in this house of precious jewels we walk (p)pon (N gahn) where
nnnn but some 're at my house N wnn baheegwing
& everything that's g(h)one before mmmmore we walk (p)pon but
some 're at my howinow N wnn baheegwing
& everything that's more ( ) won't be (be!) be poor but some
're at my house N wnn baheegwing
& everything that's now & living to be old & blesst nhawu but
some 're at my howinow N wnnn baheegwing
because I am the boy who blesses/blisses to be old but some
're at my house N wnn baheegwing

Zzmmmm 're lovely N nawu nnnn but some 're & are at my howinouse
N wnn baheegwing
Zzmmmm 're lovely nawu N nnnn but some 're & are at my house
N wnn baheegwing
Zzmmmm 're lovely N nawu nnnn but some are & are at my howzes
nahht bahyeenahtnwing but nawu nohwun baheegwing

A LETTER TO DAVID McALLESTER, 1968, ON THE BEGINNINGS OF TOTAL TRANSLATION

Box 117
Steamburg, N.Y. 14783
July 23, 1968

Dear Dave—

It's being a very good summer here in all ways, & I'm certainly getting a much clearer picture of the possibilities & limits of carrying on this kind of work on the spot—of my doing it, that is. The best results so far are with Dick Johnny John—who's to be my Indian "father"—& that because he's a natural translator himself & has become involved personally in the recording, transcription & translation of the songs & other materials. I think there's a sense too that the older men in their 60s & 70s have left the younger ones like Dick (he's about 54) in a tight position, that the ceremonies etc. are dying with them, & that he wants very much to hold onto those for himself & his sons. While people here are generally aware of that problem, the procedure has always been for each generation to pick up the longhouse songs with very little actual teaching, & even if there's now a changed situation in the men's growing inability to commit these things easily to memory, loss of Seneca as a 1st language, etc., they postpone the necessary assistance or the work of putting much of it on tape. And there's of course the "sacred-secret" connection you spoke of with relation to Frank Mitchell, still very strong here … & applied within the group (I'd guess) as well as towards us outsiders.

For that last reason too I've gone very easy about intruding too much into the sacred areas, reassuring myself that my 1st concern this summer is with technique rather than substance. In some ways too I find the secular music (woman's dance songs, etc.) the most exciting fact for the moment, because it's a really ongoing & creative form, however light the words & vocables may be in contrast to the medicine ceremonies, etc. The principal singers are very prolific & responsive to some of the influences & events we have in common. They all have tape recorders, for example, & one of them at least—Avery Jimerson—uses them in the process of composition. He has a whole array of equipments that makes his diningroom look like a professional recording studio: 3 tape recorders, 2 large amplifiers, 2 standing studio mikes, etc. After a song comes to him & he has the basic form of it set, he plays the lead (on waterdrum) onto a tape, then accompanies himself with horn rattle as chorus, getting the two voices onto a single tape, so as to simulate an actual performance by the Singing Society. He can then listen & (he says) begin to cut away the parts that aren't needed or readjust the vocables until the piece feels good enough to present to the group, who will then be able to suggest further (but generally more limited) modifications. He puts a big emphasis on technique in that sense, & I'm trying now to get him to save his discards for me, so that I can get some notion of how the songs in fact develop—a little bonus that this use of contemporary technology now makes possible.

The subject matter of the songs that use words (most don't) is sometimes also of interest in terms of its modernness, e.g. a very popular song now going the rounds (the songmaker is Johnson Jimerson of Newtown) runs roughly like this [in translation]:

> Screw it
> We'll just have to help
> (heya)
> these longhaired boys along
> We'll sing their song
> (ga-a-no-weya   heya)
> yah-yah-yah   yah-yah
> That's what it says
> We're all becoming INDIAN BEATLES
> hey heya yoooh

reminiscent of a song from the 20s by Chauncey Johnny John ("Cold Voice") that says "I can make songs like the colored people do," then runs in a string of complicated vocables to the tune of pretty redwing. There are also a number of social-protest songs about Kinzua, etc., that I've recorded, & a number of set pieces in praise of the Allegany singers or the longhouse religion, some surviving woman's dance songs in praise of the creator, etc. I've mentioned the possibility of their going to Wesleyan [to perform there], & I think they can work it out, although the problem for them is that they have jobs & find it difficult to get away. A weekend arrangement for the group (say 3–4 singers) would probably be best, with (hopefully) one of them remaining for a longer period. (Again Dick Johnny John would seem the most willing to talk about Seneca music in general, therefore the best bet from your point of view.)

With all of this (including some sacred work Dick is starting to supply) I haven't found time for much else; but the arrival of the new horse-songs has been the 2nd exciting fact for me, offering so much to work on. I find the cumulative effect of what you're doing even more astonishing than I'd expected, & very happy with some very good changes you're getting into the wording of them, either from what I'd seen previously or penciled into texts I hadn't seen before. For a while I didn't know exactly where I'd come into it, until I began to play the tape of the 10th song against your version & was thrown back to the question of how to make the English sound correspond to the sound in Navaho, both as a matter of color (rhyme etc) & compression (number of words & syllables per phrase). I began to chant along with Frank & to work-in, not vocables but little words that would play off "woman" or "son" as his "e-hye-la" & "ana yeye 'e" do off "esdza shiye'." I don't know if this is the "solution" in fact, but the results at least seem "real" to me, the one drawback being that the key words I've used in place of his vocables enter substantially into the meaning of the piece, my intrusion I'm afraid; & yet the structure as sound seems related to what he's giving, & the three repeated words (one & none & gone), while they're absorbed in the music & become almost "abstract," feel to me like a relevant statement. Anyway the chorus as I now have it reads:

> Go to her my son & one & go to her my son & one & one & none & gone
> Go to her my son & one & go to her my son & one & one & none & gone

& the opening verses read:

> Because I was the boy raised in the dawn & one & go to her my son & one & one & none & gone
> & leaving from the house the bluestone home & gone & one & go to her my son & one & one & none & gone
> & leaving from the house the shining home & one & go to her my son & one & one & none & gone
> & leaving from the swollen house my breath has blown & one & go to her my son & one & one & none & gone
> & leaving from the house the holy home & one & go to her my son & one & one & none & gone
> etc.

Whether I change the key words into something else (i.e., English sounding vocables) or not, there's no question that a "solution" of this kind would have been impossible without getting at Frank's original; nor would what I'm doing in terms of compressing some of the later sections have been possible without your notes, etc. In other words the collaboration, from my point of view, seems to be working so far. As soon as I do a little more polishing I'll be sending you a small tape on which I'll read or chant my first versions of the 10th song, also a copy of it in writing. The look of the rest of what you've sent has me very excited, particularly the way the vocables change & in the last songs seem to cut right into the middle of phrases. What I'd like, as soon as possible, is tapes of some of the others, so I can hear for myself what's going on in them; maybe the first, the eleventh, & a couple of the last ones. I have no hope of matching the precision of what you're doing, only of making a kind of poetic statement of my own that may possibly present in an immediate form some of the power & intelligence of the Navaho originals.

It would be good too if I could somehow get together with you somewhere along the line, since I find those sessions of great value all around. Would you possibly be able to come out here for the Green Corn, which is likely this year to be falling out the last week of August. It's one of the good times to be out here & would afford you the chance to look in on the workings of the song-makers, etc. If that seems possible we have lots of at least floor space in our house & would otherwise try to take care of you & Susan in royal style. Let me know & keep me further informed as things progress.

Again thanks for everything & for letting me share your workings, which I hold in the greatest admiration.

ADDENDUM. *It was through David McAllester, undoubtedly one of America's great ethnomusicologists, that I was led into the "total translation" of a series of "horse songs" from the blessingway of the Navajo hatali Frank Mitchell. The letter, above, was written early in my stay at the Allegany Seneca Reservation in New York State, where I was also engaged with Richard Johnny John in the translation of a range of Seneca (Iroquois) songs. McAllester's own translations of the aforesaid horse songs were quite as radical in their literalness & attention to Navajo syntax & expression as were my own attempts to capture the oral dimensions of the original as a form of new performance. I was of course entirely dependent on him in the process.*

A full account of my experiments in "total translation" appears on page 193 & the translation of an additional horse song—that one with the dominant color blue—on page 159.

POETICS & POLEMICS 2

EYE OF WITNESS

A Klee drawing named "Angelus Novus" shows an angel looking as though he is about to move away from something he is fixedly contemplating. His eyes are staring, his mouth is open, his wings are spread. This is how one pictures the angel of history. His face is turned toward the past. Where we perceive a chain of events, he sees one single catastrophe that keeps piling ruin upon ruin and hurls it in front of his feet. The angel would like to stay, awaken the dead, and make whole what has been smashed. But a storm is blowing from Paradise; it has got caught in his wings with such violence that the angel can no longer close them. The storm irresistibly propels him into the future to which his back is turned, while the pile of debris before him grows skyward. This storm is what we call progress.

Walter Benjamin, *Ninth Thesis on the Philosophy of History*

PROLOGOMENA TO A POETICS

for Michael McClure

....

Poet man walks between dreams
He is alive, he is breathing freely
thru a soft tube like a hookah.
Ashes fall around him as he walks
singing above them.
Oh how green
the sun is where it marks
the ocean.
Feathers drift atop the hills
down which the poet man
keeps walking, walking
a step ahead of what he fears,
of what he loves.

....

Why has the poet failed us?
Why have we waited, waited for the word to come again?
Why did we remember what the name means
only to now forget it?
If the poet's name is god how dark the day is
how heavy the burden is he carries with him.
All poets are jews, said Tsvetayeva.
The god of the jews is jewish, said a jew.
It was white around him & his voice
was heavy,
like a poet's voice in winter,
old & heavy,
crackling,
remembering frozen oceans in a summer clime,
how contrary he felt
how harsh the suffering was in him,
let it go!

The poet is dreaming about a poet
& calls out.
Soon he will have forgotten who he is.

. . . .

Speak to the poet's mother,
she is dead now.
So many years ago she left her father's clime.
His father too.
The tale of wandering is still untold,
untrue. The tale of who you are,
the tale of where the poem can take us,
of where it stops
& where the voice stops.
The poem is an argument with death.
The poem is priceless.
Those who are brought into the poem can never leave it.
In a silver tux the poet in the poem by Lorca
walks down the hall to greet the poet's bride.
The poet sees her breasts shine in the mirror.
Apples as white as boobs,
says Lorca.
He is fed the milk of paradise,
the dream of every poet man
of every poet bride.
The band plays up
the day unstops & rushes out to greet
another night.

. . . .

Is the black poet
black?
And is the creation of his hands & throat
a black creation?
Yes, says the poet man
who wears three rings,

the poet man who seeks the precious light,
passes the day beside a broken door
no one can enter. Hold it shut,
the god cries & the jew rolls over
in his endless sleep.
Gods like little wheels glide past him
down the mountain road where cats live
in a cemetery guarded by his father's star,
a poet & a bride entangled in the grass,
his hands are black
his eyes the whitest white
& rimmed with scarlet.
Hear the drumbeat,
heart.
The blacks have landed on the western shore
the long lost past of poetry revives.

. . . .

Our fingers fail us.

Then tear them off! the poet cries
not for the first time.
The dead are too often seen filling our streets,
who hasn't seen them?
A tremor across the lower body,
always the image of a horse's head
& sandflies.
A woman's breast & honey.
She in whose mouth the murderers stuffed gravel
who will no longer speak.
The poet is the only witness to that death,
writes every line
as though the only witness.

From THE SIBILA INTERVIEW: THE POEM AS AN ACT OF WITNESS

CHARLES BERNSTEIN. *Many of the poems in* A Book of Witness, *your new book from New Directions, are centered on the possibilities of the "I", and by extension, personal expression. Yet much of your work, as editor, poet and translator, has worked to decenter conventionally self-expressive verse. Can you talk about the tension between expression and construction in your work?*

That was certainly one of the driving ideas in *A Book of Witness*, something that I had had in mind before but on which I had never acted so deliberately. The question of self-expression had come to dominate many of the conventional approaches to poetry, to make poetry almost exclusively an arena for the lyric, first-person voice. Like most of us, I came out of that mind-set, and like many of us, I resisted it. My idea for poetry was that, even where we worked in shorter forms, the range of voice accessible to us, like the range of subject or vocabulary, should be unlimited. At the same time I was fascinated by certain works—largely but not exclusively ethnopoetic—in which the first person ("I" and "me") was used in ways that went far beyond the personal. I gave a number of examples in *Technicians of the Sacred* and the other anthologies, but the one that I took as template came from the María Sabina *veladas*—wall-to-wall first person but every utterance attributed to a mythic other voice:

> I am a little launch woman, says
> I am a little shooting star woman, says
> I am the Morning Star woman, says
> I am the First Star woman, says
> I am a woman who goes through the water, says
> I am a woman who goes through the ocean, says
> I am the great Woman of the Flowing Water, says
> I am the sacred Woman of the Flowing Water, says

But even before I knew about María Sabina, I was using the first person in that way—maybe derived from African praise-poems, maybe on my own:

> I am the man who held the keys.
> I asked you to forgive me.
> I was the first to be insistent and the last to leave.

I vomited.
I didn't come there often.
I was eager and alive.

I was not the least among them.
Once I was.
Once I remember being in a poor position.

I applied for membership.
I was sad.
Then I thought no longer to go on living.

I turned from you and offered you my keys.
You turned beside me and offered your position.
I had turned against them.[1]

All of that, as you point out, is a compositional as well as an expressive matter, and I'm not sure if expression or self-expression is anything but misleading when we talk about it. Looking back now, I see that in that last poem I was using the "I" pronoun to set up a series of repetitions, more for the sake of contradiction than agreement. I could switch of course to third person ("he" or "she" or "they") with similar results, but the power of the "I" and a certain fluctuation in its use—between fact and fiction—had a different meaning. It was clear that language allowed the "I" to testify, but to what was it testifying and who in any instance was the person, the "I," who was speaking? I began to feel, in that way, that an unfettered use of "I" wouldn't so much lock in identity as put it into question.

Regarding composition or construction, there was another work which helped me to launch *A Book of Witness* and to which it has some necessary reference. I had been reading a little book by the artist Jenny Holzer—*Laments*—and finding in it a still more complicated weaving of "I" utterances. For Holzer these seemed to function as narratives that formed a kind of postmodern version of Edgar Lee Masters' *Spoon River Anthology*—twelve individuated "voices of the dead" she called them, but I read each one instead as a series of overlapping voices and identities. I also had a number of other things in mind—compositionally, I mean, as well as intellectually: that the utterances would be separate from each other as I wrote

[1]The full poem appears above, page 96.

them and would form a unity only later, or however it fell out; that they would include brief "I" utterances from other poets, most of whom I would identify in the margins; and that they would constitute a long series (a hundred poems in total) where the reiteration of the form affected and changed the reading of the individual poems.

Here's one, as a sampler, that starts with a line from the Brazilian poet Jorge de Lima:

I BELIEVE IN THE MAGIC OF GOD

I believe in the magic of god (J. de Lima)
& in fire. Somebody
dangles a key on the steps.
From a hole in my chest
eyes stare out.
I run into a circle
of friends
little men with pale lips
& soft fingers.
I signal new forms of expression.
The way sand shapes hills
& water shapes fountains.
I am in their hands completely
helpless as a babe
unless the babe command the world
sending a stream of
feathers
back to earth.
A prince he is & dances
between rivers
then rides a shining rocket
to the upper air.
It brings the wolves to me
to eat out of my hand.
The streets of Rome
signal a fresh
disaster. I am one
a pope would deign to speak to
when I wave my arms.

CECILIA VICUÑA. *In the pre-face to the* New Selected Poems 1970–1985, *you speak of yourself as a witness, as I understand it not just to the world, but to your own process, which leads us to the old question of "el desdoblaje", being in and out of yourself at the same time while performing. Would you care to explore this further?*

This is a different question from Charles's, although it touches on similar ground and on the word "witness," which is, I suppose, central to my idea of what the aim of my poetry may be. In the pre-face you mention, the declaration about witnessing goes as follows: "I am a witness like everyone else to [the world, the present, as it comes and goes], and all the experiments [the poems] for me … are steps toward the recovery/discovery of a language for that witnessing." At the same time I find myself shying away from such a claim, because it seems to me I've seen and felt so little. I keep coming back to it, however, with a sense that a little may be enough and that I can use the means at my disposal to be a conduit for others—at its most intense for others who have seen and felt a lot.

In *Khurbn*, the cycle of poems I wrote about the holocaust, I opened myself to other voices, witnesses to those events, by composing, constructing, texts—my own words interlaced (collaged) with theirs. *A Book of Witness* is much more constructed, much less constrained by its thematic. Here I take the first person ("I") as voice of witness and follow wherever it leads me, while at the same time I confront the problematics of witnessing and the possible lie of speaking in the first person—in the witness's voice. I am aware here too of the degradation of the first person, both by poets close to me who disparage it and by others who restrict it to a narrow, "confessional" perspective. In the Postface to *A Book of Witness*, I speak of it as "the instrument—in language—for all acts of witnessing, the key with which we open up to voices other than our own."

When it comes to performance, however, I appear as who I am—as the presenter of my own works or of works like Hugo Ball's *Karawane* or Schwitters' *London Onion* that I've appropriated for myself. I'm not aware of acting a role other than myself; that is to say, I don't have to get into character to perform, as an actor would, but have only to work myself into the performance as a musician might. In doing that I'm aware as well that "myself" in the act of performance feels different for me than "myself" does otherwise. I like your word *desdoblaje*, which I take as a splitting apart or a breaking in two, and I think that what I've said just now may be my version of it.

Or put more simply: I hear myself speak and in that moment of performance I am both subject and object: the one who listens and the one who speaks.

KHURBN & HOLOCAUST: "AFTER AUSCHWITZ THERE IS ONLY POETRY"

In the 1970s, in composing *A Big Jewish Book* as an anthology/assemblage of poems "from tribal times to the present", I began with a dream about a "house of Jews" ("like a great black hole in space") and a quotation from Franz Kafka ("what have I in common with Jews? I hardly have anything in common with myself"), and I ended with a poem from Paul Celan addressed to fellow poet Nelly Sachs (another holocaust survivor), questioning "the dimming through light, of / Jewishness, of / your God. // Of / that."

1
With Celan, who was a poet of the human—not only Jewish—disaster of the second world war, I would like to address a theme or presence to which until a certain point in time my work only barely alluded, but which has been an ongoing subtext in my poetry and in that of much of my generation. In a period of barely half a dozen years (from 1939 to 1945) there were over 50 million state-directed murders of human beings and at least that many [far more] sufferings, maimings and tortures: a disaster so large as to be almost incomprehensible and itself only a part of the disasters and conflagrations of the past century and the first decade of the one in which we're now living. Auschwitz and Hiroshima came to be the two events by which we speak of it—signs of an enormity that turned myth into history, nightmare into fact. The horror of those events encompassed hundreds of thousands of like disasters, joined (as we began to realize) to other, not unrelated violence against the environment / the earth and the other-than-human world. By the mid-twentieth century, in Charles Olson's words, "man" had been "reduced to so much fat for soap, superphosphate for soil, fillings and shoes for sale," an enormity that had robbed language (one of our "proudest acts," he said) of the power to meaningfully respond, had thus created a crisis of expression (no, of meaning, of reality), for which a poetics must be devised if we were to rise, again, beyond the level of a scream or of a silence more terrible than any scream.

The ground against which Olson, writing in the late 1940s, set his own poetry of "resistance" (his word for it) is the too familiar ground of Auschwitz and the death camps of World War Two. Even now, when that ground has been sanitized and turned into a museum (a museum more than a shrine), the presence as exhibits of hair, shoes, fillings, glasses, prayer shawls, toys, can still bring an immediate uncontrollable sense of the reduction, the degradation that the modern world allows. I do not intend to set the Jews apart as victims, as if the lesson is only there for *us*—or the suffering. Nor do I want to see us only as victims, the innocent sufferers, though Auschwitz and the holocaust are at their most horrible the accounts of an innocent suffering. To be only the victims, as the founders of Zionism knew, was to be only partly human—a perception that has led on its negative side to the tragedy of Palestine and the ongoing wars and murders. It is for reasons like this—reasons still unresolved for me—that in writing *Poland/1931* and *A Big Jewish Book*, I did for the most part let the holocaust speak without being spoken.

The word "holocaust" was itself a block, something I'll say more about as I get into my own work as a poet, but I'll say a little about it now. I grew up during the war but not in it, and the reports of the death and suffering—*all* the deaths and sufferings—came back to us only by degrees. I was a child of the generation that rejoiced in the deaths of our enemies [and all those—whether innocent or not—connected to those enemies], and there is a burden in that from which I have long wanted to be free. There was a grandmother who wept for her dead, but I only cried for her weeping. At no point did she speak the word *holocaust* or even the word *shoah*, but the childword for me (from which I can still feel a tightness in the throat and chest) was *khurbn* (*khirbn* in the dialect of where they came from). Holocaust is a Christian word that bears the image of a total, all consuming sacrifice by fire. A totality of fire: that is, in human terms, a genocide. The fire I believe is true; the sacrifice a euphemism for the terror.

(Or if one thinks of sacrifice, the question next comes up: a sacrifice to what? To whom? And the answers come rushing back, sounding themselves like questions: to God? to Hitler? to make atonement for inherent sin? or Jewish sin? to set the circumstances for a Jewish state? And it seemed to me then and now that the word itself was false, that the questions that it raised were false, that the answers that it seemed to force only increased the sense of pain and madness. *Khurbn* was the word I knew for it: a word with a history but with no false ennoblement. Disaster pure and simple. Nothing left to say beyond the word. No sacrifice to ponder. And no meaning.)

Besides which, I didn't hear the word holocaust used in that sense until a decade or more after the event. By then much had been written about the suffering, some of it (the first witnessings in particular) in a language and a literature that we came to prize. But there was also a feeling that turned many of us from a participation in that writing: a revulsion at taking on the voice of those who suffered, of displaying our own feelings in such a way as to overshadow the terror of those times and places. It became necessary to talk outside it if we were to talk at all. But the impression of it was burned into our minds and hearts, so that it colored everything we did as poets or as artists. "After Auschwitz," wrote Adorno, "writing poetry is barbaric"; but *that* poetry he singled out as *lyrik* [lyric poetry]. Another kind of poetry came to be our crucial way of speaking: our most human/humane act.

I want to speak about two turnings in my own work as they related to holocaust or *khurbn*. "What have I in common with Jews?" Kafka had asked, as a mark of his own alienation, even from himself. As a Jew after Auschwitz there were two [principal] ways to go: to move into a new Jewish nationalism as a response to the threat against this order-of-being in particular, or to take the legacy of Auschwitz as a call to vigilance against all forms of chauvinism and racism (even those held by Jews). [I do not count the third way here, of total separation or indifference.] Most of those whom I know went the second way, there to meet with others likewise moved by those times and by the times that would follow. What was Jewish moved beneath the surface—or lived *inside* the words. A witnessing by silence.

In 1968 America was deep into Viet Nam and I was finishing a first assemblage of tribal poetries from around the world, *Technicians of the Sacred*. The war drove me to a further, deeper alienation from America, and *Technicians* led me to explore ancestral sources of my own—"in a world" (I wrote) "of Jewish mystics, thieves, & madmen." The book that followed, *Poland/1931*, was unmistakably Jewish; but ironic also, since it accepted (on the surface) a degree of chauvinism and sentimentality I would otherwise deny. Played out in part as a comic encounter, it gave me a sense too of having come into a mythic, fantastic world in which, astonished, I somehow felt myself at home. David Meltzer called it my "Jewish surrealist vaudeville," a phrase that I liked and often repeated. Beyond the irony and myth, there was I felt a history as well, but a history that fell just short of the holocaust, of that which was still not to be spoken. (It didn't have to be, of course, since everyone knew it was there without the naming.)

The opening poem of *Poland/1931* begins like this:

my mind is stuffed with tablecloths
& with rings but my mind
is dreaming of poland stuffed with poland
brought in the imagination
to a black wedding
a naked bridegroom hovering above
his naked bride   mad poland
how terrible thy jews at weddings
thy synagogues with camphor smells & almonds
thy thermos bottles thy electric fogs
thy braided armpits
thy underwear alive with roots o poland
poland poland poland poland poland …[2]

I wrote that in 1967/68, and the other poems in that book between then and 1973. I had never been to Poland but had set the parameters of the work by Poland as my ancestral place-of-origin and by 1931 as the year of my birth—not in Poland but in Brooklyn. As at the end of that first poem (with its executioners procreated by the Polish-Jewish bride and groom), you can sense the holocaust if you choose or you can find it more clearly, more at surface, in another poem, "The Student's Testimony," in which I speak of a war and a man hidden in a cellar [an uncle the circumstances of whose death by suicide was later told to us] while above him the stars draw letters across a ruined sky.

. . . .

(Auschwitz, Hiroshima.) It was as much as I wanted to say—as I thought I should say—until I traveled by car from Germany to Poland in 1988. Crossing the line I felt myself moving into a world still in ruins—an empty world—a world of ghosts. At the border, waiting, we sat in our car beside a line of trucks filled with cattle on their way to slaughter. Bellowing. The sounds were heavy—lost and painful. The air stunk of excrement, became itself an animal. I walked into a latrine to relieve myself, to

2 The full poem, "The Wedding," appears above on page 214.

piss, and I was overwhelmed by accumulated human smells. And I remembered the books of witness I had read before, the visions of a death by excrement so often written there. I felt myself (this man, this animal) in a condition of unrest as never before—and in a condition of poetry.

2

Robert Creeley—the American poet who, more than anyone else in my generation, has saved (that is, transformed) the "lyric voice" for us—writes in a later [and not particularly typical] poem:

Ever since Hitler
or well before that
fact of human appetite
addressed with brutal
indifference others
killed or tortured or ate
the same bodies they
themselves had   we ourselves
had plunged into density
of selves all seeming stinking
one no possible way
out of it smiled or cried
or tore at it and died
apparently dead at last
just no other way out.

I cite this here because of Creeley's recognition that there does in fact exist a kind of poetry to which the term "holocaust [poetry]" [or post-holocaust poetry] might still be meaningfully applied. As such it is not necessarily poetry *about* the holocaust [as here], but a poetry that characterizes what it means to be human, to be a maker of poems (even *lyric* poems!) after Auschwitz. Poetry after Auschwitz is poetry that has been touched, transformed by Auschwitz and the other terrors of our time. It is altered, transformed, down to its roots, its language, and the extent of that transformation is a measure of its test as poetry. This is not an easy test to make or take, but it is for me, with all the allowances I am willing to make for myself and my fellow poets, the measure by which our work has been, must be judged from thereon out. It underlies our discontent with regularity and clarity as a reflection of nature or of God. Reality—and let me say this as strongly as I can—is what the twisted, rotting, disbelieving dead at Auschwitz, Hiroshima, and the other hellholes of this world reveal to us. We may hide from it—and do—too often in that other mode that we confuse with poetry [and may still write or practice as "resistance"]—I mean, "the way of Beauty," "Reason's Way."

The poetry after Auschwitz is a poetry *in extremis*—a poetry at the extremities of language ... the extremities therefore of thought and feeling. It was Creeley who spoke, elsewhere, of a poem "addressed to emptiness" (the *anomie* and anonymity of the modern and postmodern conditions), but I would speak as well of a *poem addressed to ugliness*—a counter not only to anomie's numbness (its loss of law or meaning) but to that other temptation—*the temptation of the beautiful*—that we also feel. Given more time, I would trace it with you to a range of poetries—of transformations across the arts—from both before and after Auschwitz. It is *mankind in extremis* and it has its counterpart in *nature in extremis:* the terror of an angry and devouring god—the total god envisioned in the total state—made real by the imagination.

It is this that comes to me when writing, living, in a state of poetry—when I am most clearly in it. And I think of the bodies of the living dead, buried in excrement: the account of an ugliness, repeated many times over, that overwhelms us in the pages of the witnesses. "Hell upon hell of excrement," writes Antonin Artaud (of other places, other hells), locked in the mental hospital at Rodez, while the Holocaust was going on—and in the pit of his own body. But the century—of wars and holocausts [continuing as well into the present]—has worked its way into his own language and the vision that his language gives us. "With my own eyes," he writes, "I have seen falling from a great many coffins I know not what black matter, I know not what immortal urine, [from] these forms mute of life which, morsel by morsel, drop by drop, destroyed themselves. The name of this matter is caca, and caca is the raw material of the soul, whose puddles I have seen in so many coffins spread before my eyes. ... The breath of the bones has a center and this center is the abyss of Kah-Kah, Kah the corporeal breath of shit, which is the opium of eternal survival. ... The odor of the eternal ass of death is the oppressed energy of a soul whom the world refused to let live."

This, then, is also poetry's real voice—its *most* real voice perhaps, given the revelations of the Khurbn and of the century (and more) from which we have just been emerging [and which continues to assault us]. It is not an easy thing to say, since I too have been smitten by Beauty—often enough—and have felt that as an antidote to the murder and madness of the other dispensation. But that was to forget that the perpetrators themselves so often held to a cult of mindless beauty, while committing the ugliest (because most systematically conceived of) crimes and degradations—as the final issue, so to speak, of a false and lying art.

It was all of that that stuck with me, came rushing back at me in fact, when I felt myself *dibbik*-stricken on my first journey to Poland and the death camps at Auschwitz and elsewhere. I'll end this part of my presentation, then, with one of the poems from *Khurbn*—a poem with the Yiddish title "Nokh Aushvitz"—and the English title "After Auschwitz"—which says, I think, what I've otherwise been trying to say here. It follows another poem in which I've modified Adorno's comment that there can be no poetry after Auschwitz into my own declaration: *After Auschwitz there is only poetry.*

[Reads "Nokh Aushvitz" (After Auschwitz)]:

the poem is ugly & they make it uglier
wherein the power resides
that duncan did—or didn't understand
when listening that evening to the other poet read
he said   "that was pure ugliness"   & oh it was
it was   & it made my heart skip a beat
because the poem wouldn't allow it   no
not a moment's grace nor beauty to obstruct
whatever the age demanded   or the poem ...[3]

---

[3] The full poem appears above on page 313.

HAROLD BLOOM: THE CRITIC AS EXTERMINATING ANGEL

Among the uglier images making up what will emerge as the myth of the 20th Century is that of Dr. Josef Mengele—exterminating angel of Auschwitz—who separated the victims bound directly for the gas chambers from those healthy enough to be spared for terminal labor assignments. His characteristic gesture, at least in my own vision of it, was a flick of either wrist & the laconic words, "You to the right" or "You to the left."

One variant of the myth would have us believe further that Mengele, being a man of some "culture" or pretensions thereto, found the task sad but otherwise inevitable.

As goodness, we have been told ad infinitum, may sometimes spring from evil, I would have hoped that the image of Mengele's judgment (or its innumerable counterparts) might have helped us pull away from the model of man casting himself in the role of a judgmental god. At least I would have hoped so in the domain of art: an experimental ground in which such human possibilities can be played out as images. "Pour en finir avec le jugement de Dieu"—Artaud's great verbal act of exorcism—followed the savageries of Auschwitz by a couple of years, & a characteristic if milder stance of some later avant-gardists aimed to create for art & poetry a function that allowed discovery while avoiding the pretense to judgment characteristic of most critical & literary traditions.

I'm reminded of all this in going over the critical writings of Harold Bloom—a task I set myself after reading a particularly indulgent piece of his exclusionary criticism that I'll discuss below. In Bloom, more blatantly than elsewhere, the idea of the critic as exterminating angel appears with characteristic regrets, etc., but in no uncertain terms. "However diffidently I give the answer," he writes in *Kabbalah and Criticism*, "I am engaged in canon-formation, in trying to help decide a question that is ultimately of a sad importance: 'Which poet shall live?'"

I'm aware of the hyperbole, even the absurdity involved in setting Bloom beside Mengele, but I can't help feeling that he himself must have had some such comparison in mind when presenting his work in those terms. The play of much of his criticism (& by far its most interesting aspect) involves his incorporation of Jewish mysticism & myth into a description of "post-Enlightenment poetry;" & this includes, beyond a reinforcement of Bloom's six rhetorical tropes or of his "revisionist" poetics in general, the use of such a solidly traditional figure as the Malakh ha-Mavat = Angel of Death = Satan = (by a common gnostic & Blakean inversion) God as Jehovah. His criticism seems obsessed as well with the killing-off of poets—largely of course with poets killing other poets, both forerunners & contemporaries, in a veritable battle-to-the-death. Given all that, it seems unlikely to me that as "Jewish" a critic as Bloom would not, in making his assertion of a "you live / you die" function for criticism, have been struck by the image of Mengele, in much the same way that as "Jewish" a poet as myself immediately felt its presence.

I will get back to the "Jewish question" shortly—as well as the not unrelated questions of poetic struggle & canon-formation. For the moment I would like to play with (& even "mis-read") some of the key terms in Bloom's criticism, which together form a coherent if spiritually stingy view of reality & one that seems aimed (for whatever we might want to salvage from it) against much of what I take to be of most value in the poetry & art of this century.

2

Much of Bloom's energy as a critic has gone into the exposure of the blindness of poets about their origins in other poets—a blindness & an attempt at concealment that involves, most crucially, those poets whom Bloom professes most strongly to admire. This work of exposure is more than critic's busy-work, whether as simple source-study or as what Geoffrey Hartman calls, using some of Bloom's own terms, "a type of 'misreading' which helps poets to overcome the influence of previous poets"—or, as Bloom more accurately puts it, a "deadly encouragement that never ceases to remind them of how heavy their inheritance is." Bloom's involvement is intense, even personal, & what it finally reveals is his own blindness about the motives of his enterprise & its origins in what may be a deep struggle with, & antagonism toward, the very objects of his admiration. The work, in other words, is highly deceptive (to himself & others)—at least if one misses certain key confessions sprinkled through it, or if one is diverted by the radical nature of Bloom's great predecessor poets (Milton, Blake, Shelley, Emerson, Whitman, & so on) into thinking that Bloom is dealing in the present—as they in the past—with a true poetics of liberation. The approach through Bloom is in fact the reverse of any such position.

To begin with—& this shouldn't surprise anyone out there—Bloom's poetics, as he presents it, is militantly "literary." (This doesn't mean that it may not have other ends in view—political, social, etc.—but more of that later.) He is by self-proclamation an "academic critic," who presents the history of Western poetry as the work of a succession of academically based canon-makers, from the time when "Alexandria, which … founded our scholarship, permanently set the literary tradition of the school, and introduced the secularized notion of the canon"—a process which modernism (= "the Romantic psychology of belatedness") has challenged or confused but never, presumably, replaced. "Nothing in the literary world," writes Bloom in *A Map of Misreading*, "sounds quite so silly to me as the passionate declarations that poetry must be liberated from the academy, declarations that would be absurd at any time, but peculiarly so some twenty-five hundred years after Homer and the academy first became indistinguishable." (How the assembled ghosts of Blake, Shelley & Whitman would have handled that one, boggles the mind—though no doubt it provides Harold with a chuckle as well.)

What holds for the critic-as-academic-reader must also hold for the poets. That most poets who read are readers isn't the point at issue, nor that poets are "desperately obsessed with poetic origins"—& with other origins as well: personal, linguistic, cosmic, etc. For Bloom it must be tighter than that, & so he writes, in *Poetry and Repression:* "Even the strongest poet must take up his stance within literary language. If he stands outside it, he cannot begin to write poetry. For poetry lives always under the shadow of poetry." (Thus Bloom's favoring of rhetoric & so on over Wordsworth's "selection of the real language of men" or its more precise, therefore more threatening contemporary equivalents.) Or again, in *A Map of Misreading:* "Poems, I am saying, are neither about 'subjects' nor about 'themselves.' They are necessarily about other poems; a poem is a response to a poem, as a poet is a response to a poet, or a person to his parent." And the response, in Bloom's terms, is always a mis-reading, a mis-interpretation, the outgrowth of a struggle oedipally conceived: "To live, the poet must misinterpret the father, by the crucial act of misprision, which is the re-writing of the father." (Such misprision, in Bloom's account, may also involve the critic as reader, though the struggle there seems muted—not presented, for all of Bloom's exterminating passion, as a battle-to-the-death.)

In all of this, as I see it, the problem is not that Bloom takes a literary or textual approach but that he leaves us room for almost nothing else: an occasional nod toward the "reading" of nature or of experience, or a passing hint that precursors, even literary ones, may be other than poets or that the struggle may be with forces other than literary ones. Such one-sidedness is the price of obsession—his own, self-acknowledged, with the idea of influence & its attendant anxieties—& it leaves him often & inevitably at odds with his poets themselves, their poetics & self-interpretations, their views of their own & others' struggles where those contradict the needs of Bloom's particular "misprision." While Bloom is certainly aware of this, he "take(s) the resistance shown to the theory by many poets, in particular, to be likely evidence for its validity, for poets rightly idealize their activity; & all poets, weak and strong, agree in denying any share in the anxiety of influence."

The finesse of that last shot is absolutely breathtaking: an assertion of the critic's hegemony against all odds & certainly "all poets"—like Bloom's comment elsewhere that "the true poem is the critic's mind." It is as if Claude Lévi-Strauss had inadvertently confessed to Russell Means's worst suspicions about anthropologists; & seen in the larger frame of Bloom's intentions & assumptions, it drives home a separation between poet & (academic) critic, not as many of us have long felt it but toward ends that Bloom announces here & there with great forthrightness. So, he tells us in *A Map of Misreading*, "No strong poet can deign to be a good reader of his own works," nor should the critic speak for him exactly, because "this is not the critic's proper work, to take up the poet's stance." And having said that much, he goes on to question—from the critic's perspective—the term most central to the poetics of nearly all his targeted "strong poets" & to that Romantic tradition one might have thought he was defending:

> Perhaps there is a power or faculty of the Imagination, and certainly all poets must go on believing in its existence, but a critic makes a better start by agreeing with Hobbes that imagination is "decaying sense" and that poetry is written by the same natural man or woman who suffers daily all the inescapable anxieties of competition.

The key word here—since Bloom has pulled us back into the "light of common day"—is "competition." Few poets would deny their identity as natural men or women (it is, if anything, part of the inheritance of the Romantic); but the discovery that competition—not imagination!—is the central definition of the natural & human (&, ultimately, the poetic) is a point that wouldn't escape the readers of *Commentary*, say, whatever effect, or non-effect, it may have on the readers of *Sulfur.*

We are approaching the crucial split between two human possibilities that marks Bloom's doleful "deconstruction," the moral choice behind his poet-critic cleavage, whose implications, since his position isn't timeless, become much clearer, more specific & more contemporary, elsewhere in his work. Thus, he writes in the introduction to *Figures of Capable Imagination* (1976):

> Poets lie, both to themselves and to everyone else, about their indebtedness to one another, and most critics and literary scholars tend to follow poets by hopelessly idealizing all interpoetic relations. Now that the tides of aggressive ignorance, or the counter-culture, are ebbing, many of the absurd hopes that the young and their middle-

aged followers placed in an apocalypse of society are coming to rest in the arts, particularly literature, in the belief that there at least the repressed can return, a belief much encouraged by such false prophets as Marcuse and Norman O. Brown.

If this isn't Bloom at his best—& it isn't—it's Bloom giving an unequivocal context for his present disturbance. The identity of the "false prophets" isn't worth an argument, though the question of the other poets/prophets, who "lie ... to themselves & to everyone else" (but from whom Bloom derives his livelihood), should at least give one pause—the relation of Blake, say, to "counter-culture" &"apocalypse" & "art" & the "return of the repressed." A notable "misreading,"' I'd have thought, to go from Blake's dream of liberation to this hostility toward those who would presume to carry it into the present. Knowingly or not (but no critic should "deign to be a good reader of his own works"), Bloom is here playing out the archetypal role of Blake's "Devourer": the antithesis of the "Prolific," who thinks he has the Prolific/the "producer" in his chains ("but it is not so, he only takes portions of existence & fancies that the whole"). In this, Blake writes as a (true? false?) prophet, pointing to the continuing existence of "these two classes of men ... [who are &] should be enemies," for "whoever tries to reconcile them seeks to destroy existence."

If Bloom is the Devourer—the diluter of energy, the reductive agent—"revisionism" is no longer the poet's (prolific) re-visioning but an attempt to turn the unqualified "freedom" of the Romantics & their successors into a qualified & "repressed freedom": itself a product of anxiety. The Devourer, then, swallows the Prolific's "excess of delights" but seems to choke on them; or, as Devourer-turned-teacher, he laments: "How is he [am I] to teach a tradition now grown so wealthy and so heavy that to accommodate it demands more strength than any single consciousness can provide?" Unlike the Prolific—the producer—who revels in his own & others' excesses, the teacher/Devourer/critic is driven to despair & to canon-formation to relieve the stress.

As mere "academic criticism," the Bloom dilemma seems a little sad & silly. But it's never more than a short step from literature to those other areas where ideas like "freedom" & "repression" affect the actual ways we think & act as human beings. Given Bloom's own time frame & his sense already quoted of the counter-revolutionary nature of the middle 1970s & beyond, I will allow myself a political reading of one of his statements vis à vis "strong" poets & "strong" poetry in *Poetry and Repression*, that "it is only by repressing creative 'freedom,' through the initial fixation of influence, that a person can be reborn as a poet." The terms are slippery & may at first be taken as purely self-repressive &/or psychological; but while Bloom relates his work to Freudian ideas of sublimation ("Geoffrey Hartman ... calls the poetic will 'sublimated compulsion' ... [while] I would call it 'repressed freedom'"), he himself tells us that his aim isn't "so much to apply Freud (or even revise Freud) as to arrive at an Oedipal interpretation of poetic history." Nor is it simply a question of poetic restraints as a matter of technique or method. The issue for Bloom increasingly involves a response to a contemporary condition of yearning for which Bloom's own precursor poets had acted as prime movers. That response—at least the part of it that concerns me here—is threefold.

He is, to begin with, scornful of the ambitions of "post-Enlightenment poets," although the scorn is sometimes hidden behind a mask of "melancholy." "Unfortunately," he tells us in *Kabbalah and Criticism*, "we have all of us arrived too late in the day to take on such a flamboyance" as that of Emerson & Whitman "chanting ... that a large consciousness contradicts itself because it contains multitudes." But this late-in-the-day, therefore absurd flamboyance extends, we find out in *A Map of Misreading*, from "all of us" to all American poets whatsoever, "the most consciously belated in the history of Western poetry," who, "rather more than other Western poets, at least since the Enlightenment, are astonishing in their ambitions. Each wants to be the whole of which all other poets are only parts." Applied to Emerson & Whitman themselves (but also Dickinson, Thoreau, Hawthorne, & Melville), the Bloomian misreading moves from muted mockery to a diffident paternalism that only a true Devourer could master.

From such a defensive-aggressive posture, Bloom can put into question the stand of any of his great poet-precursors against repression itself. Such a strategy is at the heart of Bloom's mis-readings, in line with which he proposes, in *Poetry and Repression*, to revise "all reasonings, including my own," of such a poem as Blake's "London," since said readings "are wholly mistaken in seeing ['London'] primarily as a protest against repression, whether societal or individual." Here a cautious adverb ("primarily") keeps him from the arch-revisionist statement he seems really to be aiming at, but later he crosses the line & tells us that "Blake's poem is not a protest, not a prophetic outcry, not a vision of judgment. It is a revisionist's self-condemnation, a Jonah's outcry at knowing he is not an Ezekiel." All of which is a crazy "academic" view of a poet who shivers the boundaries of literature; who is Blake rather than Ezekiel (& no less important for that);

& whose prophetic outcry co-exists with whatever "negative and self-destructive" elements Bloom may rightly or wrongly see in him.* We have here passed from mis-reading to deception: the attempt to reduce Blake's fine frenzy to that "failure of nerve" which, if I remember it correctly, underpinned the new conservatism of the critics of my childhood. (Bloom's teachers too—to whom he once again succumbs.) The process from here on in begins to read like critic's self-projection.

The third response I have in mind is something more than that, though clearly tied to Bloom's own situation. For what Bloom does at the extreme of his deconstruction is virtually to reject the idea of "freedom" in favor of that of "repression"—terms he has already revealed to have a "social" as well as "individual" dimension (i.e., not merely "literary"). Emblematically Bloom phrases this rejection as his turning from Milton's Satan (as interpreted by Blake): a poetic creation whose influence had extended into the work of such American poetic "revisionists" as Ralph Waldo Emerson &, even, Emily Dickinson. In his characteristic manner he describes the turning not only as a matter of regret, but something deeper. "I am temperamentally a natural revisionist," he writes in *A Map of Misreading*, "and I respond to Satan's speeches more strongly than to any other poetry I know, so it causes some anguish in me to counsel that currently we need Milton's sense of tradition much more than Emerson's revisionary tradition. Indeed, the counsel of necessity must be taken further: most simply, we need Milton, and not the Romantic return of the repressed Milton but the Milton who made his great poem identical with the process of repression that is vital to literary tradition.")

In the light of current New Conservative & Moral Majority maneuvers, the invocation of the language of repression & of Milton the Puritan (or a parody thereof) as counselor-on-tradition, cannot be confined to the world of literary studies. The "we" who need the Milton of Repression is ultimately a "we" that can't be narrowed down, Bloom tells us, by "sex, race, social class," etc. "If we are human," he writes, "then we depend upon a Scene of Instruction, which is necessarily also a scene of authority

---

* Before being misled by the contrast between Blake &, say, the Hebrew prophets, the reader can check out, e.g., the self-doubt of Ezekiel 20.49: "Ah Lord God, they are saying of me: Is he not a maker of allegories?" Or Jeremiah 20.9: "There is something in my heart like a burning fire / Shut up in my bones / & I am weary of holding it in / & I cannot." Or Abraham J. Heschel in *The Prophets:* "The prophet is human, yet he employs notes one octave too high for our ears. He experiences moments that defy our understanding. He is neither 'a singing saint' nor a 'moralizing poet,' but an assaulter of the mind." [All quoted by J. R. in *A Big Jewish Book.*]

and of priority." And no matter how he tries to modify this into a middle-ground accommodation with the authoritative fathers, the stance remains contemporary with Bob Dylan's recent need "to serve somebody"—as Bloom's competition-as-creation might make a fit with the revivalist side of Milton (Friedman)'s economics.

• • • • •

I'm not refuting Bloom here, so much as indicating his obvious & admitted deviations from the line of poets (the nineteenth-century ones at least) foregrounded in his work. The spirit of that work, it seems to me, isn't revisionist but, as he himself renames it, "antithetical": almost a full turn from the re-visioning—the actual return to vision—that has marked our poetry from Blake until the present. I've found Bloom useful in clarifying some of this, & I'm in sympathy with some larger part of what he attends to: romanticism, gnosticism, & so on. At the same time I'm distressed by the reductiveness of his work, by his unwillingness to revise or revision a narrowly conservative idea of tradition & "priority." There is, in other words, no questioning of "tradition" at its roots, but a reductive assertion "that everyone who now reads and writes in the West, of whatever racial background, sex or ideological camp, is still a son or daughter of Homer." No Coyotes or Taras appear in his mythologies, no Milarepas or Li Po's among his canonized poets. Kabbala & gnosticism gain entry as maps for criticism but otherwise his "canon" is still European & his specialization post-Enlightenment & English. So it remains only those poets devoted to the idea of the prolific, exuberant, & flamboyant who have made the move to let the greater world into our work.

Bloom's narrowness helps him turn any new or liberating sense of the past into a species of "belatedness," & it allows him to disregard the forwardness that has again & again defined an avant-garde over the last two centuries. It is against such forwardness in particular that his rage seems directed—& even more particularly against the forwardness that surrounds him here & now. The poets wandering past the Bloomian woods should at least be warned of this. "A map of misreading" may sound like a step toward the openings of indeterminacy or chance or toward a free experiment with word & thought, but it isn't. Similarly, his selection of John Ashbery (Bloom's one candidate for canonization among the old "New American poets" & the New York School) may feel like a leftward tilt but is, if anything, the scorning of poetic "movements" (the attempt to draw multiple voices into the work of poesis) in favor of the single poet winnowed from his peers.

While obscuring his own critical precursors in the anti-Blakean, anti-Miltonic New Critics, Bloom's aim—against the whole thrust of visionary & revolutionary poetics—has been to maintain the process of canon-formation & the mastery of critic over poet, Devourer over Prolific, system-maker over "Inspired Man." To keep poetry within the domain of academic literature—to maintain, that is, the separation between art & life—he has devised a system that has both limited his own ability to read & to create, & has allowed him to be arbitrary in his selection of "strong" poets & "strong" poems. More than his method, it is his intention that seems so wrong & devious: a deliberate obfuscation that would reject (at least in his own time) the strong & bold in favor of those he sees, rightly or wrongly, as candidates for the purveyors of a "repressed freedom."

3

The arrogance of criticism prospers, even fattens, on the silence of the poets over whom it means to tyrannize. It is an illusory fatness, anyway, & there does come a time when some of us who make poetry are moved, for one reason or another, to break the silence & to respond in kind. For if critics are instructors, as in Bloom's view of it they are, so are poets; & it isn't always possible or useful to save ourselves the effort of that clash of instructions by surrendering the field.

What finally pushed me to a reading & a response to Bloom was his second attempt at dealing with, & dismissing, a generalized entity called "the American-Jewish poet." Since I'm a particularized version of that entity, I can be seen to have a personal stake in the matter. As a poet, of course, I'm supposed to thrive on personal stakes, while Bloom as a critic may be thought to have a need for more objective standards. But what's attractive to me in Bloom's work is that such "objectivity" is almost never there—& surely not when dealing with an entity so close to home as this one.

Bloom himself is a marvelous example of "belated" Jewish culture. It colors a large part of his criticism & it is, as I said earlier, its most interesting aspect (at least for me). This isn't a question of a down-home feeling shared by Jews, but that in dealing with certain areas of Jewish tradition, Bloom allows himself access to the kind of uncanonized traditional material for which, by a curious display of willful ignorance, he seems otherwise to have so little use. The result, in a work like *Kabbalah and Criticism*, is sometimes very useful, & similar insights turn up in his other works & intersect with a referential network that touches as well on Jewish orthodoxy & gnostic heterodoxy—non-canonical also from a Western/Christian point of view. It's my feeling that if Bloom had allowed this network to expand, he could have made an extraordinary synthesizing contribution to our concepts of poesis. But he would also have been poaching incredibly on the poet's terrain, where "all ages are contemporaneous in the mind" & everything is possible.*

Bloom on the Jewish poets is something very different. The two pieces that raise that issue are "The Sorrows of American-Jewish Poetry," which appeared in *Commentary* about ten years ago & was reprinted in *Figures of Capable Imagination*, & "The Heavy Burden of the Past" from the January 4, 1981 issue of *The New York Times Book Review*. The first piece seems to have come out of nowhere—or out of nothing more than Bloom's suspicion of, discomfort with, or hostility to, the idea of (American) Jewish poets—while the second is a review of a specific book, *Voices Within the Ark*, that presents 1200 pages, worldwide in scope, of what the editors, Anthony Rudolph & Howard Schwartz, call "The Modern Jewish Poets." The "simple" question, raised in the first essay but covering both, is "why isn't modern Jewish poetry better?" since, Bloom assures us, of the ninety American-Jewish poets in the Rudolph-Schwartz book, "only about a dozen have written authentic poems, true artifacts, and none of these alas has yet earned a place in the canon, though one or two yet may." And of those ninety American Jews (the Europeans end up only a little better at

* Bloom backs off from any such wide-spectrum synthesizing, which I assume is something he identifies, too exclusively, with the mythical "school of Pound." He is reticent as well about his relation to kabbalists & mystics, writing in *Kabbalah and Criticism:* "I myself am no kabbalist, and I hold no theosophical beliefs of any kind. I am merely a skeptic." While this is fair enough, his view of kabbala as "an interpretive and mythical tradition [rather] than a mystical one" also plays down its creative & performative side—in spite of his perception, e.g., "that the Sefirot are like poems in that they are names implying complex commentaries that make them into texts." Interestingly too, his dismissal of himself as kabbalist is coupled with a repetition of his hostility to poets who make a conscious use of precursors: "Only weak poems, or the weaker elements in strong poems, immediately echo precursor poems, or directly allude to them." (I take this as one of the most symptomatic & debilitating attitudes in all of Bloom's writings—a damning result of his critic-poet cleavage & the surest guarantee that poets will be trapped in the past rather than free it up toward future uses.)

Bloom's hands, but it's clearly the Americans he's after), Bloom further assures us that "no single figure [is included] who so far matters urgently or overwhelmingly in the poetry of our country."*

Since this is Bloom writing, I take it, in the language of "natural man & woman"—or what we used to call "the man in the street" or "average N.Y. Times reader"—I assume we can go by the ordinary meanings of those sentences. Bloom in fact makes it a little difficult to test his proposition, since he names not one American-Jewish poet in the course of his review—unlike the earlier *Commentary* piece, where he may have exposed himself by doing precisely that. Still, a casual glance at the Rudolph-Schwartz book shows that among the ninety canonless Jews are Louis Zukofsky, Allen Ginsberg & George Oppen; among those missing, Gertrude Stein. Of these, Zukofsky & Oppen (along with Charles Reznikoff) had been dismissed ten years before by Bloom for ties to Pound & Williams; Ginsberg had been tagged "Mock bardic" & had really blown it by being "beyond the reach of *criticism*" (italics mine); & Stein, as always among "academic" critics & anthologizers, had again been left unmentioned. While I'm not one to get that easily into reputations & achievements, it seems inconceivable that in the ordinary sense in which a "figure ... matters urgently or overwhelmingly in the poetry of our country," the aforementioned poets (or a dozen more if we really started naming names) could be said not to matter, or that some of those others Bloom does mention—Elizabeth Bishop or James Merrill or A.R. Ammons—could be said to matter more.

But we know already—don't we?—that Bloom is into something else: a devourer's need for reduction; a myth of poetry as a response to poetry & of person as a response to parent; & with that as the pre-set pattern, a decision by fiat as to who best fits it. So, the reduction & the claim for what matters proceed—here as elsewhere in Bloom—by a definition of "strong" poets as those who "tend to achieve an individualized voice by first all-but-merging with a precursor and then by pulling away from him, usually by way of a complex process of fault-finding and actual misinterpretation of the precursor." (This is the famous path-of-poetry-through-

* In the earlier piece he writes, under the categories of "melancholy phenomenon" & "sorrowful conclusion," that no "single American-Jewish poet of undoubted major status has established himself in a century now more than two-thirds gone." (Here, of course, his field isn't even restricted by the previous editors' choices.) The response—by a citation of poets—is obvious, though it would involve the literary equivalent of naming all-time "dream teams" without having first agreed on what game we're playing.

ignorance—as if to prove that Harold likes his poets blond & dumb.) And if we ask, before we swallow that, is that the mark of every "strong" poet, the answer from Bloom is every-strong-poet-since-the-Enlightenment. (He exempts Shakespeare & Co. as "antedeluvians" & can't conceive of primal sources like Homer & Bible as themselves "belated."*) It is Bloom's handle par excellence, & since it is, he wields it as he chooses—this one "strong" & that one "weak"—& if the parent-precursor gambit doesn't work (or if it works too well where he doesn't want it), he comes up with the "authentic poem" as the "true artifact." And so on.

As for the Jews, they fall, well, like Jews before the critic-executioner, who informs us:

> All post-Enlightenment poetry in English tends to be a displaced Protestantism anyway, so that the faith in a Person easily enough is displaced into an initial devotion to the god-like precursor poet. This, to undertake it, is hardly a very Jewish process, and yet something like it seems necessary if poets are to continue to be incarnated. However far from Jewish tradition they may be, something recalcitrant in the spirit of young Jewish poets prevents them from so initially wholehearted a surrender to a Gentile precursor, and indeed makes them nervous about the process itself.

The statement looks so crazy as I read it over, that I wonder if Bloom isn't out to prove that critics are the real madmen in the critic-poet cleavage. All of it could, of course, be argued—from any number of directions—but to accept the premises to start with is, I fear, to walk into Bloom's language trap. Its mechanism is the standard double-bind: if Jews appear too Jewish they're in trouble, & if they don't appear so, they're in possibly worse trouble. "The dilemma," he writes, "seems to be either too much tradition or too little, and while such a dilemma typifies all 'modern' poetry, it assumes acute and crippling manifestations in most verse that intends somehow to be Jewish." Still, the Jews "work on under peculiarly internalized disadvantages"—a statement, in spite of its racist implications, never spelled out more clearly than in what I've already quoted. But then, he tells us, "Jewish history [was] almost always catastrophic"—or, as they said, in my family & probably in his, "OY OY OY it's hard to be a Jew."

---

* Consider the cover-up of Mesopotamian & Canaanite influence, etc. on the Bible—as part of the true enterprise of Western canon-making up to the present.

• • • • •

I have been asked by friends—both Jew & Gentile—who have watched me tussling with the Bloomian angel, to conjecture on the root problem. Although speculation of that sort—dealing, as it would have to, with questions of literary & psychological "priority"—would turn the tables on a critic devoted to a probing of such origins, it feels uncomfortably far from my previous poetics. I can, however, speculate on some of the reasons, explicit & implicit, that appear in his own writings, & can see where my comments on those will lead us.

In *Poetry and Repression*, for example, there's a discussion of Giambattista Vico's "new science," an 18th-century enterprise that involved a return to what Vico took as the oldest strata of human thought & language: a hieroglyphics of "mute signs and physical objects" followed by a figurative "poetic" language or "poetic wisdom"—much like that "science of the concrete" (C. Lévi-Strauss) later ascribed to "primitive" peoples by the strangers who came to study them.* The true poets for Vico were the first peoples (= "gentes" or "gentiles"), "who spoke in poetic characters" & whose language, theology & social institutions he contrasted not only with those of Jew & Christian (as Bloom presents it) but of all peoples (Chaldeans, Scythians, Egyptians, Germans, Greeks, & Romans) who had gone through a development from family or tribe (= gens) to a "civilization" that brings a separation from "poetic wisdom" & the creation of a "human language" of "common uses" that he identified with "prose."

Since the Jews had also undergone such changes, it is curious how often in Bloom's discussion the distinction becomes that of Jew & Gentile, with the Christian given entry as a kind of adjunct to the Jew. (That last point, however, I find truly ambiguous.) Thus he writes: "In Vico's absolute distinction between gentile and Jew, the gentile is linked both to poetry and history, through the revisionary medium of language, while the Jew (and subsequently the Christian) is linked to a sacred origin transcending language, and so has no relation to human history or to the arts." And again: "A strong poet, for Vico or for us, is precisely like a

---

* "In devoting half his book to poetic wisdom, Vico exhibits scientific and religious wisdom seeking to know itself by recovering its own origins in vulgar or poetic or creative wisdom. In doing this, it becomes itself creative, or recreative … re-creates itself by re-creating the first science, that of augury or divination, out of which all the others grew." (Thomas Goddard Bergin & Max Harold Fisch, *The New Science of Giambattista Vico*)

gentile nation; he must divine or invent himself, and so attempt the impossibility of originating himself. … Since poetry, unlike the Jewish religion, does not go back to a truly divine origin, poetry is always at work imagining its own origin, or telling a persuasive lie about itself, to itself."* It is as if Bloom had taken one of the terms in Vico's universalizing version of a primitive-civilized dichotomy—"with our civilized natures we cannot at all imagine and can understand only by great toil the poetic nature of these first men [= gentiles]"—& had fixated on the Jewish-Gentile distinction the term implies in common usage. By so doing he can advance the standard view of the Jews as a people set against divination & graven images, etc., & can contrast "the link between poetry and pagan theology" with the "[perpetual] war between poetry and Hebrew-Christian theology." In this the Christians are somehow let off the hook by Bloom, but the Jews, himself among them, are made to live forever beyond the pale of poetry.

I can only sense that Bloom, as Jew, feels himself cut off from poetry, and that he projects this deprivation onto other Jews as if to explain & even justify this loss of poetry. In doing so he invokes the horrors of the Holocaust & the "burdens" of Jewish history:

> If one adds to the indescribable horrors of Jewish history the strength and power of Jewish religious traditions, from which most contemporary Jews are now so largely estranged, then the force of the past becomes so great as to inhibit imaginative consciousness and to stifle inventiveness. Who could be adequate to thematic concerns so annihilating, to losses so painful, so fresh, and so irreparable? (*N. Y. Times Book Review*, January 4, 1981)

Bloom is here echoing Adorno's famous comment on the impossibility of writing poems after Auschwitz, pushing it further than Adorno, & placing the curse on those Jews—whether they write as Jews or not—who can

---

* That poetry—"unlike the Jewish religion"—doesn't go back to a divine origin would seem to be Bloom's opinion or his mis-reading of Vico. In *The New Science*, in fact, Vico has it that the first language—hieroglyphic & poetic—was from an "age of the gods in which the gentiles believed they lived under divine government," etc. It was only the later ages, then, that brought a "human" view of poetry & language. Accordingly, the "gentile poets" must share with the "Jewish religion" a sense of divine origins—or, in my own terms, a sense of the "sacred" underlying all acts of poesis. Unless one argues that the Jewish revelation is "true" & all the others "false," as Bloom may in fact be doing, the Jewish-Gentile distinction is canceled at this level.

imagine the possibility of a survival into the present. This self-projection—& I have no other way of describing it—is then translated into a "double belatedness" for modern Jewish poets, "coming after the virtues and sufferings of their ancestors, and also after the main sequence of Western poetry has worked itself through and perhaps out." It would thus seem that if American poets are "the most consciously belated in the history of Western poetry" & Jewish poets are "doubly belated," the combination of the two is absolutely "catastrophic."

• • • • •

"A strong poet," then, "originates himself"; & in this re-reading of old Whitman, the possibility of all our poetry opens itself again. Such self-origination ("soul-making" in Keats's phrase, world-making elsewhere) takes many forms—including a "collaging" from the (literary & non-literary) past & present. Its constructions of identity are individual or broadly human or set in the framework of a special culture or tradition. In the Jewish instance, it has involved the work of rewriting ourselves within a real but collapsed tradition of language-centeredness & resistance to oppression. As such the collapse is more an opportunity than a threat, which Bloom, had he survived the struggles with a crippling orthodoxy ("the hand of jealousy among the flaming hair"), should have been the first to see.

But this "Jewish instance" itself, for all its particularities, is part of a larger work of human striving. The Jews like others have a history that moves from tribe to state & in that movement sets up a struggle between new vision & the literalisms of the canon-making mind. In *A Big Jewish Book* I had to make this clear, because the Jewish distinction was a trap that robbed us—even as Bloom would—of much of our power as poets.

If Jewish history is a "burden," so is all human history—I take it this is the final message of what Bloom calls his "Gospel of Gloom"—& no poet's voice should now be possible. But this is nonsense & a neurotic distortion of what the real work is all about. When Maria Tsvetayeva, herself not Jewish, tells us that "all poets are Jews," I would hope it's in this sense that she means it.

The manifestos have been writing themselves for eighty years, & Bloom has still not learned to read them.

4

In *The Anxiety of Influence*, Bloom conjures up the Covering Cherub, a figure from Jewish mythology incarnated anew through Blake's imagination. The Cherub—who in one tradition may be the Exterminating Angel himself, the Malakh ha-Mavat—guards the Tree of Life & blocks the return of fallen man to Paradise. The same figure appears in the Jerusalem temple, where the two carved cherubs over the ark (the Edenic cherub is also double) "cover" the mercy seat with their wings; & in Ezekiel the Covering Cherub represents the "Prince of Tyre," a type of the earthly city whom "I will destroy ... from the midst of the stones of fire."

Like any genuinely multiphasic image, the Cherub's surface meanings continually shift, no less so in Blake than in his Biblical predecessors. (Singular meanings—or "allegoric delusions & woe"—would in fact be an aspect of the Covering Cherub's threats to the "Inspired Man.") With Bloom, working after Blake, we get a number of set & sometimes contradictory readings, & at least one major omission, of what seems, curiously, a most obvious use of the image in Blake. The occasion for Bloom is his attempt to drive home the "anxiety of influence" as the central fact of poetic composition—of which the "struggle" between Blake & Milton provides the clearest instance. And since Milton—or "Miltons Shadow," to be more precise about it than Bloom is—is at times identified, in Blake's *Milton* and *Jerusalem*, as the "Covering Cherub," it isn't surprising that Bloom calls up the identification & generalizes the process to poets after Blake:

> For Collins, for Cowper, for many a Bard of Sensibility, Milton was the Tyger, the Covering Cherub blocking a new voice from entering the Poet's Paradise. ... In Blake he is fallen Tharmas, and the Spectre of Milton; in Yeats he is the Spectre of Blake.

But elsewhere in *The Anxiety of Influence*, Bloom tells us that "the Covering Cherub stands between the achieved Man who is at once Milton, Blake, and Los, and the emanation or beloved"—in which case the poets aren't pitted against each other, and the covering Cherub, who threatens Blake & Milton both, may in fact not be a poet. There are a number of such non-poetic readings in Blake, & one of the ideologically crucial ones—as interpreted by S. Foster Damon in *A Blake Dictionary* & here omitted by Bloom—is that "the Covering Cherub sums up the twenty-seven Christian heavens which shut out man from eternity" & by which "the truth becomes petrified into dogma and relegated to ritual":

> And these the names of the Twenty-seven Heavens & their
> Churches...
> All these are seen in Miltons Shadow who is the Covering
> Cherub...
> The Heavens are the Cherub, the Twelve Gods are Satan...
> (*Milton* 37: 35, 44, 60)

Here, of course, is the ideological kingpin of Blake's argument with Milton—the puritanical side of him (his "Shadow") that "wrote in fetters when he wrote of Angels & God" & thereby "entered into the Covering Cherub." But Bloom prefers his own psychological & literary struggles to the struggles of his "post-Enlightenment" poets against repression, authority, & dogma—that is, against the total apparatus of canon-formation both as a religious & secular phenomenon.

In place of Blake's anti-Christian /anti-canonical view, Bloom chooses to put forward the idea of the Covering Cherub as a "demon of continuity"—the enemy therefore of that "discontinuity" from the past which was "freedom" for the Romantics. By doing so, he can present the Romantics & Moderns as narrowly future-directed & hostile to ideas of poetic lineage that would—at least in Bloom's terms—psychologically diminish them & threaten their survival after death. The concept he needs to pull this off is that of an established & unchanging past—just the kind of fixed tradition (= canon) challenged by those poets who have sought a true re-visioning of the larger human past & present. To misread in this way is to conceal the "strong" (experimental) poet's simultaneous regard for lineage & the "academic" critic's desire to obstruct it.

The Covering Cherub—to pull Bloom's reading further—not only keeps the poet from the paradise of poetry but from a natural relationship to all those poets who inhabit it. It's a pretty rotten business all around, & the Cherub in this sense begins to lose his resemblance to anything like a "strong" precursor poet—even for Bloom, who writes:

> In this discussion he is a poor demon of many names (as many names as there are strong poets) but I summon him first namelessly, as a final name is not yet devised by men for the anxiety that blocks their creativeness. He is that something that makes men victims and not poets, a demon of discursiveness and shady continuities, a pseudo-exegete who makes writings into Scriptures.

But the weariness & weakness of Bloom's "poor demon" is such that Blake's words from another occasion leap to mind: "Those who restrain desire, do so because theirs is weak enough to be restrained; and the restrainer or reason usurps its place & governs the unwilling."

Who, then, is the Covering Cherub?

If we accept Bloom's version of him—& in fact we don't—are we to see him as Milton's specter or as Blake's, or as any poet's who still speaks to us from the past? How turn Shelley or Whitman into victimizers of future poets, except on the level of a trivial psychological competition? Is it a poet who tries to keep us from our poems, or someone else: "a demon of discursive and shady continuities, a pseudo-exegete who makes writings into Scripture"?

But we know, after all, who threatens us. We know who reminds us of how "heavy" our "inheritance" is; who tells us not to deign to be good readers of our own poems or to think that we can write at all "after the deluge"; who enters into Milton's Shadow—& "not the Romantic return of the repressed Milton" but the Puritan Milton of repression. And we know who proposes the discontinuities between poets & rejects those who might know their lineage too well. We know who thinks that he "can block a new voice from entering the Poet's Paradise" or who would presume "to help decide a question that is ultimately of a sad importance: 'Who shall live?'"

The game, in short, is up. The Cherub's wing droops & reveals a face a little rounder & a little softer than we might have thought: the melancholy sweet face of those "cherubs" of our childhood. That much, it seems to me, is clear. And clear also is Bloom's summation, his confession of the Cherub's fate: "He cannot strangle the imagination, for nothing can do that, and he in any case is too weak to strangle anything."

Originally published in Sulfur, *No. 2, 1981*

"SECULAR JEWISH CULTURE / RADICAL POETIC PRACTICE"

Notes for a conference with that title, organized by Charles Bernstein in 2004

1

Every time I appear in a Jewish anthology—except those of my own devising—something goes wrong. Lines are omitted or placed out of sequence, prose is set as verse or verse as prose, and footnotes are used that represent an editor's imagining of what a word might mean or a place-name represent. I believe that the God of the Jews has something to do with this—a punishment for my deliberate withdrawal from Him or Her or It. Or else, to be more Jewish about it in the manner of a writer whom I admire and have sometimes drawn from, it is as if one of Isaac Bashevis Singer's imps or demons had been there to gum up my works—not when I'm being a Jew on my own terms but when I give in to temptation and let myself be part of somebody else's order or communion.[1]

I will speak, then, *in my own terms* (on my own grounds), though with continuing doubts as to whether there is any particular "*radical* poetic practice" that can be viewed as distinctively Jewish. That isn't to say that there aren't plenty of Jews (however defined) who have been active in avant-garde (or twentieth- and twenty-first-century) poetics, still less to deny that by this time many—perhaps too many—Jewish poets have actively engaged in a Jewish version of identity writing, though I don't think that that's what "radical practice" is intended to mean in the present context. I would also say, in my own case at least, that I would be willing to construct a connection between aspects of traditional Jewish linguistic practice (much of it religious or mystical rather than secular) and current forms of poetic (i.e. language) experimentation. I have in fact done this at some length, along with a proposition that Jewish history has been marked as well by an ongoing and more obvious resistance, by *the Great Refusal*, as I once put it, *to the lie of church and state*. (I would include here synagogue as well—at least for some of us.) That resistance may not have

1 Made-up footnotes in *Norton Anthology of Jewish-American Literature;* prose changed to verse in *Princeton University Library Chronicle* (Jewish-American issue, gathered by C.K. Williams); poem truncated & missing part added to another poem, in Steven J. Rubin, *Telling and Remembering: A Century of American Jewish Poetry.*

been secular in the first instance, but it carried the mark of outsider or *outrider* traditions (to use Anne Waldman's word); or that was how it felt to me when I first turned to it.

It was in the sense of such an outsiderness—and placing it clearly in "this most Christian of worlds"—that Marina Tsvetayeva spoke of *all poets* as *Jews*—much like Norman Mailer's "White Negro" of the 1950s. That was in her poem "Poem of the End," later quoted by Paul Celan in the cyrillic epigraph to his own poem "Und mit dem Buch aus Tarussa" and by me in *A Big Jewish Book*, where it became a central proposition of the stand I was then taking.[2] My argument here wasn't for some kind of Jewish exclusiveness but toward a recognition that such resistances existed both there and elsewhere and that my address, in Tsvetayeva's sense, was to "all poets" or to all poets who share the outrider stance or to all, poets and others, who resist the rule of totalizing states and constrictive religions. I saw myself—then as now—not writing in a specifically Jewish context for a Jewish audience as such, but opening the Jewish mysteries to all who wanted them. And I dramatized some of that in the dream that opens *A Big Jewish Book*, that ends with Kafka's remarkable question & answer: "What have I in common with Jews? I have hardly anything in common with myself ..."

That last, of course, is an extraordinarily Jewish statement.[3]

2

Having gotten this far by way of introduction, I want to say something of how I came to be here, and to launch a few other comments, in no particular order but as they came to me while writing.

Like Louis Zukofsky and Charles Reznikoff, among other children of Jewish immigrants, my first language (to the age of three or four) was Yiddish. (I learned later from reading T.S. Eliot, who I know had *me* in mind, that this disqualified me as a poet within the English mainstream [& probably out of it as well], and I came to take that as a challenge and an opportunity.) My parents (unlike Zukofsky's) were avowedly secular, from late adolescence on, but my mother's mother, who lived with us from a month or two before my birth, was an orthodox Jew, though the relations between her and them were never less than cordial. The outside world—in street and school—was emphatically secular, extending even to the Jewish

---

2 Right here, in an aside, I pointed out: "Of course—conversely—all Jews aren't poets."

3 For the full text, see above, page 213.

school where I would go most afternoons for Yiddish lessons. I had no problem with my grandmother's love of God, though as the terror of the Holocaust came back to her—two of her sons and their families having vanished by then—I heard it rather as an argument—an interrogation & rebuke—that came into her nightly prayers. For myself the experience of the war—viewed fitfully but at an easy childhood distance—brought out, with regard to that, my first poetic stirrings and what Tristan Tzara, in an earlier war, had spoken of "not [as] the beginnings of an art, but of a disgust." Such in a nutshell was the story of my early turn to poetry.

I grew up knowing a little about Jewish religion and lore but almost nothing about Jewish mysticism (the richest source for a poetics, as I later found). What came to me at some time in my teens was what I felt to be a need for poetry and for the intensities & disgust that brought the poetry I knew to life. At a still later point—I don't know just when—I was surprised to find something like that intensity in the language of religion—more likely in pagan and Christian sources, I then thought, than in Jewish ones. It soon seemed to me that I wanted to steal that language and to make it my own.[4] In doing so I meant to shift the field from religion to poetry, while not denying but even emphasizing the origins of what I took as poetry in areas of religious languaging and ritual. The transfer here, as the Dada poet Richard Huelsenbeck once pointed out for his own borrowings and deformations, was from the misbelievers to the disbelievers of religion. *I wanted to stand here firmly with the disbelievers.*

The involvement with Jewish materials as such came about when it had to, coterminous with *Technicians of the Sacred* (in 1968) and with a need I felt then "to explore ancestral sources of my own," most specifically and deliberately (I wrote & would write again) "in the world of Jewish mystics, thieves, & madmen." That project—experimental through & through—began for me with *Poland/1931*, continued with *A Big Jewish Book* (as Jewish anthology or assemblage), and returned in *Khurbn*, *Gematria*, and finally in *14 Stations.* (Even so, I would remind you, I was producing a still larger body of poetry and poetry gatherings that wasn't part of my Jewish experiment *as such.*) The intention throughout was not so much to discover or exploit identity (in the ethnic/tribal sense) but to put identity into doubt or question.

4 Thus William Carlos Williams, when I met him as a student at City College: *Seize the language! Smash it to hell! You have a right to it!*

For this I applied or meant to apply the full range of modernist techniques and procedures to identity thematics, taking the resultant work, if it's right to say so, as itself a form of romantic/modernist *irony.*[5] In that sense too I saw what I was doing as the continuation of an aborted Jewish/Yiddish poetry in another language (American or English rather than Yiddish) and by every means at my disposal. Once into it I also found that I could draw from procedures and imageries imbedded in traditional Jewish sources. This was true in particular with gematria (mystical Jewish numerology), which I adapted and *secularized* as a processual form of composition, culminating in the book-length poem *Gematria* (from Sun & Moon Press[6]) and *14 Stations* (gematria turned to memorialization of the Holocaust). But *Poland/1931*, my first experiment with a constructed Jewish poetry, is also full of fragments (verbal and visual) appropriated from traditional sources.[7]

I've been involved, then, with a secularization of the mystical and supernatural, a project which I share with others going back to at least the eighteenth century, but with twists & turns of my own & reflective also of the time in which we've lived. What this involves is the transfer of a body of work and language from religion to poetry & from poetry to the domain of Huelsenbeck's disbelievers. My effort—but hardly mine alone—has been to open the field of poetry into areas of *poesis* (oral *and* written, sacred *and* secular) that have not had an adequate accounting. In so doing it was *our* intention to hold onto the energy & ferocity/intensity that we found there but without the "mind-forg'd manacles" of orthodox religious thought.

---

5 My first deliberate attempt at writing "the Jewish poem" was a mix I created by bringing together structures from Gertrude Stein's serial poem "Dates" with mystically-loaded and sexually-charged vocabulary from Isaac Bashevis Singer's novel *Satan in Goray.*

6 The final version, *Gematria Complete,* was published years later (in 2009) by Marick Press.

7 And even here, let me add, I was not alone, but entered a discourse with poets I had known or was soon to meet, like David Meltzer, Nathaniel Tarn, Jack Hirschman, Edmond Jabès, and even (from our one meeting) Paul Celan; or others, important to me at different times, like Robert Kelly and Robert Duncan. In addition the totalizing impulse of *Technicians of the Sacred* and, later, *Poems for the Millennium,* may itself have been part of a secular Jewish thrust, something, as Charles Bernstein has suggested, that could even have influenced a similar tendency in Ezra Pound and others still more obviously outside the Jewish context.

For me the process went beyond my engagement with Jewish sources, and before I assembled *A Big Jewish Book* I had already assembled "a big Indian book" (*Shaking the Pumpkin*) and before that "a big human book" (*Technicians of the Sacred*). [I would, still later, do the same with Christian & Buddhist imageries.] In those non-Jewish gatherings, the act of assemblage or construction was similar but my position was different in that I couldn't be thought of as writing from within the subject or with myself identified *as* subject. *A Big Jewish Book*, then, was an experiment along the lines of the other anthologies but with myself as a participatory subject in a shared subjectivity. With an awareness of all of that, I set out to explore what was possible *in extremis* & with no holds barred. I thought of myself as operating through a secular/poetic consciousness that set the content & form of the sacred against that of the not-so-sacred, the heretical, the heterodox, the blasphemous, & certainly the secular as such.

But even in *A Big Jewish Book* or *Poland/1931*—a plunge into a constructed world based on real witnessings & documents as "data-clusters" (Ed Sanders' term in his argument for an "investigative poetry")—if I were to play it from within, I had to perform some part of it in costume, which I did in fact with the additional aid of photographs & films, something I would never have done in the Indian instance. Similarly, when I was writing, or rather performing, *That Dada Strain*, I costumed myself again—in imitation this time of Hugo Ball & Tristan Tzara (a.k.a. Sammy Rosenstock)—but that was still another kind of identity poetics that would get us too far afield if I stopped to speak about it here.

There was a time, then, when I became concerned with "the jewish poem" as such and even wondered—in light of Tsvetayeva—where I might, if I continued, place its final boundaries. ("Jewish-American" was of far less concern to me than "Jewish," which in itself was international in scope.) In the Pre-Face to *A Big Jewish Book*, I even made a list of Jewish "topics & conflicts/tensions," with the caveat that many of these were not unique to Jews although the history of the Jews might—up to a point—offer an exemplary instance. I presented these as characteristics that still held me to the Jewish work, as follows:

- a sense of exile both as cosmic principle (exile of God from God, etc.) & as the Jewish fate, experienced as the alienation of group & individual, so that the myth (gnostic or orthodox) is never only symbol but history, experience, as well;

• from which there comes a distancing from nature & from God (infinite, ineffable), but countered in turn by a *poesis* older than the Jews, still based on namings, on an imaging of faces, bodies, powers, a working out of possibilities (but principally, the female side of God—Shekinah/Shekhina—as herself in exile) evaded by orthodoxy, now returning to astound us;

• or, projected into language, a sense (in Edmond Jabès's phrase) of being "exiled in the word"—a conflict, as I read it, with a text, a web of letters, which can capture, captivate, can force the mind toward abstract pattern or, conversely, toward the framing, raising, of an endless, truly Jewish "book of questions";

• &, finally, the Jews identified as mental rebels, who refuse consensus, thus become—even when bound to their own Law, or in the face of "holocaust," etc.—the model for the Great Refusal to the lie of Church & State.

[And I concluded]: ... it's from such a model—however obscured by intervening degradations from *poesis*, impulse to conform, etc.—that I would understand the Russian poet Marina Tsvetayeva's dictum that "all poets are Jews."

Two points to end it, and then, if I may, a poem.

There is also a curious way in which Jewish writers—contrary to Harold Bloom, say—have had an advantage, a leg up, *as poets* and as long as they maintained their sense of *otherness*, even as a counterpoint to the hominess they may have sought in the language that surrounds them & is nevertheless, for all of us, a place of exile. As my brother-in-arms Pierre Joris has written, in defense of a "nomadic poetics": "It is only when constantly aware that the writer is not 'at home' in language (or anywhere else, for that matter) that any real and critical engagement with the enemy forces is possible." It is then too that the strongest engagements with language *qua poetry* take place.

The context for such remarks is of course diasporic/dispersed, and it's in the condition of diaspora—not exclusively but largely—that our poetics (Jewish & not so Jewish) has been constructed. That has led me, in the course of preparing this talk, to wonder about the *state* of Israel and the emergence of a Jewish *home*land—whether the connection between Jews & an exilic/nomadic/diasporic poetics isn't by now distressingly anachronistic. To say "all poets are Jews" in an Israeli-Palestinian context in which Jews are the privileged insiders, is something quite different from Tsvetayeva's 1926 context "in this most Christian of worlds" and gives me the acute sense that history has somehow overwhelmed us.

I think that I may pursue this at a later point but for now it seems to me enough simply to have said it.

•

To conclude, then, I'll read a poem from *Poland/1931*, that speaks both to the persistence of Jews in history & to my bewilderment at being called on as an expert in this kind of forum. (The irony is even more obvious today than when I wrote it.)

[Reads]:

THE CONNOISSEUR OF JEWS

if there were locomotives to ride home on
& no jews
there would still be jews & locomotives
just as there are jews & oranges
& jews & jars
there would still be someone to write the jewish poem
others to write their mothers' names in light—
just as others, born angry
have the moon's face burnt onto their arms
& don't complain
my love, my lady, be a connoisseur of jews
the fur across your lap
was shedding
on the sheet were hairs
the first jew to come to you is mad
the train pulls into lodz
he calls you
by your polish name
then he tells the other passengers a story
there are jews & there are alphabets

he tells them
but there are also jewish alphabets
just as there are jewish locomotives
& jewish hair
& just as there are some with jewish fingers
such men are jews
just as other men are not jews
not mad
don't call you by your polish name
or ride the train to lodz
if there are men who ride the train to lodz
there are still jews
just as there are still oranges
& jars
there is still someone to write the jewish poem
others to write their mothers' names in light

THE POET AS NATIVE: AN ASPECT OF CONTEMPORARY POETRY & ART

Written as a talk for American Folklore Association conference on "Homo Narrans: Storytelling as Integration of Self" University of Southern California, Los Angeles, October 1979

From an interview:

Why do you write? Who do you write for?

Because Indians always tell a story. The only way to continue is to tell a story and that's what Coyote says. The only way to continue is to tell a story and there is no other way. Your children will not survive unless you tell something about them—how they were born, how they came to this certain place, how they continued.

Who do you write for besides yourself?

For my children, for my wife, for my mother and my father and my grandparents and then reverse order that way so that I may have a good journey on my way back home.

—Simon Ortiz, *A Good Journey* (1977)

Opening remarks. In my work I have no life histories but my own ... in an ongoing, maybe oblique way... and maybe, as another speaker said, "a life as it might have been."

Gary Snyder says that when he gave up his folklore studies at the University of Indiana in the early 1950s, he changed from being an anthropologist and became an informant. As poets, we are all professional informants.

I wanted to say—in the spirit of the title for this conference—that I can only speak for myself or as myself: that I will speak, here as elsewhere, as a poet concerned (in my more self-conscious workings) with the creation of meaning through language. The creation, the making of meaning is involved with self-making (or self-invention) and more ambitiously of world-making (or world-invention); and this process, which I have elsewhere called poesis, is not the work (or play) of poets and artists only but of all functionally languaged people. In their acts of poesis, all languaged people are poets, and this has in fact been the intuition of poets who might mistakenly be thought of as "elitist"— William Blake, for example, who translated the Biblical text, "Would that all God's people were prophets," into a virtual "All God's people are poets"; or, maybe more surprisingly, the French Surrealists quoting Lautréamont on the masthead of their magazine, *The Surrealist Revolution:* "Poetry must be made by all. Not by one." The search, there as here, was for a broadly human approach to creativity, to return with a renewed self-consciousness to what should be the most familiar ground for all of us (our selves, our humanness in place and time) and from which, as the poet Charles Olson wrote in quotation from Heraclitus, we have been (tragically) estranged.

We proceed by telling, and the telling by which a world is told and comes to be is our sense of myth. Myth as telling—story-telling or whatever other form it takes—is the life-work of each languaged person, which he or she may do "well" or "badly"—and who are we to judge? Its thrust is to experience and enact, not to explain the world—or to explain as after-thought, the experience of all that foremost. That experience itself is knowing—religiously as gnosis, otherwise as history, which Olson, after Herodotus this time, etymologized as knowing, going out and seeing for one's self— one's self as witness and as teller in a circumstance, an enactment in which the thing known is the thing said or spoken—for "thought," as Tristan Tzara wrote, "is made in the mouth." The intention of the one who tells that kind of story is to make his voice a witness, to put himself and those who hear him into the condition of experiencing—in response to the basic questions of self-identity and world-identity. As in the Iroquois Indian account:

> A man who was a crow was traveling. As he walked along he asked himself: "Who am I? Where did I come from? Where am I going?"

Or again: who are *we*, etc.: the question asked in the voice of the group, the people for whom the individual as poet may think himself to be speaking, giving an account.

Language (voiced or written, verbal or pictorial) creates the answers, the accounting, as an individual act that is also the culmination or recounting of those previous acts and thoughts (cultural traditions, say) of which the individual is aware. If the culture defines the limits of the things spoken of—person, actions, objects—it is defined by those things in turn. Mythology always carries with it an element of auto-mythology. Mythology as auto-mythology (experience as *mythos*) reaches its extremes in the self-projections and world-creation of tribal shamans and certain post-tribal mystics, and perhaps equally so in the work of the contemporary poet/artist as myth-maker, narrating the world and his experience of it as a story. The poet's and the artist's telling is an instance of any man's and woman's need to do the same, but with a continuing demand for a heightened self-consciousness and, often, a quirkiness and openness to change that casts doubt on its own projections. In the contemporary instance the poet/artist as rebel challenges the idea of a culturally legislated reality and seems, in the aftermath of an internationalizing imperialism, to move beyond the particulars of culture, time and place.

I will point out very briefly some of the many forms that this auto-mything, self-telling, has taken in twentieth-century poetry—modern and "post"modern.

First, in so-called "confessional" poetry (Plath, Sexton, Lowell, etc.): a widely used but unfortunate term that seems sometimes to limit the work of poetry to its suicidal fringe; that psychologizes too rapidly and escapes (in the work of its interpreters, not necessarily its practitioners) the mythic encounter with what Euripides called "not my story but one my mother told me."

Second, the long mythic poem (Pound's *Cantos*, Williams' *Paterson*, Olson's *Maximus*, Zukofsky's *"A,"* etc.) in which the created/experienced ego intersects with the experience of the past and present as multiple times and/or with a single place as center. This is the poem "including history," as Pound defined the epic. The poem *as* history.

Third, a range of poems in which cultural particulars dominate, as the poet tries to deal with the embattled traditions of American ethnicities: the idea of Acoma Pueblo continuities in the poetry of Simon Ortiz, or the struggle with discontinuities in my own *Poland/1931* and *A Seneca Journal*.

Fourth, the poet carrying his work into the public arena: as a performance in which he restores sound to writing or "talks to discover" meanings inherent in his poems or, in the case of David Antin, works through the performance itself to talk his way toward meaning—pre-eminently by telling a story.

Fifth, the poet's use of collage and assemblage as a rearrangement of the fullest range of feelings and meanings (myths) available to a culture—again the basic method of the *Cantos*, *Maximus*, etc. and, in one form or other, common to the work of many poets active in this century. (I take this as a contemporary equivalent to the traditions transmitted orally in other cultures.)

Even so called "lyrics"—short poems, etc., personal or "image-"centered—are tellings: the re-counting and/or creation of a momentary event, an experience of an action or perception or dream, or an occasion within language itself. The poet as reporter, narrates/tells "news that stays news," but (like the newsman in the practice) also makes or shapes the news. And, where experiment is possible or demanded, he or she makes new ways of making news: new strategies for language—strategies which are themselves "another kind of story."

Art and poetry are today permeated with narrative and performance: extended and full or broken into the fragments of stories told and re-told. If you, as anthropologists or folklorists, and so on, are concerned with these questions, so are we; and we look to the work that you bring from the many sources once despised as below "high culture" and set apart as "folklore." These contain both the wide range of cultures from which we learn in pursuit of a still illusory ethnopoetics and, for each of us, the still familiar worlds, the small towns and neighborhoods, the particular cultures from which we come and to which we cannot return because they are gone or we or they have changed. And that dislocation, like that of the

Iroquois crow-man, causes us to ask and to answer-in-language, as the basic poetic act, those questions: Who am I? Where did I come from? Where am I going?

From A BOOK OF WITNESS: "i-SONGS EXIST"

i-songs exist, (I. Christensen)
& I have sought them,
playing an empty hand.
i is your mother,
is a good day
& also not.
i equals nothing
in the game of numbers
where it is also ten
& jew.
i is a womb
a belly
something stolen
heart & hand.
i eats
& will be eaten.
i is a habitation.
i is go & good.
i is a power.
i is to God
a question.
i is willing.
i is i-am
but stands confused.
i is a name for ice.
i is an end.

POSTSCRIPT TO *A BOOK OF WITNESS*

A Book of Witness was my passage from one century—one millennium—to another. The first fifty poems were written in 1999, the second fifty in the two years that followed. When I came into the street that first day in the year 2000, it was one of those bright California mornings, & I was struck, very forcefully, by the curious name of the year & by a feeling that I was entering another world. While I didn't put much stock in that kind of era-shifting, my mind that morning still held an image from something I had seen on television the night before—a series of movie clips showing earlier twentieth-century views of what the coming century would be like. *Millennium* was a word I had been mulling over in that closing decade, most notably in the assemblage *Poems for the Millennium* that Pierre Joris & I put together & published in the later 1990s. The word itself, we knew, was slippery—associated as it was with a sense of apocalypse & destruction that often belied our rosier interpretations.

Witness was another word we held in common. In its twentieth-century usage it had a meaning—pathetic but real—that spoke to the horrors, great & small, that marked that time & that persist today. I had come to think of poetry, not always but at its most revealing, as an act of witnessing, even of prophecy—by the poet directly or with the poet as a conduit for others. I had also been struck by how crucial to all of that the voice was; I mean the voice in the grammatical sense, the "first person" centered in the pronoun "I." I was aware, even so, of how that first person voice had either been debased or more frequently despised by many poets—often (where despised) by poets close to me. The intention, understandably enough, was to free the poem from its lyric shackles—"the lyrical interference of the individual as ego," as Olson called it.

The loss of such expression, however, would be immense, & its elimination futile. For there are a number of ways in which that voice—first person—has been one of our great resources in poetry, something that turns up everywhere in our deepest past & present. I mean here a first person that isn't restricted to the usual "confessional" attitude but is the instrument—in language—for all acts of witnessing, the key with which we open up to voices other than our own. I am thinking here of someone like the Mazatec shamaness María Sabina (& her echo in the work of our own Anne Waldman), who throws up a barrage of "I" assertions, when it's really the voices of the gods, the "saint children" of her pantheon, whom she feels speaking through her.

There is in all of this a question of inventing & reinventing identity, of experimenting with the ways in which we can speak or write as "I." In the course of putting that identity into question, I have brought in statements now & again by other poets—very lightly sometimes but as a further way of playing down the merely ego side of "I." And I let the voices that I draw in shift & move around. I want to do that, to keep it in suspense. "I am I because my little dog knows me," Gertrude Stein wrote in a poem she called "Identity." I have written a hundred of these poems now—a century of poems—& I hope that they're both of this time & still connected to the oldest ways in which the poem makes itself.

2001/2002

[Further excerpts from *A Book of Witness* begin on page 472, below.]

GALLERY THREE

A CRUEL NIRVANA

I can hear
a water song
close by my ear
& track it
where it leads me.
It is summer
but the trees
are dead.
They vanish with
our fallen friends.
The eye in torment
brings them down
each mind a little world
a cruel nirvana.

TWENTIETH CENTURY UNLIMITED

As the twentieth century fades out
the nineteenth begins
                                    again
it is as if nothing happened
though those who lived it thought
that everything was happening
enough to name a world for & a time
to hold it in your hand
unlimited   the last delusion
like the perfect mask of death

From "14 STATIONS"

[Pre-Face] The full series of fourteen poems was written to accompany Arie Galles's monumental charcoal drawings derived from World War II aerial views of the principal Nazi extermination camps—each with an attendant railroad station—known even then to have been the sites of holocaust. As Galles worked from documentary photographs to establish some pretense at distance (= objectivity), I decided to objectify by turning again to gematria as a way to determine the words and phrases that would come into the poems. The counts were made off the Hebrew and/or Yiddish spellings of the camp names, then keyed to the numerical values of Hebrew words and word combinations in the first five books of the Bible. It was my hope that this small degree of objective chance would not so much mask feeling or meaning as allow it to emerge.

The First Station: Auschwitz-Birkenau

now the serpent:

I will bring back
their taskmasters
crazy & mad

will meet them
deep in the valley
& be subdued

separated in life
uncircumcised, needy
shoes stowed away

how naked they come
my fathers
my fathers

angry & trembling
the serpents
you have destroyed

their faces remembered
small in your eyes,
shut down, soiled

see a light
take shape in the pit,
someone killed

torn in pieces
a terror, a god,
go down deeper

The Third Station: Buchenwald

deliver me
from them

your cattle
rising

your assembly
lords of fat

deliver me
from color

The Eleventh Station: Maidanek

1
a thing
spoken
speaks me

I see
the spoken
thing

a word
hail
pestilence

& from your face
a curse
is poured out

& a bone
is set in motion
spoken

in disgust
to see
the one who speaks it

2
a foreigner,
you say,
the dew like blood

her city
broken
empty for her sake

has blessed you,
seed of them
I will pursue

& you will say
in blood:
leave me alone

The Twelfth Station: Sobibor

1
as he had spoken
from the wilderness:
be fruitful!

(& they were fruitful)

so he could blind them
with a fist
& cut them —

& she could take from them
the vision of
his cities

2
a skin
harp
& a boil

according to his words

how blind
& evil
like its skin

your words
erased

The Fourteenth Station: Stutthof

the evil water
in my dream

has emptied out
their cities

like my mouth
a hole

& in the blood
they burn

they turn them
into smoke

A further poem from 14 Stations *appears on page 334 in the visual/verbal version composed with Arie Galles.*

From THE LORCA VARIATIONS

Lorca's Spain: A Homage

Beginning with olive trees.

Shadows.

Beginning with roosters.

Crystal.

Beginning with castanets & almonds.

Fishes.

This is a homage to Spain.
This mists dogs.
This silences rubber.
This is Saturn.
Beginning with yellow.

Eclipse.

Beginning with needles.

Insomnia.

Beginning with baskets.

The Moon.

Who is naked? The imagination
(wrote Lorca) is seared.
This is a homage to water.
Beginning & end.

WATER JETS

1
If death once had a face
the water from this water jet
has wiped it out,
the August air has left no trace of it,
like other fountains
or other faces from your home town
that the sunlight & the water jet
drive from your room.
Things leave our eyes no boundaries here
other than dreams, no dreams
still precious to your heart,
its carved interior shot through with corners,
into which a grapevine grows,
fed by the water jet your fingers
once turned on, made it a place of clouds,
the perfect death's head still inside it,
& that a water jet wipes out.

2
It's night.
In the garden our hearts have turned blue.
A maid opens the water jet, lets water & roses spill out.
A century passes.
Pianos circle the earth, dark swords slice arteries.
No dust on your windows, just blood.
In the garden four gay caballeros trade swords.
A cloud breaks apart & starts quaking.
It's night.

The Return

1

To write through Lorca, to come back on Lorca's wings, to return to where you're feeling empty, like dying sweetly after love, to where a rose has left you wounded, the shadow of your childhood like a flower inside your heart, where Lorca's road trails off into a garden, in which the morning star drops colors onto a faded dress, like paint.

2

To come back on Lorca's wings, who sees his origin in water, sees his soul die in a dream, transform into a corazón forever, sees a shadow overwhelm the flower in his heart & cry goodbye, until his soul returns to him, a muddy spot from which a butterfly arises, shivering, a gust of wind in motion through his heart.

3

To see his origin in water, in the dawn, a feeble sight, the motion of her corazón, of Lorca's wings in water, making love down at the oxbow, hearing the nightingales, a love as sweet as perfume, goodbyes & reminiscences turned into songs, a girl & a muchacho turning & returning through the spray.

4

To return with Lorca only yesterday, to walk along the sea, under the stars, to see the forests becoming green forever, green with love, the shadow of our childhood like a flower, crying adios! while marching single file up to a crossroads, reciting the songs we made, white muslin shaking, trailing along the byways, the glitter that drops down from Lorca's wings, words that we write through Lorca.

Second New York Poem

El mascarón. Mirad el masscarón
como viene del Africa a New York.
(F.G.L.)

1
"They Are Gone, the Pepper Trees"

Half of it was sand
          & what remained
                    was mercury & made him
tremble,
          too afraid to rub it in
                    while visioning
a hippopotamus who stalked through
          everlastings,
                    & other animals who crossed
those endless bridges,
          whom he could bring down
                    with a spear,
their beaks grown dormant,
          their flesh nailed onto trees
                    from which he used to cut his masks,
would wear his masks around
          New York, half crazy,
                    wasn't he,
the bright gazelle mask flashing
          where he walked,
                    what joy to be among you
at this gathering,
          he thought,
                    to spend this time with you
here where the wheat rots,
          swans rut, camels
                    plod among the peppers,
in the mask that shows you fear,
          the mask dissolving into sand,
like solitude & ashes

where the light has died away
so recently,
the cat is playing with a cork,
& all things come into this other light
the phosphorous ignites
over New York, where death
's a crocodile, & sunlight
makes the world
grow darker, where a sword cuts through
my throat, my feet,
where silence covers everything,
where eyes turn white,
where time turns inside out
like valleys
rife with mutilated buds
in Africa,
inviting us to join
their dance of death.

2
"Canyons of Lime Imprisoned"

A fond farewell
at the border. See the dead
& how they hunker down,
who bring us hurricanes,
those naked masks,
those shameless tumulters,
who tempt us with strange lights
horses will ride past,
slender mounts for children,
edging their way through niches,
squeezing
into bank vaults,
Wall Street poor & empty,
roofs on which manometers
break into pieces,
& the channels they leave behind
excite the iris,
yes, & voices

cut across New York, & someone
          wears a mask
                    that looks like North America,
& someone else counts up
          the unemployed, whose numbers
                    brought together in a frozen dance,
o Lorca,
          darken the sky.
                    These herds are what we will become,
their frenzy
          will be ours tomorrow,
                    o my naked heart,
we watch the sphinx together,
          squatting inside this cemetery,
                    she with a bank director's mask
& you a chinaman's,
          your profiles soon identical
                    except that you
still sing your deep song
          while the sky fills up
                    with down, & fireflies
grow faint & then invisible.
          Time hides
                    inside you, can you feel it?
does it press against your mask?
          whose groans
                    are rising in this place?
whose blood is on our blueprints
          even now?
                    is there a formula to chart
the impetus we feel? a yellow thread
          to recollect it?
                    when I dance, the naked wife says,
it is no less for money,
          when I give you tail
                    you fade in me and die,
the stillness
          overtakes you, sky
                    is split asunder,

lime & mire splatter on the snow,
the night makes even gold
turn black for us
who wait here at our windows,
watch old columns
lit by flames,
the impetus returning
like a wheel that spins
forever
in an empty bank vault,
see it with your own eyes,
hear it cross this space
in silence,
watch her naked body
in your mirrors,
feel the sap press upward,
as if moving among mountains,
guano everywhere,
to drown in guano,
living,
buried in its canyons.

3
"I Was on the Terrace, Wrestling with the Moon"

Below us, men in iron masks
who rob a bank,
lie buried in a landscape
with the dead,
fear dripping from them,
seeds of light
under our windows,
where those who pass us groan
like swarms of cattle,
press against store windows
that reflect the sky first,
then the blood that spurts up
when you bite an apple
sweetly, sweetly
when the dancers mass around us,

others dressed like shepherds
crying silver tears,
cold earthworms,
standing on streetcorners in the dawn,
near where the young girl
rises from the flames,
still others whom you couldn't know
cut off her hands with broken shells,
the tiny drops igniting
in the air,
smear yolks between her thighs,
& beat the moon
with oars, as I do
wrestling on this ancient terrace,
watch me, watch me,
whose eyes blaze in the night like stars,
who gaze down Broadway
like a prairie,
I who offer up a mollusk
for the dead,
slam virulent guitars
against my thighs,
who wait with Lorca on a fire escape,
a pyramid behind us
to welcome our forgotten king & pope.

4
"'Don't Let the Pope Dance!' Someone Cries"

"Don't let the Pope dance!"
someone cries,
"El mascarón. Mirad
el mascarón."
It's Lorca crying,
Lorca coughing poison
over Wall Street, dreaming
of a courtyard
covered with blue mosses,

of sodomites in masks,
cathedrals where frail millionaires
adore a King,
where dancers drift around
like madmen, scorched by scarlet fever,
stung by nettles,
& it's Lorca perched atop
his pyramid, it's Lorca
smuggling rifles through the forest,
Lorca in the mask of anguish,
trapped in vines,
or Lorca in the stock exchange,
the floor collapsing under him,
it's Lorca in a mask with emeralds
for teeth, a mask
to charm the Pope back to New York,
to wear in jungles,
to stare out of on terraces,
a mask with cobras that the builders
have forsaken,
the Pope has jammed over his own,
not dancing, no,
but turning blue,
cries out with Lorca
for the mask,
it's Lorca's mask
we wear together now,
el mascarón,
he cries to us,
the mask! the mask!

Coda: The Final Lorca Variation

The end for Lorca comes
only when we let it   helpless
with insomnia
we hear him stir   we see him
reach for Saturn
rising overhead.

No homage can repay what we have lost
our false beginnings   naked crystals
bathed in the imagination
needles that sting us, rubber
that brings us down
a rooster who cries against his shadow.

Where it still smells of almonds
dogs are howling
at the moon   eclipses in the water
olive trees for Spain
& castanets
our homages stuffed into yellow baskets

offered to Lorca's Spain.

Further Lorca variations and translations appear on pages 127–134, along with an account of how the poems were composed.

FIRST NIGHT POEM, FOR JACKSON MAC LOW

Variations & Collage

1
Where Mac Low walks someone stops a clock.
    The hands are set at twenty-three.
    In the rush of air beneath his table toes are beating out a symphony.
    A man is sitting on a chair inside a classroom with black windows.
    The sun is cold against the man's cheek.
    Fingers on a keyboard send a message to the king of thumbs.
    The message to Mac Low is further coded.
    Aiming to reciprocate I offer a black sun.
    The sense of night rests in my mind: a pall of thought above the silent river, see it running through a false partition in the heart.
    I want to wear a top hat & to dance with what's her name.
    A bunch of keys is what I give you.
    In the black night no one sleeps as light as you, oh camerado.
    Dreaming of it.
    Reaching through the gauze.
    The entry to the sable night is such an opening.

It finds the dark-eyed night alive & counts the moon a stranger.

No one will leave my table but we will sit around until the mother comes with lesser portions.

Kurt Schwitters can arrive at midnight, seated in the central row, a shade beneath our nightlight.

Wrapped in a cowl the night is hanging, moaning.

It is called a cowled night—not a night the pointer nudges but a phantom presence in the hush of night.

Is it then Europe's night that hides him, England's night-raids that create a noonday night?

A long electric night?

A gala night that turns into an empty night?

An unseen night?

A night to feel & touch?

Is it a night that breaks the glamour of a lost midsummer's night?

A night that ends in death?

(The voice of Schwitters calls me in the darkness, rising like a cry of witness through the great primeval night.)

Dark wheels & axles, dark dentist drills, dark locomotives.

A ticking clock, a meat grinder, barbed-wire fences.

Dark shoes & wigs & ice skates.

Dark squads of people on a stage lit by a darkness visible as light.

A night of shining darkness.

Of darkness giving birth.

Plump swollen creatures in the night.

A night of dark-red turtles being born, of hornbilled turtles.

Pregnant with small lobsters,

sharp-nosed creatures,

fat ones swollen in the night.

Where time stands still for us inside the poem,

& only there,

the poem becomes a night poem & gives back the night.

A flower like a raven, Schwitters cries.

He names a night bird.

In love with incandescence Schwitters finds a clock & sets it right.

He & Mac Low are changing places.

Swallowing a dog a cat a rooster both are now waking up.

The clockwork world is pressing on their pupils.

An old alarm clock's hanging from a scarecrow's neck, it spells out love gone mad, a night of mystifying flowers.

Night of surprises: Kurt & Jackson two old hoofers dancing.
The world applauds their act. A nightclub swoons.
Caught in a ring of dancers they trade pronouns as the night runs on.
Night rhymes with womb & slaughter—music as sure as light & bright.
A night train rumbles into Oslo.
Kurt rhymes with Jackson, poem rhymes with face & light.
A line of poets rhymes along the lines of sight.
I walk into a hall beside my father where the walls sing silent night.
Kurt tells the story of his Norwegian flight.
We raise ourselves by inches as if we were learning to recite.
To constrain is thrilling, to explain is erudite.
We barter words with Kurt & Jackson in a garden of delight
And here begins another night poem uniting light & night.

2
Night Walk Variations

So cold a woman might stop talking
& a man, his meaning stripped from him
might hide his learning,
touching gently,
hearing how their fingers scrape against her sweater
how they rub against his cheeks

It is in memory he sees her
that in its dimness brings him peace:
the sky down almost to his fingers
slipping through them
like his memory of two o'clock
a memory of utter darkness
lost friends beside him in that water

So why this half-light when it's only two o'clock
(he thinks) & why those twigs that cut him
where he walks
                    and why the meaning
stripped from him
                    like hair that falls away
revealing only air

a single tree
a quiet feeling when he bites his lip

This is what comes to us from resting
& this from freezing
& from standing solitary
freezing once again
or finding teeth too long forsaken
finding some & seeking others
until the hills wear down from silence
standing apart

3
The first time I heard your light poems, Jackson, I was overcome with awe.
        That is—that means to say—that there are times the mind hears what can alert the mind,
        can open it to something in the world, known but unspoken,
        & leave it trembling at the sound & sight.
        Light was the voice of day for us,
        & life,
        while night, its rhyming partner, signaled sleep & death.
        That was repeated in a thousand places we both knew.
        And it was also given to us that dreams which came with sleep were an entry to a still deeper life.
        Sleep rhymed with deep,
        but you were ready to call the first collection of your works "Awaken,"
        which was a sign of light & day,
        except that when I spoke it in that other tongue
        it rhymed with night.
        So Milton told us not to follow rhyme,
        as Blake did too,
        & still we follow to our dying day.
        Those are our contraries, you'd think, the poles we need to make existence seem complete.
        Like chance & choice,
        another pair
        the work will bring together.
        That's when the light will be as lovely & alarming as the night

& the night will be the time of new awakenings.
Until then I thank you for the rhyme
that even now the time affords us.
And the hope to be together in that darkness
—Cage had once written—
fumbling around if necessary,
bumping into things,
adding to the disorder that characterizes living,
but alive.

FIRST NIGHT POEM, FOR JACKSON MAC LOW: *Written on the occasion of Mac Low's 75th birthday & in celebration of his* Light Poems *with their extensions back into the early 1960s. The "variations"— in section 2— work off the strings of words presented without fixed grammar or punctuation in the first section of his "Night Walk" (1960), & the "collage" has reference to phrases appropriated mostly from my own* Technicians of the Sacred, *& from Mac Low's* In Memoriam: Kurt Schwitters. *My translations from Schwitters'* Poems Performance Pieces Proses Plays Poetics *also play a part in this.*

A final night poem, as memoriam for Mac Low, appears elsewhere in these pages.

THREE PARIS ELEGIES

1

into my own dark sunday light approaches like the moon through feathers that's no sooner seen than sunk by blindness & the thought that everyone is dead around a city that's about to vanish as it has before sucked down an empty pocket oversized & with a smell of earth the bright adventurers of 1910 whose streets these were sharing a common grave with those who followed reaching even to the place where you and I are waiting with the friends who drop out one by one like cybermonkeys flying into mindless space

2

above a gorge we hung
& swayed
the mountains were alive to every side
stone witnesses

the air was still with only a distant puff of wind
we sat suspended by an iron wire
voiceless
no one to talk to in the world
but you & me
that revelation
I think I prize its emptiness the most
so even now arrived in paris
I sit alone
& feel it bursting from my chest
electric
final
rush of footsteps down an empty street

3

why does a well-dressed man come up to me & ask me for a handout?

(this is a dream, I think, it can't be real)

why does a smiling mother dressed for church reach out a hand to touch me shadows all around her sitting on the ground

why does she ask for help

& why do I keep walking walking past her

where there is no street or sun

even in paris on this hottest day in summer

what is the sound that comes at us around a corner sound of a wave suspended in the air of hives of bees of hands applauding in the dark

who is the man who wears a flower in his ear a shirt with many folds a vest a beard the buttons glowing like electric sparks

the more I search his features I can see his lips are gone his tongue is heavy hanging to one side & forming words that never reach me that the darkness covers

all the people on this street sit flat against a wall some open-eyed some sunk in a deep sleep

all are dressed up

the men wear business suits & blazers a cardigan a double breasted jacket a tuxedo tie & tails but have no coats or hats

their shoes are simple always a dark brown or black with marks of sand from garden walks in paris laces open sometimes sometimes without socks

& the women well dressed too although the hair of one is hanging limply with another's there are open spots that show her skull a third one has the traces of a beard a large wet stain under one armpit

just look at them & they begin to talk
the way that birds talk
feathers that the wind is blowing swirl across the square
we sit in paradise & pass a ball between us
papers at our feet

then when it's time to leave we walk around a corner climb the little flight of stairs & hear them following

the rush of music from a distant time a woman's voice becoming regular the words emerging low & high relentless openings processions

& it's picasso in the lead a little man with hairy shoulders he has stripped down to his running shorts like frank o'hara both of them now stars for minneola prep both now declare their love of evil

with apollinaire here too his head no bigger than a thumbnail flanked by gertrude stein eyes like a crazy doll's & someone looking like my father max jacob wrapped in a monk's brown cloak down which his body disappears

here in a world where there are only little people phantoms where the sky is not a sky the earth is shrinking daily under silver plastic disappearing slipping through my hands like balls in a pachinko parlor eyes revolving like red lights

to end here in la république with all the other dead the hungry ghosts under our windows a soup kitchen for the dead the ones who run the ones who squat now on the grass

they speak our frailty the doom built into life decomposition chaos anarchy *confusion worse confounded* helter skelter squalor

out of whack & out of order out of kilter out of money out of time & out of place & out of breath & out of work & out of hope & out of power

because the men who come to us though dead are just like us & stare at us like fallen princes

we welcome you to death they say their looks dividing us in two
the numbers dance again behind our eyes
the circles break
the man holding a clock up to his ear will count the silence
every day is summer

what was once alive is gone
& what has yet to be alive
is also gone

Paris
August/September
1997

AT TSUKIJI MARKET TOKYO

10/19/96, for Kato-kun

1
fish & styrofoam
& plastic wrappings
where we watched great tuna bodies
white still under frost
on carts that pass us by
here in this market without smells
a place for noble death
for fish death
we can view it from our chariot
this flat bed
moving forward—curving—in a dream
small fishes packed in rows
a giant clam like a vagina
a razor-beak *sayori* red dot at its tip
the *kimme* showing god's large eye
(he said) or under lamplight
gills still moving
fish blood seeping out
the blood of white fish with what stolen beauty
orange fins & tails of poison *fugu*
nearby eels in vats of blood & water
& the dark saws splitting flesh & bone
the severed tuna heads their mouths still open
black fish wrapped in ice
a red slash underneath its head
eye wide & dry
a cavity that cuts down deep
that lets the hand move in & out

to draw out lungs & guts
shrimps wriggling   sad survivors   in the sawdust
"insects of the sea"
my mind aswim with these
with mouths that open in the blood they float through
miles of searching filaments
like flags for death
a paradise of bubbles fast ascending
tiny eggs & sperm
each one a seedbed for a hundred kannons
breaking into life
the cry of food & sex so strong
there is no wrapper can contain it
but it fills the air
& from my mouth it issues like the dead
the voices of our fathers calling
ploughed back in the earth
without regrets
reminding us how gorgeous death is
blood of fishes staining the white flesh
red flowers & round open eyes

2
THE TALE

He walks among the others: animals & neighbors. In the land of islands someone comes to meet him, tall & with an eye that cuts through space. Immaculate. The man cries out & falls. His death comes when it does by force of nature. In this way we feel the earth shake till it draws the light around us. Lungs and guts are emptied. When the shock breaks through the crust a block of houses rises from the sea and burrows down. Its people lie beneath a wall of boulders: stones a god shakes free. They see the fish swept up into a stranger's net. The corridors are white & lined with fish blood. Death is always sudden, always comes after the fatal blow. A mallet cracks the fish skull. They blast a hole into the fish's maw. The messengers who spoke a broken language, also now stare through broken eyes. We walk among the shelters & the empty lots. Awash in Tsukiji where the boards cry out with fish death. Continue with the work he hands you. To provoke & probe. A life disrupted is no less a life. Those who were sleeping when the floats drove by continued sleeping. Those

who were awake were faster—like fathers running in & out of dreams.
The prince of tides has written this for you. The land of islands.

3
for Makoto Oda

"a great quake
"shook the earth
the old poem has it
thinking how our legs have lost their balance
books & ladders tumbling down
a dream of fish death

where the bathers in their terror move like fish
the man who has an old world in his mind
sees it return to him
the year behind him lost to sleep
a rush of water dims his eyes
the words rewoven to the present day

•

[HOJOKI—CHOMEI AT TOYAMA—1212 A.D.—KOBE 1995/96]

months passed & people spoke about the quake no longer
but a skull would sometimes turn up in the earth
heavy with water
& the aftershocks now were inside us
carried with us day by day
the earthquake hidden underneath the ground
our houses like our ashes swept away

this is how a capital can disappear
or boats be swallowed by the earth
covered by mountains
a city with dead houses (someone thinks)
how long will they be standing?
—until the wild boars clog up all your streets
—until the mountain cleaves in two

days grow darker
world knows what its equal is
an earthquake spewing havoc all around us
when the elements light up
the days go white with aftershocks & black with clouds
houses slip into the earth consumed as dust
like that stirred up by horses racing through a valley
where land gives way & blights them
trapped in the event

but when they speak the language of the gods
no words come out
therefore the masks they use are hinged
to make a show of speech

no one is free of it   no heart
escapes its vanities
but all their thoughts record the years that pass
the way the wind shadows their months
all times abandoned to its ceaseless shaking
like a dragon moving up & down
like thunderbolts that strike them dead
like smoke that covers a pagoda
waves that break on rocks
seas burying the earth

a fish
under the light

a message brought out of the shadows

fin & claw
& claw
tearing at your throat

periphery
pursuing

torn to shreds

how many years before it ends?
how dark the sin? how raw the talk that ends it?
how cruel the buddha who resides here
who abides catastrophes & fires
aftershocks of quakes that pass us by
events that raise us on their wings
then let us crash   pale billows
swelling up around the little temples
the little shorelines under water
rivers driven skyward in one final quake

•

forgotten with the dead
in glory
massive bodies hidden under frost

the words recorded
of a man beside himself who speaks
who says

"be here
"pretend

(so like the world they are
so like the man himself

the water underneath his window
still a haven for lost birds

uncertain thoughts
uncertain passage through a foreign world

finished 1.i.97

TSUKIJI: (*pronounced* tskeejee) *The great Tokyo fish market—largest in the world by several times—through which we were led by Kato Hitsuji, a young actor who worked there nights & early mornings. The visit to Japan was not long after the great Kobe earthquake, whose ruins we saw in company of novelist Oda Makoto & which brought up memories of the Kyoto earthquake of 1185 described by Kamo-no-Chomei as witness in his early thirteenth-century classic,* Hojoki.

From CHINA NOTES

for Wai-lim Yip

Tibetan Boogie

Puning Tibetan Temple
Chengde

In the post Buddha
land the boys
dressed up as monks
scuffle & sway,
the hungry ghosts
in black   like skeletons
at halloween
with skulls
& cross bones.
They dance Tibetan boogies,
dangling arms
their buttocks
swinging,
faces hidden behind
boogie masks.
The loudspeakers
erupt   with cossack
choruses,
a world of counterfeit
through which the long horns
sound, reclaiming
what was lost,
the undulations,
red in color like
the flags,
red guards in motion,
easy, red, a color
the desires of young monks
in ancient songs:

the girls beneath the walls
like tigers
wild but beautiful.

Along the way
the visitors burn incense,
bang tibetan bells,
spin prayer wheels,
thirty in a row,
for which they pay, they
sway & smile,
they pick out robes
& dance in them,
they pose for photographs
(I step into the image
—see me see me—
& screen my eyes)
the awkwardness of tourists
bowing at a shrine,
the face of Guanyin staring back,
1000 eyes, 1000 arms.
A string of plastic bags
hangs from her belt
the memory of lamas,
old & young,
of governors & thieves
who came here,
foreign ghosts who coveted
the inner temple,
stripped gold from teeth
& tiles, who robbed
the country blind,
left it captive
to its future days   the past
a theme park for the dead,
gifts of an emperor,
the king of clocks.
Theirs is a world of spectacles
like yours   a world
from which no traveler returns,

once entered,
but all who come here
count the time
between the courier's arrival
& where we walk
upstairs & downstairs
numbering our days.

The Poet At Chin's Mausoleum

1
he loves to watch
images of power
more than images
of love   but knows
that both are momentary,
mindless
knows what he sees
& hears
not what he says

2
Mao is a copy of Chin
our friend says

—he with black beard
& flowing hair—

the return of privilege,
while the poor fall back

3
the more they eat
the more they feel the need
to go on eating

The Poet In A Field Of Tombs

1
The Poem as Landscape

the loneliest place
I've never seen
or felt before
the earth gone dead
after a conflagration
leaving a flat world
distant from the dunes
& mountains
clumps of earth
cast up   small tufts
with tiles
or broken bricks
as coverings
with sticks & wires
left for markers
generations of the dead
each ghost
into its tomb   each tomb
a little world
more than 10,000
down the ages
each one set apart
in desolation from
the others

2
Inside the Tomb

the entry to that world,
the fence to heaven

•

human head with body
of a snake

•

a crow with three legs

sun & fire

•

ugly frog:

the moon

•

a bird makes music
& makes rain

•

a fox with nine tails

happy days

•

this bear holds up
the roof

•

an oil lamp
dropped down from above
to eat the air

•

a turtle in the river
brought up words

& so began
the art of books

•

a man
a woman
wearing silk

two servants
at each side
who have no mouths

The Treasures Of Dunhuang

Performance Version

1

a faceless buddha

•

a black buddha

•

buddhas with silver mustaches
& chin hairs

•

three transvestite buddhas

•

buddha with heads
around his head—
dozens of whirling heads

•

2000 buddhas

•

crouching buddha—
slits for eyes—
looks sleepy

•

a buddha with a dozen faces
& a thousand hands with eyes

•

buddha holds a fern—
he wears a scabbard
& the scabbard grows a hand

•

rays stream from buddha's eyes
—or tears

•

eyes wide in terror
open anguished mouth with fangs
he holds a dish with flaming ryes
but haloed

can this be buddha too?

•

thin buddha
starving buddha

sitting hand to chin
& smiling

2
a meditating buddha
a practicing buddha
a preaching buddha
an enlightened buddha
a thinking buddha

a musing buddha
a performing buddha
a didactic buddha
an irradiated buddha
a pragmatic buddha

an absentminded buddha
a fabricating buddha
an authoritative buddha
a radioactive buddha
an obstinate buddha

an oblivious buddha
a counterfeit buddha
an imperative buddha
a degenerate buddha
a disobedient buddha

a paralyzed buddha
a vicarious buddha
a tyrannical buddha
an apostate buddha
an anarchical buddha

an anarchical buddha
a disobedient buddha
an obstinate buddha
a pragmatic buddha
a thinking buddha

an apostate buddha
a degenerate buddha
a radioactive buddha
an irradiated buddha
an enlightened buddha

a tyrannical buddha
an imperative buddha
an authoritative buddha
a didactic buddha
a preaching buddha

a vicarious buddha
a counterfeit buddha
a fabricating buddha
a performing buddha
a practicing buddha

a paralyzed buddha
an oblivious buddha
an absentminded buddha
a musing buddha
a meditating buddha

3
a buddha behind bars

•

black buddha face
with marble eyes

•

five bodhisattvas
in a row
each with a flower

•

how big this buddha's hands are

•

buddha's palms
lie open
waiting for stigmata

•

two buddhas sit together
one without a forearm
one without a hand

•

guardians
with knotted muscles
on their chests

a lion face
upraised
& baying

buddha
like a warrior
in armor

•

a giant painted
buddha

his hands that look
like feet

his feet
gargantuan

push past the garment's
fringes

beneath the image of
a dragon

& a snake

•

the buddha on the right
is dark with age

an old man's face
& bald

what does he know of man's fate
or of woman's?

•

beyond the door
buddha lies dying
a choir of mourning monks
behind him

•

a paradise of buddhas

everlasting bliss

A COMMENTARY ON CHINA NOTES

The *China Notes* come from a trip in 2002 that brought us out as far as the Gobi Desert & gave a chance to see some of the changes & continuities throughout the country. I was traveling with poet & scholar Wai-lim Yip, who lives near us in San Diego & is best known here for *Pound's Cathay* & other books, & had a chance to read poetry in five or six cities & to observe things as part of an ongoing discourse with Wai-lim & others. The ancient beauty of some of what we saw played out against the theme park quality of other simulacra of the past, as in the poem "Tibetan Boogie," or the lavish growth of cities everywhere we went. Among the older sites & sights, Chin's (or Qin's) mausoleum is the center around which the ceramic armies at Xian were buried (& many living workers besides), & "the field of tombs" is close to Dunhuang & Yang Pass, which Pound mentions as the Gate of Go, & Wang Wei before that: "west of Yang Pass there will be no friends." So a sense of beckoning wilderness/wildness in a landscape already cut into to serve the human need for power & control.

From AN ORACLE FOR DELFI

For Demosthenes Agrafiotis

The Stones Of Delfi (I)

1
the stones speak

2
the stones laugh

3
we—like all poets—
have a taste for stones

THE STONES OF DELFI (II)

here is an edge to stone,
here is a cry with splinters driven
into the bone   the clavicle

responding in pain
here where the pain is nearly solid
gravitates toward stone itself

the voice in stone is letters
broken marks   the small men chipping
writing on the walls

will build a world in stone
where we can live   & find it
beautiful & lonely

the mark of higher cultures
but once shattered into shapes
becomes so primary

it takes your breath away
—those loplop columns
arising toward the sky at delfi

no civic order merely
architecture   but the promise of
new wildernesses

where the stones speak
the stones laugh
towering above their witnesses

the stones drop to the earth
we sow them into place
& watch them grow

like giants
broken bodies of our pasts
false signatures

inscribed by wars
that never end
that leave a chaos always

a paradise of stones

At Mykines

1
in the royal house
a fire pit & smoke hole
at the center

around which men would sit
the walls renewed with
paintings
every year

with goat bells somewhere
in the distance

2
with goat bells somewhere
in the distance

or goblins of these mountains
little people

at this time of year

3
making echoes from its walls
we look for goats

invisible, whose lonely bells
are clanging in the air

4
snowcapped arcadia
beyond   small puffs of smoke
marking the Argive plain
where we were too +

+ I too have been there

The Silver Trade

by workers
strapped into a cage-sized
space

poor slaves,
whose children finish up
the job

to bring the silver
to the light

Cape Sunio, Greece
December 1992

Spetses In Winter

1
was more like maine's
dark coast   the way
we walked around it
combing the ground for shards

& in the rain we found
Marina's shrine

(not Mary's, someone said)
in which she stood

triumphant,
sandaled foot on
devil's head,
her face lit

by a crazy smile

2
the wind rose
& the weather—lost to us
in greek—reported
sleet & snow across
the isthmus

oh the pleasures of
the single cotton cloth
& inner heat

3
"does an indian eat eggs
"the way a greek does? (D. Agrafiotis)

From A BOOK OF WITNESS

Language belongs to the saint children.
They speak and I have the power to translate.
María Sabina

THE CASE FOR MEMORY

I was amok & fearless
twice deceived
for which I sought out
satisfactions

in a tree.   Too carelessly
I reached for love
& beaten down
I found you
in a froth or frenzy
spent my days around
the pan yards.
I would ask no help from those
whose trust is weak
but I would buy the latest
& the least.
I live for something practical
—the case for memory—
I set one foot into the space
the others leave abandoned.
Not your lord or slave
I meet you
in an equal clash of wills
& face you down.
I only touch the ground
on Sundays

A Cruel Nirvana

Half dead
is still alive
& half alive is too.
So keep it rolling
I declare.
The others mingle in a room
atop the city
where a fire burns.
They sing.
I sing among them.
Then I push my way through
with my thumbs.
I eke a living
from a stone.
Hard knocks are bound to follow.

I can hear
a water song
close by my ear
& track it
where it leads me.
It is summer
but the trees
are dead.
They vanish with
our fallen friends.
The eye in torment
brings them down
each mind a little world
a cruel nirvana.

A Real Man

Mangled fingers
push the stones aside.
The scars run deep.
Hate suits
the human face
far better
than a mask
The price of happiness
is wisdom.
Stones that interfere
with speech
will interfere with sleep
no longer.
Soon he wipes away
the stain.
The motor seems outrageous.
Back & forth
he walks.
I watch the fathers
growing
throwing caution to the winds.

My body hovers
in an air
the man can hold forever
in his sights.
I do not trust his way
of dealing.
He & I
are brothers
for this moment
only.
Watch his fingers closing.
He is a real man
when he murders
is he not?

I Can't Say Who I Am

I can't say who I am (A. Baraka)
but go for it
& speak
as if I knew it.
Time is half the story
so is death.
I run from shadows
to avoid old people
maddened by God.
I follow animals
whose eyes at night
mirror my face.
Seeing myself asleep
I touch my arm.
I celebrate
new forms of sex.
I am frantic
knowing that nobody
has a way out
or a face
more marked than
mine.

I was not
born live. (J. Holzer)
The case for memory
grows weaker
day by day.
The more I know myself
the less I am.
I hold on to a name
because it suits me
but the voice behind it
never was my own.

I Come Into The New World

Voices are dumb until
I speak for them.
Knowing the sound
I find myself between
two fires. One
is dark green, one
the color of my mind
asleep. I come into
the new world
where the thought of death
no longer rankles.
It will be good to be
a stranger always
to know the terms by which
we visit back & forth
& sideways.
In the morning I will wear
a suit with shoulders
big as boards. My clothes are
silver plastic.
When I step into the car
it starts to fly.
I play games with
children
where I make

a nose
into an ear.
Like a clock my heart
moves closer
to the burning babe
& stays there.
I will now count
the century
by ones & twos.
This morning
all the voices in my dream
spoke with one voice.
I feel privileged to be here
among you.
From now on
we will live
on borrowed time.

January 1, 2000

Eager To Break Through Language

I proceed along a path
that others
make for me
before they die.
The winds blow in from space.
I still do not exist (N. Mandelstam)
but with a name like theirs
I play the game of *being*.
Eager to break through language
& touch life
I crack my head against
a mirror.
I hack at a false body
with a stick
pushing the flames apart
until the heart appears.
It is imperative to plant a garden

to share a common fate
with those called creatures.
Proud possessors
of a *geist*
they turn from me
the more I beckon.
I can no longer
face the music
though no one asks me
if I can.
I meet you backwards
out of shame.
The Baltic beckons.
Knowing
that the dead possess
a terrace
I ask permission to attend
the bride.
They call for silence
while my ear fills up
with grace.

I Am That I Am

I am that I am
the god trills.
(He is no more a god
than I or you.)
We see his little boats
ride to the shore
& watch our fathers
like our children
muscle through the waves.
There is a cry
like anybody's
in my throat.
There is a crowd
that fails to see
how our flesh flakes off.

All eyes discern me
where I fall.
No one demands
the tribute
that I cast aside.
I cannot bear it
when they foul my nest.
All that I keep
from those who
sleep beside me
is the calculus of
who they are.
I scorn old people &
discount their days.
I add the numbers
to the newly born
without a thought of
how or why.
I puzzle my old
ways & hide
my fecklessness.
Today is Saturday
forever.
The book is ending
where the book
began.

[Further poems & the pre-face to *A Book of Witness* are presented elsewhere in these pages.]

From 50 CAPRICHOS AFTER GOYA

The Sleep Of Reason

for Clayton Eshleman

Words imprinted on a sign
by Goya   glowing
white against a surface
nearly white:
the sleep of reason
that produces monsters.
He is sitting on a chair
his head slumped
resting on his arms
or on the marble table,
pencil set aside,
his night coat open
thighs exposed.
All things that fly at night
fly past him.
Wings that brush an ear,
an ear concealed,
a memory beginning
in the house of sleep.
His is a world where owls
live in palm trees,

where a shadow in the sky
is like a magpie,
white & black are colors
only in the mind,
the cat you didn't murder
springs to life,
a whistle whirling in a cup,
gone & foregone,
a chasm bright with eyes.
There is a cave in Spain,
a fecal underworld,
where bats are swarming
among bulls,
the blackness ending in a wall
his hands rub up against,
a blind man in a painted world,
amok & monstrous
banging on a rock.

The World A Masquerade

Hats the men wear
—striped—
atop their heads
so ugly & so cruel
the murky air
won't hide them.
One averts
his eyes, the other
stares at you
with hatred
fierce enough to freeze
your blood.
A third one sits,
a lump down on the ground,
his good eye riveted
on empty space
or on the rump of someone
bending over

—man or girl—
with hat pulled tightly
over ears,
in deference to
the woman in the mask,
her gown adorned
with spanish laces.
Nadie se conoce,
Goya writes,
but all are gay
deceivers,
the world a masquerade
for those like you
who run from it   for those
like me who stay.

The Company Of Men

Those who are *real* men
stroke their knives & wait
under the rocks, their guns
at ready. Mindless
their eyes are, like the eyes
of reptiles, tight
the flesh over the bone,
the blood like snow
dyed pink. It is
the company of men
that shapes the world,
some who are friends
& others
in it for the sport.
They chew & pick their teeth.
The end of strife
unmans them. Life is death
& death
is what is lost,
retrieved,
& lost again.

Men who are *real* men
rub their skin
with death, a paste
of fat & ash.
They marvel at
the splintered tree
behind them,
the papers strewn about,
wine spilled,
the sky a blister.
They will go to war
& you, because
your time is drawing nigh,
will wait in wonder,
trembling to be born.

Tight Stockings

Tight stockings
make a man's balls swell
they say. They play
love like a game,
place a slippered foot
on a bidet & rock around
the clock. Old women
count the days,
the hours left behind,
the thrusts made
by the perfect pelvis.
Some body with a name
like yours   steps
from his clothes,
a dream of women in
tight stockings
filling half his brain,
the other half
long gone.
A chair goes up in flames.
The man remains inside

a burning house,
the sand dissolving
in the pit.
He dreams about his own leg
stuffed into its silk,
the fit of which
is like a miracle
& heats him.
Few of them remember
what began it,
thinking
they were always there.
Now that his pants
are halfway down
he looks at them
with wonder,
thinks that they're halfway
up.

All Who Will Fall

A swarm of little birds
with heads of men
& women,
this is his dream
& yours.
The mothers in the world below
hold back a laugh   a fart
that dances in the air
between them. One is old
& holds a bone
between her fingers,
watches how a daughter
prongs the screaming
bird man, props him
on another's lap,
the spittle from his mouth
against her dress.
All who will fall,

like these,
have one commitment,
it is not to you
but to the air
they ride on.
Some are angels,
some are myopic men,
the one atop the tree
a woman known for envy,
hidden thoughts,
a fountain at her source.
Adrift or flying
backwards,
theirs is the fate of sailors.
Bind them pluck them.
Those who have enough of dreams
wake every morning,
ready to be the slaves
of those who dream for pleasure,
naked & wounded,
eager like them
to kill.

To Speak As Who You Are

To speak as who you are,
say "I"
then streak across
the tiled floor,
little naked birds
your feathers stripped from you.
Lost, without wings
you feel the heaviness
of time, like those
who stalk you,
those who strike the air
with brooms
& banners,
signatories

to your days on earth.
Old women sneer,
young women snicker,
the door that opened onto China
fills with light,
the stubs of feathers
sting you,
in the air above them
shadow of a hawk
without a head
is looming   waiting
for the kill,
the carcass to be cast aside,
like paper,
like a poem in a dream
unread but endless.
You are the last of Goya's
birds   the fatal product
of his will,
a face without a name.

That Which We See In Goya

A woman made to wear
a fool's cap
& to ride a mule.
The road clogged up with watchers,
men on horseback,
shadows on a glass,
an eye gone dead,
a change of fortune.
Time is running
backward.
That which we see
in Goya
comes alive. It is
the punishment men dream
who live in fear
of women,

bang their bells
in anger.
Deep inside
the mind
there is a drawing
still to do.
Here are the men
whose backs are turned
against us,
others with sticks,
with curled hair
shoulder length,
unkempt,
& eyes that travel
sideways,
ready for the kill.
Nobody can call them back.
A stadium erupts
in flames. A stand
of fathers
draws a clamp around
her neck.
The past & future
intersect. God's
word is spoken,
strands you
in a foreign clime.
A fell arrest.

A Donkey & A Monkey

Disciples of a donkey,
do they come
to learn attitudes
& platitudes
stamped on their reptile
minds? *That parrot,*
this carrot (Tatehata A.)
are other signs for sure.

A donkey & a monkey
facing off   caprichos
that the monkey plunks
on *la guitarra*,
soundlessly,
the donkey following
in wonder,
strangers clapping hands
& crying *hey*,
olé.
A donkey like a monkey
reads a book,
a monkey like a donkey
listens.
He sees a pair of
donkey faces,
lines of A's across
a chalkboard,
easy aces,
donkey silhouettes
in grey,
a spunky donkey
in a coat, his muzzle
pressed against
the dead man's chest
the best he has
to show   hello,
caprichos!

A COMMENTARY FOR CONCEALMENTS & CAPRICHOS

50 Caprichos after Goya and *A Book of Concealments* that follows were a two-pronged followup to the earlier hundred-poem work, *A Book of Witness*, with some notable changes in strategy & composition. In *A Book of Witness* I was concentrating on the rescue of the first-person voice as our principal instrument of witness—not only the personal "I" but the possibilities of a real if sometimes fictive "I" across a range of experiences, my own & at choice moments those of others, mostly recent poets from whom short & often cryptic phrases were appropriated & put in play. By contrast the poems in *A Book of Concealments* suppress or conceal the witnessing "I" but draw from more distant "romantic" predecessors & from my own accumulated works by collaging as italicized inserts small fragments of poems already written & published, while *50 Caprichos*, written simultaneously, compensates for the largely missing "I" by allowing a give-&-take responsive to the dance of images in Goya's early opening to states of spirit & mind that many of us would later come to share.

The title A *Book of Concealments* is based, almost literally, on a medieval Jewish mystical text, *Sifra diSeni'uta*, a section of the Zohar from which I drew lines & images that appear sporadically throughout, not as the mapping of a nonexistent god, but as an intimation, in both *Concealments* and *Caprichos*, of an imagined world embedded in the real one.

From A BOOK OF CONCEALMENTS

THE TIMES ARE NEVER RIGHT

Warm days hanging
over San Diego,
where streets
slide into murky
canyons. What
is this but
home & what
is home
but a misnomer?
Pisces has shifted
into Aries.
Aggravated
bumps shadowing
the server's
arms are no
concern to anyone
yet called to our
attention show
a strain, a fearsomeness
hard to conceal.
The times are never right.

A skin of air is over
everything. The sun
flows like a liquid,
all the universe we see
has never happened.
There is no truth to time
except for birthdays.
In a city under siege
a ceremony
gathers, scattering
the birds.
We live forever
in the instant,
in the house we share.
A groom & bride
are figures,
smaller than a thumb
& little reckoning
how short
the passage between
death & life.

20.iii.02
for Diane's birthday

A Man In Love With Death

A man in love with death
is still a man.
He sees his hands bleed
with another's cankers, sees
the blood cold in his eye,
a rosy episode
smeared over walls & door.
The others enter through it,
sit beside him.
What does he hear?
Where does a life
begin & end?

How fast? How far?
Who but the dead
can claim an end
to numbers?
In his head he learns
to count them   with his hands
they are more real
than right.
Deceit of numbers
raising questions in the mind
that's helpless
& of doors that will not
shut   the others
waiting for a door to shut
behind them   for his voice
to be a voice
that speaks for them,
one of the lonely
dead.

The Mystery Of Evil

for Oda Makoto

The mystery of evil
rests in *God*,
no less in *terror*.   [*gematria* = 42]
Fathers who shun the world
cry scandal
where they spawn,
eyes dark as dungeons,
a wool beard
on every face.
Men grow transparent
in their rages,
oblivious the more
they claw with
longing
at each other's flesh.

The mystery of terror
rests in God,
no less in evil.
Poems are written
to the dead,
the ones
who do not speak nor share
a common language.
In the air of caves
a figure like a god
lies broken.
His glasses tumble to the ground.
His breath smells sweet to everybody.
Fools find places
where they track the stalkers,
legs that cross a line,
a line that dwindles to a point,
a point that shatters.
Stars collide.
The words of poems
go up in smoke.
Mothers brandish babes
like weapons.
There is no
boundary dividing
life from art.

Oceanside Pier: Among The Fishers

The line, more tangled than
the fishing lines at Oceanside,
hangs from a hundred different mouths,
coronas colored in a hundred ways
each one around a brilliant
orifice, bright droplets
white & yellow,
yellow,
red,
the red of circles,

a debris of spirit that the mind
can shape as words,
as sounds more true than words are,
waiting on a pier
above the mackerel-crowded seas,
to hear, to know, to celebrate,
to walk among the fishers,
lines of men & women
phantom residents
of phantom towns,
who fish by day,
go forth at night
into a world inhabited
by dolls,
a mannikin romance,
a gaffer wedging mussels from
black columns,
hearing voices
from below the earth
of animals,
the worlds we haven't seen
more real
than those we have.

The Sorry Mystics

Little Infinite Poem

Infinity intrudes,
posits a world where everything,
repeated endlessly,
is possible.
A world caught in a mirror
too vast to be contained.
Infinities of mirrors.
The ones who see it
falter, their hands
break the glass.
They are the sorry mystics,
misfits from

the middle states,
we spy them
on a distant planet,
lost from time.
Another world contains them,
world on world,
another grain of sand,
each grain a world.
Another town to walk through,
hand in hand.
Another one like you
to be there   always
whom you will not know
but she will write her name
on stones.
Out of the earth
a farmer will dislodge
great stones
like gods
a paradise of stones.
Another earth
is theirs   who claim
a signature
in stone, a number
greater than
infinity, mapping
a mindless world.

A Double Schism

There is a pope
who waits for you,
a pope who sits on cushions,
paints his fingernails
a shade of red
so much like blood

it scares the dead away.
The men who stare at
their own faces
on the screen,
who write on air,
declare
his holiness.
By night the father
breaks apart,
halfway inside the window
cut in two.
He is four fathers
now, his eyes
awash with tears,
with bells that sound off
in his skull
A double schism
links to
double happiness.
The four who are
our fathers
call themselves
the pope.
They name their brides
America & point
their tongues
at heaven.
They are everything
his mother
wanted   ministers
of grace.
A trickle down his leg
is sign of rapture.
Two plus two is five.
The fathers without
issue are the lords
of those who do.

A Deep Romantic Chasm

for Michael McClure

A deep romantic chasm
beckons him   it leaves no time
to hide from light
in spite of circumstances,
& the way the street
flows like a stream
from no source,
nowhere.   This season
with its birds
newly arrived,
the first one on a fence,
mortal as you,
a harbinger of days to come.
Another word,
a false return,
the spoken still unspoken
carries us off.
The cavern of the universe
widens each morning.
My head fills up with dew,
the father writes,
having no home but where
his shadow leads him.
In greasy shirtsleeves, heavy
lids, blotched faces,
the men pursue
a trail of tears,
unbuttoned   captive
to a dream,
a starless galaxy,
the deeper sky
a field of images
measureless & mindless,
absent their god.

Romantic Dadas

for Jeffrey Robinson

A late night party
where Romantic Dadas
cut a rug   too iridescent
to resist
our smug caresses.
How will we begin
addressing them,
by name or by a face
that turns away from you
unseen, leaves scarce
a trace behind.
Mister Novalis,
or if that isn't
your real name,
drop it right now
& try another.
He is too determined,
too far below
his average height
for anyone to count.
Aside from which
there are the odors
of the women
who surround him,
so many that the walls begin
to press his skull.
He has to break away
to make an outcry
in the name of Dada.
I & I & I are left
without a place
ulterior to place,
to run or hide.

The Persistence Of The Lyric Voice

for Scott McLean

He will keep writing,
will he not,
as you will.
A pressure like a finger
builds inside
his chest
& travels upward,
somewhere between
the trachea
& glottis,
pushes the fold aside
& breaks.
Imagined speech.
It is the same for everything
we say   we think we know
the speaker but the speaker
escapes our observation.
It is this concealment
that reveals
the truth of poetry
no less authoritative
than the other
in full gusto.
From the direction of his voice,
an absence & a grief,
his profile is a kind of blue.
The footfall of a wanderer
crosses the open field
in daylight.
Let the *spirit* rise
until its *mind*,
the untranslated,
untranslatable,
in which the lyric voice
resides   mind's matter
& its coming forth
by day.

In The Book Of Concealments

everything is concealed,
therefore the book
runs out   the pages
still glued together
must be torn
apart. Hello again,
dear little dove,
we have agreed to be
your crazed pursuers.
Standing on a pebbled beach,
the sand pushed back,
thousands of shining
jelly fish obstruct
our passage.
We have to strain
to read,
the letters even now
escaping, twisting
back & forth,
the world so soon
engulfed.
In the book of concealments
on the final page
we find the secret written,
words askew,
a distant swarm of hummers
darkening the land.
The armies never stop.
The men who fish
are fishers,
draw their lines across,
two threads, one side
in red
one side in black,
the eye of man
shut tight.
What are the words they proffer,
paper thin?

"You are the prince of waters"
reads the missive.
"I have loved you."

Postscript To A Book Of Concealments

There is a burnt book
that remains a book,

a hidden book
which, if it opened,

would tear the walls
of time down, let

the false world
infiltrate &

overwhelm
the real.

June 2008

POETICS & POLEMICS 3
TOWARD AN OMNIPOETICS

In the grand collage signs flash green against blue, black against white, red against yellow. Enlarged pupils of the emerging doctrine attend the hidden teacher of the increasing sound.
And all the signs rime.

Robert Duncan, *Bending the Bow*

THE BOOK SPIRITUAL INSTRUMENT

for Edmond Jabès & Alison Knowles

I meet him in the book—or what he takes to be a book.
Or I meet her in the book that she had made & sing with her the praises of construction.
It is you, when all is said & done,
it is you & your strong voice
that sets us free.
For these the Dream Book is another matter, it is a marker leading to the mind or leading where the mind will intersect with daylight.
She builds a platform between windows.
Sunlight rushes in from either side
a book of sunlight.
But from all this we turn aside: we run from it and find her running with us.
In a street named for a forest & a sword, our friend was dreaming of a desert.
It was a desert different from the desert that we knew,
a desert different in its absence.
How could I ever be a desert person?
How could I be descended from a desert people,
homeless,
harmless,
when what they spoke about was only forests?
The desert in the book was truly different
& was only in the book.
The book was where she lived & where we walked.
Trees were in its pages,
dark with leaves.
Edmond was with me in the dream & in the forest
& was reading from a book.
The woods were full of strangers.
The desert was a life away.
In the valley just below we saw a cloud of smoke—blood-colored—emerging from a single chimney.
In it a woman stood as in a book.

Within the book worlds came together.

THE ANTHOLOGY AS A MANIFESTO & AS AN EPIC INCLUDING POETRY, or THE GRADUAL MAKING OF POEMS FOR THE MILLENNIUM

Talk first presented at the Modern Language Association December 30, 1995, modified for presentation at the Boston Alternative Poetry Conference July 18, 1998

I would like to go back over my own relationship to anthologies & to contrast it to a general discomfort I have with anthologies as such, before entering into a discussion (however it falls out) of *this* anthology or of "the anthology as an epic poem and/or a manifesto." In 1979 I had done five anthologies, the most recent of which (*A Big Jewish Book*) had been published by Doubleday the year before. It was with relation to this that Charles Bernstein, who was then editing the important (poets') journal of poetics, *L=A=N=G=U=A=G=E*, asked me to write a piece on my own work &/or "on anthologies." I began it with a quote from Gertrude Stein about the new & the old, since the anthologies I had then made were a conjunction of modernist poems with ancient or culturally distant works of near-poetry that I wanted (in Robert Duncan's words) to "bring into their comparisons." What Stein wrote (words that I've quoted a number of times since, as I have a way of doing with quotations) was: "As it is old it is new and as it is new it is old, but now we have come to be in our own way which is a completely different way."

With that as epigraph, what I tried to do was to distinguish two, at least two, kinds of anthology (a point that seemed to me self evident): those that *deceive* me/us by a false sense of closure & authority, as over against those that I had hoped to do with regard to the *past* & those still more rare & useful ones that opened up & thereby changed the *present*. (Both of the latter I took, rightly or wrongly, as instances of a single impulse.) The canonical anthologies we all know as the great conservatizing force in our literature(s), against which—as artists of an avant-garde—many of us have had to struggle. As gatherings of acceptable/accepted poets their conservatizing thrust is evident; as gatherings of contemporary poets it is to rein in or exclude those moves that challenge too overtly the boundaries of form & meaning or that call into question the boundaries (genre boundaries) of poetry itself.

The other possibility of anthologies is to use the form as a kind of manifesto-assemblage: to present, to bring to light, or to create works that have been excluded or that collectively present a challenge to the dominant system-makers or to the world at large. In my time the great American work of this kind was Donald Allen's (1960) *New American Poetry* (replete with its appended section of poetic statements/manifestos), but also LaMonte Young & Jackson Mac Low's *An Anthology* (as a manifesto of the 1950s/60s Fluxus movement), and Emmett Williams' *An Anthology of Concrete Poetry* as a first summary & presentation of the movement of that name. Still earlier works were Pound's Imagiste gathering & later *Active Anthology* or (better yet) Louis Zukofsky's "Objectivists" anthology of the early 1930s (a prime example, that, of the construction of a movement through a book—& little else by way of publication).

From these I sensed the possibility of the anthology as (1) a manifesto; (2) a way of laying out an active poetics—by example & by commentary; & (3) a grand assemblage or collage: a kind of art form in its own right. My first anthology, *Technicians of the Sacred*, grew from premises (theory) *within* experimental modernism, rather than from critical authority situated outside it—what Tristan Tzara implies in his (1918) *post*modern divergence, that "Dada is ... not a *modern* school ... [nor] a reaction against the schools of today ... [but] more in the nature of an almost Buddhist religion of indifference." Beginning in that general area I was able to explore an open-ended range of deep cultures, of culturally embedded poetries & related language works, many of them subsumed as poetry by resemblance to contemporary work & in that comparison also opening the range & giving a new depth to the experimentally modern. So too I used the last quarter of the book for a section of commentaries that not only gave some ethnographic context to the traditional pieces but allowed the entry & comparison (for better or worse) of a number of more contemporary works (an early revival of Gertrude Stein & a mix of new & old voices, of the modern & the postmodern: André Breton, Diane Wakoski, Tristan Tzara, Gary Snyder, Anne Waldman, Allen Ginsberg, Ian Hamilton Finlay, Simon Ortiz, Hannah Weiner). This was of course the hidden (secret) heart of the collection, what made it (I hope) not a book of antiquities or orientalisms or primitivisms, but a manifesto for our time: each commentary a pointed statement of a way of poetry long overlooked.

All of the anthologies I've assembled since then—by myself or with others—have shared in this; or, to use a key word of the 1960s European Situationists, who helped so much in the development of a strikingly "appropriative" postmodernism, they have been a *détournement* (a turning or a twist) on the structures & presumptions of those fixed anthologies that continue (like the darkness) to surround us.[1] After claiming it as a right, I later found that I had gotten leverage to continue & to expand this work & (with Pierre Joris as a powerful co-worker) to construct an assemblage of the twentieth-century that would bring together (on a global scale) works entirely of this time that had been (the greater part of them at least) too often kept beyond the pale or, if present, had been kept from those comparisons, those co-existences that were so real to our generation of poets *throughout the world.* In that sense I would bow also to those many others who have been our companions, even forerunners in this attempt: cultural hunters & gatherers (or, simply, formal & experiential innovators), who recognized that the common work cut across boundaries; that alliances & strategies were international, intercultural, in scope; that it was possible to seek wholeness or completeness while knowing that we never would achieve it; that the explorations & discoveries of a new poetry & art were precisely what made the attempt at wholeness possible.

That work, which Pierre Joris and I called *Poems for the Millennium*, is now complete and its two volumes and 1600 pages (some twelve years in the making) are generally available. The first volume ("from fin-de-siècle to Negritude") covers the century up to the second world war and is the first such gathering to put the avant-gardes and movements of that time into a place of principal consideration. With that in mind we were able to devote whole sections to six of those movements (Futurism, Dada, Expressionism, Surrealism, the American "Objectivists", and the African & Caribbean Negritude poets) and to draw on individual voices from a still wider range of languages and cultures. And we were able to show too—if it needed showing—that multiculturalism and avantgardism were not incompatible but historically, though not inevitably, related. Our last section, in that sense, was devoted to ethnopoetic explorations from throughout the century.

The gathering—in so far as it smacked of "anthology" in the ordinary sense—was replete with problematics & anxieties. This intensified of course with the second volume, which moved us into the (almost) present; moved us, literally, into a time & poetry in which we shared. The tough thing here—and we knew it from the start—was that as an anthology (& I

1 In *Poems for the Millennium* such détournements extended to the overblown subtitle (*The University of California Book of Modern & Postmodern Poetry*), the Board of Advisors (largely themselves experimental poets), the quasi-scholarly commentaries, & the various other accoutrements & paraphernalia of the *official* book.

mean a largely *contemporary* anthology) it had to be a flawed book—a compendium of absences as well as presences; & we knew too that there was no way that it would not be read as an anthology in that sense. For me, though—and I'm sure this holds for Pierre as well—it was conceived, like other gatherings of mine or his, as something else: an *assemblage* or pulling together of poems & people & ideas about poetry (& much else) in the words of others and in our own words. That *imago*—that representation of where we've been and what we've lived through—is something in fact that I would stand by—like any poem. (It's also why we've allowed ourselves to end the book—as epic poem jammed full with histories & voices—with two poems of our own.)

What is missing from that gathering exists in the still greater gathering we carry with us—as a mental, a spiritual, construct. It is in this sense that every one of us has his or her anthology, that every one of us, given the opportunity, could bring it into some kind of form or structure in the outer world. At the end of a joint interview with Chris Funkhouser, following the publication of volume one, Pierre suggested that as far as future projects went, the two volumes were (for us at least) "the anthology to end all anthologies." To which I added that the only anthology still left to do was "an anthology of everything." In saying that I suppose there was an echo of Mallarmé's intuition that "everything in the world exists in order to be put into a book." By that measure, of course, Mallarmé continues to be a guardian angel for the work—one of those who led us into the domain of the impossible, which is really where we want to be.

POEMS FOR THE MILLENNIUM: A FIRST PRE-FACE

Volume One: From Fin-de-Siècle to Negritude

(with Pierre Joris)

> *Know this:*
> *the only game I play is the millennium*
> *the only game I play is the Great*
> *Fear*
>
> *Put up with me. I won't put up with you!*
> — AIMÉ CÉSAIRE

1 *To pick up at the turning …*

The book began under far different conditions—in the middle 1980s, with the reality of the "cold war" and of the "specter of communism" (K. Marx) still haunting Europe and the world. These were among the defining circumstances of our time, and while they continued it seemed that the twentieth century as we knew it would never end—that it would outlast its final decade and that the context of the life from which our poems arise would remain, largely, the way it was for us. With the changes of the 1990s came the strange sense of a return to the century's beginnings: a time dominated by nationalism and ethnic conflict, when totalitarian ideologies were still in their early stages and science and technology were on the move toward new and ever faster transformations. It was circumstances like these to which the century's first modernists were responding politically and artistically. The difference was in their sense that the norms of the culture were—like its politics—open to unprecedented changes, which they accepted exuberantly or from which they recoiled with equal passion. For most of those represented in these pages, such changes were centered in the conditions of their work as poets and artists—an intuition or prophecy, as William Blake had put it in the century before, that "poetry fetter'd, fetters the human race," or, by extension, that poetry set free, can free or open up the human mind.

The intention of this gathering is to trace the history of that intuition—and its attendant poetry—from *then* to *now.* From its earliest emergence—out of the eighteenth-century Enlightenment and into the seedbed of a radical Romanticism—it reflected a tension between the growth of totalizing nation-states and repeated declarations of the rights of "man." In the ensuing conflicts, poets were not only "unacknowledged legislators" in the ideas they projected (Shelley), but transformers of and through the language in which the work was written. What began to take shape, then, was the idea of poetry as an instrument of change—a change that would take place foremost in the poem itself, both as a question of language and structure and of a related, all-connecting vision. Such a change—deepseated, not cosmetic—was felt to be a virtual reinvention of poetry (or any other art), even (for some of its practitioners) of language itself. So Tristan Tzara, as spokesman for post-rational Dada, would quote Descartes as an informing slogan: "I would like to believe there were no other men before me." And yet, as we will say again and again in these pages, a new past was also being fashioned in the process—many new pasts in fact.

The form of the work we have assembled is that of a synthesizing and global anthology of twentieth-century modernism with an emphasis on those international and national movements that have tried to change the direction of poetry and art as a necessary condition for changing the ways in which we think and act as human beings. While the first volume of the anthology runs—historically—from the beginnings of modernism to the middle 1940s, its emphases come largely from concerns of the later twentieth century as the editors and their contemporaries have experienced them. These emphases include

* an overall sense that what has characterized the century's poetry has been an exploration of new forms of language, consciousness, and social/biological relationships, both by deliberate experimentation in the present and by the reinterpretation of the "entire" human past;

* poetry-art intersections, in which conventional boundaries between arts break down, sometimes involving generalized art movements (Futurism, Dada, Surrealism, Fluxus, etc.) led by poets and with the presence of a poetics at their centers;

* experiments with dream-work and altered forms of consciousness (from the outburst of Surrealist dream experiments in the 1920s to the psychedelic experiments of the 1960s, the meditative experiments of the 1970s and beyond) in which language itself becomes an instrument of vision;

* a return to a concept of poetry as a performative genre, from Futurist and Dada soirées, sound-poems and simultaneities to the "new orality" and the expanded performances and textsound works of the "post"modern (post-World War II) decades;

* language experiments, including the sound poetry and textsound works mentioned above, as well as experiments with visual and typographical forms, attempts to develop a non-syntactic (abstract) poetry, and explorations of new languages and those sub-languages that had long been at the fringes of accepted literature;

* ethnopoetics and related reassessments of the past and of alternative poetries in the present: a general enlargement of cultural terrains directed by the sense of an ancient and continuing "subterranean tradition" with the poetic impulse at its center: a widespread attack on the dominance in art and life of "high" European culture, leading in the later part of the twentieth century to a proliferation of movements stressing an exploration and expansion of ethnic and gender as well as class identities;

* an ongoing if shifting connection to related political and social movements ("surrealism at the service of the revolution," etc.) during what became heroically, sometimes disastrously, an age of ideologies;

* an overall sense of excitement and play ("to work in the excitedness of pure being ... to get back that intensity into the language" — G. Stein) that must be brought across to show the work of the century in all its color and as the poetry "that might be fantastic life" (R. Duncan).

It has been our hope throughout that we could accomplish all of these ends without turning the selection of authors into the projection of a new canon of famous names—rather to have the anthology serve a more useful function as a mapping of the possibilities that have come down to us by the century's turning.

Finally, by way of starters, it should be clear that we have not been looking for any more certainty regarding form or content than what the work itself allows us. In that sense we've welcomed the problematic, even the contradictory, into the poetry that we've brought together here. Thus, if an awareness of the "new," say, seems central to these projects, it is often balanced, sometimes overbalanced, by an obsession with the "old" and "ancient." This represents a problematic and an issue, as do polarities of high and low (in language, diction), of symbolism and realism, lyric exuberance and "objective" precision, hermetic condensations and epic expansions, minimals and maximals, verses and proses, sacreds and seculars, maleness and femaleness. While the predilection of the work is to push things to their limits, even those limits (and that predilection) may be called into question—as in the Dada poet's turning on the Dada work: "The true Dadas are against Dada." (T. Tzara) Or put another way: at the core of every true "modernism" is the germ of a "*post*modernism."

2 *Of what makes a history and what it is ...*

It is the persistence of such issues (political and cultural as much as formal) that makes a history of the "modern" and the "avant-garde." For the better part of two centuries, the western world and then the world in general have been witness to a revolution of the word that's simultaneously a revolution of the mind and (consistently or not) a revolution in the (political, material, and social) world itself. Much of that is already implicit in romanticism," but it's "modernism" (at least the experimental modernism projected in these pages) that takes it all the way—through a sometimes unrestrained attempt to change both word and thought. On the simplest level, the Romantic poet carries along a still traditional, if increasingly shaky, image of the poem—its formal structure or poetic "line"—as in that side of William Blake that writes (but noticeably minus all punctuation)

> Mock on Mock on Voltaire Rousseau
> Mock on Mock on tis all in vain
> You throw the sand against the wind
> And the wind blows it back again

while the emergent new poet (Blake again) blasts the line apart, casts off "the bondage of Rhyming" and "Monotonous Cadence," to produce "a variety in every line, both of cadences & number of syllables." Thus:

> To cast off Bacon, Locke & Newton from Albions covering
> To take off his filthy garments, & clothe him with Imagination
> To cast aside from Poetry, all that is not Inspiration
> That it no longer shall dare to mock with the aspersion of Madness
> Cast on the Inspired, by the tame high finisher of paltry Blots,
> Indefinite or paltry Rhymes: or paltry Harmonies.

The difference here is what Rimbaud will later call us to, writing in the final quarter of the nineteenth century that "the invention of the unknown demands new forms" or, again along those lines, "one must be absolutely modern."

The story of the modernism that characterized the twentieth century goes back at least to Blake or to Hölderlin at the start of the nineteenth—poets who took traditional verse to its limits and then stepped across the line into unprecedented "freedom." With Baudelaire (another key figure), the old verse was more persistent, however much he was (in Rimbaud's view of him) the first "*voyant*" or "seer," and was, with Novalis or with Edgar Poe in his extraordinary *Eureka*, an early master of the (so-called) prose poem—a form that Lautréamont and Rimbaud, somewhat later, brought to a first fulfillment. In their positioning between the old and new, most of the nineteenth-century forerunners resembled Emily Dickinson, whose recognizable metric was accompanied by a revolutionary sense of off- or near-rhyme and by the use of hyphens/dashes to call her own set rhythms into question. Only with Whitman do we see the work turning irreversibly to free or open rhythms (and to the realization of Wordsworth's earlier prophecy of a demotic poetry written in "the language really spoken by men")—equaled, in a sometimes more radical and quirky way, by the sprung rhythms and soundscapes (= instress) of Gerard Manley Hopkins. Often unrecognized, unpublished or scorned in their own time, these would become the major forerunners for the century ahead. And with them as a master innovator was Stéphane Mallarmé, whose extraordinary *Coup de Dés* of 1895 both finished the nineteenth century's fade-out into symbolism and marked the beginning of the twentieth's relentless transformations.

It is with Mallarmé, then, that our view as such begins. In the works that followed his, barrier after barrier began to crumble, toward the construction of new forms, the exploration of new behaviors, and the opening of new possibilities. Early in the twentieth century this expressed itself in movements (some tightly organized, some hardly so) across the arts, as well as in the work of individual poets, acting off a new permission to write a poetry freshly invented—reinvented—in each succeeding poem. The first decade of the century was already filled with this new breed of creative innovator—in poetry as in the other arts. Stein, Apollinaire, Cendrars, Reverdy, Jacob among the cubists of Paris are obvious examples of poet-experimentalists interacting with other experimentalists. This interaction accounts also for the visual edge in Apollinaire, the verbal edge in Picasso's collages (always present, heretofore overlooked).[1] Elsewhere too the push against boundaries and restrictive definitions of poetry and language can be felt: Darío's *modernismo*, Blok's late symbolism, Huidobro's interactions with the Parisians and self-generated creationism; the multiple names (personae, "others") created by Pessoa; Rilke's breakthrough into angelic visions (prodded in part by the emergence of Expressionism and rediscovery of Hölderlin as forerunner); Pound's declarations favoring a new poetic image (or, later on, the image set in motion).

The movements of those first two decades functioned also as collaborative *vortices* (Pound's term), bringing together many individualities in a common push toward a new dispensation, aimed at a drastic change of poem and mind. Of those movements, Futurism was both the first and the first to have a poetry and a poetics at its center. Based in Italy, it was paralleled by Expressionism in Germany, the other Futurism in Russia and in central Europe, Vorticism in the Anglo world, the various new -isms coming out of Paris, and a culmination (circa World War I) in Dada, which was also the first (*post*modern) turning against movements and against modernism as such. The highly individuated poets working from within these movements included Marinetti, Trakl, Benn, Khlebnikov, Mayakovsky, Pound, and Tzara, along with boundary-breaking artist-poets such as Arp, Kandinsky, Klee, and Schwitters.

This energy—first sighted in a time of war and revolution—continued into the century's third decade and beyond, as typified, perhaps, in what Clayton Eshleman has described as the banner year of 1922. In that year Europe and America saw the publication of Eliot's *Waste Land* and Joyce's *Ulysses*, but also Rilke's completed *Duino Elegies* and Vallejo's incredibly knotty, thwarted *Trilce*. It was the decade too of the birth of Surrealism (1924), led by poets like Breton, Soupault, Aragon, Péret, Eluard, Desnos, and culminating in a poet-artist like Artaud, who turned against it with unprecedented inner violence. In its central focus on the *dream work* (S. Freud) and in its call for a strategy of moral and artistic transgression that it only (very) partially began to realize, Surrealism has colored a major area of post-Surrealist writing. At the same time it was countered, largely from the American side, by a push from "Objectivists" and others toward a poetry that would focus on the "luminous detail" and would allow thereby a reperception of the here and now—

---

1 A more detailed approach to Picasso as an actual poet appears above (page 139).

the familiar world from which (Charles Olson later wrote) we were the most *estranged.* A result—in Pound, Zukofsky, others—was to set history alongside myth and dream as areas of mind and practice to be newly rediscovered.

3 *A poetics in advance of a poetics ...*

The history of twentieth-century poetry is as rich and varied as that of the century's painting and sculpture, its music and theater, but the academic strategy has been to cover up that richness. Imagine—now—a history of modern art that left out abstract painting or collage or Cubism or Surrealism and Dada, and you have a sense of what the literary histories (in America for certain) look like to those of us who know that similar things exist in poetry and that many of the earlier moves and movements—but Futurism, Dada, and Surrealism in particular—were essentially the work of poets. It is this realization—so obvious and so deliberately concealed—that the first of our two volumes is intending to express.

A characteristic of modern art (and poetry) so defined—but this carries into the "postmodern" as well—has been the questioning of art itself as a discrete and bounded category. Some such radical questioning of art and of its boundaries is what defines our sense of an "avant-garde" and of some form of "deconstruction" as a strategy for coping with the inherited (authoritative) past. (Both of the terms in quotes are themselves now under question—the result of two centuries of abuse in the former case, of two decades in the latter; or as David Antin puts it elsewhere: "When I hear the word 'deconstruction,' I reach for my pillow.") In an essay on Robert Wilson's "theater of images," Robert Stearns writes (in a configuration we would share with him): "The avant-garde might be characterized as those creators who do not take their environment and its traditions at face value. They separate and view its elements and realign them according to their own needs."

This description (while devoid as yet of social/revolutionary purpose) is general enough to include the great range of strategies and stances in experimental poetry and art. Since nothing around us is (ideally) taken for granted and the conclusion or intention of the work (again ideally) arises or emerges from the work itself, the work by definition is experimental: its outcome unknown, its process crucial. Such experiments/redefinitions/reconstructions may work with and on structures, ideologies (contexts and contents), materials and technologies, or (in any instance) combinations of all of the above. From our shared perspective as poets of a certain place and time, we see the coming together of these possibilities as (still) the great opportunity of art and poetry as these cross into a new millennium. We would want to go so far as to suggest that the experiments of the twentieth-century avant-gardes can be viewed as prologomena to the realized workings of the century to come.

While the basis for most of these new poetries has been a drive toward social—even spiritual—transformation, the experimental moves on their structural/compositional side have involved a range of procedures that bring out the opaque materiality of language as a medium as against a "romantic" view of language as purely a transparent window toward an ideal reality beyond itself. These have included developments (from Mallarmé and Marinetti on) in visual, typographic and concrete poetry; in primarily English language experiments (from Pound and Williams to Charles Olson and beyond) with "projective verse" and composition-by-field; in systematic chance operations (Duchamp and Arp the early prompters, Mac Low and Cage the leading latterday practitioners); in variations, foremost, of montage and collage from throughout the century. Along with such quasi-formalist moves, more strictly ideological/ideational experiments permeated Dada and Surrealism during and after World War I, Negritude (broadly defined) by the start of World War II, Beat and Beat-related poetry in the 1950s and 1960s, street poetics in the 1960s, and aspects of feminism and other liberationist movements over the last three decades. Equally extreme but often less recognized experiments involved the materials and media of poetry—from the obvious return to poetry as an art of live performance, to the creation of a new electronic poetry (soundtext, *poésie sonore*, etc., grounded in its Futurist beginnings), the rudiments of a computer poetry (leading to recent hypertext and cyberpunk experiments, etc.), and the beginnings (toward the other end of the technological spectrum) of a poetry without sound in the culture of the deaf. And along with this there have been persistent thrusts to raise demotic, colloquial, common speech as the language of a new poetry and culture. Taking many different forms and challenging many longstanding prejudices and language barriers, this marks a key point at which language experiments and politics meet.

This is a much larger field of experiment and change than has been brought forward, say, in recent controversies about "the death of the author" or "non-referential writing" and similar textual/intertextual modes of conceiving writing and the world. The field is still larger in that the old rules and basic definitions within each art have increasingly and deliberately been set aside or reversed. The imageless (non-representational) art which characterized the American and European mid-century has been matched (in deed if not in prominence) by a wordless poetry: the *lautgedichte* of Hugo Ball (early) or the *poésie sonore* of Henri Chopin (late). Other moves from within language have included those as obvious as the development of a *free* verse (an oxymoron, as William Carlos Williams taught us) and the *parole in libertà* (free words) of Marinetti; experiments in the prose poem and the aphorism and their questioning of the boundaries between prose and poetry; nonsyntactic, antisyntactic and "totally syntactic" poetry from Gertrude Stein to the Language Poets of the 1980s; and a poetry of elementary forms—letters and numbers—that works with reduced alphabets (Otto Nebel in the 1920s) or extended ones (Isidore Isou in the 1950s) or that reads numbers as words (Kurt Schwitters) or words as numbers (neo-gematria and beyond).

Similarly, the boundaries between the arts have been dissolving into an age of blended media (intermedia) and hybrid forms of poetry and art. The distinctions between word and picture, action and text, have broken down. Definitions of high and low art have fallen away: the primitive chant, the pop song have become parts of the poet's arsenal—new instruments at our disposal. The language of everyday speech collides with or expels the exalted language of an older poetry—like the art that seeks to break the boundaries between itself and everyday life, to reenter the mundane world or to elevate the mundane into art. At the same time that some poets have reclaimed prophetic and visionary functions (the most expansive claim of all), they or their contemporaries have been altering the physical nature and location of the poem: new shapes of books (the Cendrars/Delaunay "Prose of the Transsiberian" a prime example); new materials to print on (metal, acetate, film and video); poetry as sculpture in the early works of Kurt Schwitters ("*merzbau*," etc.) or the later ones of Ian Hamilton Finlay; the poetry reading and performance, moving poetry off the page and into the cabaret, the theater, the lecture hall, the gallery, the coffee shop, the loft, the prison, and the street. Writes Michael Davidson of a postmodernism that extends one thrust of the modern presented in these pages: "The boundary to what is possible in writing is a fiction created by and within writing. Only when the boundary is recognized as moveable can it become a regenerative element in art, rather than an obstacle to its growth."

The twentieth century may be known by its push against the boundaries. Where once the definitions were apparent and the frame known, we have now come into the open, have taken up a stance outside the walls.

The most interesting works of poetry and art are those that question their own shapes and forms, and by implication the shapes and forms of whatever preceded them. But it is possible for one to become a master of poetry (or even a doctor of poetry) and still be ignorant of all this. (It may even not be possible to do so without that kind of ignorance!)

It is our intention in this book to bring that much to light.

RECONFIGURING ROMANTICISM: THE FANCY AS DUENDE & CAPRICHO

My contribution to a projected volume of essays, edited by Jeffrey Robinson under the tentative title "An Active Poetics", as a followup to Poems for the Millennium, volume three: The University of California Book of Romantic & Postromantic Poetry.

1

In the course of assembling *Poems for the Millennium*, volume three, I was engaged in two—at least two—companion works. This wasn't at all strange but fit, maybe too neatly, into a view that I like to put forward—that the composition of large structures like the Millennium volumes is inseparable from my other activities as a poet and that this would hold true for other poets engaged in what Robert Duncan, I believe it was, spoke of as the construction of a "grand collage" and as "a poetry of all poetries," a type of work practiced in one form or another by many a modern or postmodern poet/artist. Looking back at my earlier works, the first of the anthology/assemblages, *Technicians of the Sacred* (1968), was paralleled by first experiments with "total translation" as a form of composition from oral sources, but also by the beginnings of *Poland/1931* as an exploration, I wrote, "of ancestral sources of my own in a world of Jewish mystics, thieves & madmen." The followup, *Shaking the Pumpkin* (1972), an anthology of American Indian texts, was also a catalyst for *A Seneca Journal*, while *A Big Jewish Book* (1977) continued the work of *Poland/1931* and led to first experiments with *gematria* and other forms of traditional aleatory procedures. In the same vein I wouldn't separate *Revolution of the Word* (1974) as its American counterpart from *That Dada Strain*, both celebrations of our Dada and modernist predecessors.

Romanticism, as Jeffrey Robinson and I came at it, was a catalyst for us as well, much as it was for those who came before us. In Robinson's case, though his primary life's work has been as a devoted and innovative scholar of British Romanticism, he has accompanied the scholarship as such with an ongoing series of original poetry texts drawn or collaged ("spliced") from the work of poets, both Romantics and Moderns/Postmoderns, who were central to his studies and enthusiasms. For myself what I had to overcome was my own prejudice against fixed forms—shared with many in my generation—in order to see anew the challenges to form and content that were set in motion by the Romantics and a number of others who had preceded them. As a matter of nomenclature Jeffrey Robinson and I began to talk between us about "experimental romanticism," although I'm not sure if that phrase came into the actual writing.

With that as our target, experiment and transformation appeared both in aspects of Romantic writing that were largely subterranean and, even more surprisingly I thought, at the heart and core of the Romantic project. An aspect of this, from my side at least, was that the Romantics and those we called the Postromantics began to feel like contemporaries, less magisterial figures and more like fellow poets with whom we could enter into a free and easy discourse. In large part, if this doesn't sound too arcane or abstract, we rode on Jeffrey Robinson's recovery of the "fancy," salvaging it from Coleridge's otherwise brilliant and long-lived dichotomy of fancy and imagination. The two terms—fancy and imagination—had otherwise been historically synonymous, whereas Coleridge made imagination not just his "shaping spirit" but a binding spirit that reconciled and thereby froze deep conflicts of image and idea. In relation to this "the fancy" appeared as a secondary or degraded or trivialized faculty, an arena of "mere" image making and escape, rather than a liberatory force—for play and invention—the field par excellence of the experimental and visionary. In this sense I would think of *imagination qua fancy* less in Coleridge's sense as reconciliation and closure than in Keats's definition of "negative capability" followed immediately by his criticism of Coleridge: "Several things dovetailed in my mind and at once it struck me what quality went to form a Man of Achievement especially in literature and which Shakespeare possessed so enormously—I mean Negative Capability, that is when a man is capable of being in uncertainties, mysteries, doubts, without an irritable reaching after fact and reason—Coleridge for instance would let go by a fine isolated verisimilitude caught from the penetralium of mystery, from being incapable of remaining content with half knowledge." Or Whitman in an equally famous passage:

"Do I contradict myself? Very well then I contradict myself, (I am large, I contain multitudes)." That being said, I would as well speak of imagination as of fancy, the good-of-it being, always, in the meanings, not in the nomenclature—an acknowledgment in any case of their fluidity, both before and after Coleridge, with the invocation of the one often sliding curiously into an invocation of the other. I thought of all this again in the process of working through a series of poems that I was composing alongside the major work of construction or assemblage that Robinson and I were engaged in. The series in question (fifty poems in all) was my response to Goya's *Caprichos*, a work of imagination or fancy that we included in *Poems for the Millennium*, both as a touchstone of an emerging Romanticism and as a forerunner of the expressionist and surrealist side of a modernism yet to be. The images that Goya gave me helped, as with other forms of ekphrastic writing, to launch a succession of my own images and fancies, an interaction across space and time that I've often tried to practice. In the opening poem, for example, I begin with Goya's well-known self portrait, a figure slumped over a table on which are written the words *"El sueño de la razón produce monstruos."* From that and from the bats and owls that fly around him comes the following, not a literal account of Goya's image but a journey into places where the Fancy leads me on my own:

> His is a world where owls
> live in palm trees,
> where a shadow in the sky
> is like a magpie,
> white & black are colors
> only in the mind,
> the cat you didn't murder
> springs to life,
> a whistle whirling in a cup,
> gone & foregone,
> a chasm bright with eyes.
> There is a cave in Spain,
> a fecal underworld,
> where bats are swarming
> among bulls,
> the blackness ending in a wall

his hands rub up against,
a blind man in a painted world,
amok & monstrous
banging on a rock.[1]

In the course of which I became aware, as I should have earlier, that *caprichos* as a term was most commonly translated as "fancy" or "fancies", which after Coleridge at least would effectively conceal what Goya was unleashing here. Yet it is precisely in his "caprichos" that Goya shows us the fancy as "a power, not a work … a struggle, not a thought," as Federico García Lorca wrote of that related or perhaps identical power he called *duende.* In Lorca's case too the word in question went back to an earlier source that belied the characteristics that he ascribed to it—a hobgoblin or imp to start with and a driving force among those Flamenco singers and dancers from whom he took it. Dramatized by Lorca as engaged in a fierce creative struggle (chthonic, even demonic, in his telling) it also released, as he described it, a sense of unprecedented formal and visionary transformations: "The duende's arrival always means a radical change in forms. It brings to old planes unknown feelings of freshness, with the quality of something newly created, like a miracle, and it produces an almost religious enthusiasm."

It is this force or something very close to it that Jeffrey Robinson captures in his aforementioned description of "fancy" with perhaps a greater emphasis on the transformative or experimental side of the process, as well as the playfulness of the original folk presences that in no way diminishes the power of what's at work or play here. The search on this side of Romanticism is less toward resolution, then, and more toward struggle and conflict, with a resultant *liberatory* thrust (the adjective is Robinson's), a newfound openness of form and thought. In the process Goya's caprichos operate at white heat, burning away appearances to let new worlds emerge, kept hidden otherwise by "mind-forged manacles" in Blake's words and inherited conventions of the "really real." For me at least the convergence of Blake and Goya is essential to their time and to the times that lead from them to us.

---

1 The complete poem, "The Sleep of Reason," appears above on page 480.

2

Having plunged into a new series of poems, *50 Caprichos after Goya*, just as *Poems for the Millennium* (the third, romanticism volume) was getting under way, and with Blake's sense of "the Fancy" and Lorca's "duende" always in mind, I moved toward the following concluding poem, in my terms and, I hope, in theirs:

CODA, WITH DUENDES

Duendes sound a last
hurrah   they squeeze
a bellows, scrub a dish
with greasy hands,
a whisper
in an ear bent down
to listen.
No one sees them.
Over every duende
falls the shadow
of a greater duende.
Holy moly!
Is this not a black sound,
Mister Lorca?
Pissing olive oil
I isn't what *I* seems
to be   a poor
partaker
barrel overturned,
the wine *I* swigs
gone rancid.
There is now an end
to everything.
What is flesh
they suck no more,
they drive the foul caprichos
out of sight.
Caprichos, Goya, Lorca,
all my duendes,
locked into a cage

at dawn, evading
sleep & dreams,
those whom they leave
behind them, fathers
raising arms
to heaven,
screaming through
their empty
mouths like caverns
black holes
where all light
is lost.
Now is the time.

If this, then, was my interplay with Goya and Lorca, the discourse and engagement with Romanticism was linking—deliberately on my part—with still other aspects of the poetry I was then composing. At the turning of the century and the millennium I had written and published a long series of poems—*A Book of Witness* (2001)—in which I explored, among other matters, the first person voice as integral to the poetic act of witnessing, even of prophecy (itself an inheritance from Romanticism)—by the poet directly or with the poet as a conduit for others. I mean here a first person that isn't restricted to the usual "confessional" stance but is the instrument—in language—for all acts of witnessing, the key with which, like Keats's "chameleon poet," we open up to voices other than our own. There was in all of this a question of inventing and reinventing identity, of experimenting with the ways in which we can speak or write as "I." In the course of putting that identity into question, I brought in occasional and very brief first person statements by other contemporary poets—very lightly sometimes but as a further way of playing down the merely ego side of "I." The continuity with the first two volumes ("modern" and "postmodern") of *Poems for the Millennium* seems to me obvious, no less the relation to Romantic poetics (as in the case of Keats and others), which I had still more fully to explore.

Shortly before Jeffrey Robinson and I started on our Romantics project, I was beginning a new series of poems—*fancies* perhaps in the sense of Blake and Goya—in which the operative thrust was to suppress the "I" as it had emerged in *A Book of Witness*, and to let world and mind interact absent direct first person intervention. The title I gave it, *A Book of Concealments*, was drawn from a medieval Jewish work, *Sifra diSeni'uta*, from which I also drew, as with *A Book of Witness*, occasional and very brief statements or phrases but without further citation. The idea of *concealment*, in contrast to that of *witness*, had many implications and was a driving force behind the work as such. Not least of course was the concealment of the singular first person pronoun, as if that in itself might counter what Keats had called the "egotistical sublime" or Charles Olson "the lyrical interference of the individual as ego," a challenging if imperious directive in the first place.

Midway through the work and with *Poems for the Millennium*, volume three, already underway, I dedicated a poem to Michael McClure, with whom I had an ongoing discourse about Romanticism and Romantics as those entered into the poetry and poetics of our own time. The poem's title, "A Deep Romantic Chasm," drawn from Coleridge's seminal and truly fanciful *Kubla Khan*, led me to consider using the Romantic poets in *Millennium* as I had used the modern and postmodern poets in *A Book of Witness* and to break down in other ways the barrier between the poems in *Concealments* and the large assemblage I was simultaneously composing. In the process I separated a group of poems under the title "Romantic Dadas" and had those published as a limited edition artist's book, but all remained integral to *A Book of Concealments* and were included as such in the final publication. The result is that the last third of the book (25 or 30 poems) has a score or more of such insertions, as in the following, with the Baudelaire appropriation noted in the margin and a short sentence from an earlier poem of my own set likewise in italics:

Concealed Assassins

Those who are masters
needn't talk,
but signal with a secret
nod or wink,
concealed assassins
brought into the mix.
Involuntary tears,
a dream of executions, (C. Baudelaire)
smoke
rises between our teeth.
The ones who loved us
die not one by one
but now en masse,

the presence of the dead
in every corner.
The wretch who testifies
may also sing,
capturing the ebb & flow
of tides, the pressure
blood breeds
where it stokes the body.
Once to stand there,
hapless,
to sense the joy
in failure
only the wise
can know.
Someone will lift
a burden
from our eyes
& we will witness
worlds unseen.

Looking back now I can only surmise that the work of assemblage and that of original composition were, for me at least, deeply co-dependent. Certainly the poems in both *Concealments and Caprichos* (later published as a single book) would have been different were I not engaged then in the construction of *Poems for the Millennium.* By the same token I needed just that sort of engagement to feel myself in an active exchange with those poets whom Jeffrey Robinson and I were weaving into our larger composition. It is something like this that I found years ago in Pound's construction of "an *active* anthology," and the use of the word "active" in the title of the present volume again brings that thrust to mind. Whatever it is that goes to create a *canon*—a word and concept we could well do without—or to perpetuate it through a canonical anthology or series of such, an active and thereby transformative idea of anthology, as of our lives in general, is by far the greater work to aim at.

The fancy (as capricho and duende) demands nothing less of us.

A ROUND OF RENSHI & THE POET AS OTHER: AN EXPERIMENT IN POESIS

1

I first heard about *renshi* from Hiromi Itō, a remarkable and justifiably celebrated Japanese poet and writer, who has also been our neighbor in Encinitas, California, for most of the last two decades. Her presence among us goes back to 1991 and to my first visit to Japan, a contact I hadn't had before but have been able to repeat six times since then. My host for the Tokyo part of that trip was Hisao Kanaseki, a distinguished scholar and translator of Gertrude Stein, who was also compiling a book of American Indian traditional poetry with some acknowledged adaptations from my own *Technicians of the Sacred* and *Shaking the Pumpkin.* Kanaseki arranged a roundtable reading and dinner for me at a large and presumably newfangled restaurant in the Ginza, and a few days later, at a private dinner in his home, he introduced me more directly to Hiromi, who signaled her intention, which I barely understood at the time or even now in retrospect, to come to California as my student in American Indian culture and related matters. That was the beginning of my acquaintance with Japan and contemporary Japanese poetry and poets, but it connected as well to ideas about poetry that had been a dominant concern of mine from as far back as I can remember.

There was a time—now a good half century in the past—when poets of my generation were discovering themselves as part of what Donald Allen, in the great and seminal anthology of that name, was calling "the new *American* poetry" (emphasis mine). The connection he asserted there with jazz and abstract expressionism and other good things was incredibly seductive—for me and most of the poets around me—and yet there was something disquieting about it also, something that rhymed too easily with the idea of an "American century" or an American hegemony and seemed to belie the other connections and genealogies that many of us felt. The break with British language and stylistics was one thing, but to my mind at least it went hand in hand with the discovery and recovery of other poetries on a nearly global scale.

It was with something like that in mind that I met with Donald Allen for the first and last time—sometime in the early 1960s. Allen explained to me that unlike the poets in *The New American Poetry*, I was a part of what he called the international school of poetry. This stung me at the time but after a while made perfect sense to me, and I began to ponder the different ways that I could play his designation to the fullest. My own work I knew was continuous with radical modernisms and postmodernisms that were situated well beyond our shores, and this I thought held for all but a handful of my contemporaries, the few like Olson and Snyder, say, who pushed the American stance to its limits. By the time I appeared in the revised edition of *The New American Poetry* in 1982, the Vietnam war, among other events, had intervened and may have shaken confidence in a purely American moment.

There is a tension of course between the particularities of place and language (the "localism" that Olson wrote of) and the idea of a poetry that translates, reaches across borders. Both I've come to think are necessary, and in the years since my first book—*New Young German Poets* published by City Lights at the heart, let me say, of the "new American poetry"—translation and travel have allowed me to test and experience the interconnectedness between poetry and poets physically and linguistically at a considerable remove from each other. In some sense too I was likely testing my own otherness, my closeness to or distance from the place from which my parents came. And my experiments with forging a new ethnopoetics was a further exploration of poetic particulars and poetic transmissions across boundaries of space and time.

With all of that behind me, with all of that in mind, I responded to the invitation to come to Japan in March 2010 to engage with Hiromi Itō and others in a round of *renshi.*

2

Renga, the traditional and well known form of Japanese collaborative or linked writing, has its modern counterpart in *renshi*, generally practiced with projective or open forms but always with the shadow of the ancient orders somewhere in the background. While the practice of *renga* goes back at least 800 years and follows a wide range of traditional rules and constraints, *renshi* is tied closely to the freeing of verse during the upsurge of a new poetics in the half century and more of Japanese "postwar writing." Its notable Japanese practitioners include Makoto Ōka and Shuntarō Tanikawa, key figures of the modernist or postmodernist "postwar" groupings, and an occasional foreign participant, such as British poet Charles Tomlinson in the late 1990s. Far better known in the West is the still earlier collaboration across four European languages by Tomlinson, Octavio

Paz, Jacques Roubaud, and Edoardo Sanguinetti (*Renga: A Chain of Poems*, 1971), though that one without a Japanese participant.

My own brush with *renshi* came last March, during a four-day event in the southern Kyushu city of Kumamoto in which I was the fifth wheel with Tanikawa, Hiromi Itō, Yasuhiro Yotsumoto, and Wakako Kaku. For this the chosen site in Kumamoto was the happily alternative Orange cafe and bookstore, as a result of which the place for writing, unlike some other *renshi* that I know of, was open rather than private, a small area at the rear of the equally small cafe, which was however closed off to outside business during our time there. Even so, people came and went freely, which only enhanced the sense of writing in public—in-the-open, so to speak. That and the relative speed required gave it—to my mind at least—a performative and improvisatory feeling, while responding—always—to what came before and after. For all of that it was the sense of *writing* that dominated the proceedings—pen and paper augmented by the computers that all six of us brought to the event. At the end the Japanese poets used brush and ink on long strips of exquisite Chinese paper to transcribe their work in calligraphic form, as did Jeffrey Angles who functioned—largely for my benefit—as our principal translator. To top it off there was also a public reading and discussion, a paying event that drew over four-hundred people to an auditorium adjacent to the city's Literature Museum, where the calligraphic poems hung like banners from wires overhead.

While the *renshi* event went a long way toward clarifying any sense I had of a connection with Japanese poetry, both contemporary and traditional, I would have to go back to the 1950s at least, to recall how Japanese poetry and culture began to enter our consciousness. It had something to do with the aftermath of the war and the possibility for some of us of travel to Japan, but that was not my own case, since I was still settled in New York and my only real possibilities for travel were eastward (to Europe) and southward (to Mexico). I had however begun to read and to be startled by some of what I was reading. Notably at that time it was translations of Japanese Noh theater that I think had the greatest impact on me. Arthur Waley and Ezra Pound were the dominant translators of course, and what came through in the wake of their translations was not only a dynamic dramatic and poetic form, but a poetics associated with ancient figures such as Zeami and Kanami Motokiyo. Their concept of *yugen*, which LeRoi Jones (Amiri Baraka) took for the title of his early poetry magazine, stood alongside Lorca's *duende*, Koranic *ta'wil*, Hebraic *kabbala*, and ancient Australian *alcheringa*, as touchstones for the emergence of a radically new/old poetry.

There was more than that of course, and for a time (and with more than time on my hands) I gave myself to the language—a year's study of Japanese at Columbia, following two years (against my will) of army service. While I've retained very little of the actual language, my sense of some of its grammatical and syntactic strategies was of great importance to me; but not only that. By the end of that year I was able to translate a few poems by Fuyuhiko Kitagawa and a part of Yukio Mishima's *Mizu no Oto*—something that greatly surprises me in retrospect. I also attended a class of Donald Keene's and for a while I was scheduled to publish his translation of Bashō's *Narrow Road of Oku* for an independent press that I was then co-directing with David Antin, but we sadly failed to do so. The press's name was Hawk's Well Press, after Yeats's play *At the Hawk's Well*, itself derived from Yeats's early fascination with Noh theater. An accompanying little magazine of mine, *Poems from the Floating World*, also had a Japanese-derived title, not in the familiar *ukiyo-e* sense of an urban pleasure world (though something of that too) but as it turns up in an old Japanese Buddhist text that I only came across recently: "The [floating] world [*ukiyo*] is one in which happening gives way to happening, illusion follows illusion, and all of it is nothing but a phenomenon void of substance." To top it off a series of my poems from the early 1960s, *The Seven Hells of the Jigoku Zoshi*, had its source in the hell-scrolls of that name, but brought definitively, I would like to think, into the immediate and continuing present.

It wasn't until the 1990s, however, that I began to spend time in Japan and made actual and sometimes surprisingly close contact with a number of my Japanese contemporaries. The first time there, as I mentioned earlier, was through Hisao Kanaseki, and the next couple through Hiromi Itō, but once the visits started, they took on a momentum of their own. Better than that, they carried with them a sense of collaboration that wasn't, I knew, *exactly* collaboration, but in the act of being and performing together, it might as well have been. And needless to say too, some of my visits to Japan also resulted in a number of poems that I wrote and that have remained of considerable importance to me.

For me, finally, the culminating work in Japan has been the recent *renshi* event in Kumamoto, in which I participated alongside Itō, Tanikawa,

Kaku, and Yotsumoto, with the last of whom I have been collaborating on a translation of the poems of the Japanese "dada poet" Nakahara Chuya.[1] That the five of us could work, as we did in Kumamoto, across languages and cultures, vindicated for me the sense I've long had of poetry, for all its cultural and linguistic specifics, as an international enterprise at its deepest and even sometimes at its most superficial levels. This is something that I've written about elsewhere but that may still be worth repeating here.

The result of that and how we got to it is what I'd like to take up next.

3

The openness of *renshi* was the first thing that came across. I had read enough about *renga* to recognize how rule-bound that was—not only the *tanka* or *waka* form with its strictly fixed lines and syllables, but thematic commands and prohibitions (seasonal, geographic, imagistic, and so on), and the way that poems linked or bled into each other, sometimes openly, more often by a kind of subtle indirection. In advance of my own participation, I had read a number of books, to get a better feel for *renga* as the traditional underpinning for *renshi*, while aware that *renshi* practice, in so far as it had developed, was formally open and left the linkages in the hands of the individual participants. In the present instance, Tanikawa, as

---

1 A DIGRESSION. Of the five active participants, Tanikawa and I were the oldest, born four days apart in December 1931. There was no question of the deference paid to him, which he took in stride, and I had the sense that some of it got attached to me as well, though it was a little harder to respond from my perspective. He comes across as a physically taut and emotionally self-contained person—under these circumstances at least—and was the only one of us who went off frequently to write in private. One of the leading postwar [post]modernists, his reputation at home is far-reaching, enhanced as a writer of popular children's books and as the translator of *Peanuts* and Mother Goose into Japanese.

The two women poets, Itō and Kaku, also have a pop side, Itō as a translator of Doctor Seuss and author of a number of books on childbirth and child rearing, and Kaku as a musician and a lyricist for films such as Hayao Miyazaki's anime classic, *Spirited Away*. In Itō's work this has to be measured against the transgressive sexual extremes in both her poetry and fiction, yet neither she nor Kaku seem to feel this as any kind of rupture. At the end of our public performance, Yotsumoto, a younger counterpart to Tanikawa, had Kaku set one of his *renshi* poems to music and accompany him on guitar as he performed it *karaoke* style. (I joined the two of them on a Seneca Indian horn rattle, which I often use in poetry performances.) Here the ease in moving between literary and popular forms is also something to be noted.

the senior figure and acknowledged *renshi*-master (*sabakite*), only asked that the individual poems be kept short (between four and fourteen lines, I think he said), that some attention be paid to poems preceding and following one's own, and that linkages be subtle or mysterious rather than direct or obvious.[2] We were also encouraged to avoid competition and to go easy on the confessional or expressionistic side of things. Then, as the work unfolded, allusions to earlier works and sources came into play, a practice in which I was happy to engage, as a further instance, let's say, of what I speak of elsewhere as "othering" or "writing through." (Itō in this regard drew all her texts directly from earlier, largely oral, sources.) And there were passing references too to matters that came up in our conversation—dinner talk, a lot of it—which would be more difficult to reconstruct but had a resonance for some of us that may or may not carry over to those who read us.

As if to underscore the contemporaneity of what we were doing, the opening set of the *renshi* event began before we arrived in Kumamoto. We made the link by email, with the leadoff slot given to Itō, who was the local organizer along with a group of others who had named themselves—curiously, I thought—The Kumamoto Literature Band. As would be the case throughout, every poem in Japanese was immediately translated into English, and every poem of mine into Japanese. The order in which we wrote was also set beforehand, switching a couple of times along the way. So, by the time Diane Rothenberg and I left San Diego, I had the first five poems stowed in my computer, and by the time we arrived and met a few of the others at Mount Aso (still a ways from Kumamoto), some of the talk (but not most of it) was already turning to the poems.

Hiromi's opening gambit was a response, she later told me, to a criticism at an earlier *renshi* event that she had been too personal, too

---

2 A SECOND DIGRESSION. Of all such "distant links" (*soku*), the fifteenth-century poet-monk Shinkei wrote in his *Sasamegoto*, a masterwork of renga poetics and of poetics over all: "A *soku* poem is said to be one wherein it does not matter that the upper and lower part are put together in a seemingly unnatural and arbitrary way so long as they cohere in the mind." (For which see *Murmured Conversations: a Treatise on Poetry and Buddhism by the Poet-Monk Shinkei*, translated by Esperanza Ramirez-Christensen, Stanford University Press, 2008.) My own inclination here is to see this, as with much of Shinkei's poetics, as a forerunner to the principle in modernist collage, of bringing together disparate elements in a single field and, as Pound or Reverdy might have had it, letting them cohere. In that sense the very process of *renga* or *renshi* might be seen in itself as an instance of poetic collage.

I-centered in what she wrote there. (She also didn't care to write short pieces, she said, her own work known for its expansive form and, even more so, for the outrageously sexual and transgressive nature of its content.) So she decided on a strategy of total appropriation and armed herself with a stack of books—mainly from ancient and oral sources—as a repository of works from which to draw her poems. And because we had started at Mount Aso, the four lines she tossed down were from a song chanted by young women dressed in white who come to feed the local gods in the yearly Onda Festival at Aso shrine:

Let us offer up a song, may the gods
Of these fields bear witness
The gods look down, the farmers
Plant the fields and are glad

These lines set the tone, then, and were followed by Tanikawa's linked response, which picked up the idea of festival and planting, plus something more:

The children form circles and play in the forests
Where the leaves of visitor's language flourish

Even in the land of roots
There are seeds waiting to germinate
Or so my great-grandmother used to say

I knew, in writing after Tanikawa, that I couldn't answer directly even if I tried, that there were things that weren't open or clear to me as outsider, and yet enough came through, aided by hints thrown at me by Jeffrey Angles—as translator—and a little too from Hiromi. I was the "visitor" here and the "leaves" were "pages," as they are with us, or "words," as they are with them. I also knew the "land of roots" as an ancient formula—in the Japanese origin myth *Kojiki* and elsewhere—for the subterranean world of gods and ghosts. So I took it all as an invitation to play out my role as visitor or guest or stranger and to see how far I could move between my own resources and theirs. As a first instance I found myself following the syllable and line/strophe structure of the traditional *tanka* or *waka* (5-7-5 7-7), something I wasn't likely to do in any other circumstance including the rest of the *renshi* event. The result follows, and then some words about it:

the future rising
as does my name red mountain
summit high above

the earth below in darkness
hole the fathers called sheol

soon to be with you
on Aso not *Death Mountain*
in the other poem

beneath which looms the shadow
of a visionary fish

… all of which was more allusive than anything I would later do but was needed, I thought, to bring our worlds together or to make a stab at linking them. In doing so I brought in my own Japanese name (*Akayama* = Red Mountain = *Roten Berg*), which I had given myself many years before, and juxtaposed it with the name of the mountain/volcano (*Aso yama*), where we were heading, in contrast to the mysterious Death Mountain (*shide no yama*) that I found in a seventeenth-century "death poem" by a Buddhist poet/monk named Shiyō. Also, once Tanikawa's "land of roots" gave me an opening, I introduced ancient Jewish *sheol* as a great-grandmotherly accounting of my own. And as a further nod in his direction I appropriated a phrase, "the shadow of a visionary fish," from a poem of his, to end the poem and, as far as I could, to put my own authorship in question.

Such questioning, it seemed to me, was crucial in this kind of work. So I wasn't surprised when Kaku followed me with a poem that, though I didn't recognize the source at first, had a larger than life quality, an attempt, about which I might otherwise be dubious, at mythopoetic speech:

Come, please,
My red, burning fluid!
From my crumbling bosom
Through my chest and arms
To the villages beneath the mountains

Things seen with the eyes
Washed away, burned to ashes
Bring a beginning to this world
Once again after so many times

For Kaku all of this involved both a relation to the Greek Eurydice—suggested by the "death world" references from me and Tanikawa—and an immersion into the ferocious sexuality of the *Kojiki*, in which the creator gods Izanami and Izanaki fuck and give birth to the islands of Japan and multiple lesser divinities.[3] Still alive here it was a world like what I knew from *Technicians of the Sacred* and elsewhere, though I couldn't pin it down precisely until the source was disclosed to me. Yotsumoto, when he linked to it, took the "red fluid" as menstrual blood but transferred it from dreamtime to the scene of a woman watching a kitsch diorama of a volcano at the Aso Museum and feeling her period come on, for which he used an old-fashioned Japanese term and, for better or worse, spoke it in the woman's voice:

Standing before the diorama
Gazing at the mechanized plumes of smoke and flows of lava

My monthly visitor caught me off guard

There is another me who watches silently
As I let out a sigh of relief

---

3 A THIRD DIGRESSION. As the oldest surviving Japanese book, the *Kojiki*, or "Record of Ancient Things," completed on "the twenty-eighth day of the first month of the fifth year of Wado" (A.D. 722) is an attempt to keep a grip on matters already at some distance from the compilers and to establish the "origins" of the Japanese court and nation on (roughly) native grounds. It is, at the same time, "a compilation of myths, historical and pseudo-historical narratives and legends, songs, anecdotes, folk etymologies, and genealogies." (Thus: Donald L. Philippi, the composer of a long-standing translation.) Like other such works it begins with the generations of the gods and follows their creation of and descent into this-place-here. The fecundity and sexuality of those early gods—like Izanaki and Izanami in the present instance—is an example of surreality (= *poesis*) as an attempt to comprehend and thereby to possess the world. The following, for example, is from Yoko Danno's recent translation: "When Izanami was delivered of the fire deity Kagu-tsuchi, her genitals were severely burnt and she was seriously ill in bed. She vomited and in her vomit a pair of ore deities came into being. In her excrement arose a pair of clay deities, and in her urine the female deity who controls irrigation water and the young deity full of procreative force whose daughter is the food goddess Toyo-uke."

That ended the first set of *renshi* as a mix of myth and dream with words and voices from the non-mythic present and past—an expanding field that could accommodate the several minds at work here.

It was in this spirit that the game continued.

4

The thirtieth and final poem of the *renshi* event fell to me as "visitor" and gave me a chance to consider or reconsider the entire process—the experimental side of it at least, as a test of poetry under special circumstances. The moves up to then had been easy enough, a cool kind of writing that I didn't find at all displeasing, and a chance, as Robert Duncan had once put it, "to exercise my faculties at large." On top of that—and not to be ignored—I was doing it out in the open and immersed in a language that I barely understood. It seemed to me too that Kaku, writing in the slot before me, had been pushing toward some kind of conclusion, to which I felt an affinity, but had to consider it, along with a specific request from Tanikawa, as an invitation to formulate my own coda here, a kind of capsule poetics as I conceived it. The conclusion of her short poem ran like this:

> *... We put logic to rest*
> *We celebrate the outrageous*
> *The last song remaining*
> *Is our offering*
> *To the world*

And mine, as an alternative conclusion, was a reference both to my present predicament and to that other, distant world in which I lived and wrote:

> *people speak at me*
> *& I don't understand*
> *except my name & yours*
> *& little words like* koko & asoko
> *& those that aren't words at all*
> *but sounds remembered*
> *first as sounds*
>   the small nouns
> crying faith *(he wrote)*
> *what poets always knew*
> *what still astounds*

If the work we composed was communal, as I thought it was, then what I wrote here as a final "offering" would hold for all of us, bound by the *renshi* process itself to what the others had presented. What I was doing from my own perspective was calling up certain elemental terms for poetry—the sounds that change as we move from language to language and the crucial but easily neglected words like *koko* and *asoko* ("here" and "there") or the "small nouns" in the quote above from George Oppen. The rhyme—almost terminal rhyme—came pretty much on its own and with a sense of its probable untranslatability into Japanese, where rhyme has always been beside the point. I realized too that were these thirty poems to be published, my preference would be for mine to remain in English, however crucial translation may have been to the *renshi* event as such. The distance or otherness of the English would show, as I conceive it, a further willingness to abide by the principles of something-like-collage.

While my poem brought the *renshi* part of it to a close, the poetics of the event continued outside and beyond the actual writing. The discussion at the public performance concentrated on the individual linkages at the heart of *renshi*, but also got into questions of appropriation, orality and writing, collaboration, even the way in which my presence as guest changed the nature of the *renshi* itself. For me it was enough to see the *renshi* event as an experiment in writing, and as such I thought of it as raising several distinctive but related questions.

Collaboration was the key word here, not in any easy sense but as a way—not for the first time nor the last—to put the self or self-as-author into question. The result wasn't, as it surely has been elsewhere, a collaboration by consensus, two or more authors working together on a single text. Rather each poem within the total *renshi* was written individually and juxtaposed with what had come before, while bringing still others (by quotation or appropriation) into the field of the poem. (This last was done consistently in Itō's case, sporadically by all the others.) And sometimes, writing in the same space and needing to translate, to work between languages or even between idiolects, a series of small changes and reconsiderations (modifications) might come up for discussion but never dilute the mystery and the force of what the larger work had brought together. In this way *renshi* as collaboration could also be taken as a form of collage—not the clear and consistent product of one mind but "a juxtaposition of disparate materials without commitment to explicit [syntactic] relations between elements" (D. Antin), or in the present instance, isolated and quasi-independent poems brought together by the principle of collage and the rules of distant linkage in the *renshi*.[4]

Also tied to collaboration was the act of writing in public as performance, first around a small table in the Orange cafe and bookstore, then in a room upstairs where the poets wrote out their poems calligraphically, and finally in the large auditorium of the Literature Museum. The effect of all that had a curious resemblance to those traditional rituals through which I had sat for hours and days in the Allegany Seneca longhouse and elsewhere—including the welcome breaks for meals and conversation (those also, as Richard Schechner once reminded us, a part of the ritual). And still more crucial here—as there—was how the deep past, theirs and mine, came into it—myth and poetry (or myth as poetry) with a suggestion of the sacred or numinous, the trace of gods and goddesses in whom we no longer believe but whose presence is still felt in the words that evoke them. All of these come into the poems here and elsewhere by processes of appropriation or othering, another aspect of collage applied to both the past and present, from ancient sutras and creation myths to satellite dish and morning news, to the sound and feel of David Antin's [talk-poem] *hiccups*, accompanying my accounting here, if it should come to that.

---

4 A FOURTH DIGRESSION. Another set of *renshi*—the fifth of the present session—gives a sense of how the poems come together "without commitment to specific [syntactic] relations." Even in Angles's off-the-cuff translations, below, the sense of disparate sources and idioms comes across, the degree of fusion as much in the minds of the beholders as in those of the authors:

Oh, my beloved, darling husband!
If this is what you insist upon doing
Every day I will strangle to death
One thousand people from your land!
*

Pandemonium seeping from an article on the page of the morning news containing all the shocking news
Women's sobbing leaking between the lines of the story
War cries filling the table of events

Voices packed tightly within the letters
In the voices, there is only breath
Only emptiness discreetly returned to silence
*

With Antin in mind too, I'm aware of how close the *renshi* event comes to the practice of improvisation, or if not improvisation, a form of accelerated writing, with any persisting constraints or turns imposed here by the interplay with others. For this, my presence may have had a contrary effect, introducing a series of short breaks or pauses while Angles translated each poem of mine into Japanese and theirs more loosely into English. Yet it was the translation, exactly, that was the key to the most far-reaching experiment of all—the *renshi* as an exercise in transcultural writing and a test, for me at least, of the degree to which I could think of myself and them as *international/intercultural* poets—at least for the moment—or could think of poetry as a bridge rather than a wall or, like language itself, both a wall and a bridge. What made it easier for us of course was that the differences of language and culture had already been weakened, so that we shared a contemporaneity and with it a by now similar sense of poetry. (That we had English—in varying degrees—as a kind of lingua franca might also be noted.)

Still *renshi* is not primarily an experiment but very much a game, and treating it as an experiment in writing and poetics—a chance to test the possibilities of poetry under circumstances different from any I had

---

Hiragana, katakana, kanji, and western letters
Moving back and forth between the synapses
Of the left hemisphere of my brain
Meanwhile my hand and fingers go on strike
A raptor draws a circle over the satellite dish
*

Passing through
Will sweep all illness away, they say
Will change one into infinite blue—
The body whole
*

840 million thoughts
the sutra says
come every night
& overwhelm the sleeper
looking for a place
to hide
for which he writes
his death poem
as a perfect circle

The sequence of poets here is Itō, Yotsumoto, Tanikawa, Kaku, and Rothenberg—a detail of authorship that may or may not be needed in the final publication.

known before—is a willful act on my part but one I had in mind throughout the four-day session. My own work as a poet, like that of most poets I know, is largely carried on in private, yet not without a sense even so of other voices, other poets, who constitute for me an often cited "visionary company" or, as I have it elsewhere, a *paradise* of poets. Treating authorship as collaboration, then, and performance as ritual puts into question that other side of poetry—our separation from each other by the realities, if left unchallenged, of cultural and individual identity. The further step would be to treat *all* acts of poetry as collaborative at heart, a great collective and collaborative enterprise—like language itself. In the critical divide between an oedipal view of poetic kinship and an absorptive and universal one, a conflict to which some attention has been paid by Harold Bloom and others, I and other poets of my company stand firmly with the latter view.

Originally commissioned & published in Critical Inquiry, *volume 37, number 4, summer 2011, alongside David Antin's talk-poem "hiccups."*

From THE MEDUSA INTERVIEW: TOWARD AN OMNIPOETICS

with Rodrigo Garcia Lopes
[circa 1999, revised 2012]

(1) *The connection between language & reality has been a major focus of your poetry & poetics. It seems that we've crossed a long way from Blake's "doors of imagination" to Bill Gates's "Windows 98". I'd like to start our interview with this provocation as well as pointing out the medium by which this interview is being taken: the e-mail. How do you think that this Media Age—of TV, internets, consumerism, & rapid technological advances—is affecting the language of poetry written today (& specifically in the U.S.)? How do you think poets are responding to this so-called "Globalization"? Retaking the anxiety posed by Marjorie Perloff in* Radical Artifice, *"Given the particular options (& nonoptions) of writing at the turn of the twenty-first century, what significant role can poetic language play"?*

The question has a special relevance for me, I suppose, since I've long been engaged in a project that involves an interplay of very new & very old forms of languaging & representation. I think that one of the principal allures of poetry—even or (maybe) especially for many of our most "experimental" poets—has been the sense of engaging in a process—a way of thinking & of saying—that has until very recently been universal both in space & time. The time factor is a measure of its oldness, & the emergence of a "new" poetry over the last hundred or two hundred years has almost always been accompanied by declarations of "re"covery / "re"discovery at the heart of every new invention. This is clear enough in U.S. poetry, where someone like Ezra Pound, whom we take as radical—structurally radical— from The Cantos on, insists on pushing the time frame back & expanding it horizontally or culturally to a range of earlier initiating moments: first Anglo-Saxon rhythms merged with Homeric shaman journeys down among the shades in Canto One; then in his other & his later writings with the Chinese Book of Songs, the African "Gassire's Lute" as given by Frobenius, erotic poems of ancient Egypt, re-castings of neglected Provençal & Roman poets. This was what put him in conflict with Marinetti & the Futurists—a "tale of the tribe," as he named it, but curiously—in that fascist mind—a greater tribe than privileged race & nation might have led us to expect.

The same spirit of newness & transformation with relation to the past & present (what I used to speak of as "an ongoing attempt to reinterpret the poetic past from the point of view of the present") infused the work of many of us in post-World War II America—Olson, Duncan, Snyder, Kelly, Waldman, Schwerner, among the major ones from my perspective. And there were others too, outside of the U.S. as such—Tzara with his projected gathering of African & South Pacific poems; the Surrealists who set up a bureau (under Artaud!) of research aimed in that direction; & the French Negritude poets & their counterparts in the Spanish "new world."

The Russian Futurists are possibly exemplary here. Unlike the Italians with whom they shared that name, they dug enthusiastically into their own prehistories—the past a necessary part of all that future. Malevich was a kind of folk artist before he made himself a Suprematist, & their rough & very lovely hand-made books had sources in an old, popular, very low-tech form of book making. And Khlebnikov & Kruchonykh are a mix throughout of science fiction laced with *zaum* as futuristic glossolalia. (Khlebnikov makes the connection back to religious chants with undecipherable word-sounds.)

I would, I think, want to suggest a pendulum moving for many of us between those same poles. In my own experience I remember a time—the 1960s, a part of the 1950s—when an anti-technological impulse was very strong. It wasn't a Luddite, machine-wrecking thing for most of those I knew who shared some part of it. There was in fact an ongoing interest in machines, a use of machinery for traveling, writing, publishing & making images, or even (in the old wilderness of mountains & rivers or the new urban wilderness of cities) cutting logs & building houses; & by the 1970s there was an acknowledgement (within the art world certainly) of a new territory that brought art & technology together. What we've come into today—what you're asking about directly—is an extraordinary immersion in the world of high technology—even for most of us for whom the past is also opening & deepening.

More specifically the question comes up about "this Media Age," beginning with the fact that we're conducting this interview by e-mail. I find this no more surprising or threatening in itself than were the telephone, say, or the typewriter earlier in the century. Quite the contrary. The first thing that strikes me about our situation is that we're communicating between California & Brazil—that we're doing it rapidly & with the luxury of setting it in writing—as we could as well by voice, although the costs of doing that in detail would be more prohibitive. With some more effort too we could deliver what we're doing through the internet, could publish it, so to speak, without relying for approval on an intervening publisher who might be hostile or at least indifferent to our project. In this one week—in January 1999—I've been in touch with France & Germany & Mexico & Greece & Yugoslavia & England—most of it by e-mail, some of it by fax & phone. And you & I might also—through a network or community of which we're a part—meet together before too long in any of a number of places to which poets like ourselves can be transported across borders that are meant to keep us separate.

What this does is to further a globalism—the kind of globalism (not "globalization") that I've always wanted & that I would not shy away from. It also insulates us—in our cyber-giddiness—from problematics that some of the other instances you cite still hold for us. The problem with most technologies—including poetry at the low-tech end—is that they're double-edged. Like other means (or *media*) they can be used in good or bad ways—even *evil* ways, or what we used to think of à la Hannah Arendt as the ultimate "*banality* of evil." If the magic of the old sorcerers & shamans could be used—as "black" or "white" for good or evil purposes—it's true in much the same way for all that we class as "media." In this way the internet tempts us as poets with the sudden ability to publish & disseminate over a wider network than older means afforded us as *individuals*. But it acts as a similar conduit for an ever expanding commercialism but—still more distressing—for the ugliest forms of racial & gender hatred (among other matters), with consequences still to be determined. Or maybe it's a balance—what we want on one side & an ongoing banalization of word & thought on the other. Also I recognize—as we all do—the further encroachment of a monoculture, which I suppose is felt outside the U.S. in the growing hegemony of English & in the Americanization of the popular media, with whatever consequences those may have. For us up here it may make the globalism question seem much less threatening, may make the opening of new lines of communication seem an out & out gain with scant sense of the losses.

Going back, however, to my own awakenings post-World War II, I recall being driven by a sense of un-ease—a feel about a language that had been corrupted by propaganda & mindless sloganeering—& more insidiously, because more omnipresent in the time that followed, by the vacuities of (well-made) advertising & the developing role of news[reality]-as-entertainment. That made some of us look toward poetry as the "other" language—a language for calling language into question—the banality of language as underpinning for the banality of evil. The new technologies give us a bigger opening—or seem to—to let that otherness emerge. It is still a language & a process I prefer—a way of "othering" that brings a range of poetries together in my mind. But the greater push, I must admit, is overwhelmingly in the opposite direction.

(2) *In the last years, several anthologies of contemporary American poetry have appeared.* From the Other Side of the Century: A New American Poetry 1960-1990; Postmodern Poetry: A Norton Anthology; The Heath Anthology of American Literature; American Poetry Since 1950: Innovators & Outsiders: An Anthology; *as well as yours (& Pierre Joris's)* Poems for the Millennium: The University of California Book of Modern & Postmodern Poetry. *1) Why is there this urge to anthologize at this end-of-century? 2) In a recent interview, Brazilian poet Haroldo de Campos rejected the term "post-modern" as applied to poetry: "We are still in modernity," he says, "only if we accept that Mallarmé is already post-modern in relation to Baudelaire." To critics such as Jameson, postmodernism points to an emerging & different cultural logic. Do you believe in a postmodernism in terms of poetry & poetics? 3) How would you place "Millennium" within the context of this debate?*

There's "*this* urge to anthologize," as you put it, & then there's *my* urge to anthologize, which has been going on for some time now. (Since the 1960s, to be exact.) And one can easily say that the end of a century—in this case a millennium as well—is always a retrospective occasion. But three of the anthologies you mention in particular—Messerli's, Hoover's, & mine & Joris's—also represent the public (re)appearance of a certain kind of work after a period of time in which that work was grossly underrepresented. Earlier—in the 1960s & 1970s—there had been a blossoming of experimental & avant-garde gatherings—what I've spoken of elsewhere as manifesto-anthologies. The memorable ones from my perspective were Donald Allen's *The New American Poetry*, Emmett Williams' *An Anthology of Concrete Poetry*, & the Fluxus-oriented *Anthology* edited by LaMonte Young with assistance from Jackson Mac Low. The success of the Allen book in particular encouraged larger publishers to open up to the new poetries—in my own case Doubleday & Random House, who were the publishers of *Technicians of the Sacred, Shaking the Pumpkin, A Big Jewish Book, & America a Prophecy*, all of them works within a single ten-year period. All of these books of course had a range outside the present, but the pasts that they represented were heavily colored by a sense of radical transformations of poetry & poetics, & were presented along with later & very experimental contemporary works. And in the 1980s—even as the larger publishers were pulling back from manifesto-anthologies—the so-called Language Poets were able to use the anthology as a means for manifesting & displaying their own new departures.

By the 1990s—against a backdrop of cautious instructional anthologies—an underground constituency had built up—a relatively large group of writers & readers in search of works to represent & to update the changes since the 1960s. While middle-ground poetry still asserted itself, the take-over was far from complete, & many of us, who had come into some form of public place, found that we were able to act—Douglas Messerli through his own Sun & Moon Press, Paul Hoover through convincing the arch-middle stream publisher Norton that a big "postmodern" anthology was needed, & Pierre Joris & myself through an arrangement with a major university press. (To these I would also add Eliot Weinberger's *American Poetry Since 1950*, which appeared in both a North American & a Mexican [Spanish] edition.)

Let me say a little, then, about *Poems for the Millennium* before responding to your question on postmodernism.

Both Pierre & I had been living with a sense that what we valued most in the poetry of our time—what we shared with many others—had been almost systematically omitted from, or marginalized in, the anthologies & literary histories then current. This was true not only for the immediate present but for the near past—in shorthand terms, not only for "post"-modernism but for the modernism that came before it. The great movements from the early part of the twentieth century, for example. While we cherished the work of individual, even solitary, poets, we wanted to bring the larger movements back into the picture: Dada & Surrealism, Futurism, African & Caribbean Negritude, & the work of the North American "Objectivists." These we felt were missing elsewhere, & with their absence, there was also missing a sense of poets engaged with their own self-definition as artists & as the makers of their own poetics. The mix of poetry & poetics was something we worked to bring out—& the sense of poetry being the center of a program, a proposition or a set of propositions working in the public sphere. And writing in the United States—now, at the turning of the century & the millennium—we also thought it vital to insist (again) on the global dimensions of modern & "post"modern poetry—following several decades of insistence on the centrality & hegemony of a presumed "American moment."

In doing this we brought the distinction between "modernism" & "postmodernism" into the subtitle of our book. Here there was an advantage—chronologically—in distinguishing one half of the twentieth century from the other. But we made it clear—as I have always done, I think—that we saw a continuity between the two halves—sometimes oppositional, at other times developmental. My own first encounter with postmodernism (I will now leave out the quote marks around *post*) came in the mid-1970s—a written interview, much like this, with the critic & editor William Spanos. At that point, certainly, I felt myself to be a part of an ongoing poetic revolution—"post-nuttin" [post-nothing] as Jackson Mac Low once put it—& felt postmodernism to be a critic's term & not a poet's. (None of the poets I knew at that time spoke of themselves in any such way.) So I insisted—& would continue to insist—that postmodernism was an ill-defined term because it depended on a prior definition of modernism, & that such a prior definition was still up for grabs. Over the years—as postmodernism became a part of our time &, still undefined, a part of our vocabulary—I became more prone to use it & to use it as an extension in particular of one form of early modernism—the more experimental & overtly revolutionary—that was often in conflict with the institutionalized version still current then & now. And I came to believe that modernism & postmodernism were like some kind of twin birth—closely related & ready, always, to call each other's birthright into question. For this I would frequently cite Tristan Tzara's statement in the days of Dada: "You are mistaken if you take Dada for a modern school, or as a reaction against the schools of today. ... Dada is not at all modern. It is more in the nature of an almost Buddhist religion of indifference. … The true Dadas are against Dada."

That was postmodernism as I could use it, & that was postmodernism too in relation to your previous question. I believe that something like that was what De Campos had in mind when citing Mallarmé & Baudelaire; & I would want to extend it, say, to Tzara & Mallarmé, & then to the work of my own generation in relation to Tzara's, & that of some further generation in relation to ours. Still, it would be better to do without those terms.

(3) With a global & wide-range focus, "Millennium" aims at tracing the international history of poetry since the 19th century. What thoughts come to you when you look at this anthology together with Technicians of the Sacred *and* Shaking the Pumpkin*? What parallels more immediately come to your mind between primal & contemporary poetical procedures?*

I've answered some of this already, so I think this answer will be brief. One point that I didn't mention about *Poems for the Millennium* is that while it aims, in your words "at tracing the international history of poetry since the 19th century," it sees (or we see) that history as including most of the poetry in *Technicians of the Sacred* and *Shaking the Pumpkin.* In both volumes of *Millennium,* to start with, we have sections of ethnopoetic workings, taking these as something that came to light along with experimental modernism & aware too that many of the traditional practitioners—those in particular grouped together in an oral poetry section in volume two—have been contemporaries of ours in the century now ending. (Others, of course, are from a past that's truly past.) The ethnopoetics section of volume one ("A Book of Origins") is the concluding section of that volume—a mix of ancient, deeply rooted works & related discoveries among ourselves. "It is impossible," we say in a prologue to that section, "to present the work of a radical or innovative modernism without mapping at the same time some features of the old worlds, brought newly into the present & viewed there as if for the first time, to help to show us where we are."

In the "pre-face" to *Technicians of the Sacred*—the first of the big anthologies & the one that launched me into ethnopoetics—I set out a number of parallels between (as you put it) "primal & contemporary poetical procedures." What stands out most clearly is the relation of traditional oral poetry to the modern reinvention of poetry—both sung & spoken—as a vocal & performative art. The "new American poetry" of several decades ago—fueled by the energies of Olson & Ginsberg & others—emphasized the role of voice & breath as the physical/bodily basis for composition & for poetry as a liberating/spiritual act. The "dark" side of that comes up in what a poet-companion of mine, Clayton Eshleman, speaks of as "grotesque realism" & an "American grotesque": "an immersion in the lower body; not the body of the individual, the 'bourgeois ego,' but the body of all: the 'brimming over abundance' of decay, fertility, birth, growth, death ... unfinished, exaggerated; ... protuberances & apertures prominent." (Interpreted thus by Eliot Weinberger in *Poems for the Millennium*.) From such a vantage point connections are made—beyond Rabelais & De Sade among the earlier Europeans—to a world of primal tricksters & sacred clowns or—following the lead of our Surrealist predecessors & others—in the dreams & visions that are our common patrimony as human beings. And with this I can also connect the concern with chance-determined (or *undetermined/indeterminate*) art—in the Chinese *I Ching*, in various African forms of divination, in the poetry & related art of Jackson Mac Low & John Cage—coming to a focus where Cage, defining "indeterminacy," declares:

> IF THERE WERE A PART OF LIFE DARK ENOUGHT TO KEEP OUT OF IT A LIGHT FROM ART, I WOULD WANT TO BE IN THAT DARKNESS, FUMBLING AROUND IF NECESSARY, BUT ALIVE...

In all of this I see a questioning of God & World—crucial to our own work as I understand it & necessary to any final acceptance (or rejection) of a world & god bound up with death & suffering. And I also find in this a point where "primary" & "contemporary"—as you call them—come together; like the words of the old Crow Indian song, "addressed"— in Robert Creeley's words—"to emptiness":

we want what is real
we want what is real
don't deceive us.

(In all of this I'm also writing in a very personal way, & I'm trying to construct the anthology as a book or as a long poem or narrative. But the problem with anthologies is that everyone takes them as attempts to be definitive & neglects that you're really just telling another kind of story.)

(4) It is frequent to hear claims about the impossibility of an avant-garde today, as well as complaints about the scarcity & poorness of contemporary poetical production. I feel that Millennium *brings a more positive stance, emphasizing the possibilities, the "revolutions of the word" still to come, not their closure. Thinking specifically of the international experimental traditions you gather in* Millennium, *do you see that poe(lit)ical movements are possible or desirable today? If they exist, where would they be occurring?*

It's my belief that those "revolutions" are inherent to poetry as we've made it & will continue to be so into the foreseeable future—as long, at least, as ideas of freedom & transformation (change) remain a part of our outlook over all. I don't say that with any certainty, however, because revolutions are an area in which authority—the wisdom or the will to get it done—is, unlike some other things, a matter for the very young. So while I feel, as ever, ready for those kinds of revolution, it's not for me to say.

Revolution—if that's still the going word—is something more than a change of style or fashion. So when you're playing with the words & come up with a portmanteau like *poe(lit)ical*, you're hitting on the dual characteristics (poetical & political) of what was once the avant-garde & certainly the avant-garde of art & poetry that formed itself as *movements*. For those in the early days of experimental modernism—Futurists & Surrealists & Dadas—the ambition was to transform society & consciousness together, & it was only when the social transformation was separated from the poetic one (under the pressures of communism on the left & fascism on the right) that the avant-garde project put itself in question. In the post-World War II time, the poets of the avant-garde—whatever avant-garde there was—were no longer so quick to place their art, as the Surrealists once had it, "at the service of the revolution." The general tone, as in words from the Cobra poet Christian Dotremont that we cite in *Poems for the Millennium*, was "against all *isms*, against all that implied a system." This meant—for many—a politics against a politics, but with a leftward tilt & keeping, over all, a freedom of occasion—where & when to act. And the occasions included a widespread opposition to war & to resurgent forms of nationalism & racism, but also a reawakened sense of the poet as a spokesperson for peoples & species under siege.

The result by the 1960s was the appearance of a new "dialectics of liberation," political & personal & marked by a sense of resistance, of breaking free (in word & act, mind & body), while retaining a more-than-formalist conception of the poem as vehicle-for-transformation. As Allen Ginsberg wrote, drawing from an older source: "When the mode of the music changes, the walls of the city shake." And the Japanese "postwar poets" (in a "demand" voiced by Ooka Makoto): "Bring back totality through poetry."

That anyway was where I found poetry—in the days in particular of the postwar & the cold war. Even in a movement, say, like that of the American "language poets"—the emphasis falling on that key word "language"—the underlying issues remained political & existential. Indeed, as Charles Bernstein put it, "In order to fully develop the meaning of a formal rupture or extension, we need a synoptic, multilevel, interactive response that accounts, in hopefully unconventional, antiauthoritative ways, for sexual, class, local-historical, biographical, & structural dimensions of a poem." Or, in Ron Silliman's words, which still ring true to me: "[A] critique of reference and normative syntax ... situated within the larger question of what, in the last part of the twentieth century, it means to be human."

Other movements, like those grouped around ethnic & gender identity, were & remain more overtly agenda-driven & sometimes, from my perspective at least, lose the sense of how a "revolution of the word" relates to those other revolutions. But even here, as I've stated above, there are language questions at issue—black voices / white voices, female voices / male voices, dialects & dialectics, written word & shouted word. Such language issues—the whole slew of them & more—are still the heart of our poetics, though what the future holds is never amenable to easy guessing or glib prophecy. Certainly, as I see it, the work is far from done, & the challenge of a poetry & a counterpoetics is as much needed as ever. That in the end it may be a largely losing proposition is also possible, but I can only act as if it isn't.

POSTSCRIPT. On the matter of revolutions of the word & how they might exist today, that brings me back to your first question—the future of poetry in the computer age. ... I would urge—but with some limitations placed upon that urging—that the globalism of the internet opens up the possibility of a worldwide avant-garde. The limitations, given the dominance of English & other hegemonic languages, involve the threat to cultural & regional particulars. Against this, perhaps, the internet, the web, offers a new arena for visual, performative, & interactive modes, moving (sometimes at least) in multiple cultural directions. The number of such web sites & displays is in fact enormous, so that watching the experimental work already triggered—the technical ease in its construction—there's a sense, isn't there, of a futurism that has come into its future.

All of this—& more—is what I've more recently come to call an *omnipoetics.*

NEW POEMS:
DIVAGATIONS & AUTOVARIATIONS

I hold dark matter
in my thoughts
like ancient prophecy.
On Mondays
I adjust the hanging
clock. The galaxies
are deeper images
than once we knew.
Their absent light
confounds me.
Now the unreal
dwarfs the real.
A woman
like the sun
cries out
in shallow French.
I feel my arms
grow lame
& work
against me.
The moon
glows red.
Great distances
are mine. I plot
their numbers
but I know
that every universe
contains another.
There is no end in sight
& no beginning.
The stars stay dark
in mirrors
until your fingers
counting them
have dropped away.

From DIVAGATIONS

DIVAGATIONS (1)
The Birth of Time

Results run backward gathering in force until	
they end up in some sort of cavern miracu-	
lously well lit & everyone there feels surprise	
& wonder. They are more like phantoms than	
like little men a symptom of the way they	
cough & breathe.*	* bob & weave
From the depths the girl at center rises,	
edges toward the stooping man* & calls him	* [maybe the *stupid* man
father.	is what you meant]
She is a distant runner, trained to smash	
against the wind & carry on until some place	
draws nigh—where the whole point of speed	
is relaxation.*	* execution
It fits & lessens our predicament, although	
no final strategy permits it.	
Even so.*	* Ebb & flow
My hand in yours allows a sleep in which	
each dream is like a hole in paradise.*	* a holy paradigm
The more you fall through it* the more it	*stall in it
takes you to the birth of time.*	* of rhyme

DIVAGATIONS (2)
A Field on Mars

Hunted from their places,* fierce* & hungry*	*pastures *skinned *angry
hordes & nomads plunge into our streets.	
The word is *desiccation*,* somewhere that	* desecration
was fertile once & now, battered by a hostile	
wind, becomes a field on Mars, a world more	
lonely than the world allows.	
Behold the grandmother, her skin a dirty grey*	* [trying to see it in his mind]
as if the light were of a foreign color, absent,	
hidden from the hole in which she dwells.*	* she smells
These are no children's games—or are they?	

Cards slapped on a table, thrown against a
wall, brought as a pack down on the willing skin.
*Saints alive!** — * [words her ghost called forth]
The call to battle rattles the savage mind, a
premise from the present yet no less exotic.
Granted: that their funds are toxic comes as
no surprise; that the lack of means betokens a
further struggle; that nations once deprived
rise in their millions.* — * with their minions
It is a thought on which to dwell, shaken* — * rousted
from sleep.

DIVAGATIONS (14)
The Sound of Water

With every new invention* what was long — * extension
hidden launches into space.
Spectacular, the groundlings cry, the baby
plutocrats who live this side of Russia.
There are so many here, so little time to
push your way between them, trembling,* — * mumbling
where the owners of your lives, intrepid,
brutal, face off for a final round.
The sound of water* was the title but the — * slaughter
words were not the same.* — * the name
In tune with which a long procession fol-
lows, baring their teeth like rows of dia-
monds, glittery like glass or little poniards.
Colorless green ideas sleep furiously, the banner
reads, back to the dawn of childhood dreams.
Up stands the captain, head in hands, the
thought renewed in dullness, triggering a
voiceless rage.* — * age
Command, condemn, control.
The age* of oligarchs begins anew. — * rage

From every corner of the heimat those who
buy their circumstances sally forth.
All is forgiven, all is not forgiven.
The word is *divagations*, is it not?* * [or is it?]

DIVAGATIONS (16)
Where Memory & Dream Are One

In the dream I stretched out almost motionless, the words I tried to speak caught in my throat & nearly choking me. The place was filled with faces, like a giant hall,* a kind of nightclub with the sound of distant music ringing in my ears. Someone to the right of me, another sleeping figure, said its name was *Stille* or *die Stille*, which was clear enough in German but I couldn't find the proper English* word for it. Even more puzzling, I was aware, if vaguely, that it was taking place in Russia, & that the strangers with us were from the newly minted* class of Russian billionaires. I tried to point it out to those around me, that this Russia was far different from the one we once imagined. I was overcome with grief & longing—emotions in my dreams, rarely in waking—& alarmed at the water that had started rising in the hall. I had long loved the word *cockeyed* & mouthed it as a sure* expression of my thoughts. It came back in a flow of rhyme* I spewed forth for the other sleepers. Was this hall a mausoleum & the sleepers all of those I knew in life, now safely stacked away, forever? I stepped down from my perch & tried to swim among the beds & tables, following the voices of the rich

* a mall
* Yiddish
* favored
* a pure
* of time

that led me to an outer courtyard. Even here the word *tsunami* rattled in my ears, my fingers groping for a ladder that was out of reach. Was it the inland sea,* I wondered, a lake with putrid birds, a bog, a fen, a mash of crimson bodies, more than I could count? My shoes had little lights attached,* enough to lead me down a narrow causeway, the end of which was darkness more dense than death. *Time is abolished* was the line that came at me—*the world is o'er.* I thought if I could start to sing, the words would carry me across, *but what?* A song about a king, a bird, a fallen tree, all too romantic. The pressure of the ooze under my feet that pulls me down, that sends an ache up through my legs,* makes me wonder that my heart can still keep beating. I would rather sleep or crawl back to the hall, the place from which I came. But where? in which direction? with what name to name it? *Stille* or *die Stille*, if they ever found me here, would anybody understand me?* These were what I feared: the hangman, the exploding bombs, the curtains blocking sight, the holy fools, the drifters, the march of time, the rosary of skulls, the wings of love, the broken blossoms, the children's games, the hostile wind, the duendecitos. For me the oldest memories are those of being lost: a hall of celebrating giants, a cellar with a furnace burning bright, a point where memory & dream are one. I crawl my way toward waking, still bereft.

* the sea of reeds

* [was it my dream or his?]

* my groin

* [in what language? what account?]

DIVAGATIONS (20)
The Final Word Is Desecration

The bang & clang of hasty* hammers take me — * nasty
half away from sleep & hanging free.
    The quality of noise invades my music,
even the words that scrape against each other,
crash & clatter till they break apart.
    The final word is *desecration*, words like
pebbles in a blender,* ground to dirt. — * grinder
    Mismatched, misshapen, mise-en-scène,* — * miserere
the ear of the commander* sharper than his
eye. — * the director
    There is no beauty left to tell, no sky
exploding into clouds, no reason to cry out for
life, only the march of time that puts all time* — * all rhyme
in question.
    Funny season starts again: the chatter on
the wire turns to words, the words to smiles
too deep for tears, the tears & smiles too deep
for words.
    Where time* is endless all we know as
time* dissolves, the future & the past become — *rhyme *as rhyme
a timeless* present. — *rhymeless
    This is also testimony, shared with Goya &
a paradise of others, poets,* where the memory — * brothers
of poems will be forever lost.
    Only tread here softly, lest the voice of
someone hidden* hides your own. — * other
    They are all the shadows of my mind,
those whom I love & bury with my own.

FROM THE JIGOKU ZOSHI HELLS: A BOOK OF AUTOVARIATIONS

One should be able to rework an old work at least once—to make sure that one has not fallen victim—to one's nerves or to fate.
—Henri Matisse to Gino Severini

And again:

When you have achieved what you want in a certain area, when you have exploited the possibilities that lie in one direction, you must, when the time comes, change course, search for something new.

Variations On The Hell Of Measures

How can any of you know what it feels like
to count coins in Hell?

Hell has windows as the skin has numbers, & the sun flashing on the sidewalk blinds the little customers who bathe in it.
In my head as on my flesh the poems appear, responding to my call.
My palms turn violet & blue, smoother than Chinese silk.

My room is filled with rain, as Hell with fire, while an eyebrow slightly raised signals deceit.

The other Hells are kept in store.

A Hell of numbers follows one with rhymings.

Ribs grow heavy.

The night is meant for grief no lotions over legs or fingers can assuage.

Lost in the smoke we wait for day to come, for coins to burn the swindlers who demand them—like a brand.

Crates pile up.

Windows break.

Death makes the mind turn white.

Hands open Hell for others.

Let its fires trap the birds who fly through them.

Let disaster make them all turn black.

Let them cry out with pain, the counters filling up with cloth in boxes, broken open in the night, unmeasured, boxes smelling of the sea, the intellect imprisoned in their darkness, knowing the right questions but afraid to ask.

Make it pliable like wax & let it drip over the outlaw's' cashbox.

Words have their birth in it, & metals drawn out of the earth & melted give us coins.

The years ahead are green.

The bedposts where we rest are iron.

Our eyes are iron too & blind us.

Call it Hell.

VARIATIONS ON THE HELL OF THIEVES

The thieves, the thieves, the lovely thieves are no more.

When a wind blows
in from the sea, a door
swings open & light
white as Hell
nearly blinds us.
Night begins later,
the skin on my fingers
flakes off. A rank wind

shakes the ladders
we climb on,
the earth more distant,
for which we still
hunger, the sea
filling up with our tears,
our voices lost
in the wind.
Thieves who scour
our shores at evening,
whose voices sound under
our windows, whose tears
hide our pain,
cry out with one voice,
past shadows & windows.
One voice for
earth & one voice
for water,
& thieves dressed
like thieves,
a Hell like
no other, a house
overlooking the sea,
on a night
when coins
ring & death
has a voice,
like a thief's voice,
earth returning
to earth,
then to water,
a voice
thieves dissemble
in dreams.
Thieves & a sea
& a chimney
down which thieves
clamber. More
thieves in the snow,
skin & hair

growing white.
A shadow that thieves
spill like blood,
like the voice
from a stone,
the voice
of the dying.
Thieves & voices,
shore, wind, & sea,
tears & eyes,
fingers spinning
a thread,
in fear of the sky
& the earth,
of thieves
lost at sea,
a grave
& a stone
left for thieves
where thieves
vanish.

VARIATIONS ON THE HELL OF GRIEVING WOMEN

Because she breathed too wildly in the sun
Because the sun had risen for her because it fell into her lap
Because she held a bird between her legs, eyeless, but the face
still
warm, still tender
They have left her

Mornings are never the same.
Some bring wounds while others bring love.
The rose in her hair is alarming.
Her shadow is too.
Under a lingering star the wind drives a boat.
It is dawn.
Dawn is never as tender as night is.
And if somebody cries when it's morning,

forgive her.
She lives near the center,
away from the hills & the beaches.
Her gut is heavy with water.
It throbs.
Magnetos start fires,
& houses & bridges burn down.
Her face is the face of a bird,
leaves no traces
when caught in your wheels.
Between cities & suburbs eyes stare,
milk runs dry.
She knows sorrow.
A road runs down to the sea.
We change places.
In her womb a chimera waits to be born.
It is time to leave town,
the moon halfway risen to guide her.
She has sores on her lips,
shadows falling like rain.
The sea has turned into Ocean.
With death on her hands
she sleeps in a room without doors.
The wind drops seeds on her lap.
Soon death will lodge in a convent;
a highway will vanish in rain,
its autos in darkness.
Casinos & ferries will crumble.
A river as green as a salamander
sleeps in her spine.
Her voice flows over her teeth
like the blood on her window.
Like comets & echoes.
Like shadows.
A flower drops from her fingers.
Her shawl soaked with rain,
she ties it back with a hairpin.
The rain doesn't stop.
It reaches down to the roots.

Is the road to Hell strewn with bandages?
A virgin is praying in silence.
Locked in their offices who counts the rain?
Dawn brings hunger.
A birth takes place in a graveyard,
a wake in a spa.
A submarine sun can't be seen.
A second sun over the factories
lights up the tiles.
Fibers wrap around stones
& stones shine like glass.
Eyelids burn.
Throats go dry.
Rain traps horses in stalls & spiders in sand.
Outside her room a trolley runs by.
Night beginning, a sundial goes dark.
Her veins fill with lymph,
her mind with blue shadows.
Blind as a lion, now dead,
she knows sorrow.
Shadows cover the shore.
Flowers die.
Even the sunlight won't heal them.
Fear everywhere.
Desperation.
Nothing to say.

Variations On The Hell Of Smoke

The houses of men are on fire
Pity the dead in their graves
& the bones of the living

1
First he saw graves and after that saw ashes strewn around & molten metal. The man was standing at his door, his mind so steeped in blood, he seemed adrift in darkness. Children spun around him, changing places, scooping sand that burned like glass. So hot, he thought, will it

not scorch the bird atop that pine tree? I'll call them fire-raisers & I'll watch them running through the smoke & how the smoke drains color from their skin, the man thought.

2
Dead waters like the sweat that issues from his skin, like thunder that assaults him, that the man feels in his marrow, that his eyes search in the darkness. Spaces open in his blood & fire from the sun invades his darkest places. Shadows in the morning, long & thin & hot, fall on his skin, his arms, & sear his mind.

3
And from the roofbeams fire rises skyward. Bones in the desert sands, so small & frail, are all he sees. The images of cities disappear. The places where the man walks even now are hot & glowing through the smoke. On the man's skin little teeth are biting, leaving traces, red & green. The smoke is harbinger of death, & where the smoke is thickest, he will raise a torch & set the bones on fire. When he sees them flaming, he will rest.

4
A man is what he is, not what he seems. For those whom we call, the living clouds turn golden in the sun, black in the rain. All that is hidden from his eye still issues from his voice but leaves his eyes in darkness. With a stick he hobbles between places, feels the veins inside his right eye throbbing & his left eye blinded by the smoke. Will the fire-raisers flee on metal wings, those whom the man calls fire-raisers, & will the fires they have wrought remain? Will he then have an eye to look not one to see?

5
Houses no longer homes, how hot the clouds are that enclose them. Between his teeth a cry shakes down the clouds, the rain breaks on the house in which the man, bereft & lonely, hones his sight. More bones, more sand, & still more bones. A hot night follows and his house sinks slowly in the earth. Why do the children spin around us? They are the ones the fire sweeps away. The fire frozen in the Hell of smoke.

A COMMENTARY ON THE JIGOKU ZOSHI HELLS

In the 1990s I composed a series of thirty-three "Lorca Variations," above, systematically drawing vocabulary, principally nouns, from my previously published translation of Federico García Lorca's early gathering of poems, *The Suites*. I later made use of this method of composition for homages to Jackson Mac Low, Octavio Paz, & others as a step beyond translation but with an idea of translation—or what Haroldo de Campos called "transcreation" & I called "othering"—as one of the defining characteristics of poetry as a whole. The obvious difference in the variations presented here is that I apply the same procedure to an earlier work of my own, *The Seven Hells of the Jigoku Zoshi*, a series of *eight* poems (not *seven*) drawing themes but not specific images from ancient Japanese painted scrolls of that name & their accompanying verbal descriptions. The first publication of that work goes back to 1962, & it has remained in print for many years now as part of the first gathering of my selected poetry, *Poems for the Game of Silence* (New Directions, 1971). As with other variations—other translations for that matter—the procedure, if it works, doesn't so much annihilate the original version as bring it into a new dimension, where both versions can lead an independent if interlinked existence. The fifty year gap between them adds its own strangeness to the mix.

Some selections from *The Seven Hells of the Jigoku Zoshi* begin above, page 65.

A POEM OF MIRACLES

for Jack Collom

1 /
A miracle
more ordinary than
the grass
under our feet
the hot sun
as it dazzles
eyes & skin

so many memories
blending into one
we have no place
to go but where
we are   no nearer
to the end
than to the source

2 /
A miracle
open on all sides
toward which
the mind moves slowly
& the eye
as in a dream
opens & shuts

clouds without rain
cover the sun
the animal that sleeps
over our skylight
knows neither rest
nor waking
only a dream

3 /
Turn of the hand
by which a perfect
bird comes into
view   a flight
over the heads of some
no mystery
in what we see

we walk away
from it   no sooner
gone when something
ever bright

a flash of wing
assails us
heretofore concealed

4 /
The real comes first
the fancy a far second
hard to tell apart
still harder in the dark
the eye too weak
the skin still weaker
like the mind

the origin of species
hides its birth
the contours of the real
the hand feels
& the eye imagines
only later
in singular pursuit

5 /
A miracle
to make the seen
forerunner
of the unseen
the animal you see
its metamorphosis
deferred

imagination
lurks here
brings concealments
into light
the world inside
the mind
turns upside down

6 /
A miracle
to live a life
in celebration
knowing fear
& feeling death
he finds the poem
more to his taste

they call it fancy
a game of chance
or choice
that pulls the mind
back from the literal
opens a door
to the imagined real

7 /
A miracle
from which
the other miracle
proceeds
the owl living
night long
in the palm tree

a flight of pelicans
brown shadows
east of where the sun
touches the ocean
a miracle of distant bodies
voices from the sky
sounds absent words

8 /
A miracle
the sun crushed
by its clouds

the mind retreats from
blood lines
staining the horizon
raining down

the word is *firmament*
a cracked sky
over the sun & moon
imagined trackers
behind which
light seeps forth
a field of stars

9 /
A miracle
our lives that pass
a barrier
the evil wind
is not so evil
but brings us words
to string into a poem

nowhere to go
but up & out
the miracle
even to know
that knowing ends
having all tried & failed
against the odds

10 /
A miracle of darkness
hides the light
itself a miracle
in which infinities
escape us
& we plunge on
in hot pursuit

the ocean capped
by scarlet clouds
a miracle or not
the sand below
is pink
or mauve or amber
open & shut

11 /
A miracle
the light a miracle
the night a miracle
the sea a miracle
the tree a miracle
the bird a miracle
the word a miracle
the rain a miracle
the brain a miracle
the time a miracle
the rhyme a miracle
the breath a miracle
the death a miracle
the light a miracle

12 /
A miracle
to have been here
& to vanish
as the time ends
no more real
than anything we know
or run from

in my hand
all touch astounds me
color of the dead
is also touch

their faces & their voices
press against me
touch by touch

13 /
a miracle
that words are green still
after an age of dryness
that the rising sap
fills leaves & shoots
the sun still bright
in the engulfing dark

is an illusion   barely known
a deeper darkness
hiding all
the firmament unhinged
a miracle
that from this transient place
a universe is born

14 /
sheer accident denotes
a further miracle
the dish falls
from my hand
& finds the ground
an apple shows
the marks of teeth

a rush of things
more real than words
or less
the time has come
to add up what we know
it floats in air
I reach for it

15 /
the grass sweats
words turn green
a finger signals
a new miracle   the sky
leads into empty space
the mind is helpless
to address or fill

only in the little world
can we both love
& kill   the solipsist
is king here
waiting for the end
of time   & knowing
that it's endless

16 /
a miracle
by which the dead
animal & man
lie fallen
never to rise again
but sanguine
in their dissolution

the slow progression
into flesh
& out again
continues while the world
does   only then
no trace of mind remains
truer than this

17 /
a miracle
the small worlds
& the vast

the way the blood appears
sudden & hot
the sun at daybreak
lighting the wound

the firmament persists
over the sun & moon
the deeper image that it hides
where light & dark
change places   a time
that makes a mystery
of time & space

18 /
A miracle
to place a foot
on solid ground
& know the earth
rotates 1000 miles an hour
at the equator   barely
an inch at either pole

the ordinary
rise & fall
of how we breathe & move
steps taken
in the rush & crush
of galaxies
dark more than light

19 /
if time is endless
what we feel as time
deceives us
with the miracle
of what we feel
the ordinary push of days
against the grain

a miracle
the lie of beauty
dazzles us
deceitful elf
duende & capricho
hiding pain & hunger
ready to explode

20 /
a miracle
the earth collapsing
into ruin
while the larger world
survives   or say
the human ceases
gone astray

& leaves a trace behind
a breath or whisper
ready to become a word
the picture in the mind
is not a picture
until you call it forth
a pixel at a time

21 /
a miracle
where none exists
to call your own
mind into being
then to touch the hairs
the skin from which
they spring

the ordinary smells
that sex brings
& the heat
rising from the depths

a history contained
a touch of fingers
not the first or last

22 /
the final letter
names the end
& vanishes
the miracle of sound
absorbed   the body
freed to speak
its world

a miracle
the tread of foot
on earth   the earth
a further miracle
the firmament
no longer there
to stunt our view

23 /
a miracle
of sequence   numbers
covering a wall
the sky itself a field
of numbers
numbers as an alphabet
a game of numbers

lightly drawn & lightly
peppering the mind
inscribed in dreams
the dream of hunger
leading to a world
counted & numbered
engrafted in the flesh

24 /
a miracle
the flowers in the garden
grow tacky
& decline   the path
to the miraculous
not what we thought
or ever reckoned

but to draw breath
day by day
waiting for the breath
to be exhausted
the flow of blood to dry
the miracle of death
the greatest miracle

25 /
a miracle
to wake up from a dream
& count the dream
itself a miracle
the flower in the dream
as ordinary as
the flower awake

& spoken in your voice
the word is such a flower
broken & adrift
the sound reverberating
more a miracle
than what the eye sees
or the mind knows

26 /
a miracle
to have been spared this far
the beauty in the little known

the everyday repeated
at a finger's touch
to translate what we know
to what's barbaric vast & wild

the book of witness
opens   all the words we have
are theirs & lead us
eyeless whispering
the years themselves
a miracle
over against a world of pain

27 /
CODA
for Diane

A miracle
the unseen
overtaking us
the larger world
in darkness
darker than the mystery
of birth

the miracle resides
in what we see
& touch   so good
to be here
& to bow to you
my dearest friend
in darkness

as the poet said

30.viii.11

A CHRONOLOGY & A MEMOIR 2013

Revised from an earlier version commissioned & published by Editorial Azougue, Rio de Janeiro, as a preface for Etnopoesia no Milenio, *2006.*

Born 1931 in New York City, the son of Jewish immigrant parents who made their New World journey, from Poland to America, ten years before, I grew up in Brooklyn first and then the Bronx, at a time of depression, war, and holocaust. My education, from early years through university, was in the New York public schools, and sometime around my sixteenth year I set out to be a poet. That determination, I later thought, was a response to the debasement of language in the world at large and a desire to change or renew that language by any means at my disposal. For that I thought the language that I sought was ineluctably connected with poetry—both what the past had given us and what we had to fashion on our own. Along the way I suffered setbacks from the conservative poetics and politics that had come to dominate the 1940s and early 1950s, and I was further waylaid by two years of army time in the near aftermath of the Korean War. Because of that, however, I spent eighteen months in Germany (in 1954 and 1955), during which time I struggled to write poetry and began to divert myself with the pleasures of translation. I also had the chance to discover Europe in the company of Diane Brodatz, whom I had married in 1952 and who has remained my dearest friend and companion to the present time.

When I returned to New York in 1955, there was already a group of poets waiting for me: David Antin, who had been with me at City College and through and with whom I met a number of others: Robert Kelly, Armand Schwerner, George Economou, and later Paul Blackburn, Jackson Mac Low, Rochelle Owens, Clayton Eshleman, and Diane Wakoski. Our interests—looking back at them—were centered on the reinvigoration of a full panoply of avant-garde strategies that had been disrupted by the "new criticism" and the mainstream poetics of the immediately preceding generation. My own first shibboleth was what I named "deep image" and saw as a kind of neo-surrealism with roots in a range of traditional and still neglected poetries and visionary practices that informed my subsequent move into the exploration of a genuine and, I thought, a *necessary* ethnopoetics. My approach to poetry, then and after, was deliberately intercultural and global, and in the process it led me to alliances with other poets and still other groupings of poets—Beats, Black Mountain, Concrete, Fluxus, Textsound—that I saw increasingly as part of a great collective effort "to bring back totality through poetry" (in the words of the Japanese poet Ooka Makoto).

By the end of the 1950s I began to publish and increasingly to perform my own poetry. My first book-length publication was an anthology of translations, *New Young German Poets*, that Lawrence Ferlinghetti had commissioned for City Lights Books in 1958. I had also, like many other poets of my generation, begun a press of my own, Hawk's Well Press, which served as a vehicle for some of those closest to me at the time and for my own first book of poems, *White Sun Black Sun* (1960). My second small book, *The Seven Hells of the Jigoku Zoshi* (1962), was with *Trobar*, a press and magazine published by Kelly and Economou; my third, *Sightings* (1964), was again with Hawk's Well Press and printed in the same volume as Kelly's *Lunes;* and my fourth, *The Gorky Poems* (1966), was published in a bilingual (English and Spanish) edition by *El Corno Emplumado*, which Margaret Randall and Sergio Mondragón were publishing out of Mexico. A selection of poems, *Between: Poems 1960–1963*, was published in 1968 by Fulcrum Press in London; another selection, *Poems 1964–1967*, was published by Black Sparrow Press in 1968; and a larger selected poems, *Poems for the Game of Silence*, was published by Dial Press in 1971 and reprinted by New Directions in 1974.

During the 1960s I also began to assemble examples of tribal and oral poetry from Africa, America, Asia, and Oceania that would form the basis of my first large anthology, *Technicians of the Sacred*, published in its initial version in 1968. (An expanded edition, incorporating additional poetry from Europe, appeared in 1985.) This marked the beginning of a series of large anthological assemblages devoted both to ethnopoetics and to an exploration of experimental and avant-garde poetry and poetics: *Shaking the Pumpkin: Traditional Poetry of the Indian North Americas* (1972), *America a Prophecy: A New Reading of American Poetry from Pre-Columbian Times to the Present* (with George Quasha, 1973), *Revolution of the Word: A New Gathering of American Avant-Garde Poetry 1914–1945* (1974), *A Big Jewish Book: Poems & Other Visions of the Jews from Tribal Times to the Present* (a.k.a. *Exiled in the Word*, 1977), *Symposium of the Whole: A Range of Discourse Toward an Ethnopoetics* (with Diane Rothenberg, 1983), *Poems for the Millennium: The University of Cali-*

fornia Book of Modern & Postmodern Poetry in two volumes (with Pierre Joris, 1995 and 1998), and *A Book of the Book: Some Works & Projections About the Book & Writing* (with Steven Clay, 1999). I also joined the anthropologist Dennis Tedlock in founding and editing *Alcheringa* (1970–1977) as "the world's first magazine of ethnopoetics," and I followed that on my own with *New Wilderness Letter*, a magazine of poetics and ethnopoetics across the arts.

The work in ethnopoetics and on the attendant assemblages was a catalyst as well for my own poetry. I began to put a greater emphasis on performance, a part of that tied in with procedures for the translation and subsequent performance of oral and ritual poetry that I called "total translation." At the same time I began to work collaboratively with musicians and composers—Charlie Morrow and Bertram Turetzky most notably, but on other occasions with Philip Corner, Pauline Oliveros, George Lewis, and the klezmer group calling itself The Klezmatics. There were also theatricalizations in the 1980s of *Poland/1931* by the Living Theater and *That Dada Strain* by the Center for Theater Science and Research, a Living Theater offshoot. I engaged in poetry readings throughout this time—twenty or more in an average year, both in the United States and overseas—and wrote and lectured on performance, also teaching workshops on poetry and performance at universities and other venues. (I had written the Broadway version of Rolf Hochhuth's play, *The Deputy [Der Stellvertreter]*, in 1964, but that was a very different matter.)

For two years—1972 to 1974—I lived with my wife and our son Matthew at a Seneca Indian (Iroquois) reservation in western New York state, where I worked on the completion of the American Indian anthology, *Shaking the Pumpkin*, but also my own book of poems, *A Seneca Journal* (1978). At the same time I continued a very different but curiously related project—or so I thought—"to explore ancestral sources of my own in a world of Jewish mystics, thieves, & madmen." The immediate results were *Poland/1931* (poems, 1974) and *A Big Jewish Book* (1977, later revised as *Exiled in the Word*). The principal publisher for my poetry by then was New Directions, and in the following two and a half decades they published a string of poetry books: *Vienna Blood* (1980), *That Dada Strain* (1983), *New Selected Poems* (1986), *Khurbn & Other Poems* (1989), *The Lorca Variations* (1993), *Seedings & Other Poems* (1996), *A Paradise of Poets* (1999), and *A Book of Witness* (2003), as well as a collection of essays, *Pre-Faces* (1981). Other books during that time came from a number of smaller publishers, as well as a range of books in translation—into many languages, but principally French and Spanish. At the same time I was actively engaged in translation from a number of languages—sometimes on my own, sometimes in collaboration with others—and in the 1990s and the first decade of this century I published books of translation from Lorca, Schwitters, Picasso, and Vitezslav Nezval, as well as a book of my selected translations, *Writing Through: Translations & Variations* (2004).

Other works during that first 21st-century decade followed the same trajectory, connecting poems and poetics, as those that came before. My latest big project published in 2009 was a third installment of *Poems for the Millennium* (co-edited with Jeffrey Robinson)—a radical reassemblage of nineteenth-century poetry, tracing a line of experimental romanticism and postromanticism as it underlies our present workings, while my terminal book for New Directions, *Triptych* (2007), brought together *Poland/1931* and *Khurbn* (poems deriving from the Holocaust) with a new series of poems, *The Burning Babe*. I also assembled a second gathering of my poetics, *Poetics & Polemics* (2008), and coming into the second decade of the century, I published three new books of poetry: *Gematria Complete* (2010), *Concealments & Caprichos* (2010), and *Retrievals: Uncollected & New Poems 1955–2010* (2011). At the same time I began to work on what may be my final anthology/assemblage, a gathering of "outsider and subterranean poetry" from paleolithic times to the present, and as before I've accompanied this with the composition of several new series of poems, some of them "autovariations" on my own work from previous decades.

With all of this I find that the work has been cumulative, that it has permitted me to change while not losing track of, rather incorporating, most of what came before. I hope that someday this will be seen as a whole, the way I try to see it now, but that it has even come this far is more than I could have imagined.

TITLES FROM BLACK WIDOW PRESS

TRANSLATION SERIES

Approximate Man and Other Writings by Tristan Tzara. Translated and edited by Mary Ann Caws.

Art Poétique by Guillevic. Translated by Maureen Smith.

The Big Game by Benjamin Péret. Translated with an introduction by Marilyn Kallet.

Capital of Pain by Paul Eluard. Translated by Mary Ann Caws, Patricia Terry, and Nancy Kline.

Chanson Dada: Selected Poems by Tristan Tzara. Translated with an introduction and essay by Lee Harwood.

Essential Poems and Prose of Jules Laforgue Translated and edited by Patricia Terry.

Essential Poems and Writings of Joyce Mansour: A Bilingual Anthology Translated with an introduction by Serge Gavronsky.

Essential Poems and Writings of Robert Desnos: A Bilingual Anthology Edited with an introduction and essay by Mary Ann Caws.

EyeSeas (Les Ziaux) by Raymond Queneau. Translated with an introduction by Daniela Hurezanu and Stephen Kessler.

Furor and Mystery & Other Writings by René Char. Edited and translated by Mary Ann Caws and Nancy Kline.

The Inventor of Love & Other Writings by Gherasim Luca. Translated by Julian and Laura Semilian. Introduction by Andrei Codrescu. Essay by Petre Răileanu.

La Fontaine's Bawdy by Jean de La Fontaine. Translated with an introduction by Norman R. Shapiro.

Last Love Poems of Paul Eluard Translated with an introduction by Marilyn Kallet.

A Life of Poems, Poems of a Life by Anna de Noailles. Translated by Norman R. Shapiro. Introduction by Catherine Perry.

Love, Poetry (L'amour la poésie) by Paul Eluard. Translated with an essay by Stuart Kendall.

Poems of André Breton: A Bilingual Anthology Translated with essays by Jean-Pierre Cauvin and Mary Ann Caws.

Poems of A.O. Barnabooth by Valéry Larbaud. Translated by Ron Padgett and Bill Zavatsky.

Poems of Consummation by Vicente Aleixandre. Translated by Stephen Kessler

Préversities: A Jacques Prévert Sampler Translated and edited by Norman R. Shapiro.

The Sea and Other Poems by Guillevic. Translated by Patricia Terry. Introduction by Monique Chefdor.

To Speak, to Tell You? Poems by Sabine Sicaud. Translated by Norman R. Shapiro. Introduction and notes by Odile Ayral-Clause.

forthcoming translations

Guarding the Air: Selected Poems of Gunnar Harding Translated and edited by Roger Greenwald.

Pierre Reverdy: Poems Early to Late Translated by Mary Ann Caws and Patricia Terry.

Jules Supervielle: Selected Poems Translated by Nancy Kline and Patricia Terry.

Boris Vian Invents Boris Vian: A Boris Vian Reader Edited and translated by Julia Older.

MODERN POETRY SERIES

ABC of Translation by Willis Barnstone

An Alchemist with One Eye on Fire by Clayton Eshleman

Anticline by Clayton Eshleman

Archaic Design by Clayton Eshleman

Backscatter: New and Selected Poems by John Olson

The Caveat Onus by Dave Brinks

City Without People: The Katrina Poems by Niyi Osundare

Concealments and Caprichos by Jerome Rothenberg

Crusader-Woman by Ruxandra Cesereanu. Translated by Adam J. Sorkin. Introduction by Andrei Codrescu.

Curdled Skulls: Poems of Bernard Bador Translated by the author with Clayton Eshleman.

Endure: Poems by Bei Dao Translated by Clayton Eshleman and Lucas Klein.

Exile is My Trade: A Habib Tengour Reader Translated by Pierre Joris.

Eye of Witness: A Jerome Rothenberg Reader Edited with commentaries by Heriberto Yepez & Jerome Rothenberg

Fire Exit by Robert Kelly

Forgiven Submarine by Ruxandra Cesereanu and Andrei Codrescu

from stone this running by Heller Levinson

The Grindstone of Rapport: A Clayton Eshleman Reader

Larynx Galaxy by John Olson

The Love That Moves Me by Marilyn Kallet

Memory Wing by Bill Lavender

Packing Light: New and Selected Poems by Marilyn Kallet

The Present Tense of the World: Poems 2000–2009 by Amina Saïd. Translated with an introduction by Marilyn Hacker.

The Price of Experience by Clayton Eshleman

The Secret Brain: Selected Poems 1995–2012 by Dave Brinks

Signal from Draco: New and Selected Poems by Mebane Robertson

forthcoming modern poetry titles

An American Unconscious by Mebane Robertson

Memory by Bernadette Mayer

LITERARY THEORY / BIOGRAPHY SERIES

Revolution of the Mind: The Life of André Breton by Mark Polizzotti.

Clayton Eshleman: The Whole Art by Stuart Kendall (forthcoming)

LOUISIANA HERITAGE SERIES
(Second Line Press imprint)

New Orleans Poems in Creole and French by Jules Choppin. Translated by Norman R. Shapiro.

Dinner at Antoine's (forthcoming) by Francis Parkinson Keyes

Crescent Carnival (forthcoming) by Francis Parkinson Keyes